Religious Resurgence
and Politics
in the
Contemporary World

SUNY Series in Religion, Culture, and Society

Wade Clark Roof, Editor

Religious Resurgence and Politics in the Contemporary World

Edited by

Emile Sahliyeh

State University of New York Press

Published by
State University of New York Press, Albany

For information, address State University of New York
Press, State University Plaza, Albany, N.Y., 12246

Library of Congress Cataloging in Publication Data

Religious Resurgence and Politics in the Contemporary World /
    edited by Emile Sahliyeh.
        p.   cm.—(SUNY series in religion, culture, and society)
    ISBN 0–7914–0381–5.—ISBN 0–7914–0382–3 (pbk.)
    1. Religion and politics—History—20th century.   I. Sahliyeh,
    Emile F.   II. Series.
    BL65.P7R47   1990
    291.1′77′09048—dc20

10 9 8 7 6 5 4 3 2 1

Contents

Contents

Foreword

By the late 1970s and early 1980s, a number of highly politicized religious groups, institutions, and movements, surfaced in different parts of the world. Although of different faiths and sects, these groups shared a common desire to change their societies and even to change the international order. While some have confined their activities to the realm of political protest and reform, others have intervened more forcefully in politics, and some have resorted to violence in pursuit of their objectives.

This trend toward the politicization of religions has left a question mark over some of the central assumptions in the literature on modernization. In particular, modernization in the West has been accompanied by a reduction of the role of religion in society and politics. Modernization-development theorists posited that the interrelated components of modernization (including technological advancement, economic growth, urbanization, education, communication, and burgeoning mass media exposure throughout the world) would enhance the trend toward secularization of societies and lead to a decline in the influence of religion. Rather than fading away, traditional religions continue to occupy a central position in the political landscape of many societies. In a number of countries today, religious revivalism and fundamentalism seem to be direct products or by-products of modernization. In some cases, religious resurgence came as an expression of cultural authenticity, while in others it helped in coping with the unsettling emotional, intellectual, economic, and social consequences of modernization. Thus, religious revivalism has implications for modernization, development, political participation, and stability very different from those widely expected in the scholarly and policy-making communities.

In view of the substantive and theoretical significance of these issues, a conference was convened at the University of North Texas on April 5–6, 1988. Over the course of those two days, twenty-two scholars undertook the task of analyzing the phenomenon of religious political activism in different parts of the world. Four themes dominated the discussions. These included the need to draw attention away from excessive preoccupation with the negative aspects of religious resurgence and its extremist and violent manifestations; to place this phenomenon in a conceptual and historical context; to explain the true motives and reasons behind the revitalization of traditional religions; and to assess the limitations, positive contributions, and future prospects of religious resurgence. This volume is a by-product of that conference.

The Conference on Religious Resurgence and Politics in the Contemporary World was sponsored by the University of North Texas, Texas Woman's University, and by a host of religious denominations and public interest groups and associations. On behalf of the organizers of the conference, I wish to extend my deepest appreciation to the following for their generous financial support: the Janet and Chester H. Roth Foundation; the Lily Endowment Foundation; the Denton Campus Christian Council; the National Association of Arab Americans (Dallas/Ft. Worth chapter); Austin College; the Chaplain's Office of Southern Methodist University; Texas Woman's University; and the University of North Texas (Chancellor's Office, College of Arts and Sciences, Department of Political Science, Student Association, the University Union, and the Union Program Committee); as well as the following local congregations— the Division of Higher Education of the Christian Church (Disciples of Christ), Grace Presbytery, NT/NL Synod of the Evangelical Lutheran Church in America, Synod of the Sun Presbyterian Church USA, First United Methodist Church, Catholic Diocese of Ft. Worth, Christ the Servant Lutheran Church, Cumberland Presbyterian Church, First Christian Church, First Presbyterian Church, Jewish Congregation of Denton, St. Andrew Presbyterian Church, St. Barnabas Episcopal Church, and Trinity Presbyterian Church. The faith that these groups and institutions placed on the intellectual value of such a volatile topic made the convening of this conference possible.

Special thanks are extended to the Reverend Ivan A. "Ike" Orloff of the Denton Campus Christian Council; Wilkes Berry, Associate Vice President for Academic Affairs, Texas Woman's University; John A. Booth, Chair of the Department of Political Science, the University of North Texas; and Denton community leaders Lynn and Jerry Cott, Sundown Ranch, for their efforts in organizing the conference. The tireless efforts of the Reverend Mr. Orloff, in particular, ensured the success of the conference; he was also responsible for raising most of the funding. Thanks also go to the members of Pi Sigma Alpha (the Political Science Honor Society, the University of North Texas), particularly to Gregory P. Pynes and Ivor Weiner, for their help during the conference. Linda Strube offered invaluable help in editing the manuscripts and in corresponding with the contributors. I also wish to thank Rosalie Robertson, Editor, SUNY Press, for her continuous support and kindness. Finally, I am grateful to the contributors for their patience and prompt co-operation in editing and revising their chapters. I hope that their scholarly and collaborative efforts will help in providing for a general explanation of religious resurgence—its future prospects and implications for modernization, development, and secularization. It is also my hope that this book will serve as a resource book on religious resurgence in different parts of the world.

Emile Sahliyeh

Part I. Explaining the Phenomenon of Religious Resurgence

The following four chapters provide a general explanation of the phenomenon of religious resurgence. In chapter 1, I deal with the topic of religious resurgence and political modernization.

In chapter 2, Anson Shupe attributes the persistence of religion to two factors. First, the assumption of the globalists, that the world is becoming a single economic entity, ignores the role of religion in perpetuating particularistic religious loyalties and prejudices. Such theories are frequently secularist and neo-Marxist with often an implicit antireligious prejudice that dismisses religion as an important active force in urban societies. Second, instead of bringing people closer together, the advancement in communication highlighted their differences, thus disproving the expectations of communication theory.

In chapter 3, Joe Barnhart contends that the conditions generating magic and religion are as prevalent in contemporary technological societies, as they were in preliterate societies. Since science as a cognitive system is not the prevalent ideology of North America, supernatural religions and schemes of magic will likely continue to thrive far into the future.

Donald Eugene Smith does not believe that religious resurgence is a universal phenomenon unique to the late twentieth century (chap. 4). He asserts that the experience of Catholicism, Hinduism, Islam, and Buddhism in this century demonstrates that religious resurgence is a recurrent phenomenon. These four religions experienced periods of political activism followed by periods of passivity. Smith concludes that the political resurgence of religion has been most visible in political opposition movements.

1

Religious Resurgence and Political Modernization
Emile Sahliyeh

In the 1950s and 1960s, many social scientists argued that modernization would reduce the political significance of religion and diminish individual attachment to religious values. Students of social development hypothesized that exposure to education, urbanization, the presence of opportunities for modern employment, technology, scientific advancement, as well as the formation of new and more complex social organizations, would inevitably lead to the spread of secularization, pluralism, and political differentiation throughout the world. These changes were also expected to lead to the adoption of new values and modern life-styles that would sharply clash with religious traditions. It was thought that with the spread of modernization, traditional religious institutions would decline or disappear and religion's grip over various cultures and societies would be loosened. Rather than being a force for collective action, social control, and political mobilization, religion would simply become a private affair for the individual.[1]

Ideas about the separation of religion from politics were based upon the observation of the Western experience, which suggested that the process of secularization would not only persist, but would also be irreversible in an increasingly industrialized world. Based upon this Western experience, secularization was expected to be a universal phenomenon that would be replicated in other areas of the world. Under the impact of modernization, conventional societal outlooks and organizations would be undermined and traditional religions would be shoved aside.

Governments in different parts of the Third World were expected to increasingly utilize secular as opposed to religious symbolism to legitimize and consolidate their rule. Nationalism, rather than religion, was expected to provide citizens with a locus for their political allegiance and identification. The active role played by several religious groups in the anticolonial struggle in the first few decades of the twentieth century and the manipulation of religious symbolism by some of the national secular elite in the postindependence era, were not seen as serious challenges to the secularization model. On the contrary, the political influence of religious parties and leaders, plus the overall influence of religion over public life—including law, the economy, education, and morality—were expected to be replaced by secular norms.[2]

The 1970s and 1980s, however, have proven such expectations to be wrong. The political revitalization of religious groups in the United States, Latin America, the Middle East, and other areas of the Third World during these decades, seriously undermined many widely held assumptions about modernization. Urbanization, advancement in education, and occupational diversity, did not lead to the decline in the importance of religious values and the rejection of traditions. On the contrary, the social upheaval produced by modernization resulted in a renewed interest in traditional religions. Why was this so?

This volume explores this intriguing question from a variety of perspectives. No single theory, concept, or approach can fully account for the recent political resurgence of religion. The contributors to this volume credit religious revivalism to an assortment of reasons and forces. These reasons can be grouped into three broad categories: the presumed incompatibility between religion and modernization, crisis theory, and resource mobilization.

THE LIMITS OF UNILINEAR, DETERMINISTIC, SECULAR MODELS

Marxism-Leninism and liberal pluralism have been the two paradigms that have dealt with the role of religion in society, which have underestimated the role of religion as a dynamic modern force. Several contributors argue that the limited utility and applicability of the secular model are rooted in the pro-Western biases that pervade the literature on modernization, social development, and communication. These secularization assumptions and predictions contain many inaccuracies about the future and the role of religion in modern societies.

One such shortcoming pertains to the assertion in the modernization literature that along with the spread of scientific knowledge and modern communications, our belief in religion would fade away and that the diverse cultures and religions in the world would gradually be replaced by a singular global community. This assertion, however, did not conform to reality since religion remained an important factor in the politics of many countries in different parts of the world. The emergence of several religious movements and groups throughout the 1970s and 1980s demonstrated the resilience and persistence of religion. More precisely, the rise of the new Christian Right and other religious groups in the United States have questioned the validity of the unilinear secular model of political development even within Western industrialized democracies. Rather than being replaced by new secular norms, traditional religions and religious institutions persisted and proved to be capable of adjusting to the requirements of political and economic modernization.[3]

In some parts of the Third World, religion served as an agent of modernization and social change. In Latin America, for instance, the Catholic church has played an increasingly active role in political, economic, and social development efforts. In South and Southeast Asia as well as in the Middle East, religion continued to assume a central position in the political life of these societies. In some cases, including Iran and the Philippines, the clergy played a leading role in the overthrow of the established regimes.

Whether it was the Islamic Revolution against the shah, the Catholic church's support for the Solidarity Workers Union in Poland against the Polish government, the role of the Catholic bishops in the downfall of the Marcos regime in the Philippines, or some of the Evangelical churches' opposition to apartheid in South Africa, or the liberation theology of the Catholic church in Latin America, religion provided the political opposition with powerful symbols for mass mobilization against the established order.

Another deficiency in the literature on modernization revolves around the separation between religion and politics. Theorists of social development and communication argued that modernization would lead to the depoliticization of religion because they asserted that the relationship between religion and politics would remain conflictual and contradictory. Contrary to these assertions, however,

the decoupling of religion from politics and the privatization of religion have not been universal certainties. On the contrary, religion
and politics are inseparable in many parts of the world.[4] This is
most evident in the Middle East where, unlike Christianity, Judaism
and Islam are intimately linked with politics.

The modernization literature's depiction of religion as a traditional political force incapable of modernization and adaptation to
change is equally misleading. Experiences in Poland, the Philippines, South Africa, the United States, Latin America, India, and
the Middle East, lucidly demonstrate that religion continues to be a
viable political force in the world today.

Finally, rather than contributing to the demise of traditional
religion, modernization has revitalized several religious groups
and movements. The modernization of such groups equipped them
with the necessary resources and motives to engage in politics.
For instance, the movement of conservative Protestants from rural
areas to urban centers in the southern parts of the United States,
endowed them with various personal skills and resources, including advanced education, money, and modern means of communication. Evangelists then used such assets to promote their
interests. Similarly, in the Middle East, there arose a literate middle
class that was attracted to Islam. Followers of the Islamic movement believe that their religion and its values and teachings are
not outmoded concepts; rather, they continue to be relevant
and functional precepts that provide inspiration and guidance
to Muslims.

RELIGIOUS RESURGENCE AS A RESPONSE TO CRISES

Other contributors to this volume see in social crisis a partial
explanation for the political revitalization of some religious groups.
This approach treats religious resurgence as a result of the multifaceted crises that we face in the twentieth century. These authors perceive a generalized "crisis atmosphere" that stems from the
inconclusive modernizing efforts of secular elites in the Third
World, growing disillusionment with secular nationalism, problems
of legitimacy and political oppression in many developing countries, problems of national identity, widespread socioeconomic
grievances, and the erosion of traditional morality and values both
in the West and in the Third World. The coterminous existence of
several or all of these crises in much of the contemporary world
provide a fertile milieu for the return to religion.[5] Religion provides

the aggrieved with a sense of refuge, guidance, comfort, and a sense of discipline to cope with the complexities of life.

Inconclusive Modernizing Efforts

Efforts at modernization and secularization in the Third World have often been disappointing. Despite the erosion of traditional social, economic, and political institutions and the downgrading of traditional patterns of societal organization, modern institutions were not sufficiently established to meet the material needs of the population or to respond to its political demands and interests. Despite the wide range of hopes and aspirations that were generated by economic, political, and cultural contacts with the West, the economic and social benefits of modernization were distributed unevenly among the developing societies. While the interests of the elite were served well by the process of modernization, the living conditions of the poor worsened. The gap between both groups became so wide, that it fueled public outrage in many Third World countries. In this connection, Augustus Richard Norton and Karandeep Singh argue that the economic deprivation, social exclusion, and political underrepresentation of the Shi'a in Lebanon and the Sikhs in India, aroused a militant religious movement. As Norton argues, advancement in education and improvement in the transportation and communication systems eroded the geographic isolation of the Shi'a.

The Third World's quest for modernization through the emulation of either Western capitalism or Soviet and Chinese socialism, was frequently inconclusive. Rather than leading to economic prosperity, autonomy, and self-sufficiency, such pathways to modernization increased economic dependency upon the outside world. The political revitalization of religion can therefore be seen as part of the Third World's quest for political, economic, and cultural autonomy and authenticity.

From the perspective of religious groups and movements in developing countries, secular elites not only failed to modernize their societies, but were unable to end their countries' dependence upon the West. Religious movements therefore wanted to establish a way of life for the individual, the society, and the state, away from the influence of Western ideologies.[6] The resulting socioeconomic grievances generated two contrasting types of religious resurgence. A progressive liberal and, in some cases, a revolutionary type of religious resurgence was experienced by Iran, Egypt, and some parts of Latin America. By contrast, the response of Central American Protestants to underdevelopment was mainly conservative. The sexual permissiveness and other liberal practices associated with culture change in the United States have also generated a conservative response among the traditional Protestants.

Crises of Legitimacy and Identity

The crises of identity and legitimacy in many Third World countries are also partly responsible for the political resurgence of religion. These two crises are the result of the ruling elite's inability to substitute modernized institutions and norms for the traditional values and patterns of interaction. As the new secular norms stood on shaky grounds, many regimes of the Third World utilized religious symbolism and co-opted religious groups to legitimize their rule.[7]

Many Third World leaders used considerable power to control the state and to suppress political opposition. The crisis of leadership was further compounded by the corruption and the authoritarianism that characterized the domestic behavior of many of the developing countries. The crisis of legitimacy became more acute with the importation of Western and socialist ideologies by Third World regimes to their traditional societies. Such alien ideologies forced the local population to look for indigenous and authentic points of reference and allegiance. Still, in other societies, regime legitimacy has been seriously questioned by the incapacity of the secular elite to meet the growing needs and demands of the local population for economic, social, and political modernization.

In some cases the problem of legitimacy resulted from the military weakness of the regimes. The defeat of the collective Arab armies of Egypt, Syria, Jordan, and Iraq at the hands of the Israelis in the 1967 June War, and Arab continued military inferiority vis-à-vis the Jewish state, laid the foundation for Islamic revivalism in the second half of the 1970s. The loss of the war was viewed as punishment by God for the Arabs' neglect of their Islamic religion.

In other Third World societies, the presence of external threats to a new ethnic identity furnished fertile grounds for individual and mass allegiance to religion. In South Africa, Pakistan, Iran, Ireland, the West Bank, Gaza, and India, the revitalization of religion was initiated by the concern these societies held for the preservation of their national ethnic identity and cultural purity in the face of mounting outside challenges. For instance, there has been a fusion of religion and Polish nationalism to counter the Communist regime. The Catholic church maintained the Polish nationhood in times of crisis and operated as the guardian of human rights for Polish workers. Similarly, religious resurgence in Iran came as a reaction to the policies of the pro-Western secular shah. In addition, Islamic revivalism among the West Bank-Gaza Palestinians surfaced as a reaction to the emergence of extremist religious Jewish groups in Israel.[8]

The Catholic church in Latin America, according to Michael Dodson, experienced a crisis of identity in the wake of popular demands for political and economic modernization during the 1950s and 1960s. The church's traditional alliance with the state and with the landed aristocracy prevented it from criticizing the widespread poverty and oppression. Its insensitivity to these problems led to a decline in the church's position. This was evidenced in the popular appeal of conservative Protestants and leftist ideologists among the poor. Such a crisis of identity resulted in a religious renewal by the Catholic church, which eventually sided with the poor against the economic and political inequality in the region.

The Unsettling Social and Intellectual
Consequences of Modernization

While the failure of economic modernization efforts was partly responsible for the resurgence of religion in many of the Third World societies, the social consequences of modernization and secularization and the resulting moral vacuum were behind the political revitalization of conservative religious groups in the West. Despite the high standard of living enjoyed by Western societies and oil-producing states, there has been a renewed interest in religion. This was brought about by the widespread feelings of dislocation, alienation, and disorientation resulting from the process of modernization and from the rapid disappearance of habitual lifestyles and traditions. Religion would presumably restore traditional family values and give its adherents a sense of continuity and direction. In this connection, conservative Protestants in the United States believed that their value system, way of life, and social institutions were all being threatened by a permissive new culture. The breakdown in community values, the erosion of the traditional sex roles, liberalization of rules governing abortion, the banning of prayers in public schools, an increase in the use of drugs and alcohol, and the rising rates of divorce, were sources of deep concern for the conservative Protestants. These challenges to established social norms prompted conservative Protestants to become active in politics.

Many of the North American evangelists' social and moral grievances are also found among the Islamic peoples of the Middle East. Whether in Egypt, Iran, Syria, Jordan, Kuwait, or Palestine, Islamic groups believe that the integrity of their social values and institutions is threatened by the incursion of Western culture and civilization. These groups are particularly concerned with preserving the unity of their families and with protecting their youths against the "wild ways" of Western culture.

The unsettling consequences of modernization go beyond social and economic grievances. Some of the contributors to this volume argue that the process of modernization has destabilizing ramifications. Rather than providing individuals with certainty and tranquility, social change has unleashed a wide range of psychological, ethical, and intellectual problems. In such an environment, religion not only provides us with refuge, but emotional and intellectual stability as well.

In summation, the multiple crises that confront different societies in the contemporary world account for the political resurgence of religion. The case studies in this volume indicate that in times of crisis, religion offers its adherents a point of reference, a sense of guidance, and discipline, as well as a refuge.

RESOURCE MOBILIZATION

The socioeconomic, psychological, and political grievances and frustrations associated with the process of modernization, are insufficient by themselves, to provide for a comprehensive understanding of the phenomenon of religious resurgence. The political activism of present-day religious groups and religious movements can also be explained by employing a resource mobilization model. This model contains three components. First, a religious group's involvement in politics is not possible without the presence of opportunities that allows these groups to form independent organizations and to engage in politics. Second, the political vitality of religion is also dependent upon the presence of a variety of resources, including political leadership, organizational structures, communication networks, manpower for recruitment purposes, funds, and ideology and economic and social status. These resources will determine the nature and the degree of the reaction of the aggrieved persons. Third, such religious groups cannot be expected to be politically active without the presence of incentives, reasons, and motives that induce them to organize.[9] The combination of these conditions can account for the transformation of religious groups that have been traditionally politically passive, into groups that are strategically active.

The Presence of Opportunities

The element of opportunity is, to a large extent, a function of the presence or lack of governmental tolerance or encouragement toward the activities of religious groups and movements. In order to broaden their political constituency or legitimize their rule, governments and opposition alike frequently manipulate religious symbols and co-opt religious groups. The net effect of the secular elite's co-optation of these religious groups has been the creation of a congenial and receptive environment for the political resurgence of religion. The co-optation of the religious groups has been exercised by democratic and authoritarian secular elites alike. In the United States, as Kenneth Wald points out, the leaders of the conservative secular right in the Republican party allied themselves in the late 1970s and 1980s with the conservative Protestant movement, in order to broaden their electoral appeal. Those conservative secular leaders provided the evangelists access to political power and offered them organizational resources, financial support, and lobbying experience. The availability of such assets added to the strength of the evangelical Protestant groups.

The experience of the Gush Emunim settler movement in Israel was similar to that of the new Christian Right in the United States. Since 1977, the Likud ruling bloc encouraged the Gush Emunim movement's efforts to settle the West Bank and the Gaza Strip. In return, the Likud received from Gush Emunim, ideological and political support.

In many parts of the Third World, both the support of the government and the secular elite aided the political revitalization of religion. In an effort to legitimize and consolidate their rule, progressive Third World leaders began to invoke the notion of religion. This is particularly true for leaders such as Nasser of Egypt, Zia al-Haq of Pakistan, and Jafar Numeiri of Sudan, for whom the diminished utility of a socialist revolutionary and anti-imperialist rhetorical foundation led them to invoke religion in order to justify their hold over the state's power.

Sadat of Egypt, Khadafi of Libya, and al-Habib Bugaiba of Tunisia also utilized religious symbolism to build up their domestic legitimacy and to neutralize leftist critics. After coming to power in September of 1970, Sadat sought the support of the emerging mass-based Islamic movement. As Louis Cantori points out, Sadat's encouragement of the construction of many new mosques throughout Egypt, his program that released thousands of followers of the Muslim Brotherhood from jail, and his legalization of the official publications of the movement, significantly increased the power and the prestige of the Muslim brothers. With its enhanced power, the Brotherhood movement served as an intermediary between the government and the Egyptian people at large.

The manipulation of religious symbolism and religious groups was not just confined to the progressive secular authoritarian elite as other traditional regimes or rightist military dictatorships co-opted the religious groups to legitimize their rule beyond coercive power. Countries like Morocco, Saudi Arabia, and Jordan utilized Islamic symbols and encouraged traditional Islamic groups to combat radical political tendencies in their countries and to scuttle demands for political participation and democratization. In Central and Latin America, some rightist military dictatorships have recently supported or favored the conservative Protestant churches.

Unlike the liberation theology espoused by a segment of the Catholic church, evangelists did not constitute any challenge to the Central American dictatorships. The political marginality of the conservative Protestants, their support for the status quo, their advocacy of "salvation in Heaven" for the Latin American poor, and the financial support that these groups received from their mother churches in the United States and the Reagan administration all account for, as argued by Laura O'Shaughnessy, the increasing popularity of the evangelists in Central America.

Religious resurgence in the 1970s and 1980s also received further impetus from the political opposition in many Third World countries. By this time, religion has become a potent political force for the opposition to use in order to defend itself against incumbent regimes. Indeed, in many places of the developing world religion had become the only vehicle for the articulation of popular grievances. Regardless of whether it was the Philippines, Poland, South Africa, Latin America, India, or the Middle East, the incumbent regimes found it exceedingly difficult simply to close down churches, mosques, temples, or synagogues. This is contrasted with the ease with which those governments were able to clamp down upon newspapers, political parties, trade unions, and student and women's organizations and associations.

The Availability of Organizational Structures and Political Resources

Without minimizing the significance of the role and political opportunities made available by the secular elite, the political revitalization of traditional religions was the result of their possession of certain assets and resources. The exposure of these religious groups to advanced education, sophisticated communication networks, and improved quality of life, have increased their capacity to be politically active. For instance, in the United States, modernization enabled members of the conservative Protestant groups to allocate time, energy, and money, and to effectively utilize electronic media for a sustained engagement in politics.

The crystallization of a leadership class also assisted in the politicization of the already existing traditional religious groups. The access of this leadership to modern mass media—including TV, radio, printed material, and communal associations—enabled them to disseminate their ideas among their followers and to increase their recruitment potential.

The emergence of a charismatic religious leadership has also been crucial for the political revitalization of religion. The presence of Ayatollah Khomeini in Iran, Imam Musa al-Sadr and Muhamad Hussein Fadelalla in Lebanon, and Pat Robertson and Jerry Falwell in the United States, among others, have facilitated the process of religious indoctrination, recruitment, and organization of the politically, economically, and socially discontented in their societies. Through the teachings and the appeal of their message, those religious leaders give hope to their adherents in overcoming their particular grievances.

In addition, churches, mosques, and temples have often served as sites for mass demonstrations, strikes, and other forms of political protest and dissent. These places of worship harbor the important ingredients necessary for political mobilization since they provide a vehicle for face-to-face communication and interaction in mass assembly and offer social services at little or no cost.

According to Louis Cantori, in Egypt there are nine-thousand private, humanitarian, religious organizations run by the movement of the Islamic Brotherhood, which render social welfare and health services in addition to day-care centers and elementary education.

In Central America, the Christian base communities offer self-help economic projects as well as food and agricultural cooperatives for the local population. In the Israeli settlements on the Palestinian-occupied lands of the West Bank and Gaza, Gush Emunim offers educational, municipal, police, and health services to the settlers. Shi'ism in Iran has been conducive for collective action facilitating access to public goods. The organizational structure, bureaucracy, communication networks, and independent financial resources of the Catholic church enabled the clergy in Latin America, Poland, and the Philippines, to venture into the thorny realm of politics.

The sacred texts for the Christians, Moslems, and Jews also serve as valuable resources for mass mobilization and control. The high moral standards embodied in these holy books, as well as their commitment to social, economic, and political justice, provide politicized religious leaders with powerful moral leverage over their followers.

The Presence of Motives

Just as resources and assets are indispensable for the political revitalization of religion, so too is the presence of motivation—incentives. The process of modernization, along with advancements in science and technology, posed serious challenges to traditional religions that have prompted liberal theologians to interpret their sacred texts along more contemporary lines. The religious modernists placed a high priority on the adjustment of their traditional religions to the most up-to-date findings of science and modernization.

Similarly, the widespread social, economic, and political inequities in different parts of the world caused theologians with a progressive orientation, to eschew their traditional political passivity and assume the leadership of the political protest movement. Lonnie Kliever contends that these theologians enlisted the power of religion in order to bring about equality between the sexes, the races, the classes, and between the developed and undeveloped world. Such motives were behind the emergence of liberation theology in Latin America.

The church served as a mobilizing agent for economic development and political liberalism. The 1972 declaration of martial law by Marcos, and the assassination of Benigno Aquino in August 1983, prompted, according to C. Neal Tate, the Philippine Catholic church (which was neither as active or liberal as some of its counterparts in Latin America) to play an active and visible role in the downfall of the Marcos regime. Similarly, the presence of two cultures in Egypt in the late 1970s (i.e., the affluent minority and the vast majority that are poor) provided sufficient motives for the political revitalization of the Islamic Brotherhood movement. The poor quality of the Egyptian government's public services prompted the Islamic Brotherhood movement to assume the functions of social welfare and education. There has also been a renewed commitment on the part of the Brotherhood movement toward higher moral standards. This commitment is manifested in the increased number of pious men and women, the emphasis on proper moral behavior, the frequent use of traditional Islamic attire, and a growing hostility toward Western culture.

Israel's decisive victory against a combined Arab army in the 1967 June War and its capture of vast portions of Arab land, including East Jerusalem and the West Bank, provided sufficient incentives for the emergence of Islamic and Jewish religious movements. In Israel, as Mark Tessler points out, the result of these developments was the emergence of the Gush Emunim settlement movement. To a growing number of Israelis, the victory in the 1967 war ushered in the beginning of the messianic age and the recreation of the kingdom of Israel. The Gush Emunim, which is an offshoot of the National Religion party (NRP), added to the NRP's tradition of the observance and application of the Jewish law (as interpreted by orthodox rabbis) the idea that the West Bank and Gaza Strip are integral parts of the biblical land of Israel.

In some cases, religion can provide what otherwise seemed to be unacceptable personal political risks. In this connection the cultural religious traditions of the Shi'ites in Lebanon and Iran, and the Sikhs in India, have furnished the people with strong motives for risk-taking. Both religions exalt salvation through martyrdom and personal sacrifice. The suicide missions launched by members of the Shi'a community against Israeli military targets in southern Lebanon attest to their serious commitment to die in the name of the cause. Likewise, such religious traditions provided strong motives for the Iranian and Sikh masses to participate in the violent rebellions in their respective countries.

CONCLUSION

Despite the exposure to modern media, education, urbanization, and scientific advancement, the late 1970s and the 1980s were marked by the political revitalization of traditional religions in many countries. This political revitalization of religion challenged many of the assumptions of the literature on modernization of the 1950s and 1960s. The social upheaval and economic dislocation that were associated with modernization led to this renewal of traditional religions.

A comprehensive explanation of the resurgence of religious movements and groups mandates the employment of several perspectives. The contributors to this volume ascribe religious revivalism to the limitations of the secular model as well as to the crisis theory and resource mobilization model. These sets of factors are used by the contributors in their efforts to explain religious resurgence. Chapters 2–4, present a general explanation for the phenomenon of religious resurgence.

2

The Stubborn Persistence of Religion in the Global Arena
Anson Shupe

Not so many years ago, some notable observers of religion forecast its demise as an important independent variable in political, economic, and sociological change equations. Secularization, industrialization, and scientific advancement had presumably dealt religion a mortal blow from which it was not expected to recover. More than two decades ago, Anthony F. C. Wallace, a former president of the American Anthropological Association, wrote:

> . . . the evolutionary future of religion is extinction. Belief in supernatural beings and in supernatural forces that affect nature without obeying nature's laws will erode and become only an interesting historical memory. To be sure, this event is not likely to occur in the next generation; the process will very likely take several hundred years, and there will always remain individuals or even occasional small cult groups who respond to hallucination, trance, and obsession with a supernaturalist interpretation. But as a cultural trait, belief in supernatural powers is doomed to die out, all over the world, as a result of the increasing adequacy and diffusion of scientific knowledge . . . the process is inevitable.[1]

Wallace's statement might seem an extreme example, but was not so different from those of other observers pessimistic about the future of traditional religion. In 1965, the well-known Harvard theologian Harvey Cox expressed the same conventional wisdom.

The rise of urban civilization and the collapse of traditional religion are the two main hallmarks of our era and are closely related movements. . . . What is secularization? . . . It is the loosing of the world from religion and quasi-religious understandings of itself. . . . The gods of traditional religions live on as private fetishes or the patrons of congenial groups, but they play no role whatever in the public life of the secular metropolis. . . . It will do no good to cling to our religions and metaphysical versions of Christianity in the hope that one day religion or metaphysics will once again be back. . . . They are disappearing forever and that means we can now let go and immerse ourselves in the new world of the secular city.[2]

More recently, various social science theories of "globalization" and an emerging "world economy" have virtually eliminated the role to be played by religion in the future development of the planet. Even the futurist John Naisbitt in his popular 1982 book, *Megatrends,* devoted only a single page to religion, hardly allotting it much relevance for the educational, economic, and political changes he envisions now underway.[3]

Yet it is becoming increasingly apparent that organized religion is a stubbornly persistent and often integral factor in contemporary national and international politics. Religious sentiments and religious structures are being mobilized, or themselves doing the mobilizing, to create important trajectories of social change. This generalization is true across a disparate set of nations and world religions: from Malaysia to Northern Ireland to Iran to China to Nicaragua to North America to Egypt to Poland to Japan to Latin/South America and to the Caribbean.[4]

Whether the political agenda is one of terrorism, insurrection, or institution-building, the prophecy of religion's dwindling presence has been thus far empirically disproven. It will not do to try to dismiss the religious factor as an epiphenomenon or as some simple last gasp backlash against social change. Whether one claims that religion is enjoying a general resurgence, or that it has been a factor all along but ignored, is less an issue than determining how much of an impact religion is having and in what ways.

THE SECULARIZATION MODEL UNDER RECONSIDERATION

Ironically, the premature announcements of a decline in the importance of religion once seemed solidly grounded in mainstream social science. The demystification of religion inherent in the classic secularization paradigm posited a gradual, persistent, unbroken erosion of religious influence in urban industrial societies. It was the grand assumption of macrosocietal theories. Reviewing this model, Phillip E. Hammond has written, "A linear image dominates Western thought about society." This image can be discovered in such concepts as industrialization, modernization, rationalization, bureaucratization, and urbanization. Secularization implies a unidirectional process. It assumes that society moves from some sacred condition to successively *areligious* conditions in which the sacred evermore recedes. The first three generations of sociologists repeated this assumption so often that they came to accept it as a *fait accompli.* Only the recent generation has begun to question it.[5]

Nineteenth-century theorists such as Auguste Comte, Emile Durkheim, Ferdinand Toennies, Max Weber, and Karl Marx all prepared Western intellectuals for this expectation. Thus, many contemporary social scientists have assumed that as modernization swept across the globe, religion would, conversely, lose its grip on culture. Any sway it might continue to hold over individuals would eventually be transformed, for instance, into forms of *privatized* belief, where religion would become merely a personal matter anchored in individual consciousness, rather than remain a collective force with mobilizing potential for social change.

Attempts to salvage the secularization model have interpreted evidence of burgeoning religiosity in many contemporary political events to mean that we are witnessing merely a fundamentalist, antimodernist backlash against science, industrialization, and liberal Western values. This approach is intellectually akin to burying one's head in the sand and analytically as fruitless. Jeffrey K. Hadden, in his 1987 presidential address to the Southern Sociological Society held in Savannah, Georgia, criticized such attempts to "reduce" the key role of religion in what the model suggests should be largely secular struggles. Religious fervor, he noted, is often dismissed as ethnic hostility or as class struggle, typically explained away as an isolated exception to unremitting trends of secularization and seldom recognized as part of a larger global phenomenon.[6]

A reexamination of the secularization model as a hypothesis and not merely as a foregone conclusion, has been proceeding for at least two decades. Hadden cites four important factors that prompted this effort.

First, there is the very looseness of the concept "secularization," as well as ongoing attempts by scholars to refine it. Many such attempts at revision began inevitably to move more toward becoming critiques.

Second, there is the undeniable fact that statistics on popular religiosity (e.g., church attendance and religious book buying) from polls and surveys do not support the outcomes that secularization logically should produce. Religiosity is on the ascent in the industrialized West, not the reverse.

Third, the emergence of new religious movements in the post-World War II era, not just those of the cultic variety, but also those reinvigorating older groups, e.g., the charismatic Christian phenomenon, belies any popular loss of interest in religious meaning. Membership in traditional denominations may in many cases be on the decline, but more innovative religious forms have gained.

Fourth, even with the advent of religious television and other religious media in the West, religion has been a visible, significant factor in political mass movements, whether it be the American civil rights movement, the Northern Ireland struggle of independence, the civil war in Lebanon, or the Moral Majority in the United States.

During this postwar period, scholars have written books and organized conferences that critiqued the implications of the secularization concept.[7] Andrew M. Greeley's 1972 book, *Unsecular Man,* challenged American sociologists to defend their notion of a waning influence of religion in American society in the face of persuasive statistical evidence that showed it to be alive and well, even thriving. Drawing on a range of studies, Greeley asserted that basic human religious needs and bedrock religious functions have changed very little since the Ice Age, and those changes that did occur have made religious questions more critical in the modern world.[8] Likewise, the Lutheran theologian Richard John Neuhaus has written:

> Flying in the face of the facts, the conventional wisdom has until very recently been that America is or is rapidly becoming a secular society. . . . Americans *are* as peculiarly religious as they have been thought to be in the past, and probably even more so.[9]

The theoretical returns from this resurgence of sociological interest in religion thus far have been promising but limited. If anything, the challenge we now face is how to replace the concept of secularization, no matter how defined, with more viable alternatives. Theorists have come to realize how far social science still must travel to achieve meaningful conceptualization and theorizing *on a global level.*[10] Intriguing terms such as *prophetic religions, resacralization,* and *global fundamentalism,* must be put to the test of comparative inquiry and interdisciplinary scrutiny before their usefulness can be evaluated.

THE RELIGIOUS FACTOR IN THE GLOBAL ARENA

During the 1970s and 1980s a new interdisciplinary perspective developed out of comparative, historical, and economic theories. This theoretical framework has been generally referred to as *globalization.* That is, it postulates the globalization of nations and societies into a single, integrated, evolving "world system" of economic and political relations.[11] This new conceptualization can be described as a series of "processes by which the world becomes a single place, both with respect to recognition of a very high degree of interdependence between spheres and locales of social activity across the entire globe *and* to the growth of consciousness pertaining to the globe as such."[12] Globalization is heavily informed by Marxist and neo-Marxist economic deterministic assumptions. Thus, it also adopts the "strong version" of the secularization hypothesis (and a faith in the ultimate demise of organized religion as a significant social force). Other than occasional, atavistic manifestations of temporary cultic or doomed revitalization fervor, religion is assumed to be a spent, ephemeral force in the global arena.

That events have not worked out so neatly can be attributed to at least two sets of consequences of the globalization process that were unanticipated by its theorists.

The first set of outcomes concerns the electronic revolution in mass communications, beginning with the telegraph and culminating in satellite/laser technology. Recent advances in commercial and governmental applications of this technology have led many observers to suggest that as citizens of a planet now linked inextricably by transmitters, satellites, receiver dishes, and cable television networks and relays, we have become a truly global community. Instant communications now facilitate instantaneous awareness of events on the opposite side of the globe and make them part of our daily reality. Two decades ago the media gurus Marshall McLuhan and Quentin Fiore optimistically prophesied that electronics and automation would make it virtually mandatory that every person-adjust to the world's sociopolitical environment as revealed by mass media in a way that would render international populations truly part of one global "village."[13]

Such prophets optimistically assumed that cultural inter-changes and contact *via* electronic communications would militate against prejudices, stereotypes, and misinformation. But in fact, mass media communication have exacerbated, not dampened, the sorts of intergroup/interfaith sensitivities that lead to tension. It is true that computers and satellites can speed information and images from one distant point to another at unprecedented speed. But, as the media expert Ben H. Bagdikian asked over a decade ago: Is faster necessarily better? Or, one might add: Is it more likely to result in a reduction of tensions? Bagdikian reminded those persons enthralled by hi-tech communications that communication systems are amoral. They can transmit lies, errors, and paranoia as efficiently as truth, accuracy, and reality. Bagdikian questioned whether there were always disadvantages to the swiftness and pervasiveness of mass media.[14]

In other words, the two-dimensional and superficial portrayal of events in much electronic news may actually contribute to a rise in interfaith hostilities rather than promote understanding or tolerance. This is because the mass media deal more easily with caricatures and particularistic details, as do traditional societies where religious tensions are deeply ingrained. Flag-burnings and mob protests do not lend themselves to dispassionate reflection. The media, particularly television, encourages simplistic reductions of issues into black and white as well as into the archetypal scenario of villains and heroes. And conflict, rather than harmony, is more marketable as "news" because of its drama and glamour.

In such a medium those groups adept at reductionist, absolutist, and simplified frameworks of reference will excite and mobilize news consumers. "Mediagenic" causes, in the final analysis, will prosper. Nowhere in all this symbolic exchange are there signs that peace and brotherhood are automatic outcomes. The expansion of religious television programming in North American society, as just one example, has resulted in a tremendous amount of controversy and conflict both in religious and political spheres. On one hand, religious broadcasting has aided in the mobilization of voters to participate in New Christian Right political campaigns and in other social movements, such as the Pro-Life crusade. On the other, it has helped to bitterly polarize millions of conservative and liberal

Americans, Christians and non-Christians alike, on a highly emotional issue from which no one seems willing to retreat.[15]

The second set of outcomes deals with the calculus of the globalization process, *per se*. It is now apparent that there are certain "opposing trends" within globalization, as the American sociologist Roland Robertson has criticized,[16] that the concept's original formulators did not anticipate. As nation-states expand their "spheres of operation under the guises of enhancing the quality of life," among other things, they cross over institutional boundary lines into religious (or quasi-religious) realms. Governments become embroiled in disputes and conflicts over values in the realm of what the sociological theorist Talcott Parsons termed, *telic matters*.[17] Telic matters are those ultimate concerns of destiny, meaning, and justice that occur as questions to all thoughtful human beings and that religions purport to resolve.

Robertson and Joanne Chirico argue that the modern state well-nigh invites religious encroachment precisely because it is increasingly concerned with matters traditionally associated with the religious domain.[18] Moreover, in their view, the globalization process itself raises religious and quasi-religious questions.[19]

The result is that any secularization trajectory that accompanies globalization, because it involves culture conflict and challenges to the truth claims of various traditional religions, is ultimately self-limiting. There is, to put it simply, a ceiling effect on secularization that eventually comes into play. At some (as yet imprecisely specified) point, globalization sets in motion the dynamic for a search for ultimate meaning, values, and *resacralization*. In other words, secularization turns in on itself and generates the very conditions for a resurgence of religious influence (albeit perhaps an innovative or unconventional religion). Successful quests for such answers, as Rodney Stark has persuasively argued,[20] are inevitably religious and frequently theistic. Secular, atheistic philosophies have little to say on questions of life and death.

Secularization, as a part of the globalization process, in the larger picture is cyclical, not unilinear.

Robertson has emerged as the most persistent critic of economic deterministic globalization theory. In his view, secularization is actually a dialectical unfolding in which pressures for universality (toward globality or global consciousness, as globalization theorists recognize) vie with the persistent reassertions of pressures for particularism (toward redefinition of religion along sectarian and frequently nationalistic lines). For Robertson, secularization is not a one-way, nonrecursive movement on an evolutionary continuum of increasing Gezellschaft urbanization, industrialization, and desacralization. Rather, both Gemeinschaft (folk) and Gesellschaft (urban) modes of societal style continue to emerge in spiraling counterpoint, with important implications for religion when it appears as a factor in global relations.[21]

On a less grand scale this is the middle range empirical message of important research conducted over the past decade by the sociologists Rodney Stark and William Sims Bainbridge. In a series of studies on cult formation, sect expansion, and the conditions surrounding marginal religions' success/growth or demise, they have found a fundamental pattern of "exotic fringe" religious groups thriving in those parts of the United States (and elsewhere) where secularization, arm-in-arm with other "modern" trends, has presumably had its most advanced impacts. New religions, in short, thrive where secularization has most seriously eroded traditional religious practice and allegiance, and do worst where secularization has not yet achieved some general but unspecified level.[22] There is no evidence in their research, nor in accumulated data elsewhere,[23] that secularization drives out religion once and for all.

In sum, globalization theory has ignored religion, which has proven to be to its detriment as a macrotheory of internationalization, since spiritual matters are continuously integrated into evolving questions of global order. Globalization trends, including secularization, create structures and contexts that eventually confront larger questions of meaning, national identity, and the purpose of human existence. In such a confrontation, religion serves as a powerful tool for legitimacy, definition, and counterdefinition.

Activities of the general social movement known as the New Christian Right in the United States, during the past decade, aptly illustrate these contentions. Scores of scholars in numerous books and professional journals have analyzed the origins, dynamics, momentum, and meaning of this conservative Christian moral-turned-political movement.[24] In the United States, the world's most materialistically and technologically advanced society (and one that earlier commentators clearly held in mind as they badly forecasted the downfall of Christianity and similar traditional faiths), a brand of conservative religion was believed to have had its last hurrah some fifty years earlier. This alleged passing occurred during the short-lived fundamentalist victory of the conviction of the high school biology teacher John Scopes for teaching evolution in 1925.

Thereafter, fundamentalist Christians seemed to recede from the mainstream of American culture.

The movement literally resurrected its social and political muscle following the great liberal social movements of the 1960s and 1970s. The creation of the Moral Majority by Lynchburg, Virginia, fundamentalist Baptist pastor Jerry Falwell in 1979, did not herald the birth of this resurgence. In fact, the New Christian Right's origins were some years earlier. However, Moral Majority, Inc. came to symbolize this conservative development with its bold label and strident righteous pronouncements. After 1980 and the election of Ronald Reagan to the presidency, at least, no one was speaking in the confident 1960s theological rhetoric of the "Death of God."

Research on the phenomenon of televangelism during the past decade has addressed the two aspects of globalization theory that are most problematic where religion's exclusion as a significant independent variable are concerned: the lack of convincing widespread evidence that religion is fading from the contemporary scene as either a public or privatized concern, and the impact of the electronic media in conveying messages, coalescing social movement agendas out of diffuse grievances, promoting movement leadership, and mobilizing constituencies out of passive audiences. In the case of the American New Christian Right, the free-market capitalist nature of radio and television, greatly expanded by the existence of videotape and satellite technology as well as cable networks and favorable governmental regulatory laws, has propelled televangelism into the forefront as a catalyst for religiously based political activism.[25]

Televangelism helped provide ways to galavanize and reinforce older social movements: civil rights, anti-Vietnam War, homosexuality, and feminism. With hindsight we can say that it was no doubt inevitable that evangelical, charismatic, and fundamentalist Christians, who had been underestimated by many modern commentators as any kind of significant sociopolitical force, would not make the mistake of underestimating the potential of electronic media.

Some observers arrogantly and/or ignorantly dismiss the multibillion-dollar-a-year religious programming industry as purely entertainment, or as a laughable parody of *bona fide* religion. However, as the 1988 primary/caucus efforts of former televangelist-turned-Republican presidential contender Pat Robertson demonstrated, even the initial sensational (if not long-lasting) mobilization efforts built in large part on televangelism's fruits, can be alternately alarming or intriguing in their political potential. The Robertsonian/Falwellian/New Christian Right legacy is far from dissipated in American culture. And this is just one movement within a single pluralistic culture. The profusion of such movements worldwide is astounding.

CONCLUSION

A sociological overview of the interface between religion and political tensions in the world today finds that there are few nations or cultures where the sacred and secular realms are not intimately entangled. A massive resacralization of basic human issues in various cultures is underway, perhaps emerging in protest against secularization, but certainly arising in the moral vacuums often created by it. Religion has become a rallying point for political activism worldwide because of its nonrelativistic nature. It is a motivational source for drawing on heroic myths of resisting oppression and reform. It offers the associational structures and collective opportunities for aggrieved persons to come together and establish consciousness-of-kind. This is as true of the New Christian Right in the United States, as it is of religion in predominantly Islamic, Buddhist, Hindu, and Communist countries.

This does not mean that social science is ready to, nor necessarily should, abandon the secularization model as a whole. This model offers powerful insights into religion's interaction with given institutions, particularly the state and economy, in industrial societies.

But the model is in need of serious surgery. In particular, its deterministic unilinear evolutionary assumptions require considerable research and modification. There is no organized society on record in anthropology, archaeology, or history that does not show some evidence of religious cults and rituals. Perhaps it is time to stop anticipating a future end point to religion's prominence in human affairs and to treat the institutionalization of the sacred with the same expectation of continuity that we unquestioningly give the economy, the polity, and the community.

3

The Incurably Religious Animal
Joe Barnhart

In an attempt to answer the questions of how fundamentalism can thrive in a climate of modernity, I raise the broader question of how *any* strain of religion thrives at all. Why has not religion simply perished as a behavioral and ideological dinosaur? Why has religion flourished in a country like the United States, where pluralism thrives and where technology (including high tech) invades virtually every household and school? Why do over 90 percent of Americans still profess belief in God in the space age? Why in the age of astounding advances in medical research do people believe in faith healing, miracles, and even in life after death?

An answer lies in the inescapable fact that the conditions that gave birth to early and primitive strains of religion have not significantly changed since the emergence of *Homo sapiens*. Furthermore, there is no indication that they will be extinguished so long as the species survives. The conditions in question have been described by various phrases. I choose to refer to them as those conditions that generate in individuals the *intense consciousness of their finiteness*. To the degree that any human response is motivated or affected by this specific form of consciousness, to that degree it may be described as religious in its concern.

To say that members of the human species, like all other animals, are finite, is to say that they perish, suffer the various frailties of the flesh, and experience degrees of defeat and loss. Members of the human species, by becoming conscious of their finitude and forthcoming death, set themselves apart from most if not all other species. Since the objective conditions that breed the intense consciousness of finitude have in some ways changed only superficially, there is little hope (or threat) that the religious concern will be eliminated from the human species. By presupposing the religious concern as a relatively independent variable, social scientists along with philosophers and historians may seek to understand empirically how specific institutional and cultural forms of the ubiquitous religious concern not only emerge and grow in historical settings, but become a part of the settings.

The myth that a nonreligious secular worldview will become the reigning ideology around the world is perhaps a remnant of the nineteenth-century postmillennial Christian version of what the philosopher Karl Popper calls the doctrine of "manifest truth."[1] According to the postmillennialists, as the Christian message travels around the globe, it will enlighten the heathen, who will be readily drawn to the manifest truth of Christ. Accordingly, this progress of enlightenment will culminate in the establishment of the Kingdom of God on earth.[2]

Many who hold to the "manifest truth" of a secular nonreligious worldview have expected the blessings of modern technology and electronic communications to wean the devotees of the historic religions from their creeds and magical ways and to deliver them into a more scientific orientation. Proponents of this particular secular hope or faith have been painfully surprised, however, by the robust ability of even the most dogmatic from among the historic religions to utilize, for their own purposes, the benefits of modern technology and electronic communications. Indeed, they have utilized these ingredients of modernity and at the same time have successfully rejected one of the other primary ingredients, namely, the scientific outlook. Televangelists, for example, using state-of-the-art television studios and technology, will cast out demons on camera and, on occasion, will cast demons out of malfunctioning electronic equipment.[3] Ironically, in some cases, those explicitly religious traditions that have adopted much of the scientific way of viewing the cosmos, have been the least successful in utilizing the electronic media to communicate their message.

There is no basis for the claim that a general resurgence of religion came about in the 1980s in America or in the Middle East. There was no general resurgence because religion had not gone into decline in previous decades. What appears to have been a revival of religion in general, therefore, was in reality a shift of influence in the competition among various strains of religion. The fundamentalist wing of Protestantism, Islam, and Judaism in the 1980s gained greater influence largely at the expense of the more moderate wing.

It is misleading to think of a democratic nation, to say nothing of all the nations of the world, as capable of developing a secular ideology and practice of the kind that replaces religion of every strain. A secular democratic state with an open society is not the absence of religion but the condition of compromise and tolerance that the various and diverse religions in the land have attained in the perpetual competition with one another. It is the condition in which no one church or coalition of churches gains disproportionate aid from the state in competing with its rivals. The free access clause and the establishment clause in the U.S. Constitution express this ideal of equal treatment in an open society. The wall of separation between church and state is the logical consequence of each church or religious coalition successfully preventing its ecclesiastical rivals from gaining state support in the competition.

In the 1950s and 1960s, the more liberal and moderate strains of Christianity and Judaism in the United States mobilized their resources and symbolic network to effect major social and political changes. Martin Luther King's religious tradition joined other traditions and forces to bring about a favorable climate for legislation and court decisions advancing the civil rights of minorities.

In the 1980s, Jerry Falwell's Moral Majority, Inc. represented a shift away from symbols of minority rights to symbols that stress the recapturing of what fundamentalists, some evangelicals, and other conservatives perceived as losses they had suffered in recent decades, especially losses in what was judged to be a radical shift in the moral climate of the nation.

Several writers, acknowledging surprise at the ascendancy of fundamentalism and evangelicalism in the 1980s, ask how such an antiquated worldview could surface in a sea of modernity. By *modernity* is meant at least a cluster of developments that sail under such flags as modern technology, medical research, electronic communications, space travel, and, above all, the astounding progress in the physical and social sciences, and literary criticism.

In answering the question raised as to how fundamentalism survives in a sea of modernity, the question might be turned around. How does modernity survive in a sea of fundamentalism? Modernity, as just defined, may be thought of as not a great sea, but as a river running alongside, and sometimes into, other rivers. The scientific outlook is not the predominant outlook of the United States. Indeed, it is unlikely that the average college or university graduate in the United States could write an informed two-page paper on the concept of natural selection. The recent resurgence of fundamentalism may be seen in some respects as the inability of modern science to fulfill an unrealistic expectation, an expectation that is not bred within the scientific framework itself. The popular expectation that science would cure the malady of human ignorance was itself born of a magical way of thinking.[4] In reality, science guarantees that the condition of human ignorance will never be cured. This seems to create the curious paradox that scientific growth will continue to help generate the condition that breeds religion. This point needs elucidating.

First, the growth of scientific learning entails the opening of new vistas that were closed to earlier generations of scientists. In exploring vast new vistas, however, science invariably creates for itself new problems, puzzles, and cognitive difficulties. In short, with each new plateau of scientific learning arrives a new sense of ignorance previously not experienced because the questions and cognitive difficulties could not even have been formulated. The physicist Stephen Hawking today worries about problems and questions that the great Sir Isaac Newton could not express because physics in the seventeenth century lacked the theories and models that would have made such questions intelligible.

Second, the scientific enterprise has built into it a certain modesty and tentativeness that makes it vulnerable when competing with the dogmatists who demand "the absolutes" or "ultimate answers." Science must—in order to remain science—refer to its conclusions as conjectures, hypotheses, and theories. Science, as a cognitive enterprise, is a self-correcting process. While scientists as individuals might be as dogmatic as any televangelist, the scientific *institution* is so structured that the scientific theories and claims presented within the scientific arena will be scrutinized and exposed for error. As Karl Popper points out, science incorporates observation tests and requires of its theories that they be falsifiable.[5] Any given scientist might be dogmatic and even clever in protecting his favorite theory from falsification, but his colleagues will keep demanding that it be articulated in a falsifiable form and will subsequently seek to look for its weaknesses. The best criticisms of Darwinism have been offered, not by the poorly informed creationists outside the scientific community, but by scientists who are themselves evolutionists.

The progress of science, far from overcoming the human consciousness of finitude, contributes to it at especially the *cognitive* level. The *emotional* response to the cognition awareness of finitude to which scientific progress exposes individuals is the religious concern intensified. The point here, is that while science as an institution and tradition tends to counter dogmatism, members of the human species are not predominantly scientific animals. They have historically been more inclined to turn to magic and to putative unshakable answers to their unnerving doubts and questions evoked by the shattering experiences of life that keep reminding them of their vulnerability or finitude.

It is often forgotten that science is a rigorous discipline that is not only relatively new in the history of the species, but available to a staggeringly small percentage of the species. The by-products of science in the form of technology touch an increasingly larger number around the globe, but even then the ubiquitous concern with finitude is not significantly reduced. Indeed, a new faith in technology has arisen and is frequently expressed by individuals who are given also to magic, supernatural religion, and the predilection for miracles.

At the moral level of modern human existence, science and technology not only have helped individuals by reducing vulnerability and finitude in the face of crippling and lethal diseases, but have also generated new problems that intensify consciousness of finitude in new and unexpected directions. The astounding advances in medical research alone, for example, feed the consciousness of finitude by generating new *moral* dilemmas in the attempt to apply the medical advances to concrete cases. The ancient hankering for a quick and authoritative answer plays, in turn, into the hands of electronic shamans who step in with proof-texts to resolve the unnerving moral questions and dilemmas.

It is unlikely that shamanism, magic, and the longing for miracles in the face of severe crises will disappear. Professor Francis L. K. Hsu, past president of the American Anthropological Association, is probably correct when he writes,

> Contrary to a common sociological belief, I think greater secularization in the United States will be accompanied by more widespread and intense involvement with supernatural dogmas and other activities which provide the individual with affective refuge.[6]

Magic and technology will continue side by side, as will science and the demand for supernatural intervention. The "God of the gaps" is guaranteed continual resurrection just because science and technology will continue to create new gaps both in knowledge and in the moral life, gaps that theology will temporarily fill in with promises and grandiose proclamations. Emotionally, the modern and postmodern members of the species are as finite as their preliterate forebears. Religious strains of every variety (theistic, nontheistic, polytheistic, animistic, etc.) will, therefore, continue unless one or two strains are able to gain sufficient power and economic resources to force or induce its rivals to submit. But even then, underground strains will thrive with bewildering diversity. The human species is indeed the rational animal. It is also the magical animal, intensely conscious of its own incurable finitude, but always trying to either deny or transcend its finitude.

4

The Limits of Religious Resurgence
Donald Eugene Smith

The belief that in the 1980s we are witnessing a global revival of religion with far-reaching political consequences, must be qualified by careful analysis. Those who have popularized this belief point to the new political activism of American clergymen (Falwell, Robertson, and Jackson); the radicalism of Catholic priests and liberation theology in Latin America; the growth of Islamic fundamentalism in the wake of the Iranian Revolution; Sikh separatism in India; and so forth. All of these developments are important and must be analyzed on their own terms, but the interconnections that link them are either weak or nonexistent. Liberation theologians and revolutionary ayatollahs may be aware of each other's existence but have not influenced each other very much.

Religious resurgence is not jumping over cultural boundaries like a global prairie fire. The Iranian Revolution has unquestionably exerted a major influence throughout the Muslim world, but both ethnic and sectarian factors (it is Persian and Shiite) have imposed serious limits on its exportability to Arab and Sunni societies.

If the prairie fire metaphor must be rejected, it is not to suggest that these religio-political events transpiring now in various parts of the world are random coincidences. Rather, they emerge from a set of relationships linking religion, culture, and society, which is common to many parts of the Third World. This chapter is primarily concerned with the Third World; the limits of religious resurgence in the West (explored in chaps. 5, 6, and 7) are more obvious.

A religious designation tells us more about the character of a

Third World society than any other. Thus, to know that a particular society is predominantly Hindu or Buddhist or Muslim or Catholic, tells us a great deal, because religion is the central component of culture in all these societies. In traditional societies of the past, before the dislocations brought about by Western imperialism, education and law developed under the aegis of religion, the clergy had an important role in the function of social control, and the legitimacy of government rested squarely on religious notions. The traditional ruler was viewed as either a god or as an agent of a god.[1] Current expressions of religious resurgence are rooted in this historical reality, which still resonates in contemporary culture.

THE PATTERN OF THE PAST

There is no unique generalized religious resurgence sweeping the Third World; rather, a survey of the last sixty years shows that Hinduism, Buddhism, Islam, and Catholicism have all experienced periods of intense political activity followed by periods of quiescence. The present situation must be seen as part of the same pattern. Religious resurgence is a cyclical phenomenon. What has changed in the present situation, perhaps, is mainly the growing awareness of these events by the Western world, and the perception that they might be related to our interests.

In the 1920s and 1930s, religion was an important component in the nationalist movements that challenged Western rule. In Muslim Algeria, Egypt, and Indonesia, clerical leaders and religious ideologies appealed to Islamic consciousness so as to oppose European imperialism. The first great nationalist leader of Burma was a Buddhist monk, while in India Mahatma Gandhi drew millions into the political struggle through a universalized theory of nonviolence, inspired by his Hindu tradition. The religious resurgence of this period was remarkable, but it weakened, and when independence was finally achieved after World War II, secular nationalism was firmly in control.[2]

The one exception to this generalization is the case of Pakistan, in which a Westernized lawyer of secular predisposition mobilized the Muslim minority to demand recognition as a separate nation through the partition of India and through the creation of a new Muslim state. Since 1947, Pakistan has struggled with the problem of turning a Muslim state, which it is in fact, into an Islamic state, an elusive ideal fraught with endless complications. Nevertheless, for the Muslim world the birth of Pakistan in 1947 must be reckoned a major event of religious resurgence, overshadowed only by the Iranian Revolution thirty-two years later.

The 1950s and 1960s witnessed an explosion of political Buddhism in Burma, Sri Lanka (Ceylon), and South Vietnam as secular nationalism was repudiated. The monks became powerful political actors, leading to the assassination of Ceylon's prime minister in 1959, the enthronement of Buddhism as Burma's state religion in 1960, and the Buddhist-led overthrow of the Diem regime and successor governments in Saigon. By 1970, however, the Buddhist resurgence had spent itself and only vestiges remained of the former dynamism.

The 1960s saw the rise of Christian democracy in Latin America, inspired by the social encyclicals of the Catholic church and determined to promote real social change by democratic means. A marked departure from Catholicism's traditional role as ideological legitimizer of the status quo, Christian democracy came to power in Chile and Venezuela, but in the former country raised expectations it could not fufill and was defeated by the Marxist Allende in 1970. As an expression of Catholic resurgence, Christian democracy has had its day on center stage, but in various countries is still a live option.[3]

More radical elements were active in the Church from the 1960s; revolutionary priests like Father Camilo Torres opted for solidarity with Marxist groups and armed participation in the effort to overthrow the government. The development of liberation theology must be seen as an authentic Catholic response to poverty, inequality, and dependence, however discomforted some might be by its implied legitimation of violent change.[4]

The year 1979 was a banner year for religious resurgence, with the Sandinista Revolution in Nicaragua installing several Catholic priests in top leadership positions, while the Ayatollah Khomeini issued his final call for martyrdom and overthrew a shah who commanded the most powerful military force in the Middle East. Religious ideology and clerical leadership were always secondary in the Nicaraguan Revolution, but in Iran they dominated and furthermore, set the agenda for the revolutionary state.

One primary theme is common to all these revitalized religious movements. To assess the extent and the significance of religious resurgence, the remainder of this chapter will concen-trate on the three Asian religions—Buddhism, Hinduism, and Islam. The basic thesis is that the limits of religious resurgence are far more important than most contemporary writings would suggest.

BUDDHIST RESURGENCE AND RELAPSE

In exploring the pattern of cyclical religio-political activism and quiescence, it is useful to examine in some detail the case of Buddhist resurgence in the late 1950s and early 1960s. Events in Sri Lanka, Burma, and South Vietnam were almost as dramatic as the 1979 Iranian Revolution, but didn't attract much attention in the West.[5] Resurgent Buddhism did not threaten Western interests, and so these events were largely ignored or dismissed as curiosities. If Buddhist monks overthrew governments or assassinated a prime minister, they did not storm U.S. embassies.

In a setting of relative freedom, the Buddhist monks have unique advantages as potential political activists. They start with the highest social prestige of any group in society. "I take refuge in the Buddha; I take refuge in the Dharma; I take refuge in the Sangha," the layman intones. (The Sangha is the order of monks.) The not unusual sight of a university professor prostrating himself before a monk half his age is some index of this phenomenon. The monk's distinctive appearance, with his yellow robe and shaved head, is a political asset. As a celibate without family responsibilities, the monk can afford the risks of political radicalism more easily than most laymen. The pattern of communal residence, with up to eight-hundred monks in a single cluster of monasteries in Mandalay, means that large numbers can be easily mobilized for a political demonstration.

In Burma, U Nu's policy of promoting the revival of Buddhism undoubtedly encouraged the monks to believe that they were entitled to a place very near the center of power. Various Sangha associations became prominent actors on the political scene. In 1959 the well-organized Union Presiding Monks Association, at its annual conference attended by some one-thousand abbots from all parts of Burma, passed a resolution demanding that Buddhism be declared the state religion. U Nu made this resolution the central issue in the 1960 election campaign; the monks gave him unstinting support, including house-to-house canvassing, and he won a landslide victory.

After amending the Constitution to fulfill his election promise, however, the prime minister sought to do something to reassure the alienated religious minorities. He proposed another amendment to safeguard minority rights, and immediately faced the most militant opposition of the Buddhist monks. He was denounced in pamphlets and from public platforms by the Union Sangha League, the All Burma Young Monks Association, and numerous other clerical organizations. About two-thousand monks picketed all entrances to the building in which the joint session of Parliament met, and stopped all M.P.s who supported the new amendment. The prime minister, however, had gotten wind of the monks' plan beforehand, and got most of his M.P.s to their seats at 4:00 A.M., before the picket lines were thrown up. His amendment was passed, but U Nu faced a sullen and hostile Sangha that he could not win back. The loss of Sangha support was an important element in the deteriorating political situation that led to the military coup of 1962.

Events in Sri Lanka were more dramatic. Ven M. Buddharakkhita in the early 1950s formed the United Monks Front, which in time became a powerful network linking monks throughout the Sinhalese-speaking areas of the island. He forged an alliance with S. W. R. D. Bandaranaike, who combined democratic socialist leanings with an intense commitment to placing the Sinhalese language and Buddhist religion at the center of national life. The monk became vice president of Bandaranaike's Sri Lanka Freedom party, and the United Monks Front became a major actor in the election campaign of 1956, with monks plotting strategy, giving campaign speeches, and publishing devastating attacks on the Westernized United National Party, then in power.

After Bandaranaike's sweeping victory, the United Monks Front attempted to function as a kind of supra-cabinet, getting its favored candidates appointed to cabinet and other high posts, and expecting to be consulted on major policy issues. A power struggle between Bandaranaike and Buddharakkhita ensued, and when the prime minister refused to grant a government contract to a new shipping company in which the monk had a large financial interest, the break became final. The prime minister was assassinated by a monk in 1959, and Buddharakkhita was convicted as the archconspirator behind the yellow-robed triggerman. The Buddhist public's revulsion at the results of these clerical interventions in politics was intense but temporary, and monks have occasionally returned to dabble in politics though on a far more modest scale.

The 1956 election destroyed the secular, Western-oriented political consensus of the island, and while the Sinhalese Buddhist majority received substantial symbolic and material benefits, the minorities were seriously alienated, particularly the Tamils (the largest linguistic majority). For the next nine years there was not a single Tamil in the cabinet and state-subsidized schools were nationalized (striking a heavy blow at the Catholics, in particular), while Buddhist universities were created and Sinhalese Buddhist culture was vigorously promoted by the state. Tamil grievances and a separatist movement remain one of Sri Lanka's most serious political problems today. The Sinhalese-Tamil conflict is, to the best of my knowledge, the oldest more or less continuous ethnic conflict in the world.

Despite the assertions of activist monks that their political interventions are motivated by the desire to promote Buddhism, overwhelmingly, the authoritative spokesmen for the Sangha have insisted that all such mundane activities are contrary to the Vinaya code of monastic discipline.

There is an important point to be noted in examining the limits of Buddhist clerical intervention in politics: the yellow robe that is the source of political effectiveness, also bars the monk-politician from grasping power directly. There has never been a monk serving as premier or as cabinet minister. To become a prime minister or member of the cabinet a monk would have to leave the Sangha, but casting off the yellow robe would deprive him of the potent symbol that had brought him within range of political power in the first place. At the highest level, therefore, there are built-in frustrations in store for the ambitious political monk.

Early Buddhism had no divine blueprint for society. It emerged in a complex Hindu society that had already addressed the problems of social organization, law, and political theory. The Buddha rejected Brahmanical domination and the whole caste basis of society to the extent that members of all castes were welcomed into the Sangha. Caste was made irrelevant within the monastic order, and the general egalitarianism of Buddhist teaching was bound to have some impact on society at large, but social reform, per se, was not the Buddha's purpose. In terms of his perception of the problem, extrication from the cycle of rebirth is as difficult in an egalitarian society as in a hierarchical caste society.

There is no such thing as Buddhist law for the regulation of society. Aside from the elementary morality of the Five Precepts (which forbad killing, stealing, sexual misconduct, lying, and the drinking of alcohol), Buddhist doctrine devoted little attention to the laity. The Buddhist concern for organization and regulation was turned inward, to the development of the Sangha, creating a detailed code for the internal life of the monastic order.

As we have seen, contemporary political Buddhism, led by both laymen and monks, has scored some impressive victories. But what is to be done with political power once it is attained? There is much vague rhetoric about Buddhist ideals of equality, justice, virtue, and compassion, which are expected to motivate the rulers, and certain symbolic acts that amount to decorative Buddhism, but no ideological guidelines to suggest what policies a good Buddhist government should pursue.

By way of illustration, it is useful to examine the State Religion Promotion Act of 1961, enacted after U Nu's great electoral victory, and the adoption of Buddhism as the state religion of Burma. The act provided that Buddhist Scriptures would be taught to Buddhist students in all state schools, and in the universities and colleges where there was sufficient demand. On Buddhist sabbath days the state broadcasting system would broadcast religious programs; government offices and schools would be closed; and no liquor would be sold or served in any shop, restaurant, or public place in a hotel. Buddhist Scripture classes would be offered in prisons, and all state public libraries would be provided with a complete set of texts and commentaries. Arrangements would be made for the teaching of Pali (the original language of the Scriptures) in state schools, and Buddha images would be installed in every court building. In short, the act provided for a decorative Buddhism unrelated to the realities of social, economic, and political life.

Buddhist monks and laymen are capable of effective political mobilization to the extent of overthrowing or replacing governments, but have not demonstrated any inclination to change the structure of society in any fundamental way. Buddhist political forces can overthrow governments, but not lead social revolutions. The Mahayana Buddhist monks of South Vietnam, led by Ven. Tri Quang, mobilized the opposition to the Diem regime, which was overthrown in 1963. After the monks had toppled their *third* successive government, American correspondents were puzzled by Tri Quang's extremely vague replies to their questions about the Buddhist program for the country. The fact was that Buddhism provided no ideological guidelines.

By 1970 the Buddhist resurgence had spent itself and few vestiges remained of the former dynamism. The Iranian Revolution of 1979 may have had a great impact on the world in general, but not on the Buddhist world. Too many Buddhist monks and laymen have recent memories and clear perceptions of the limits of religious resurgence.

HINDU RESURGENCE AND INDIAN SECULARISM

India, with a population equal to that of Africa and Latin America combined, must necessarily loom large in any effort to generalize about the Third World. In assessing assertions that a global religious resurgence is in progress, we must ask to what extent it has affected Hinduism, and to what extent Hindu resurgence has affected politics.

The partition of India in 1947 created a Muslim-majority state that proclaimed itself the Islamic Republic of Pakistan and a Hindu-majority state, which proclaimed itself the secular Republic of India.[6] The Indian Constitution of 1950, still in force, gave no special recognition to the religion of the majority and enshrined the principles of secular democracy. The Indian National Congress, founded in 1885, had led the struggle for independence based on a noncommunal, secular Indian nationalism, and the framers of the Constitution did not even consider the possibility of a religious state after Islamic Pakistan became a reality. While India's forty-two-year record as a democratic secular state is far from perfect, there has been no major movement to turn it into a Hindu state.

India's secularism has not been brought about by repression, which was an important ingredient in Kemal Ataturk's secularization of Turkey. From 1947 to the present, Hindu-oriented political parties have been free to present their candidates and programs to the electorate, but with very limited success. Over the decades, the fortunes of the Indian National Congress have declined, particularly at the state level, but the major beneficiaries have been regional parties in South India and Marxist parties in West Bengal and Kerala. With regular elections every five years, the Hindu parties have failed to mount a serious challenge to the secular state.

A most important factor is the ecclesiastical structure of Hinduism, or rather its absence. Hinduism is a vast tropical forest in which every conceivable form of doctrine, ritual, and social practice has been permitted to flourish. There is no organized clergy for Hinduism as a whole but a wide range of religious specialists, including gurus of sects, temple priests, and wandering holy men.

The contrast at this point between Hinduism and its offshoot Buddhism, could not be more complete. Wandering holy men, *sannyasis*, provided the partial model for the early Buddhist monkhood, but the organizational genius of Buddhism led to a Sangha of remarkable effectiveness in modern mass politics. In India there has been no clerical challenge to the secular state comparable to that of either the Buddhist monks or the Shiite mullahs.

A further factor mitigating the political potential of Hinduism is caste. The Hindu extremist is brought face-to-face with the troublesome facts that caste is (1) central to the traditional Hindu conception of society, and (2) disruptive of efforts to weld a united Hindu identity. The hierarchical and antiegalitarian basis of caste constitutes a real problem for those who would mobilize the Hindu masses for an attack on the secular state.

What has plagued India throughout the entire period of its independence and remains a most serious problem is communal conflict. It is important to understand the nature of this problem. In many cases religion has little to do with Hindu-Muslim or Hindu-Sikh violence. As is argued in chapter 18, the conflicts have to do with competition for power, turf, and resources. Religions provide the symbols of group identity, and in an economy of perpetual scarcity violence erupts all too easily.

Many of the Hindu-Muslim riots in the cities of northern and central India started with personal conflicts that spread to larger segments of both communities. Some of the riots were instigated for political reasons, for example, to embarrass and destabilize the party in power, but others appeared to be spontaneous eruptions of violence, which quickly escalated. The primary role of government in such cases is obviously to restore law and order; the complaint of the Muslims is frequently that the government is lax or discriminatory in its protection of the minority. Communal disturbances of this type are not primarily political but a reflection of the socioeconomic strains of a plural society.

The Hindu-Sikh conflict has been more centrally concerned with the religious ideology, places of worship, and clerical leadership of the Sikh minority. It has also been more centrally political in that Sikh activists have frequently clashed with government forces over policy issues. In 1966 a Sikh agitation succeeded in securing the partition of the old Punjab state on linguistic grounds resulting in a new Punjab with a Sikh majority. More recent events have included a Sikh secessionist movement (Khalistan) opposed by New Delhi, the tactics of terrorism by Sikh extremists, the use of the Golden Temple in Amritsar as headquarters and arsenal of the movement, the storming of the temple by the Indian army, the assassination of Prime Minister Indira Gandhi by two Sikh bodyguards, and a horrendous eruption of anti-Sikh violence by Hindus in retaliation. In early 1989, the Indian government was seeking to restore normalcy in the Punjab, and there were signs that the

Khalistan movement, which was never supported by a majority of the Sikh community, was waning.

The strains that communal conflicts have put on the secular state are serious, but there has still been no major political force that has advocated the abandonment of secularism in favor of a Hindu state.

ISLAMIC REVOLUTION AND ITS REPERCUSSIONS

It is important to note that what is called Islamic resurgence, need not proceed from a mass movement, but may be simply a new manifestation of that most venerable function of religion, the legitimizing of government. Behind the ostentatious program of Islamization carried out by President Ziya-ul-Haq of Pakistan (1977–1988) lay the pressing need for legitimacy of a general who came to power in a military coup. The element of political calculation in the manipulation of Islam over the past forty years has produced considerable cynicism among the educated classes of Pakistan. Ziya's democratically elected successor, Benazir Bhutto, enjoys the distinction of being the first woman prime minister in the Muslim world, despite the protests of many *ulama* (clergy). In the short run, at least, democratic elections appear to have superseded Islamic symbolism in legitimizing power.

Islamic resurgence undoubtedly presents the most serious challenge to modern conceptions of the state, primarily because of the centrality of law, the *shari'a,* in Islam. In its most radical form, fundamentalists reject the modern legislative state on principle, for all law is the expression of Allah's will, which has been revealed. The corollary, in the case of the Islamic Republic of Iran, is that the functions of defining and executing God's law must be performed by those who know it best, that is, the clergy. The reign of the ayatollahs goes far beyond symbolic acts to the center of state power.

The Iranian Revolution must be regarded as one of the major events of the twentieth century.[7] It came as a shock to those who saw inevitability in the process of modernization that had transformed the West and that was now transforming the Third World. The revolution sent shock waves around the world, and it took a decade for many observers to come to terms with it.

From exile in Iraq and France the Ayatollah issued his call for martyrdom, and the anti-shah processions grew from hundreds to thousands to two million marchers. Drawing on a specifically Shiite emphasis on martyrdom, the Ayatollah accomplished an unprecedented mobilization of the Iranian masses and overthrew a shah who commanded the most powerful military force in the Middle East.

Religious ideology and clerical leadership dominated and set the agenda for the revolutionary state. Khomeini and his colleagues set about the task of creating in the Islamic Republic of Iran something unprecedented, a state governed by the clergy of Islam. As the revolution completes its first decade it is necessary to ask: How successful has it been in transforming state and society in Iran, and what will be its lasting impact on the rest of the Third World?

It must be noted first that the Khomeini regime astonished everyone by its internal stability, surviving the assassination of major clerical leaders, the Iraqi invasion, and the unremitting hostility of the United States. The revolutionary ideology it propagates has given encouragement to dissident Islamic groups struggling to overthrow authoritarian secular and traditional regimes.

Nevertheless, the prospects for the Islamic Republic appear bleak in the wake of the death of Khomeini, the severe military setbacks in the eight-year war with Iraq, and a devastated economy. The holy war against the "infidel" Saddam Hussain had produced a large and steady supply of new martyrs, useful in sustaining revolutionary fervor, but had distracted attention from the more fundamental task of defining and implementing the ideal of the Islamic state in the last quarter of the twentieth century. Iraq's Shiite majority did not rise up to support the Iranians, as expected, and after the loss of a million lives the world is still without a workable model of the Islamic state. The most important single characteristic of the Islamic Republic of Iran, governance by the clergy, is inconceivable in virtually all of the Sunni Muslim countries.

Throughout much of the Muslim world, Islamic fundamentalists in opposition can plausibly point to the failures of various secular movements and policies (nationalism, socialism, and capitalism) and assert that Islam has not yet been tried. But after a secular regime has been overthrown, as in Iran, religious resurgence must deliver the goods. As the Iranian Revolution completes its first decade, its most outstanding achievement remains the overthrow of the shah.

CONCLUSION

Religious resurgence in Third World countries is an important phenomenon, but should not be thought of as something that suddenly burst on the global scene in 1979. Aside from the cyclical aspect that makes decline predictable, various factors operate to limit the impact of religious resurgence. Oppositional politics is the forte of religion, and the arena in which it has achieved its greatest successes.

The most basic limit of religious resurgence is in moving beyond the oppositional role to institutionalize some vision of a modern religious state. Very few serious efforts have been made in this direction, and none can be counted a clear-cut success. From the early nineteenth century, traditional religio-political systems were disrupted or destroyed by Western imperialism, and it is doubtful that Humpty Dumpty can ever be put together again.

For better or for worse, a multifaceted process of secularization over the past century and a half has largely severed the connection between political power and the sacred. Few kings remain, and the survivors are no longer divine. A revolutionary movement, as in Iran, can revive the vision but only for a time.

In 1988 we are witnessing in the two Communist giants, the USSR and China, a conscious government-directed movement away from ideological politics toward the pragmatism of economic growth. With a growing consensus on the centrality of the marketplace linking these countries, Japan, Western Europe, and the United States, it is difficult to see a strong future for the religious variant of ideological politics.

Part II. Religious Resurgence of the Conservative Protestants in the United States, Central America, and South Africa

This part of the book is devoted to an examination of the political revitalization of the Protestant evangelists in the United States, Central America, and South Africa. In chapter 5, Kenneth D. Wald ascribes the rise of the new Christian Right to four factors: the practices of the new permissive culture that sharply conflict with the deeply held social values of the conservative Protestants and their substantial personal skills, the access to organizational structures and communication networks, and the co-optation by the conservative secular right of the Republican party.

Allen D. Hertzke and Ronald Nash, in chapters 6 and 7, respectively, dismiss the alarmist warnings of an imminent threat to American democracy and secularism posed by the conservative Protestants. Hertzke contends that the American system is capable of accommodating and channeling the political demands of even the most militant religious groups. Nash agrees with Hertzke's basic conclusion and points out that Americans overreacted to the evangelist movement and distorted its message. He concludes that the religious traditionalists behave in a manner similar to liberal interest groups who attempt to promote their cause by appealing to courts and by using modern media to spread their views.

Chapters 8 and 9 examine the Protestant religious movements in Central America and South Africa. Laura Nuzzi O'Shaughnessy traces the history of the Protestant church in Central America and accounts for the rapid growth of the evangelical sects in this area. Lawrence Jones points out that the evangelicals in South Africa are deeply divided along racial lines over the question of apartheid. He emphasizes, however, that the division in the Evangelical church is not merely a function of race, but more of a fundamental difference in the analysis of the sources for the political crisis in South Africa.

5

The New Christian Right in American Politics: Mobilization Amid Modernization
Kenneth D. Wald

Today a topic of widespread interest that generates impressive academic labor, religion and politics has only recently emerged from a period of sustained neglect by students of American politics. While they acknowledged the contribution of religion to American political development, most political scientists had dismissed religion as a fading variable incapable of sustaining electoral conflict in the modern United States. The revival of interest in religion among students of American politics has been due largely to the emergence of the so-called "New Christian Right" in the late 1970s. This development forced even the most secular-minded of scholars to acknowledge the potential political relevance of the religious factor.[1]

The New Christian Right (NCR) is a generic label meant to encompass a variety of organizations that gained national political prominence as advocates of moral traditionalism in public policy. The best known of the groups, the Reverend Jerry Falwell's Moral Majority, has recently ceased operation but is survived by Christian Voice, the American Coalition for Traditional Values, the Roundtable, and a number of other specialized organizations that share the goal of restoring a distinctive moral dimension to American politics. Under the impetus of this movement, the American political agenda of the late 1970s broadened to include a new emphasis on policies toward abortion, changing sex roles, the public status of homosexuals, drug use, sexual behavior and standards, prayer in public schools, and obscenity and pornography. These issues were not new to political discourse, but they attained an unaccustomed salience by virtue of the energetic efforts of the newly organized alliance.

In the decade since this new movement has appeared upon the national scene, it has enjoyed some successes and endured notable failures as well. It was credited with a major role in the election of Ronald Reagan to the presidency and the Republican capture of the U.S. Senate in 1980, and subsequently enjoyed privileged access to members of the Reagan administration. But as witnessed by the defeat of a school prayer amendment to the U.S. Constitution and the Democratic recapture of the U.S. Senate in 1986, it has frequently been unable to convert access into policy success. The current status of the movement remains a subject of debate. Is it more noteworthy that the Reverend Pat Robertson, an NCR standard-bearer, managed to mount a credible campaign for the Republican presidential nomination in 1988, or that the campaign collapsed relatively early in the nomination process? Whatever the answer, it seems likely that the NCR has become a permanent player in national politics, a force whose influence is likely to wax and wane with a changing public agenda.

The purpose of this chapter is to account for the emergence of the NCR as a significant force in modern American political life. As we shall see, that task is complicated because the NCR appeared to contradict the "natural" evolution of democratic political systems under the impact of modernization. Rather than destroy the foundation of religiously based political conflict, as social theory had predicted, modernization actually revitalized traditional religious communities and equipped them with the skills, organizations, and motivation to engage in political activity. This chapter first explores the puzzle of the New Christian Right, and then examines the role of social development in empowering conservative religious groups.

THE NEW CHRISTIAN RIGHT AS AN INTELLECTUAL PROBLEM

The emergence of the New Christian Right posed a daunting intellectual problem because it so fundamentally challenged the reigning model of politics in advanced industrial societies. As surely everyone knows, politics in modern societies is nothing but the organized expression of economic differences. Unfortunately for this theory, the debates about abortion, feminism, pornography, and other social issues do not conform to any recognizable economic division; rather, they represent a form of *cultural* conflict in which the contending sides are defined principally by attachment to distinctive clusters of values acquired through socialization to primary group norms and reinforced by continued social interaction with like-minded members of social groups.[2]

The persistence of such cultural conflicts in the late twentieth century ran counter to the predictions of modernization theory. Social theorists had long forecast that exposure to education, advanced technology, urbanization, and complex social organizations would diminish the size of the population committed to supernaturalism, undermining religious values or consigning them to the private realm. Thus purged of loyalties to "primordial" social forces, voters would make political decisions primarily on the basis of interest and ideology. In such a political environment, the dominant *issues* would arise from debates over the economy and foreign policy, the predominant *actors* would be secular elites drawn from interest groups, and the characteristic *methods* of political conflict would resemble corporate public relation campaigns, rather than religious crusades.

The resurgence of cultural conflicts in the political life of a highly developed society suggested the limits of modernization theory and its associated vision of politics. Discarding the assumptions of the classic theory of social development, initial explanations of the New Christian Right treated the movement as the joint product of a nationwide religious revival and a widespread rejection of the liberal trends in major social practices. According to some accounts, the 1970s witnessed a renewal of religious commitment in American life comparable in scale and intensity to the "Great Awakenings" of the eighteenth and nineteenth centuries.[3] This heightened religious consciousness created a large potential constituency for appeals to moral traditionalism. Such appeals became credible, it was argued, among the many Americans who felt themselves under siege from the rapid social change that swept over the country in the wake of the Vietnam War.

Despite the appeal of such an explanation, it rests on premises of dubious validity. Extensive survey data on the nature of religious commitment challenge the assumption that Americans experienced a general religious resurgence during the 1970s. While Americans remained strongly committed to religious institutions and values in the 1970s, trend data on affiliation and commitment leave the strong impression that continuity, not revival or secularization, has been the predominant pattern of religious attachment in postwar America.[4] One is hard-pressed to find evidence of widespread religious resurgence in these data. Similarly, trend data on American attitudes to social issues belie the claim of massive resistance to the liberalizing social ethic associated with the late 1960s. In fact, polling data suggest that most of the social trends denounced by the NCR—recreational drug use, changing sex roles, tolerance for "deviant" sexuality, and liberalized abortion—were actually *gaining* favor with the general public when the NCR first began organizing.[5] Thus, neither the claim of a religious revival nor the assumption of massive social conservatism constitute an adequate explanation for the emergence of the New Christian Right.

Subsequent survey research inspired by the Christian Right has enabled us to identify more precisely the social basis of support for moral traditionalism. These empirical studies tend to indicate that support for NCR goals is most strongly apparent among a distinctive subculture that comprises adherents of theologically conservative Christianity.[6] More specifically, opinion polls disclose that the core constituency for the NCR is composed of evangelical, fundamentalist, and charismatic Protestants, groups located principally (but not exclusively) in the southern and midwestern "Bible Belts." Further support for this portrait of NCR supporters emerges from historical detective work mapping NCR activity in elections for the U.S. House of Representatives.[7] The typical constituency that has experienced an NCR candidacy is distinguished by a preponderance of theologically conservative Protestants. Though otherwise divided on issues of theology, church governance, and worship, these religious groups apparently cohere in defense of Christian orthodoxy and its continuing primacy in public policy.

By narrowing the base of supporters to this distinctive subculture, we no longer need to rely on an explanation of the NCR that posits massive revivalism or social conservatism. However, we have merely exchanged one puzzle for another. How could a movement emerge among a constituency that had for so long forsworn political action in favor of "soul-winning" and was, according to modernization theory, declining in both numbers and social influence? Following their public defeat in the Scopes "monkey trial" of 1925, traditionalist Christians largely withdrew from the national political process, cultivating a theology that stressed the need for believers to separate themselves from corrupt secular institutions and practices, and to concentrate instead on regenerating individual souls by evangelism. This separation was never complete, of course, but it effectively discouraged conservative Christians from entering major political controversies as an organized movement. Overcoming this tradition of political indifference was made all the more difficult by the corrosive effects of modernization on the core beliefs of fundamentalist Christianity. The long retreat from politics, coupled with the expected decline in traditionalist Christianity, made it very difficult to envision a strong religious presence in American political life.

THE ROLE OF SOCIAL CHANGE

To summarize the argument to this point, the emergence of the New Christian Right cannot satisfactorily be explained as the consequence of a widespread religious revival in American life, nor as the result of a sudden popular revulsion against the liberalization of long-established social practices. Survey data indicate that neither of these phenomena appears to have occurred. Rather, support for the NCR has been concentrated among a particular community of religious traditionalists, comprising mostly evangelical, fundamentalist, and pentecostalist Protestants. Explanations for the NCR need to focus on this core constituency, addressing, specifically, how a powerful national movement could arise among a marginal population that was, until recently, noted for its indifference or outright aversion to organized political activity.

The most promising approach, so I will argue, emphasizes three interrelated changes in the traditionalist experience. Due to a variety of social changes experienced over the last half-century, religious conservatives now possess expanded *political capacity* in the form of personal resources, greater *political accessibility* through institutions with high mobilizing potential, and increased *impetus* for political action due to more frequent contact with social practices that challenge traditional values. Ironically, the catalyst for these changes has been the very process of social modernization that was once thought likely to eradicate religious traditionalism or render it negligible. Instead, the process of social change has seemingly revitalized the political potential of religious conservatives.

The magnitude of the social transformation experienced by conservative Protestants genuinely warrants description in terms of a social revolution. At mid-century, the locus of Protestant traditionalism was rural and small town America, particularly the South, and the typical fundamentalist lagged well behind the national norm in standard indicators of socioeconomic attainment. Largely as a consequence of the modernization of the South, a region heavily populated by conservative Christians, this portrait is much less accurate today. The educational, income, and occupational status gaps between conservative Christians and other religious groups have narrowed appreciably. Evangelical and fundamentalist Christians have established a significant presence in urban areas, particularly in the rapidly growing metropolitan parts of the Sunbelt, and in affluent suburbia. In these communities, religious traditionalists now occupy a wide range of middle-class and nonmanual positions that would once have been the exclusive preserve of mainline Protestants. This process exposed theological traditionalists to well-equipped and professionally run public school systems, but also furnished them the wherewithal to support extensive networks of educational institutions that attempt to maintain and propagate the faith.

Because of data limitations, it is difficult to document the full extent of this transformation. The principal problem is the lack of reliable baseline information on the various trends that have together constituted the process of modernization. The Bureau of the Census, normally the best source of social data, has provided only fragmentary data on religious groups from a single study in 1957. Though sample surveys by academic institutions have filled in the picture for the contemporary period, large-scale polling on religious affiliation did not develop until the 1950s, when the transformation was well under way. Beginning the comparison when the affected communities were in midpassage will surely diminish our appreciation for the social metamorphosis experienced by religious traditionalists. Comparison is further hampered by variations in sample coverage and procedure, changing operational definitions of religious groups, and discontinuities in the social categories by which data were reported. These problems will further understate the magnitude of socioeconomic differentials in the early stages of the social transformation or the leveling that has since transpired.[8] All these factors notwithstanding, comparisons between early inquiries and more recent findings will still help to illuminate the magnitude of social change experienced by religious traditionalists in the era since World War II.

Table 1 reports changes in the level of urbanization over the last thirty or so years. In the early 1950s, the three religious categories with a high proportion of evangelicals—Baptists, Methodists, and "other Protestants"—were concentrated primarily in nonmetropolitan settings; by contrast, most of the other major religious

TABLE 1

Place of Residence for
Selected Religious Groups

	1950s			1970s
Group	% Non-metropolitan	% Small Metropolitan	% Large Metropolitan	% Urban
National	41	28	30	83
Baptist[a]	53	32	16	70
Methodist	49	29	22	73
Other Protestants	51	26	22	—
Episcopalian	22	25	53	90
Lutheran	48	22	30	78
Roman Catholic	26	28	45	89
Jewish	1	15	84	98
None	35	26	38	89

SOURCE: Donald J. Bogue, *The Population of the United States* (New York: Free Press of Glencoe, 1959), p. 700; Wade Clark Roof and William McKinney, *American Mainline Religion* (New Brunswick, N.J.: Rutgers University Press, 1987), pp. 135–136.

[a]For the 1950s, the "Baptist" category includes all races and denominations. The figure for the 1970s is limited to white Southern Baptists.

groups were found in the more densely populated areas of the country. While Baptists and Methodists still lag behind other groups in rates of urbanization, the gap has narrowed appreciably since the 1950s. More importantly, the absolute level of urban residence has risen to over two-thirds for Baptists, and approximately one-fourth now live in large metropolitan areas. These findings support the conclusion that many members of traditionalist Protestant denominations have made the transition from a peripheral rural culture to a modern urban environment.

The traditionalist religious groups have also made substantial gains in educational attainment that bring them much closer to the national norm. (See table 2.) In the 1950s, Baptists were strikingly less well-educated than all other religious groups, trailing Episcopalians by an average of 4 years, Lutherans by almost 2 years, and Catholics by 1.5 years of formal schooling. In the 1970s, Baptists still trail these comparison groups, but the deficit has been cut roughly

TABLE 2

Educational Attainment for
Selected Religious Groups

Group	% Less Than High School Degree	% High School Degree	% More Than High School Degree	Median Years
	1950s			
National	53	28	19	9.5
Baptist[a]	65	24	11	7.8
Methodist	51	28	21	10.7
Other Protestants	61	21	19	9.3
Episcopalian	22	25	53	11.8
Lutheran	57	29	14	9.6
Roman Catholic	54	32	14	9.4
Jewish	34	33	33	11.4
None	60	18	22	9.2
	1970s			
National	33	52	14	11.8
Baptist[a]	45	46	6	10.9
Methodist	26	59	12	12.2
Episcopalian	15	51	34	13.8
Lutheran	29	59	12	11.9
Roman Catholic	31	57	12	11.9
Jewish	15	48	38	13.9
None	25	50	25	12.9

SOURCE: Bernard Lazerwitz, "A Comparison of Major United States Religious Groups," *Journal of the American Statistical Association* (September 1961): 573; Bogue, *Population of the United States*, p. 704; Roof and McKinney, *American Mainline Religion*, pp. 112–113.

[a]For the 1950s, the "Baptist" category includes all denominations. The figure for the 1970s is limited to Southern Baptists. The median figure also includes nonwhite Baptists.

in half. Methodists, another group with a sizable evangelical component, have gained parity or even exceeded groups that led them in the educational rankings thirty years ago. Moreover, data not shown in the table reveal that the educational level of young evangelicals has moved even closer to the average of other religious groups, portending a continuing convergence that is likely to eliminate the remaining educational differentials.

The comparison of income profiles over time is notoriously hazardous because of changes in the value of the dollar and the sensitivity of income questions in surveys. The data that are available for this purpose, presented in table 3, show a pattern of eroding differences similar to what has already been observed for urbanization and education. In the 1950s, Baptists, Methodists, and "other Protestants" were significantly overrepresented in the lowest income category and correspondingly underrepresented among the most affluent. The tendency persists today for Baptists, but to a much less marked degree than it was manifested in the 1950s. The "surplus" of poor Baptists has been halved in comparison to Episcopalians and Roman Catholics, while Methodists have gained to a point where they resemble groups that used to outearn them by a substantial margin. These gains in income are consistent with reported changes in the occupational stratification system gleaned from meager data. In the 1950s, only about one-fifth of all Baptists practiced nonmanual occupations, in comparison with one-third of all Lutherans and Catholics, and two-thirds of all Episcopalians. Recent surveys reveal that self-described evangelical Protestants have come much closer to the pattern of occupational distributions among other Protestants and Catholics.

No social transformation could be as simple or linear as the one just sketched out. No doubt the reality of the process was a good deal more subtle and uneven than it has been portrayed, and the process of adjustment to a new social environment was probably less smooth than this account suggests. Traditional religious communities did not suddenly appear in urban areas in the 1950s, but could be found there in some degree at the turn of the century. Similarly, religious traditionalism has not altogether cut its ties with its rural past or abandoned other features in the process of modernization. Nonetheless, the social transformation of traditionalist Christianity was sufficient to contribute in a major way to the emergence of the New Christian Right.

The first way in which modernization contributed to political resurgence was through its impact on the political capacity of religious traditionalists. Sustained political activity—as opposed to ephemeral protest or momentary rage—is facilitated by personal

TABLE 3

Total Family Income for
Selected Religious Groups

Group	% $0–$4,000	% $4,000–$7,500	% $7,500+
		1950s	
National	38	43	19
Baptist[a]	47	42	11
Methodist	41	44	15
Other Protestants	50	39	11
Episcopalian	13	41	46
Lutheran	36	48	16
Roman Catholic	31	51	18
Jewish	17	41	42
None	43	35	22

Group	% $0–$10,000	% $10,000–$20,000	% $20,000+
		1970s	
National	36	34	30
Baptist[a]	41	37	23
Methodist	34	34	32
Episcopalian	25	31	44
Lutheran	32	38	31
Roman Catholic	31	35	34
Jewish	22	29	50
None	34	34	32

SOURCE: Lazerwitz, "Comparison of Major Religious Groups," p. 574; Roof and McKinney, *American Mainline Religion*, pp. 112–113.
[a]For the 1950s, the "Baptist" category includes all denominations. The figure for the 1970s is limited to white Southern Baptists.

resources.[9] The affluent citizen has an advantage over the impoverished even in something as elementary as registration and voting. Someone who enjoys a comfortable life style will have the physical energy to follow political affairs, and even the transportation to travel to a registration site when necessary. With economic advancement comes a greater realization of the personal consequences of governmental policy and a sense of personal responsibility for public policy. Perhaps even more importantly, the educational background and job skills of a middle-class occupation provide the cognitive sophistication and self-confidence that may be necessary to comprehend political news and to maneuver through the shoals of government agencies. Such personal resources—money, time, energy, and freedom—become increasingly important with every additional increment in political activity beyond the first step of voting. That is why survey data show a progressively widening social gap between campaign contributors, organizational activists, candidates for office, and the like.

The development of an indigenous middle class has proven to be a prerequisite for successful political mobilization.[10] By equipping a segment of a previously rural population with advanced education, material affluence, and organizational skills, modernization converts a politically inert mass into an alert constituency, sensitive to its interests and capable of responding to new situations. Modernization also hastened the emergence of a leadership class that fills the role of mobilizing agent. Throughout American history, political assertion by disadvantaged minority groups has waited on their urbanization. As Protestant traditionalists have undergone the move to the cities, they too have acquired the capacity to engage in political action and an elite with the necessary skills to become activists, organizers, and political entrepreneurs. From this perspective, the political resurgence of conservative Protestants represents the latest wave in a pattern of ethnic succession to political influence.

ACCESSIBILITY: THE ROLE OF ORGANIZATIONAL RESOURCES

The political advantages associated with urbanization do not stop with enhanced personal resources. Social transformation further promotes political resurgence by developing the organizational capacity of mobilizing agents. In the case of religious traditionalists, four key institutions have emerged to play a critical role in stimulating political action—the local church, denominational or quasi-denominational religious networks, the so-called "electronic church" of religious broadcasters, and allies from the secular conservative movement. The accessibility to mobilization by these agencies is another consequence of the social revolution that has overtaken religious traditionalists.

The religious institutions of traditionalist Christianity have prospered in the move to the cities.[11] In many communities, energetic pastors have presided over the development of what have become known as "superchurches"—massive congregations with thousands of members occupying large and well-appointed complexes of buildings. These institutions resemble corporations in their wide array of member services, large budgets, and mastery of complex technology. The larger of these churches may stand at the hub of a network of integrated institutions that includes schools, camps, nursing and old-age homes, medical facilities, and travel agencies. Perhaps the ideal type is the Thomas Road Baptist Church in Lynchburg, Virginia, which has grown under Jerry Falwell's tutelage from a congregation of thirty-five meeting in a factory room, to "a vast and mighty institution with some sixty pastors and about a thousand volunteer helpers and trainees . . . [with] separate ministries for children, young people, adults, elderly people, the deaf, the retarded, and the imprisoned."[12] Even churches that have not grown that impressively have achieved levels of prosperity and vitality that far outstrip the modest, rural places of worship that many traditionalists recall from their childhoods. Such institutions are clearly the product of modernity, their parishioners coming from the ranks of the newly affluent urban service sector, their clergy no longer itinerant and self-taught but possessing seminary educations and considerable management skills.

In the process of organizational development, churches have acquired both political interests and formidable potential as mobilizing agents. Interest arises from the increased interaction with public authority that accompanies the diversification of church mission. To cite one example, a Church day school "is subject to governmental regulations on zoning, taxation, health and public safety, professional standards, wages and working conditions, racial integration, curriculum, and standardized testing."[13] Any action taken in these areas exposes the Church to substantial legal liability. The church may be well-equipped to act on these interests by virtue of its cohesive congregants. Church members are connected by communication networks, sustained by fellow congregants who may share their views, and subjected to direction from authoritative individuals.[14] These features constitute valuable resources should political action be contemplated. The church may be the target of mobilization by candidates, the base of political power for members, and the font of resources in the form of volunteers, contributors, and campaign personnel.

Once again, the traditionalist churches seem to be following a well-trod path. Research on the dynamics of the civil rights movement has revealed the critical role played by the black church in that crusade.[15] The church supplied leadership, a communication network, a locale for organizing, and a haven where spirits could be raised and commitment revitalized. When Catholics attempted to build an anti-abortion movement in response to the *Roe v. Wade* decision of 1973, or when Jews sought to raise funds for Israel in 1967, both groups turned to the preexisting local religious institutions as the infrastructure. Evangelicals are the latest group to rely upon the church as a base for political action.

Besides the local church, conservative Protestants have also benefited politically from the availability of two additional types of networks, the denominational tie and the electronic church. These two institutions add to the mobilizing capacity of religious traditionalism by furthering its resource and communication base. The denominational tie is credited with helping to build some of the pioneering NCR organizations by facilitating contact between issue entrepreneurs and likely allies in various churches. Though Jerry Falwell belongs to the independent, nondenominational wing of conservative Baptism, he built Moral Majority around fellow pastors who were members of the Baptist Bible Fellowship.[16] Christian Voice seems to have relied on the Assemblies of God as a mechanism to disseminate its concerns and political plans. Deep involvement in the Southern Baptist Convention aided the founder of Religious Roundtable in building up interest in common political action among members of that denomination.

Though the electronic Church has recently become something of an embarrassment to conservative Christianity, it nonetheless has been another source of mobilizing capacity for those who seek to direct religious traditionalism to political ends.[17] Drawing on the tradition of revivalism in American Protestantism, the modern phenomenon of "televangelism" dates from the late 1950s when a ruling by the Federal Communications Commission encouraged local stations to begin the sale of airtime to religious broadcasters. Prior to that ruling, stations had been required to donate air time for religious broadcasting and had favored the more established mainline forces within the Protestant, Catholic, and Jewish communities. These churches were unprepared to win bidding wars with the entrepreneurial ministries that had long been accustomed to financing their operations by intensive fundraising. In fairly short order, the available broadcast time was committed overwhelmingly to the aggressive pastors of conservative Protestantism. Television and radio became a means for the minister to expand his audience beyond the walls of the church and to claim a regional or even national congregation. While most religious broadcasters used technology simply to broadcast regular worship services, a few developed ministries built completely around video congregations. Largely overlooked or dismissed by secular critics, the superstars of televangelism developed intense followings among regular viewers who provided the funding to maintain the programming and to undertake outreach efforts in other countries.

The political capacity of these independent ministries was first displayed in the 1980 "Washington for Jesus" rally. A crowd estimated at between 250,000 and 500,000 people gathered for twelve hours on the Mall to listen to speakers urging national repentance for a variety of crimes. This impressive assembly appeared in the nation's capital "because powerful radio and television preachers from all over America used their programs and publications to invite their constituencies . . . [and] then tapped into the infrastructures of their multifaceted communications organization to help get people aboard buses and airplanes and private vehicles en route to Washington." Audiences do not simply do what television announcers ask of them, so it must be asked what enabled the televangelists to produce such an impressive degree of compliance. What made the invitations credible, argue Jeffrey Hadden and Anson Shupe, was the capacity of the televangelists to create a context in which viewers and listeners learned the "appropriate" connection between faith and political conduct. By consistent repetition of a common scenario, the televangelists convinced the audience that the palpable social problems they observed in their communities were the inevitable consequence of social policies that had denied fundamental religious truths. Sizable portions of the audience became persuaded that a national day of repentance would favorably impress God and so set America back upon the path of righteousness. The example suggests why access to religious constituencies through broadcasting is another factor that promotes the political capacity of religious traditionalism.

The final mobilizing agent worth mentioning consists of the secular conservative leaders who helped in the formation of some of the NCR organizations and provided advice and resources to the entire movement. Following the defeats of the Republican party in 1974 and 1976, a number of the most ideologically oriented Republican theorists set out in search of a new coalition capable of restoring their party to competitive status. Their attention was drawn to evangelical Christians by the success of a number of grass-roots campaigns waged on behalf of "traditional values" in such diverse arenas as a textbook controversy in rural West Virginia, a referendum on gay rights in Miami, and the national effort to prevent ratification of the Equal Rights Amendment to the U.S. Constitution. Discovering a population largely outside politics except when "moral issues" inspired fierce political action yet a constituency with well-regarded leaders and strong lines of internal communication, they set out to enlist the traditionalist Protestants in their "New Right" alliance.[18] As part of this effort, they recruited selected pastors for leadership positions, provided them with access to other conservative elites and organizations, and served as advisers on matters of tactics and strategy. The patronage of experienced conservative activists probably hastened the progress of the Christian Right and wed it firmly to the Republican party.

Accessibility to mobilization, one of the key factors in stimulating the NCR, is clearly a by-product of the modernization process that religious traditionalists have undergone. The urban migration concentrated conservative Protestants in strong churches, a process that unintentionally facilitated their capacity for political action. As the conservative denominations grew apace, they acquired the organizational links and technological sophistication that would also enhance potential political activism. The existence of this ready-made infrastructure presented an inviting prospect to secular conservatives in their mission to knit together a national majority on behalf of traditionalist values.

"TRIGGER" ISSUES IN THE CONTEXT OF MODERNIZATION

Neither personal resources nor a well-developed organizational framework will be deployed for political purposes in the absence of some "trigger" issue or concern. A trigger issue is especially important when mobilizing a group like religious traditionalists who have consistently forsworn political combat. It is my contention that modernization supplied such a trigger by greatly increasing the probability that religious traditionalists would encounter social practices that challenged traditional social norms. The perceived challenge was so salient that it eventually overcame the tradition of political disengagement.

Most explanations of the Christian Right take it as axiomatic that the movement emerged as a reaction to a variety of liberalizing trends that swept over American life during the 1960s and 1970s. The various disturbing trends, summarized in the concept of "secular humanism," include changes in traditional sex roles, relaxed norms about sexual behavior in general, and the development of a permissive ethic in social conduct. I do not doubt that these practices genuinely outraged people who had been socialized to respect traditional sex role distinctions, to regard homosexuality as an abomination, to treat sensate pleasures as sinful, and, in general, to favor Biblically based restraint as a key to social order. That is, I accept the Christian Right's claim that it wishes to restore what it sees as "traditional values" in American public policy.[19] But I do not think that this alone is sufficient to account for the rapid countermobilization of conservative Christians against what they see as public policy gone astray.

Conservative Christians have been estranged from American culture since at least the 1920s; the denunciations of social corruption heard on the airwaves today echo similar complaints from the great revivalists of a generation ago. Why are the contemporary evangelists so successful in prompting their audiences to seek political redress? One strand of the answer is that traditionalists, by virtue of their migration to the complex and pluralistic urban environment, are much more likely to encounter life-styles and social practices that pose a direct challenge to their own views of right and wrong. When traditionalists were concentrated in rural communities lacking any strong rivals, they enjoyed dominion over the local culture. Through this control, they could ensure that public values reflected the conservative social consensus of traditional Protestantism.[20] Local control of critical institutions enabled them to ward off any threats to the dominant value system. Political action was unnecessary except for those rare instances when outside forces impinged on local norms.

The situation changed due to a number of forces, including television and the expansionist federal government, which were viewed as the carriers of alien values threatening to social traditionalism. But the challenge was even more intense as a consequence of the urban presence. In the large towns and cities where evangelicals migrated, they found themselves no longer in the overwhelming majority but as merely a new set of players competing for influence. The city was home to many of the forces that struck at the heart of the social values that had sustained the traditionalist universe. Living in a pluralist environment enhanced the probability of direct contact with unsettling social practices.[21] And when traditionalists appealed for the restoration of order, they found themselves unable to count on the support of political authorities who might themselves be receptive to the social trends that outraged the conservative Christians.

Thus the process of modernization, which had already given traditionalists substantial personal resources and enmeshed them in institutions capable of sustained political action, now gave them a reason to transfer these new qualities to the political realm. Modernization exposed them directly to practices that were abhorrent and perceived as directly threatening to traditional ways of life. These were not distant threats that could safely be ignored from a secure environment but immediate challenges that were visible on the streets, in the schools, and even in the homes. Contact lent an urgency to political mobilization sufficient to overcome a long heritage of indifference to the political process.

CONCLUSION

Scholars have increasingly called into question the assumption that modernization inevitably spells death for traditional religious values. This chapter challenged another strand of modernization theory, the belief that advanced social development will diminish the intensity of political conflict over "cultural" values. As we have seen, the modernizing processes experienced by American religious traditionalists brought them from a position of political marginality, to the center of the political process. This transformation was a function of increased personal resources, organizational encapsulation, and contact with challenging social forces—three factors intimately connected with the modernization process. A cursory examination of other chapters in this volume will reveal the universality of this scenario. Around the globe, as in America, traditional religious communities appear to flourish politically in the supposedly inhospitable climate of modernization. These findings should prompt scholars to examine more closely the adaptive capacity of religious traditionalism, recognizing what was once so aptly described as the modernity of tradition.

6

Christian Fundamentalists and the Imperatives of American Politics
Allen D. Hertzke

The political resurgence of Christian fundamentalists in the United States has sparked a flood of scholarly analysis, much of it insightful and penetrating.[1] Yet the field suffers at times from the cultural gulf between researchers and their subjects; few professors, especially at elite institutions, are members of fundamentalist churches. Indeed, the vast majority of political scientists, sociologists, and theologians appear hostile to, or at least ambivalent about, fundamentalists and the world they represent. It is not surprising, consequently, that normative biases sometimes slant empirical studies of conservative Christians.

Indicative of this are two related lines of inquiry, one that assesses popular support for the fundamentalist agenda, and the other that purports to show the lack of fundamentalist commitment to tolerance and democratic pluralism. In each case, the research methodologies employed (constructs of opinion surveys) have allowed scholars to draw conclusions supportive of their apparent original biases. This chapter seeks to demonstrate that when we supplement this kind of research with a close assessment of the strategic political realm, a different picture emerges, one in which some fundamentalist concerns (as tempered by tactical political choices) resonate with a broader public and fundamentalist leaders sometimes appear willing to compromise and adapt to pluralist conditions.

Let us consider first the question of popular support for the New Religious Right. The literature suggests that such groups as the Moral Majority lack public backing.[2] Following the lead of Emmett Buell and Lee Sigelman, several studies have employed "feeling thermometer" scales that show, not surprisingly, that most people do not feel "warm" toward the Reverend Jerry Falwell. These studies then mistakenly leap to the conclusion that this indicates a general lack of public support for the New Religious Right, ignoring public backing for facets of the fundamentalist agenda (e.g., school prayer), and ignoring the fact that Falwell's now defunct organization represented only a small portion of a much broader movement.[3] Other studies compare fundamentalist ideology or rhetoric with the broader public, and find great disparities. The problem here is that these scholars assume that fundamentalist leaders do not adapt their agenda in light of strategic realities, that they pursue purist and therefore unpopular goals.

This leads us to the question of fundamentalist religion and its supposed closed-mindedness and antidemocratic proclivity. Often the fundamentalist constituency is viewed as intolerant, paranoid, reactionary, uneducated, and suffering from status anxiety.[4] A common methodology is to analyze fundamentalist Christian responses to survey questions about homosexuals or Communists—an approach that appears to indicate that conservative Protestants are more intolerant of diversity, less accepting of pluralism.[5] The problem, once again, is that this value-laden literature ignores the actual behavior of these individuals and their leaders in the public square, thus underestimating the extent to which they may accommodate themselves to diverse views in actuality. Moreover, this research conveniently provides a rationale for liberal academic intolerance of those viewed as intolerant: pluralism is for everyone except those we feel do not embrace pluralism.

It could well be that fundamentalist religion does lend itself to less tolerance; it may be that fundamentalist leaders frequently express a paranoid and overblown rhetoric; it may be that some of their positions are not widely supported. But what happens when "fundamentalist ideologues" confront the hard and seductive reality of practical politics in America? That is the question I have explored in my research over the past four years, research that has involved interviews with religious lobbyists and congressional members and staffers in Washington, as well as discussion with, and observation of, participants in the 1988 presidential campaign, including political consultants, national campaign managers, journalists, caucus goers, and convention delegates. The conclusion I have drawn is that there are powerful forces in American politics that moderate and channel even the most militant religious political "witness." Moreover, the modest influence fundamentalists exercised in American politics has not been without some public support. Indeed, tempered elements of the fundamentalist critique of modernity are increasingly being picked up by elites in diverse circles.

RELIGIOUS WITNESS AND THE CONGRESSIONAL MILIEU

To a greater extent than many academics anticipated, national fundamentalist lobby leaders have adapted to the congressional norms of compromise and incrementalism.[6] The reasons should not be surprising. For those groups that want to win tangible concessions and not just "witness" to their faith, a decision to lobby Congress implicitly means doing so on its terms, by its rules. Compromise, newcomers learn, is an essential component of the political art, the way to build majorities. Shifting alliances, moreover, mean that there are no permanent friends or enemies; one's adversary today may be an ally tomorrow. This potential for strange bedfellows in turn demands a certain deference and mutual respect. Finally, congressional petitioners learn quickly that most policymaking is necessarily incremental; the way you build coalitions is to craft agreement on marginal changes rather than on long-term (and more fundamental) goals.

What is astonishing is the evidence that the fundamentalist newcomers have accepted this reality more readily than some of their liberal church counterparts. In response to open-ended questions, for example, lobbyists for the liberal "mainline" churches conveyed the tension they experience in simultaneously wanting to win political victories, and yet "witness" to their faith with "prophetic," radical stands. They know from experience that tirades about the inherent evils of capitalism and depictions of America as an oppressive empire reduce credibility on the Hill, yet some hesitate to accept that their message needs to be made politically palatable. Fundamentalist leaders, on the other hand, have chosen, for strategic reasons, to accept the norms of the Washington milieu. They want to win.

Evidence of this can be found in the way in which fundamentalist leaders analyze their own situation. For example, Roy Jones, former chief lobbyist for the Moral Majority, assessed their strategic dilemma this way. "In 1981 the Moral Majority went through a difficult period. We didn't have victories, and we needed victories for our membership." Jones then conveyed that pragmatic, incremental strategies were the means chosen to gain victories, however partial, and he accepted the implications of that assessment. "Incremental approaches take us out of the business of being radical. We are not for radical change; we're for incremental change." This sentiment was echoed by the lobbyist for Concerned Women for America. "I have difficulty on a purist approach on abortion or tuition tax credits. We have to eat the elephant a bit at a time. We have to accept partial victories."

The fundamentalists learned, too, that the art of compromise demands that issues be framed in the most broadly appealing way, even if that means taking a less purist stand. With the passage of the Equal Access Act in 1984, which sanctioned student-led religious clubs in public high schools, they learned that they can "pick up the marginals," those moderates and liberals who might not share their long-range goals, but who can support a particular initiative. Indeed, this lesson came out again and again in the interviews, as this statement from Jones attests:

> For the first three years of our existence we framed the issues wrong. We pushed for school prayer, but we framed the issue in terms of how prayer in schools is good. But some people feel that prayer in school is bad. So we learned to frame the issue in terms of "students' rights". . . . We are pro-choice for students having the right to pray in public schools.[7]

From abortion to prayer to tax credits for child care, fundamentalists are attempting to craft proposals that have broad appeal, in large part because of their need for successes to maintain direct-mail lists. And to make a compelling case, as Jones put it, "We can't afford to say 'God settled it; that's it.' " In the process of lobby mobilization, consequently, leaders of the New Religious Right are simultaneously conducting a massive civics lesson for their contributors. Their long-range goals may be radical, but their instructions to grass-roots followers mundanely endorse the pluralist rules of the game: "Be respectful when you write congressional members; use arguments they can understand; don't threaten; don't rely on scripture," and so forth.

A notable challenge in the Washington system is, of course, its enormity and complexity. The dispersion of power in Congress and the multiple veto points in the legislative process make it tremendously time-consuming to lobby on even one issue. This means that even the most well-heeled interest groups make strategic choices. As one lobbyist put it, "You can only lobby on two or three issues a year, so you have to pick your targets carefully."

This is most difficult, apparently, for some of the liberal Protestant churches, whose numerous social ministries churn out policy positions with the alacrity of presidential campaigns. The United Methodist Church book of resolutions, for example, is a hefty two volumes, and covers virtually every issue on the public agenda. Consequently, the director of the Methodist lobby in Washington must choose the issues on which to concentrate. After a lengthy interview it was clear that this was not an easy task for the minister in charge, in part because he resisted making decisions where they might have the greatest success. Indeed, he compared the Methodists unfavorably to their fundamentalist adversaries. "They're smart. They are employing the same tactics with more vigor, more vitality. We have a thousand issues and they have five and they go for it."

For the fundamentalists the imperatives of maintaining grassroots networks, and the desire to win some real victories, necessitate clear tactical trade-offs: only a few issues will be the focus of major lobbying efforts each legislative session. Thus, strategic conditions generally guarantee that their greatest effort and success are on those issues, such as school prayer, pornography, abortion, and parental choice in education or child care, where their concerns resonate with a broader constituency.[8]

The norms of Congress and the requisites of organizational maintenance, as we have seen, constrain and channel the efforts of fundamentalist lobbyists. Thus, these leaders, in attempting to influence public policy, are themselves shaped by participation in the national public square, and they are simultaneously trying to bring their followers along in that accommodation. The question is whether similar tempering forces exist at the electoral level as well.

PRESIDENTIAL POLITICS AND THE MEDIA GLARE

If the congressional system is about practical accommodation, one might think the campaign trail is less so, and perhaps rightly. For campaigning necessarily involves emotion, heightened rhetoric, and exaggerated appeals. But there are constraints here, too, that channel religious activism, in part because the unrelenting media spotlight can expose and magnify insulated thinking and quirks of character.

The presidential campaign of Pat Robertson in 1988 is an illustration of the practical constraints that conservative Christians face in contemporary politics. Robertson's announcement, coupled with supporting petitions signed by three million supporters, was met with considerable fear and trembling among Republican party regulars. Moreover, his stunning early successes in party conventions and caucuses ignited apoplectic rejoinders from state Bush lieutenants. Peter Secchia, state committeeman in Michigan and a Bush supporter, described the Robertson contingent as "looking like the bar scene from Star Wars," while William DePass, a county GOP official in South Carolina, said it was similar to a "Nazi meeting."[9] Robertson's downfall, however, was largely his own doing. His proclivity for misstatements—what his campaign manager called "funny facts"—created doubts at the very time when he needed to demonstrate steadiness and competence. No doubt Robertson will be more careful in the future, but that very carefulness creates a dependency on the consultants and experts whose advice has a logic independent of the insulated world of charismatic religion. These specific circumstances, then, suggest broader lessons about the imperatives of national campaign politics that Robertson—or other candidates of similar persuasion—must understand and accept in order to mount credible efforts.

What are the special constraints Robertson (or someone like him) faces? First, one must accept the fact that most national journalists are a secular lot with a jaded view of televangelists in particular, and a suspicion of evangelical Christianity in general. Their reporting will reflect those biases and will contribute to the perception that "religious fanatics" are invading the political realm. Second, these sentiments are shared by a large portion of the Republican political establishment. Culturally there is a yawning chasm between the blue-blood (country club) Republicans and the fundamentalist populists who are demanding a prominent place in the party. Combine all this with the fact that, after the Bakkers and Swaggart, public sentiment appears wary of national charismatic figures—and the political task is formidable indeed. This context was very much on the minds of the Robertson campaign staff, whose efforts were aimed in large part at reducing Robertson's "negatives" among the public. His widely reported misstatements, however, particularly the assertion that the Bush campaign might be behind Swaggart's downfall, undermined these efforts. As Marc Nuttle, campaign manager for Robertson, put it:

We had gotten the negatives down from 45 to 32 percent with the general population, and down to just 15 to 20 percent with our [evangelical] base. Then, we had about four funny facts and Swaggart and we lost 20 points in negatives overnight.[10]

What this implies is that Robertson needed to do a better job of reassuring potential supporters and even opponents that he is a reasonable man and competent leader. But to do that he would have to submit himself even more to the discipline imposed by campaign experts, consultants, pollsters, and the like, who in turn would mold his message for the broadest appeal. This dependence on the campaign staff is heightened by the exceedingly complex nature of presidential campaigning. Nuttle summarized what it takes to run a presidential campaign:

> You have to know the media markets around the country personally. You have to know about polling, how to write the script for survey questions. You have to know how to craft a national strategy, how to set up an organization in fifty states. You have to know how to get a speech-writing staff going. You must get a shadow cabinet together. You must know the top press, the bureau chief for the *Washington Post, N.Y. Times, Wall Street Journal*, etc. You must know and have credibility with reporters. You must have personal contacts in the departments of Defense, State, and Treasury. You must understand campaign finance.[11]

The point here is that any candidate running for president must submit to the advice of those who have this kind of knowledge, experience, and access. And the likely result is that success gained in the electoral realm will be bought at the price of pragmatic adaptations to the strategic environment. Once again, there appear to be forces that move participants toward an accommodation with the system they seek to change. This is not to suggest that they do not make an impact in their efforts, but that they do so within boundaries imposed by the system.

FUNDAMENTALISTS: ADAPTATION AND ELITE LEGITIMACY

The challenge for fundamentalist political leaders is to harness the energy of their supporters, yet to channel it into politically productive ways. Jerry Falwell learned early that he had to discipline his social movement to maintain credibility. He had to disavow a supposed Moral Majority state leader who declared that homosexuality should be made a capital offense; his lobbyist had to squelch attempts by another local organization to make pornographic cookies a major issue. Pat Robertson, too, is learning that to achieve greater leverage in national politics he must accept the unwritten rules of the game. All of this suggests that the desire to achieve a degree of national elite legitimacy forces these leaders to accept conditions they did not have to live by in the early, militant phase of their emergence. It is this process (*co-optation*, as it was pejoratively termed by radicals in the 1960s) that such fundamentalists as Bob Jones fear will dilute the purity of the conservative religious witness.

However, in airing the grievances of their constituents, fundamentalist leaders have achieved a modest degree of elite legitimacy, if not for themselves personally, then for elements of their withering critique of modernity. Yet if the examples that follow illustrate the ways in which concerns of fundamentalists are being picked up and legitimated by elites, they also demonstrate the dependence of the fundamentalists on intellectual elites to transmute their concerns into acceptable forms.

Consider the following illustrations. For a time the Equal Rights Amendment (ERA) enjoyed a kind of hallowed status among cultural elites; it was "politically correct" beyond question. Thus, Phyllis Schlafly's opposition caught supporters off guard because she was able to mobilize women, not men, to oppose an amendment ostensibly for their own good. To supporters, of course, Schlafly was viewed as a right wing joke and her minions as benighted housewives sadly unprepared for the gifts of modernity. Schlafly, however, prevailed, and a reassessment is now under way about the merits of the ERA and the wisdom of the effort that went into it. In a sympathetic analysis, Jane Mansbridge concluded that the forces promoting the ERA were self-defeating, lending the opposition their most potent arguments. This was because American feminists could not concede any compromise on the issue of absolute equality between the sexes, and thus were led to conclude, for example, that the ERA *would* result in women serving in military combat, and that it *would* eliminate any preferential treatment for women in work situations.[12] This proclivity is analyzed more harshly by Sylvia Ann Hewlett, who argued that the obsession of American feminists for abstract equality—as embodied in the ERA battle—kept them from understanding that strict legal equality would do nothing for the concrete conditions many women live under. Hewlett concluded that the European emphasis on social benefits—day care, maternity leave, and the like—provided women with tangible resources to balance their families and their jobs without losing work seniority, and that the ERA therefore might have had the effect of eliminating these obviously preferential benefits.[13]

In a slightly different vein we see a growing acknowledgment that the public schools have indeed become places of secular indoctrination, as the fundamentalists claimed. In court cases and protests, fundamentalist parents and pastors averred that school textbooks were biased against their religious and moral beliefs. These people, of course, were initially dismissed as modern day book burners.[14] Then serious scholars began to explore the issue and found that the fundamentalists were largely correct. Paul Vitz of New York University, for example, in a systematic analysis of the content of public school texts, concluded that they went out of their way to exclude any recognition of the role of religion in American history and society, and that they clearly did evince a hostility toward orthodox belief. Moreover, the words *marriage, wedding, wife,* and *husband* hardly appear, owing to the new age bent in the texts to embrace every conceivable alternative to traditional family arrangements.[15] Other studies have corroborated this basic finding, including one done by the fundamentalist *bête noire*, People for the American Way.[16] This awareness of the hostile atmosphere in the schools, in fact, led both houses of Congress to pass the Equal Access Act with overwhelming majorities. During the debate, congressional testimony and news reports were filled with horror stories: school officials demanding that a blind girl stop reciting her rosary on the school bus, teachers confiscating a girl's valentines because a Christian cross appeared on them, a school principal in Alaska instructing teachers not to utter the words, "Merry Christmas"; the list went on and on.[17]

Consider, too, a tale of two law suits featuring Robert Coles of Harvard. Coles was asked to testify on behalf of a school district in Tennessee, which was being sued by Christian fundamentalist parents who objected to specific stories assigned in literature classes. Coles testified that such tales as the Wizard of Oz were not patently harmful to children or their religious beliefs. Then came the Alabama case, in which parents claimed, more sweepingly, that general textbooks were promoting the religion of secular humanism. Again Coles was called in to defend the school district, yet after reading the texts he concluded they were "crap," "psychological trash," that they did indeed promote a militantly secular worldview, and that he would not want his kids reading them. An illustration of the material he found offensive was a tenth-grade home economics text that offered Jesus and Gandhi as examples of the "irrational-conscientious" character type whose "repressed hostility makes them cold and unfeeling." The plaintiffs quickly adopted Coles's deposition.[18]

Another interesting case is Nat Hentoff, civil liberties writer for the *Village Voice* and professed atheist, writing in the Moral Majority Report of his conversion regarding the issue of abortion. Hentoff had been exploring the civil liberties implications of the medical nontreatment of infants born with defects. The more he probed, the more he became convinced that acceptance of abortion did, in fact, constitute a slippery slope toward tolerance of infanticide and euthanasia.[19]

In short, concerns of conservative Christians have been legitimated in diverse elite circles. There is the Cornell professor Richard Baer's devastating critique of values clarification.[20] There is Tipper Gore's effort to expose the pornographic, violent, and satanic content of some rock lyrics and videos, not to mention the ongoing concern about the impact on children of violence and sex on TV. Some feminists now vehemently attack the culture of pornography, and Edward Donnerstein's path-breaking research indicates that violent smut may indeed affect young men in ominous ways.[21] Or take Ken Kesey's assertion that instead of assigning *One Flew Over the Cuckoo's Nest*, high school teachers should assign the Bible.[22] Notable also is the scholarly evidence that parochial schools are far more successful with educating disadvantaged students than are public schools or private prep schools, indicating that support of a religious community is valuable for learning and achievement.[23] Finally, and perhaps most dramatically of all, we see the Reverend Jesse Jackson, visionary on the left, railing against drug abuse, calling upon young people to shed the comforts of the video culture, and challenging students to develop self-discipline and diligent study habits—traditional values.

What is happening is that on issues relating to cultural change and moral stability, fundamentalists have apparently articulated, at times forcefully, at times ineptly, what many others were thinking. More profoundly, perhaps, they have exposed, along with evangelical moderates and conservative Catholics, the paradoxical nature of the human liberation sought by secular and religious leftists. As the great John Wesley understood so well, for oppressed peoples to be liberated from their subjugation they must be imbued with a sense of morality and discipline and a family structure that sustains them. Yet the contemporary spirit of "liberation" is antithetical to traditional restraints on the individual imposed by marriage, moral codes, religion, and law. Thus, those hurt most by the libertarian drift of society—by feminist and *Playboy* attacks on the family, by the drug and porn invasions, by loss of sexual restraints, and by Madison Avenue's daily appeals to the seven deadly sins—are the poor, those with the least resources to waste, with the fewest resources to fall back on.[24] Indeed, an intriguing study of the much-romanticized Polynesian people suggests that the promotion of immediate gratification and promiscuity were tools of social control used by rulers to subjugate the masses. The ruling class, which cultivated discipline, delayed gratification, and strict sexual codes for itself, found it easy to induce lassitude and pliability by promoting just the reverse for the rest of the population.[25]

If the fundamentalists have a blind spot, it is their lack of appreciation for the fact that modern capitalism (which they embrace) is itself an awesome engine of libertarian change.[26] But they at least appreciate the mixed blessing of unfettered capitalism better than some of the libertarian "enterprisers" with whom they share an uneasy alliance in the Republican party.

It is just too simplistic to conclude, as some political science literature does, that fundamentalists lack public support, or that they have no business trying to shape the public agenda because they are intolerant and do not accept pluralism. To assert this, however, is not to dispute that there are elements of truth in the depiction of fundamentalists that one finds in liberal academic circles. The ugly tinges of anti-Semitism circling around the religious protests against the film *The Last Temptation of Christ*, are haunting reminders that intolerance and hatred are indeed found in fundamentalist circles.[27] Yet if we fear this proclivity, we might be wise to welcome the attempt by some fundamentalist leaders to move their followers into the mainstream of American culture, where they will be forced to confront their own narrowness of vision. Who would have thought twenty years ago, for example, that some of the staunchest friends of the state of Israel would be Christian fundamentalist leaders, who dearly want to be accepted by Jewish Americans as friends and supporters of mutual aims. The genius of

American politics to produce strange bedfellows is, thus, one of the central reasons why the fundamentalist movement has taken a different turn here than elsewhere in the world.

CONCLUSION

The revival of religious fundamentalism around the globe, whether in Christian, Jewish, or Islamic forms, appears to be a profound and militant reaction against the cultural sweep of modernity—the shattering of traditional moorings that tie a people to its past. This is, no doubt, one of the reasons why international comparisons are so readily drawn. We only have to compare the radical Shi'ite denunciation of "satanic" Western culture—pornography, rock music, libertarianism, and immorality—to see the ground shared with fundamentalists in other societies. The political direction of religious revivalism, however, will be channeled by the set of institutions existing in a particular nation. Thus, an analysis of political fundamentalism in the United States suggests that there are powerful forces that constrain and temper the militancy of the American variant of religious revivalism.

These forces include: 1) a complex journalistic establishment that is largely unsympathetic to the fundamentalist right; 2) a formidable entertainment, advertising, and mass media industry whose ubiquitous messages often denigrate the concerns of Christian conservatives; 3) a set of well-established political institutions and actors—and not just the three venerable branches, but the thousands of congressional aides, lobbies, think tanks, Political Action Committees (PACs), party elites, and entrenched senior bureaucrats—that operate with their own logic and interests; 4) an electoral system that exists under intense media scrutiny and with its own norms; 5) a vast secular university system that socializes teachers in an even vaster secondary school establishment dominated by the National Education Association (NEA); 6) a highly decentralized and pluralistic religious environment that renders unity difficult even among fundamentalists themselves; and 7) a modern market economy that uproots people, shatters communities, and promises secular innovation, power, and wealth. Given these secular and religious forces, it is no wonder that fundamentalists had to expend enormous energy to make modest gains, had to shed their radicalism for more practical tactics, and had to mold their messages for broader appeal.

This analysis clearly suggests that the context of religious revivalism is a critical ingredient in determining what political manifestations will emerge. In the United States the sweep of secular modernity has been exceedingly powerful. (What, after all, do we export so well as our popular culture with its libertarian promises?) This not only constrains fundamentalist initiatives, but in light of the chaos of narcissistic culture, creates some public sympathy for their more modest goals. American institutions, in short, are secular in profound ways, and many nonfundamentalist Americans are ambivalent about the impact of these institutions on their lives. Therein lies the potential for alliances with Christian fundamentalists, who may beat back the beast, but can never defeat it alone. The more sobering question for fundamentalists (and others) is whether the beast of modernity can be defeated at all. If the answer is no—if no blend of militancy and accommodation seems to work—then the siren song of disengagement may draw Christian conservatives once again back into the womb of their protected cloisters.

7

What Do the Evangelicals Want?
Ronald Nash

Not too long ago, religious liberals in America were busy attempting to get the federal government's help for causes and programs that they supported. Reveling in their easy access to the citadels of power, these liberals enjoyed chiding fundamentalists and other Protestant conservatives for their supposed indifference to social issues—for ignoring what is called the social dimension of the gospel. "All these guys ever do," the liberals pouted, "is preach what they call the gospel; they ignore everything else."

Suddenly the shoe is on the other foot. Religious conservatives have discovered the social dimension of the gospel—although some never really lost sight of it. Now the liberals wish conservatives would go back into their churches and forget the political arena.

The recent resurgence of religious conservatism in America and the determination of many of these people to push their views and values into the forefront of public discussion is thought, by some, to pose a threat to "civil liberties, to a healthy diversity of opinion, and to the hope that we can conduct public affairs free of the divisiveness of religious factionalism."[1] As Richard John Neuhaus describes it, assorted liberal organizations believe that "the religious Right is the greatest peril to American Democracy since Joe McCarthy."[2] Of course, Neuhaus adds, the religious Right is also a financial bonanza for its critics since nothing brings in the money more quickly than alarmist reports about the Christian Right's alleged intention to take over the country.

Thus full-page advertisements in prestige newspapers inform us that the religious Right is determined to abolish the no-establishment clause of the First Amendment, impose its fundamentalist morality upon all of us through law, put politicians in our bedrooms, censor what we may read and see, and then, for good measure, blow up the world in order to force history's denouement in the final act of Armageddon.[3]

There is no question but that some people in America want the rest of us to believe these claims; perhaps the people making the claims even believe some of them themselves. But are the claims true? Do fundamentalists or evangelicals or other conservative Protestants really want to bring about this scenario? If not, what do they want? What are they actually trying to accomplish?

An important first step in answering these questions is becoming clear about who it is we're talking about. While various labels for Protestant conservatives are used, the generic term seems to be *evangelical*. Unpacking the meaning of this word, then, is a good way to begin our inquiry.

WHO ARE THE EVANGELICALS?

The meaning of the word *evangelical* has evolved over many centuries to where it is, at least in the United States, the contemporary term used to refer to theologically conservative Protestants.[4] One can normally expect that anyone who claims to be an evangelical is a Christian believer whose theology is traditional or orthodox, who takes the Bible as his ultimate authority in matters of faith and practice, who has had a religious conversion, and who is interested in helping others have a similar conversion experience. Estimates as to the number of such people in the United States range as high as fifty million, including a growing number in the mainline churches, three or four million Roman Catholics, and of course millions of black Americans.[5]

Many who seek to generate fear and alarm about American evangelicalism fail to give proper attention to the tremendous diversity of the movement. Evangelicalism in America includes at least three major subcultures: (1) the evangelical mainstream represented by Billy Graham and *Christianity Today*; (2) fundamentalism as represented by Jerry Falwell; and (3) pentecostalism for whom Pat Robertson functions as one representative.

The relations among these three subcultures can be pictured in terms of three intersecting circles in which the center circle represents the evangelical mainstream. The fact that the circles representing fundamentalism and pentecostalism overlap the center circle illustrates several things. First, it is possible to be a fundamentalist or pentecostal without being an evangelical. It is important to note here that *fundamentalism* and *evangelicalism* are not synonymous terms. The fact that our circles overlap signifies that some pentecostals like Pat Robertson[6] and some fundamentalists like Jerry Falwell have enough in common with the evangelical mainstream to be considered part of the overall evangelical movement.[7]

Falwell has never spoken for all evangelicals, even for those mainstream evangelicals who remain politically conservative. Nor has Robertson ever been *the* evangelical candidate. Many evangelicals fit comfortably into the most liberal pockets of the Democratic party. A few evangelicals find even those Democrats too conservative for their more radical tastes. Evangelicalism is as diverse politically as it is theologically. Such evangelical publishing houses as Eerdmans (Grand Rapids, Michigan) and Intervarsity Press (Downers Grove, Illinois), regularly issue books that attack the religious Right. As Stuart Rothenberg notes, it is a mistake to "treat the Evangelical community as a homogeneous religious and political force that is primed to take over the Republican Party and, ultimately, the country."[8] Anyone who attempts to lump the theologically and politically diverse factions of the evangelical movement into one homogeneous pile makes it clear that he has a defective understanding of American evangelicalism.

Pentecostals like Jim Bakker, Jimmy Swaggart, and even Oral Roberts have never been part of the evangelical mainstream. Their use of what often appeared as a mindless and self-centered appeal to personal well-being always operated with a doctrinal vacuum at its core, that left informed fundamentalists and mainstream evangelicals critical of their ministries. The recent troubles of Bakker and Swaggart along with Oral Roberts's occasional bizarre claims, are an embarrassment to pentecostalism. But there is absolutely no justification for any attempt to taint the entire evangelical movement because of the failings of a few people who, at best, operated outside of, or on the fringes of, evangelicalism.

A DIFFERENCE BETWEEN EVANGELICAL AND LIBERAL POLITICAL ACTIVITY

The first thing to notice about politically active religious conservatives is that what they are up to is essentially the same sort of thing that scores of other good American organizations have been doing for decades. The Catholic writer Clifford Kossel asks:

> Why are the liberal social individualists so worried about [religious conservatives who] push their own interests? They appear to be doing just what other good American organizations do. Corporations, labor unions, senior citizens, NOW [National Organization of Women], NAM [National Association of Manufacturers], and NEA [National Education Association] lobby in federal and state capitals, raise challenges in the courts, use radio, television, and computerized direct mailing to promote their views and get out the voters.[9]

But perhaps there is a difference after all. Kossel continues.

> While the other groups seem to be doing mostly the typical American thing in protecting some private interest or reaching for a bigger slice of the federal pie, the Moral Majority takes religion and public morality seriously. Many liberals had thought that, as far as public life was concerned, religion was slowly withering away (or at least was being domesticated) and that "absolutes" were absolutely dead. But here is a religiously based group publicly and militantly proclaiming some absolute positions for insertion into our legal and political ethos. They might even be a majority, and that is threatening.[10]

The political scientist Robert Zwier is an example of an evangelical whose liberal political views often result in his attacking politically conservative Christians. Nonetheless, Zwier finds at least one reason to defend the religious Right:

> It is unfair to criticize the new Christian Right for trying to exercise influence over political affairs. To criticize it for violating the wall of separation between church and state is to miss the important distinction between the actions of an institutional church and the convictions of individual Christians. This movement is calling upon persons, not churches, to use their votes to elect certain candidates. That is a fundamental right without which democracy is threatened. Such criticism also ignores the legitimate role which religious beliefs have al-

most constantly played in establishing this nation and building public policies.[11]

Evangelicals have as much right then to attempt to influence public policy as other organizations. After all, this is precisely what theologically and politically liberal Christians have been doing for decades.

TREATING THE EVANGELICALS FAIRLY

Many people think the evangelicals have been getting unfair treatment from the media, the entertainment industry, and the academic world. As Neuhaus points out: "The pattern in the media and elsewhere is to use the term 'Fundamentalist' in a careless way that refers to anything we deem religiously bizarre or fanatical. . . . This pattern reflects intellectual laziness mixed with an unseemly measure of bigotry."[12]

Another writer who smells some prejudice in recent treatments of conservative Protestants is Nathan Glazer, professor of education at Harvard, and an editor of *The Public Interest*, who sometimes collaborates with Senator Daniel Patrick Moynihan on articles on religion. Glazer reminds us that religious-based conflicts are not exactly new in American society. Not too long ago, he points out, Catholics were perceived as subversive so far as important American values were concerned. Glazer also notes disturbing similarities between the anti-Semitism practiced against Jews in America, and the frequently encountered intolerance of American Protestants who dare to run against the cultural current.[13]

It is hard to dispute the claim that for decades now, the values of conservative Christians—both Protestant and Roman Catholic—have been under siege in this country. This is apparent in the courts, in the media, in movies and on television, and in the schools. One thing evangelicals want is a reprieve from intolerance against their beliefs, values, and practices.

Fair treatment of conservative Protestants will begin by recognizing that many of them are new to the public arena. Perhaps they could be more informed on some issues; perhaps they could be more knowledgeable about economics or political theory. Their hearts may be in the right place and—for that matter—their positions on some issues may be correct. When they begin to master the information and arguments available to them in a growing body of writings, liberals may be surprised at how sophisticated they can become. Perhaps this explains why the evangelicals worry some liberals.

Many leaders of the Christian Right are preachers who are prone at times to rhetorical overkill. But after listening to Jesse Jackson for years now, why should any of us think that that is an exclusive trait of religious conservatives? Neuhaus urges Americans not to take everything a few spokesmen for the religious Right may say at face value. Do not caricaturize them or their positions by their hyperbolic lapses, he warns.[14] The truth is that they are not enemies of religious freedom or political freedom or freedom of speech or freedom of the press. They have made clear their commitment to democracy and pluralism.[15]

Every movement has its share of fanatics, extremists, uninformed zealots, and general all-around zanies. In this respect, evangelicalism often resembles the political Left more than it should. Evangelical centrists are dismayed whenever such individuals appear to speak or act on behalf of all evangelicals. It is unfair when such exceptions are treated as the rule.

THE EVANGELICAL REACTION IS DEFENSIVE

According to Glazer, recent evangelical actions in the public arena should be understood as defensive, not offensive. They do not represent a sudden assault on a passive and tolerant society. Rather, they are a reaction to what religious conservatives see as an attack upon them and also upon values that have played an essential role in the success of the American political experiment. As Glazer sees it, "It is the great successes of secular and liberal forces principally operating through the specific agency of the courts, that has in large measure created the issues on which the Fundamentalists have managed to achieve what influence they have."[16] Glazer provides several examples to back up his claim.

> Abortion did *not* become an issue because Fundamentalists wanted to *strengthen* prohibitions against abortion, but because liberals wanted to abolish them. . . . Pornography in the 1980s did *not* become an issue because Fundamentalists wanted to *ban* D. H. Lawrence, James Joyce, or even Henry Miller, but because in the 1960s and 1970s, under-the-table pornography moved to the top of the newsstands. Prayer in the schools did *not* become an issue because Fundamentalists wanted to *introduce* new prayers or sectarian prayers, but because the Su-

preme Court ruled against all prayers. Freedom for religious schools became an issue *not* because of any legal effort to *expand* their scope, but because the Internal Revenue Service and various state authorities tried to impose restrictions on them that private schools had not faced before.[17]

Perhaps the issue of who started these fights is now irrelevant. But it is helpful to remember, as Glazer points out, that

Dominant power—measured by money, access to the major media, influence, the opinion of our educated, moneyed, and powerful elites—still rests with the secular and liberal forces that created, through court action, the changes that have aroused Fundamentalism. What we are seeing is a defensive reaction of the conservative heartland, rather than an offensive that intends to or is capable of really upsetting the balance, or of driving the United States back to the nineteenth century or early twentieth century.[18]

Liberals have been so successful in getting their own agenda adopted that it is easy for them to forget that "America is a many-cultured society, and that religion is an important component of many U.S. subcultures as well as of the larger culture."[19] Evangelicals are simply fighting back in an attempt to restore some balance and to regain some lost respect for beliefs and values that are important to them.

THE DANGERS OF THE NAKED PUBLIC SQUARE

Consciously or unconsciously, politically active evangelicals have been pointing out the dangers in what Neuhaus has called "The Naked Public Square." As Neuhaus explains:

The naked public square is the result of political doctrine and practice that would exclude religion and religiously grounded values from the conduct of public business. The doctrine is that America is a secular society. It finds dogmatic expression in the ideology of secularism. I will argue that the doctrine is demonstrably false and the dogma exceedingly dangerous.[20]

Neuhaus understands much evangelical militancy as a protest against the naked public square. He thinks these protests can and should alert "us to a widespread pattern of thought and practice that has distorted and threatens to discredit the American democratic experiment."[21]

The truly naked public square is . . . a vacuum begging to be filled. When the democratically affirmed institutions that generate and transmit values are excluded [from the public square], the vacuum will be filled by the agent left in control of the public square, the state. In this manner, a perverse notion of the disestablishment of religion leads to the establishment of the state as church. Not without reason, religion is viewed by some as a repressive imposition upon the public square. They would cast out the devil of particularist religion and thus put the public square in proper secular order. Having cast out the one devil . . . they unavoidably invite the entrance of seven devils worse than the first.[22]

Society, Neuhaus continues, needs transcendence.

[T]ranscendence abhors a vacuum. Every society needs some transcendent referent that is the source of its sanctions, legitimacy, and direction. Otherwise it is simply a society adrift. Because Americans are, for better and for worse, an exceedingly religious people, that transcendent referent must be carried and shaped by religion. Now the most aggressive force moving, indeed leaping, into the vacuum is the religious new right. As long as other religious candidates hold back or disdain the culture-forming tasks, the religious new right will seize the attention and grow in influence.[23]

Neuhaus goes on to point out deficiencies in the political worldview of many fundamentalists. Instead of appealing to private truths, he argues, they need to do a better job of grounding their public claims on arguments that are public in character.[24] Of course, some mainstream evangelicals have been doing precisely this sort of thing for years.[25]

FUNDAMENTALISM AND PUBLIC MORALITY

Evangelicalism is a diverse movement, both theologically and politically. But frequently, or so it seems, the fundamentalists get more than their share of attention. Surely, many think, all those sinister charges repeated at the beginning of this chapter must be true. I have already admitted that, like the Left, fundamentalism undoubtedly has its share of fanatics and extremists. But responsible leaders of the fundamentalist camp have spoken out on public morality and their statements make it clear that they wish to be in the mainstream of American political life. One such statement appeared in the March 1985 issue of the *Fundamentalist Journal*, a monthly magazine that caters to fundamentalists who look to Jerry Falwell for leadership. The editorial was authored by Ed Dobson who at the time was vice president of Falwell's Liberty University. Dobson's comments under the heading of "Public Morality" deserve more attention than they have received.

First, he writes, "We believe that the First Amendment prohibits the establishment of a state religion and thereby protects the rights of all religions."[26] Of course, Dobson goes on to say, neither does the First Amendment "advocate the exorcism of God and religion from society." Falwell-type fundamentalists believe in the separation of church and state. As Dobson urges, "We believe that religion must neither dominate the political process nor be dominated by it. We must be free to worship God according to the dictates of our conscience, and we must be free to exercise our political rights as good citizens."

Dobson then turns his attention to the fact that, while exercising their political rights, fundamentalists have often been misunderstood. In an attempt to eliminate such misunderstanding, Dobson offers four points that he hopes will clarify where fundamentalists stand on public morality.

First, he writes, "We are not seeking to make America a Christian nation. We are concerned about the erosion of the basic values expressed in the Judeo-Christian tradition, and we believe we must protect those values within our society." Dobson here contradicts all those hysterics who keep claiming that Falwell and his followers want an America where every congressman, Supreme Court justice, and member of the executive branch is a born-again Christian pursuing some type of fundamentalist agenda.

Second, Dobson explains, "We are committed to an America that is pluralistic in the broadest sense. We desire to protect the rights of all minorities—whether or not they share our faith."

Third, he continues, "We are committed to principles, not political parties." It is helpful to remember that through the 1970s, the majority of American evangelicals regarded themselves as Democrats. If many of those former Democrats have become Republicans, it is because they believe that the Democratic party has been radicalized and no longer stands for the values that these people regard as important. Of course, many nonevangelicals have long since reached the same conclusion about the Democrats.

Fourth, fundamentalists "seek to influence the political process in the highest tradition of American politics. We reject the use of manipulative power politics and inhumane methods to accomplish our goals. While we may battle with others in the process, we must live with them in peace as fellow Americans." Many believe fundamentalists like Dobson and Falwell when they state: "We simply desire to influence government—not control government. This, of course, is the right of every American and we would vigorously oppose any Ayatolla type of person's rising to power in this country. . . . We believe in freedom of speech, freedom of the press, and freedom of religion."[27]

It is difficult to see anything un-American in the fundamentalist agenda set forth by Falwell's followers.

CONCLUSION

A few evangelicals are left-wing radicals. No one on the Left regards them as a threat to important American values. A growing number of evangelicals are politically liberal. No American liberal regards them as a threat to vital American values. The millions of mainstream evangelicals clearly pose no threat to democracy. Is it only the fundamentalists that bear watching? Even they—the evidence makes clear—can be trusted and deserve to be treated with the same respect as any other minority. As Dobson says:

> We are exercising our American citizenship and doing what the National Council of Churches, the National Association for the Advancement of Colored People, the National Education Association, and other special interest and minority groups have been doing for years. When others suggest that we should be silent, we wonder if their own concern is that we threaten their position in the political process.[28]

Perhaps, if we are interested in targeting un-American behavior, we should begin with those who appear interested in denying important rights of this one American minority.

Neuhaus believes "that the public resurgence of fundamentalist Christianity is good both for Christianity and for America, because it returns to the national discourse a huge bloc of citizens previously estranged from . . . 'the public square.' "[29] Politically active evangelicals, Neuhaus continues,

> want us to know that they are not going to go back to the wilderness. . . . They explain, almost apologetically, that they did not really want to bash in the door to the public square, but it was locked, and nobody had answered their knocking. Anyway, the hinges were rusty and it gave way under pressure that was only a little more than polite. And so the country cousins have shown up in force at the family picnic. They want a few rules changed right away. Other than that they promise to behave, provided we do not again try to exclude them from family deliberations. Surely it is incumbent on the rest of us, especially those who claim to understand our society, to do more in response to this ascendance of Fundamentalism—and indeed of religion in general—than to sound an increasingly hysterical and increasingly hollow alarm.[30]

It should be clear by now that I believe that the distinguished scholars I've quoted—Nathan Glazer, Stuart Rothenberg, Clifford Kossell, and Richard Neuhaus—are correct. The entry of religiously conservative Christians into the political arena is an interesting phenomenon. But it is not cause for alarm.

8

Onward Christian Soldiers: The Case of Protestantism in Central America
Laura Nuzzi O'Shaughnessy

When I was reborn I accepted military discipline, I became a soldier of Christ.

> General José Efraín Ríos Montt,
> president of Guatemala, 1982–1983;
> member, El Verbo Church, Guatemala
> branch of California-based Gospel Outreach[1]

From the beginning of their evangelization in Latin America, the worldview of many missionaries had both religious and political dimensions. A century later religious worldviews and political positions remain intertwined. Since the late 1970s, evangelical sects and faith missions have grown rapidly in Central America and are currently challenging mainline Protestant churches, as well as the Catholic church for the allegiance of the faithful.

THE ARRIVAL OF PROTESTANTISM IN LATIN AMERICA: THE EARLY YEARS

Protestantism played no role in Latin America during the period of the Spanish conquest. The Catholic clergy came to the New World at the request of the Spanish crown, and as a vital part of the extension of Spain's dominion over its colonies. The pervasive religious orthodoxy of the Spanish meant that the distribution of the Bible was discouraged until the late seventeenth century. In fact,

Protestantism had little influence in the region until the national period, when it began to play an important role as the bearer of "modernization."

In the early 1800s the first Protestants to arrive in the New World resettled in ethnic-cultural enclaves. The members of these "transplant churches"[2] fled persecution in their own nations and did not want to suffer the punishment of the Spanish Inquisition in Latin America. Thus, these early Protestant churches were not missionary churches that were actively engaged in evangelization or in challenging the Catholic church.

Evangelizing Protestantism grew slowly in Latin America after the fight for independence from Spain. In regions such as Central America, which were initially controlled by conservative forces in the postindependence period, Catholicism again was given a privileged status. For example, the 1824 Constitution of the Central American Confederation stated, "Her religion is the Roman Catholic Apostolic with the exclusion of the public exercise of any other."[3]

At the same time, postindependence liberals began to pursue commercial arrangements with northern European nations and viewed favorably the quality of life in these Protestant nations. They encouraged the influx of Protestant missionaries and tried to remove the obstacles to their colonization by granting religious freedom as an integral part of commercial treaties. By 1832, liberal governments had succeeded in modifying the Central American Constitution to allow for freedom of religion.[4] They also saw Protestantism as an ally against Catholic hegemony and as an important part of the progress of the Western industrialized nations. The work ethic, the dedication to schooling, and the importance of the individual that the missionaries brought with them, served to reinforce the separation of Church and state and the economic philosophy of liberalism that encouraged foreign investment.

The earliest missionaries, whose presence was encouraged by liberal leaders, had a great impact on Protestantism in Central America. A most interesting case is that of Guatemala, where the liberal president Justo Ruffino Barrios returned from a diplomatic visit to the United States accompanied by the Presbyterian missionary John Hill in 1882. Barrios was convinced that Guatemalan society could be improved by the infusion of Protestant values, and the Presbyterian Board of Foreign Missionaries of the United States was willing to support him.[5] The Guatemalan government paid Hill's passage from the United States to Guatemala, and President Barrios personally accompanied him to Guatemala City and donated the land upon which the Guatemalan Presbyterian church still stands to this day. Hill became the pastor of an English-speaking congregation in Guatemala and founded the Colegio Americano, which the children of Ruffino Barrios attended.[6]

In addition to the denominational churches, the Bible societies played an important role in bringing the gospel to Latin America. In the nineteenth century, both the British and American Bible societies performed an invaluable service by their distribution of the Bible to rural as well as urban areas. These Bible salesmen were among the earliest Protestants to risk persecution at the hands of the Catholic church. But they persevered, and by the early twentieth century their interdenominational evangelization was also supported by the growth of faith missions. The independent Central American Mission was founded in 1895 under the sponsorship of the Dallas Theological Seminary, to "spread Bible teachings throughout Middle America,"[7] and by 1902 the Central American Mission had missionaries stationed in all five Central American nations.

Both the Bible societies and the faith missions played an important role in giving Central American Protestantism the rich variety that it maintains to this day. Faith missions did not encourage loyalty to a particular church or denomination. Instead, they emphasized conversion to the gospel and made emotive use of the Scriptures to achieve this objective. Of particular note was the Latin American Mission founded by Harry and Susan Strachan in 1921 in Costa Rica. They devised an original strategy of tent meetings, popular music, and "fire and brimstone" oratory to hasten the conversion of the popular classes.[8] This approach has remained a dominant characteristic of several important and expanding forms of Protestantism such as Pentecostalism, which arrived in Latin America in the 1930s and is today acknowledged to be the fastest-growing Protestant group in Latin America.

North American missionaries were also subject to the fluctuations between liberal and conservative governments and to the rigors of life in a Latin American culture and climate with which they were not familiar. It is estimated that by 1916 Protestant growth in Latin America had reached 10,442 communicants.[9]

THE AMERICAN SENSE OF MISSION

We have spoken of the varieties of faith that Protestant missionaries brought to Latin America and their perceived value as modernizers. We must also look more closely at the political role that missionaries played in the early twentieth century so that we may explore the similarities with their complex contemporary role in Central America.

Intentionally or unintentionally, these missionaries also brought North American political values to Latin America. Along with the gospel the missionaries carried with them a sense of the moral superiority of their own nation and its form of governance. In a curious way, North American religious values had been combined with a sense of political righteousness since the colonial period in the United States. The puritan John Winthrop expressed the hope that this new society would be founded so that "man shall say of succeeding plantations: The Lord makes it like that of New England. For we must consider that we shall be as a city on a hill, the eyes of all people upon us."[10]

For Winthrop, the city on a hill was measured against standards that were internal to the individual and to the community in which one participated. The city on a hill was a model of how to live: the values embodied in this puritan notion are an integral part of the American psyche. Yet over time this internal notion of the moral example that Americans could set, became fused with American patriotism and developed an external dimension— it became a standard by which to measure other people and other nations.

As the United States became a stronger nation, our moral example became an essential part of the concept of manifest destiny that was first popularized in 1845 by the journalist John O'Sullivan who said it was but "the fulfillment of our manifest destiny to overspread the continent allotted by Providence for the free development of the United States."[11] Manifest destiny helped to spread the authority of the United States westward in the Mexican-American War of 1846–1848, and to the south beyond our borders in the Spanish-American War of 1898.

This period in American history is especially important for the understanding of Protestantism in Central America, because a steady wave of Protestant evangelization occurred during the latter quarter of the nineteenth century, and the beginning of the twentieth century.[12] Along with the gospel came the North American flag.

The impact of these determined missionaries was greater in Central America than in Latin America in large measure due to its geographic proximity to the United States. Even before the turn of the twentieth century, national security, U.S. interests, and the expulsion of foreign powers, were of concern to U.S. policymakers. The reader will recall the range of policy options that were utilized in Central America and the Caribbean from 1900 to 1933. North American responses included the Big Stick Corollary to the Monroe Doctrine; dollar diplomacy; nonrecognition of governments; and military interventions in Cuba, Haiti, the Dominican Republic, Puerto Rico, and Nicaragua.[13]

THE CONGRESS OF PANAMA: 1916

We will conclude this historical overview by discussing the impact of North American missionaries on Latin America with a brief discussion of the Congress of Panama of 1916.[14] The congress was composed mainly of representatives from North American churches who met to discuss the difficulties of evangelization in Latin America, and to plan a coordinated strategy for the coming years. The conference was organized by the largest Protestant denominations working in Latin America: Presbyterians, Lutherans, Methodists, United Brethren, and Baptists. Out of a total of 304 official delegates or visitors, 145 came from eighteen Latin American nations; but of these delegates only twenty-one were Latin American by birth. English was the official language of the congress, although several presentations were offered in Spanish.[15]

The mission boards of the North American churches set the agenda for this meeting. Theological issues such as the relationship between religion and science and the impact of the Bible in Latin America were discussed, as well as practical concerns such as sharing the cost of printing the Bible for Latin American distribution.

The denominations also agreed upon "comity agreements" by means of which Latin America's territory was divided among several denominations. If one mission was working in a given area, other missions should begin to evangelize elsewhere. Thus, in Central America, for example, El Salvador, Honduras, and Nicaragua were assigned to the Northern Baptists, and the Methodist church was assigned to Panama and Costa Rica.[16]

This domination of Latin American Protestantism by their parent churches in the United States was an organizational as well as a financial reality. Organizationally, the member churches in Latin America were linked to a larger network that supplied Bibles and missionaries and trained local ministers in the United States. Financially, North American mission boards raised funds within their own more affluent congregations to build churches in Latin America and to establish local schools to train local pastors. Over time it was realized that from a financial standpoint it was more cost-effective to train pastors at the local level in their native language than it was to send them to the United States.

Inevitably, organizational and financial ties led to lack of autonomy within the Latin American denominations and faith missions. For some who were embued with the Protestant ethic and North American values, lack of autonomy presented no problem. They were content with their religious role as part of an integrated whole and had little difficulty, in the 1950s, for example, espousing the anticommunism of the United States.[17] For others, awareness of the disadvantages of their relationship with their mother churches in the United States came gradually, and, by the 1960s Latin American Protestantism had reached a turning point.

THE DECADE OF THE 1960s AND THE SEARCH FOR A LATIN AMERICAN PROTESTANTISM

During the 1960s when Latin American Catholicism was experiencing a period of intense renewal, there was also unmistakable pressure upon the Protestant churches to reexamine their role and mission.[18] Small group discussions took place within the mainline churches to address Latin American concerns. These groups began to reinterpret their faith based on the prophetic traditions of the Old Testament. At the same time they began to posit an interrelationship, not a dualistic relationship, between individual faith and social mission. Protestant leaders were challenged by the young people in their congregations to reexamine their faith. Finally, as I have mentioned, the renewal in the Catholic church was a catalyst for the Protestants.

However, Vatican II provided an immediate Catholic reference point that Latin America's Protestants did not have. Thus, in their search for an indigenous Latin American understanding of their faith they had to cast off the "foreign garments" of the mother churches in the United States without a unifying directive.[19] They relied primarily on the life experiences of their own pastors and congregations, and upon their reading of the Bible. Given their divisions, and lack of doctrinal consensus, the search for an authentic Latin American Protestant identity was indeed difficult. Moreover, even if they could formulate a Latin American identity as Protestants, would a majority of them—fundamentalists, charismatics, and members of denominations and faith missions—agree upon the same definition?

The search for unity centered around two issues: (1) the working out of an indigenous identity as Latin American Protestants, and (2) the achievement of consensus on what their role should be in society. For some Protestants, as their faith evolved in Latin America, its mission changed from a private, individualized sense of faith, to one in which social commitment played an integral part. This evolution, to the extent that it gained a foothold, has in turn aggravated the conservative-progressive divisions within Protestantism. Ironically, as Latin American Protestantism developed a Latin American theology based on its own reality, the unity it sought became ever more elusive. The Conferencia Evangélica Latino-America (CELA I, II, and III) bear witness to the evolution of a progressive Protestant mission in Latin America. Some of the CLADE (Conferencia Latino-America de Evangélica) meetings, in which the more traditional Protestant views prevailed, attested to the continuation of divisions in Latin American Protestantism.[20]

By the time of CELA II (1961), Protestants began to discuss a new model for their church and to reconceptualize evangelization. Those who were arguing for a definition of indigenous Protestantism argued that the new model for the church should be one in which an emphasis on personal salvation and individualism must not allow the Christian to disassociate himself from the fate of the earth.[21]

Thus, what distinguished CELA II from previous Protestant conferences was its openness to discuss socioeconomic issues and to relate them to its religious mission. CELA II demonstrated an awareness of the conditions of underdevelopment and of the need for change within a developmental, modernizing perspective. The conference called for a model of capitalistic economic growth, increased foreign investment, the expansion of democracy, and the reconciliation of social classes.[22] CELA III would attempt to endorse more controversial solutions to socioeconomic problems.

In July of 1969 Protestants from all over the continent met in Buenos Aires to celebrate CELA III.[23] This conference has been called "a landmark in the ecumenical history of Latin American Protestantism."[24] Representatives from Pentecostal churches as well as from faith missions such as Evangelism in Depth (which evolved from the Latin American Mission) and World Mission joined the denominational churches and the World Council of Churches at this meeting. Forty-three churches and ecumenical organizations sent representatives. CELA III acknowledged the growing social consciousness that was evolving in Latin American Protestantism. While committed to developmental ideals, CELA III was more critical in its appraisals. Instead of accepting the call for democracy at face value (as CELA II had done), CELA III argued that the church should work to promote Protestant participation in the transformation of existing unjust political systems.

With the perspective of time, it can be argued that CELA III represented a determined thrust toward a new social awareness. At the same time, it must also be realized that the forcefulness of this position was opposed by more conservative Protestants in attendance. These disagreements were sharply drawn in the deliberations of the Youth Commission that presented two conflicting reports to the plenary session. The majority report called for a fundamental change in political and economic structures and expected "the church to 'commit itself' to the liberation process, thereby taking 'the gospel to its ultimate consequences' rather than continuing to be an institution that 'maintains the status quo.' "[25] The minority report, uncomfortable with the thrust and tone of the majority report, condemned all dictatorships of the right and left and wanted the conference to endorse a more "balanced" course of action. In the plenary discussions of these reports, the delegates could not reach consensus: CELA III eventually decided to refer both documents to the churches for further study.[26]

The divisions revealed at CELA III carried over into the last major Protestant ecumenical conference held to date in Oaxtepec, Mexico, in 1978. Latin America's Protestants did not resolve the differences between those Christians who advocated a social liberating mission for the Church, and those more traditional Christians who believed that liberation (and salvation) were private individual concerns that should not be confused with sociopolitical positions.

By 1982 two rival confederations of Latin American Protestants had come into existence. The first ecumenical organization, CLAI (The Latin American Council of Churches) was established in preliminary form at Oaxtepec. As CLAI became more committed to an agenda of social action, more conservative Protestants formed CONELA (The Latin American Confraternity). These divisions, to which we now turn, have continued to the present day and have political, as well as theological, repercussions within Central America.

THE PRESENT AND THE DEBATE OVER LIBERATION ON EARTH OR SALVATION IN HEAVEN

Theologically, those progressive Protestants, who did not want their faith to be an appendage of either a mother church or of U.S.

foreign policy decisions, have formed their alliances with progressive Catholics. To date, this ecumenical movement has had more success in the southern cone of Latin America than in Central America because of the reasons we discussed previously. In this union Latin America is witnessing cross-church alliances that were unheard-of eighty years ago. The reader should realize that Catholics were not delegates at the 1916 Congress of Panama; the first Protestant Latin American conference to invite Catholics to attend as observers was CELA III.

Theologically, progressive Christians believed that economic and political structures, not individual characteristics, are major (but not exclusive) causes of the widening gap between rich and poor on their continent. They believed that sin has both individual and organizational dimensions and that material poverty and the biblical "poverty of spirit" must not be confused. Most importantly, the former cannot be spiritualized but must be addressed and redressed. The Bible for these Christians has a social as well as a transcendental context. This view of faith and how one acts on a social and political level are deeply related. These Protestants frequently make reference to the prophetic tradition of the Bible and argue that they work for social change and social justice. Unlike their conservative counterparts they are not afraid of Marxism as a rival ideology that will destroy Christianity.

If it is difficult to summarize the beliefs of progressive Protestants, it is equally difficult to summarize the complexity of the beliefs of conservative Protestants. In fact, even the term *Protestant*, which has been used throughout this chapter, presents some difficulty. The Spanish word for Protestant is *evangélico* from the Spanish word for "gospel," *evangélio*. Thus, the distinction that is made in the English language between "Protestant" and "evangelical" is harder to make in Spanish. As we discuss Protestantism in the contemporary period, specific distinctions within Protestantism become necessary for our analysis.

In the North American context, Protestant groups that I have characterized as "traditional" or "conservative," would refer to themselves as "evangelicals." In Central America these conservative Protestant groups increasingly refer to themselves as evangelical. Given their vertical integration into the organizational structure of a mother church or mission in the United States, this is not surprising. Within Evangelicalism there are further broad distinctions to make between evangelicals, fundamentalists, and pentecostalists. It is a common misconception to use evangelical and fundamentalist as synonyms, but not all evangelicals are fundamentalists. With a broad stroke we can draw the following distinctions.[27]

The evangelical mainstream in the United States accepts the major doctrines of the Christian faith such as the primacy of Scripture, the incarnation of Christ, the Trinity, the virgin birth, and the gift of grace. An evangelical pastor such as Billy Graham, the journal *Christianity Today*, and colleges such as Wheaton and Calvin, are representative of this group. Frequently, their social positions stem from the primacy afforded by Scripture.[28]

Fundamentalists take the primacy of Scripture a step further and believe in the inerrancy of the Bible, a literal interpretation of God's truth revealed. They follow a strict moral code in which the individual is largely responsible for his fate. In their view wealth is a reward from God.

The third group to be discussed are the pentecostalists who believe they have the gift of the spirit and speak in tongues. Their main message is a millennial one—for them salvation in the next life is the primary goal. Earthly life is temporary and to be endured as best one can. Good works on behalf of government or a search for temporal justice are discouraged. Our nature assures that these attempts are doomed to failure.

For the latter two groups the anticommunism of U.S. policy is easier to accept because of their strict sense of right and wrong, and their view of the Bible as an explanation for the good (God) and evil (Satan) on earth. The Soviet Union, communism, or Marxism, can be characterized as satanic forces of evil; it is the Christianized United States that represents the "good." Yet if one is to ask members of fundamentalist sects about their view of political action they will argue that they are apolitical and that they do not get involved in politics.[29] Faith and political action are not related and must be kept separate: Relying on Matt. 22:15–22 they would argue that "we must render to Ceasar what belongs to Ceasar and to God what belongs to God."

Yet on Central American soil, their churches have supported the foreign policy of the Reagan administration, they have opposed the "Communist Regime" in Nicaragua, and have either reached a *modus vivendi* with authoritarian governments or offered outright support, when an evangelical such as General Ríos Montt assumed the presidency of Guatemala. Many mainstream evangelicals also supported similar policy positions as do fundamentalists, but they are more judicious in their support, and more sophisticated in their explanations.

The state, in turn, has tacitly supported the evangelical groups, especially those who offer salvation in the next life. A belief of this nature encourages earthly passivity and therefore is not a challenge to the state. Evangelical churches and sects tacitly and overtly lend their support to a right-wing authoritarian regime because it leaves them alone; and because it is frequently supported by the United States who these groups view favorably.[30]

The permeation of American values within Central American evangelical Protestantism, as well as the ambivalence produced by these values, can be demonstrated vividly by allowing General Ríos Montt, who was quoted at the beginning of this chapter, to speak for himself. In a discussion of chapter 12:12–31 of 1 Cor., Ríos Montt used this familiar analogy by St. Paul.

> America is the head of the body but North America was not only the United States. As Jesus is one, we are members of the body of Jesus; Central America is a particular member. But the head (the United States) has lost its vision and therefore Central America has lost its vision because it is humanistic. The U.S. has lost God to technology and secular humanism. The answer is the restoration of Jesus Christ in the United States. Only Christ will save us!
>
> The U.S. had a vision in World War II and in Viet Nam. Its vision came from the Bible.[31]

In contrast, it is difficult for an authoritarian regime, whether civilian or military, to reach a *modus vivendi* with progressive Protestant (and Catholic) groups who question the legitimacy of state policies. These groups, on the basis of their prophetic understanding of their faith, and on the basis of their political convictions, challenge an authoritarian regime to expand the political process to the marginalized. On the other hand, conservative Protestant groups, such as fundamentalists, accept the conditions of social marginality as the context in which they live and work. Their pastoral program is to reform the individual's bad habits (e.g., smoking and drinking), in this life, while offering greater rewards in the next life. This millennial belief has great appeal to Central Americans who face an existence of worsening poverty, while the emphasis on personal habits and discipline helps to build a community of the faithful. Moreover, the liturgy of many fundamentalist or pentecostalist churches and faith missions is captivating in that it is emotive, joyful, and shared by others in the congregation.[32] Marginalized squatters of the *barrios* of the major cities of Central America may not have employment or health care, but they have found a support group, which for many is not to be taken lightly.

If one looks at a demographic map of Central America today it is the latter forms of evangelical Protestantism (fundamentalist and pentecostal) whose numbers are increasing dramatically. It is estimated that 20–30 percent of the population of Guatemala, and 20 percent of the population of El Salvador is evangelical.[33] Overall, the number of evangelicals in Latin America has doubled in six years to fifty million.[34]

Moreover, contemporary North American missionaries in Central America are not from the mainline Protestant churches in the United States; neither are the majority of them graduates of the mainline evangelical colleges in the United States. It is estimated that of 54,000 North American and Canadian missionaries in Latin America, approximately 5,000 are from mainline Protestant churches.[35]

To look more closely at the political positions of the most active Protestant groups allows one to see the reasons for an alleged conspiracy theory. Conservative Protestant churches and faith missions offer tacit support for the status quo and, by implication, for American policy goals. Their vocal anticommunism makes it easy to give credence to a conspiracy theory: namely, that these groups (or their mother churches in the United States) are on the rise because they were financially encouraged by the Reagan administration as a conscious part of the policies of containment (in El Salvador) and roll-back (in Nicaragua).[36]

There is strong evidence to support this hypothesis when we analyze the policy similarities between some evangelicals and political decisionmakers in the Reagan administration. Also, there is the rapid growth of new churches (some of modest means that offer services under a tent but others that are new concrete structures that the local Central American communities cannot afford) as well as the televangelists such as Jimmy Swaggart and the Argentinian Luis Palau who can be seen biweekly on Costa Rican TV and heard on the radio daily. We must also include the involvement of the Christian Broadcasting Network (CBN) in raising funds for Nicaraguan "border refugees" in Honduras,[37] and the domestic electoral appeals to the New Religious Right in the United States. However, this analysis would be strengthened if it took into consideration the complexities of the Christian faith and the historical appeal of messianic movements among the dispossessed.[38]

CONCLUSION

This chapter has demonstrated that Protestantism, since its arrival in Latin America, has never been exclusively religious in content. The Protestant faith came first with liberalism, then assumed overtones of U.S. national policy goals that have continued to the present day. Currently, the religious-political situation is more volatile than it was a century ago, because many Protestants on both continents have assumed more articulated and consciously vocal political positions that have deeply polarized denominations within the United States and Central America.[39] The rapid growth of Central American faith missions and sects and their implications for established churches, both Catholic and Protestant, have yet to be studied thoroughly. In the United States, with its relative affluence and unemployment rate of 5 percent, these evangelical churches have become sources of electoral strength primarily for the Reagan and Bush presidencies, while mainline churches, for the most part, supported the presidential candidacy of Michael Dukakis in the 1988 elections.

In Central America, where real wages have declined over the past thirty years, where unemployment ranges from 20 to 35 percent,[40] and where the ravages of war are a constant factor of daily existence, a retreat from *la situacíon* and the appeal to a better life in the next world, have a powerful attraction.[41] In summary, we are witnessing a play in which religious beliefs and political choices share center-stage together. How the drama unfolds over the next decade will, in part, determine the future of Central America.

9

Divided Evangelicals in South Africa
Lawrence Jones

The fact that I'm black and living in a different township than a white suburb is a cause of division.

A pentecostal pastor from Soweto,
a member of Concerned Evangelicals

The evangelical movement has been growing worldwide and becoming more and more influential through the power of the media. But evangelicals, including fundamentalists and pentecostals of various stripes, have always been divided by factions and schisms and the movement riddled with conflict. Because of the right-wing religious coalition supporting Reagan in the United States, and conservative domination of radio and television broadcasting, the evangelical movement has seemed more ideologically monolithic than it ever really was. Outside of the United States, especially in the Third World, evangelical churches are increasingly split between progressives with grass-roots support and conservative Americans, and their local allies who enjoy easy access to foreign money and electronic media.

South Africa is a good case of such a split in the movement. Evangelicals, like many other groups, have become deeply divided over the issue of apartheid. Many white evangelicals have remained conservative or have become reactionary in response to growing black unrest. Black evangelicals have become increasingly critical of apartheid and of white evangelicals they see as supporting the "system."

The white government of South Africa claims it represents "Christian Western civilization." Consequently, the credibility of the churches has become a major issue in the black communities. Black pastors in the townships decided that they had to make Christianity relevant or else it would become totally meaningless to congregations who lived their lives under apartheid.

Many black congregations have young progressive black pastors who grew up in the townships and who shared the same daily life and suffering as the people. The shooting of children radicalized some ministers. However, because of the security legislation and the continuing state of emergency, "evangelical rallies and big street marches with banners proclaiming Christian faith are out of the question."[1]

Young black pastors working to organize youth groups in Soweto could not ignore the realities of everyday life and expect to succeed. Christianity had to be made relevant, especially to youths who found themselves in a revolutionary situation. The security forces were storming into schools in the townships and arresting students. Black pastors began to form their own groups to rethink their theology and practice and to publicly express their view in pamphlets and sermons.

The leadership of several pentecostal denominations in South Africa is now divided. These denominational groups originated in the United States and some, like the Full Gospel Church, have an American Constitution that puts effective control in white hands and relegates black congregations to a subordinate "mission" status. Church leadership is split between popular progressive black preachers in the townships, who openly oppose the apartheid system, and conservative white church leaders.

WHITE EVANGELICALS

Many whites, both Afrikaans and English speaking, have flocked into the new pentecostal churches like the Rhema and Durban Christian Center during the 1970s and 1980s. It was a tense and anxious time for South African whites because of growing black resistance against the apartheid system. From 1970 to 1980, the number of South Africans involved in pentecostal churches tripled.[2] The giant new pentecostal churches are predominantly white[3] and many of their members left so-called mainstream churches (e.g., Anglican, Catholic, and Dutch Reformed) when church leaders began to criticize apartheid publicly.

The largest of the new pentecostal churches is Ray McCauley's Rhema Ministries, situated in a white suburb north of Johannes-

burg. McCauley, a former muscleman, received his seminary training at Kenneth Hagin's Rhema Bible Training Center in Tulsa,
Oklahoma.[4] Rhema also runs a Bible College of its own that uses
videotapes of Kenneth Copeland and other American evangelicals
to train its students. The flags of both the United States and the
Republic of South Africa flank the lectern at the Rhema Bible College. American evangelists regularly visit.

Rhema has three Sunday services: two large ones, mostly
white, in the morning and afternoon in the 5,000-seat auditorium,
and an afternoon "servants service" for black domestic workers
held in a smaller room. Services are very much like American pentecostal services: there is an animated sermon with singing and music, and an altar call where people are "saved," "baptized in the
Spirit," "healed" by the laying on of hands, and sometimes "slain
in the Spirit" (they fall backward, unconscious, "under the influence of the Holy Spirit"). The huge Rhema congregation is divided
into some 250 small "household fellowship groups" or "cell
groups," led by Church elders.[5]

Like many American pentecostals, and also like American fundamentalists, Rhema is dispensationalist in theology. Dispensation-
alists believe the Second Coming of Christ, and the end of the
world as we know it, is ever imminent. But before the prophesied
catastrophes of the last days occur, they expect to be caught up in
the "Rapture," sometimes called the "Great Escape," when they
will suddenly disappear from the face of the earth and meet Jesus
in the clouds. For American evangelicals this belief functions as an
antidote to popular fears of nuclear war.[6] In South Africa, however,
belief in the Rapture has a different function. Pastor McCauley,
tongue in cheek, so described it in a taped sermon. "I'm preaching
on the great escape. Amen. And that's not going to Australia, or to
the United States or Canada."[7] His congregation knew immediately
what he meant by "the great escape" and laughed at his contrast of
the Rapture with emigration. For McCauley, as for his largely white
congregation, "the great escape," like emigration, represents a hope
of fleeing the worsening political crisis in South Africa.

In their political attitudes, members of the new, mostly white,
pentecostal churches in South Africa are generally more conservative than members of the established churches.[8] Many consider the
idea of One Man, One Vote—the slogan of the now-banned United
Democratic Front (UDF)—to be "extremist." They tend to support
both the status quo and the restrictive racial laws. Nevertheless,
many conservative white pentecostals voice the hope that South

Africa will become a model of racial harmony for the world. When asked how this will come about, they answer vaguely that God is the only answer to the racial dilemma. The huge pentecostal churches in South Africa, like Rhema and the Durban Christian Centre, do not practice apartheid within their own congregations.

Ray McCauley has publicly denounced sanctions against the white state. But Rhema also supports the white government against black resistance. For example, in April 1987 during a strike of railroad workers backed by COSATU (Congress of South African Trade Unions) against the government-controlled South African Transit Service (SATS), a student monitor and church deacon, Derek Nykamp, a second-year student, announced at the Rhema Bible College that there were jobs available at the South African Transit Service for strike-breakers and asked the students to pass the word along. Nykamp denounced the COSATU workers for "striking for Satan's purposes" and urged the Bible College students to "show the world how Christians can work."[9]

There are well-funded groups of South African evangelicals who actively support the policies of the white government and devote themselves to making propaganda on its behalf.[10] There are a variety of these groups, some of them nonevangelical secular rightists, most of them cottage industries run out of suburban homes. New organizations and coalitions of the same people are constantly being formed to issue statements (sometimes claiming to represent the opinion of millions of black Church members) in support of the white government. They produce abundant printed material and have close contact with right-wing groups in the United States, the United Kingdom, and West Germany.

One of these groups, United Christian Action (UCA), was formed in 1984 as a right-wing coalition of religious supporters of the white government. UCA regularly attacks the religious opponents of apartheid as Communists or Communist sympathizers. The South African Council of Churches (SACC) is one of their favorite targets. UCA was founded by Ed Cain, a former missionary in Mozambique, who runs the coalition from his suburban home outside Pretoria. Cain's coalition includes a white pentecostal church and several other small right-wing groups as well as a shady black bishop, Isaac Mokoena, who falsely claims to represent some 4.5 million blacks.[11] A more sober assessment of Mokoena's following estimates it as only a few thousand.[12] It is unlikely that Cain's UCA actually represents more than several thousand people. However, Cain is often quoted in the South African press as a foil to Bishop Desmond Tutu or to the South African Council of Churches. Cain also publishes a newsletter called *Signposts,* which he started in 1982. Cain's operation is well equipped with computers. His literature is distributed by some American evangelical organizations, including Campus Crusade, which quietly circulated a speech by Cain entitled, "Liberation Theology." The speech was an attack on religious critics of apartheid, particularly the signers of the *Kairos Document.*[13] The *Kairos Document* is a theological assessment of the political crisis in South Africa signed by more than one hundred fifty church leaders, whom Cain denounced as apostates and as anti-Christian Marxists.[14]

Cain got his start in right-wing politics as the editor of the newsletter of the now defunct Christian League of Southern Africa. In the late 1970s the surreptitious funding of the organization by the Information Department of the South African government was exposed.[15] Fred Shaw, the founder of the Christian League of Southern Africa, described in an interview how the money was funneled to his organization through a small group of sympathetic businessmen who acted as intermediaries.[16] The outspoken Shaw managed to alienate his allies and associates as well as his government sponsors.

Cain, as well as other members of his United Christian Action coalition, receive much of their funding in a similar way to that of the old Church League. A small group of businessmen regularly, as individuals, donate large sums.[17]

Whether or not the UCA and its affiliates are also indirectly funded by the South African government cannot be known for sure, but the pattern of funding is suspiciously familiar and suggests that the government may secretly be involved in their propaganda efforts. Such right-wing cranks, who love to write tracts denouncing anti-apartheid church leaders as Communists, may be secretly funded by Pretoria through businessmen who pass the money on in monthly allotments.

There are new right-wing religious leaders emerging and new pro-government coalitions of evangelical churches have issued statements attacking the imposition of sanctions on South Africa and denouncing the more outspoken opponents of apartheid. Some of these coalitions are very uneasy alliances. Martin L. Badenhorst, a white Afrikaner, is now the president and formerly the director of missions of the five-hundred-thousand-member Full Gospel Church of God (FGCG) and the chair of the Fellowship of Pentecostal Churches. In June 1988, Badenhorst, as a representative of his church, publicly denounced the imposition of sanctions on South Africa.[18] He oversees the black churches of his denomination. Half of the membership of the FGCG is black. In response, a group of church members in Soweto in September 1988 produced a statement sharply critical of Badenhorst, who, they wrote, "in recent times has been actively involved in right-wing, pro-government politics. Further evidence for right-wing involvement lies in the fact that some of the FGCG white ministers are known AWB [Afrikaner Weerstand Beweging, a violent neo-Nazi group] members."[19] Badenhorst, in an interview, denied the charges.[20]

Badenhorst had also helped organize a new right-wing coalition calling itself "Christian Forum."[21] The group of 400, which claims to represent 17,000,000 South Africans (including Isaac Mokoena's nonexistent millions), most of them black, met in the Johannesburg City Hall to issue their statement attacking sanctions. Ray McCauley was also there.

Some evangelical groups are directly involved with the South Africa army and the wars in the front-line states. Open Doors and Frontline Fellowship, two examples, are allowed to distribute their literature on the military bases of the South African Defence Force. Open Doors, a stridently anti-Communist ministry based in The Netherlands, published a comic book in both English and Afrikaans, which is distributed through the chaplain general's office to all the troops. The comic book portrays the struggle between "democracy" and "communism" as the final contest between Christ and Antichrist.

The founder of Open Doors, who calls himself Brother Andrew, wrote *The Battle for Africa*. This book states that South Africa has a divine mission to evangelize all of Africa, and that the international movement for economic sanctions to end apartheid is a ploy by Satan "to isolate South Africa to prevent it from fulfilling its divine commission." In a recent speech to the International Christian Embassy in Jerusalem, an American evangelical organization, Brother Andrew claimed that there's a direct relationship between Israel and South Africa. The two nations were united in an end-times scenario. In this scheme, "the powers of evil, Communism and Islam, will join forces to make war against the Lamb."

Like their American counterparts, right-wing evangelicals in South Africa are obsessed with "the spread of communism," so much so that some of them even refuse to see apartheid as a serious problem. In their sermons they attack Christians, like Bishop Desmond Tutu, who have criticized the white government, as "Communists" and Marxists masquerading as Christians.

BLACK EVANGELICALS

Blacks tend to see the world rather differently. Black evangelical pastors from the townships in the Transvaal have published critiques of both apartheid and what they perceive to be white evangelical support for the apartheid state. In 1986 a group made up mostly of black evangelical leaders from Soweto and other townships in the Transvaal, calling themselves Concerned Evangelicals, published a pamphlet that addressed the crisis in South Africa.[22]

This progressive movement among black evangelicals has been growing over the last ten years. Black students in bible colleges in the 1970s began to organize themselves to address problems within their schools such as worms in the meal; "purely American courses [in evangelical seminaries] imposed on South Africa," for example, a course in "Christian etiquette" that taught American manners,[23] and the fact that black teachers were being paid less than white teachers. Some of these students became the progressive anti-apartheid evangelicals of the 1980s.

They began "to reevaluate their own theology and practice" after the state of emergency in 1985–1986 and came to the conclusion that they, as evangelicals, had been unduly influenced by American and European missionaries who were actually hostile to their own interests as blacks, and who were themselves uncritical supporters of the apartheid system.

Concerned evangelicals have broken away from a fundamentalist reading of scripture in favor of what they call a "contextual" one. Rom. 13, for example, is a verse often used by white evangelicals to demand submission to the state. "Let every soul be subject unto the higher powers. For there is no power but of God: the powers that be are ordained of God." Read in the larger context of Rom. and its historical setting, the verse does not call for blind obedience to an oppressive system. Rather, as their pamphlet states: "It says that governments are not a terror to the people but punish wrong doers (Rom. 13:3–4). The South African regime as we are experiencing it is just the opposite of what Paul said."[24] This kind of "contextual" rethinking has led them to reject some of the conservative and legalistic tendencies of American evangelical theology.

Moreover, the Concerned Evangelicals have become the most outspoken critics of other evangelicals who, they say, preach a "status quo theology" supportive of the apartheid state. In the fall of 1987, they published another pamphlet, this one critical of a tent crusade to be held in the Vaal Triangle townships of Sebokeng, Evaton, and Sharpeville by Nicky van der Westhuizen, an Afrikaans-speaking white pentecostal preacher.

Concerned evangelicals questioned his motives. The government had been trying to break the resistance of the Vaal townships with a variety of strategies,[25] and van der Westhuizen is a leader of the International Fellowship of Charismatic Churches (which includes Rhema Ministries), a confederation of white churches that the black evangelicals consider "famously progovernment." After meeting with van der Westhuizen and considering his case, the Concerned Evangelicals decided his tent crusade had no relevance to the day-to-day problems of the black communities and called on participants to reconsider their support.[26] As they wrote in their critique:

> White preachers who go into the embittered black communities have a subtle awareness that the ulterior or indirect results of their preaching will be to bring some kind of political sense into black heads. It will help black people to see the dangers of the feared communism. Alternatively, there is a malicious belief that "Jesus is the answer" to the political problems of this country. Jesus is adored as a durable broom that will endlessly sweep away the mess that is being daily produced by the South African political system. People are exhorted to let Jesus into their hearts, and that when He is in their hearts, He will in turn change the stubborn hearts of their slave-drivers. It is again observed that this white-preached gospel is only an antidote against black political anger, and that those who are fired with this kind of gospel become bereft of all earthly concerns.[27]

Concerned evangelicals blocked Nicky van der Westhuizen's planned crusade and effectively shut him out of the Vaal townships.

Black evangelical ministers said that one of the reasons why they formed their loose network was to counter the impression that all evangelicals in South Africa equated opposition to the apartheid state with "communism." For blacks, this equation is simply unbelievable, a kind of bizarre fantasy. But for many white South Africans, as well as for many American evangelicals, the idea that communism, not apartheid, is the major problem in South Africa seems perfectly reasonable, even self-evident. The two separate worlds of white suburb and black township are repeated in the conceptual worlds of whites and blacks. This crucial difference in perception, even more than race or theology, defines and divides two very different kinds of evangelicals active in South Africa now.

The word *Communist* has been applied so loosely and so frequently in South Africa to any and all opponents of apartheid that it has become an almost meaningless term. Marxist literature is banned and there are few real Communists who know much about Communist doctrine, especially in the black community. Ironically, however, because of the state propaganda, "communism" has become almost synonymous with opposition to apartheid and, consequently, has gained some measure of prestige among black youths in the townships.

Concerned evangelicals sharply criticized this "fixed idea" of conservative evangelicals.

They are so obsessed and pre-occupied with what they call the "threat of communism" to the extent of blessing any regime in the world that is anti-communist however evil and corrupt it may be. They have put their eyes so much on their conception of the "evil" of communism that they cannot see the evils of the systems within which they are living, and, in most cases they are part of the perpetrators or beneficiaries of these systems.[28]

Theologically, for Concerned Evangelicals, this fixation on communism as evil and the corresponding deification of Western capitalist culture, has become a kind of idolatry.[29]

Recently in South Africa, some of the black churches see themselves as an emerging "third force" in the conflict between the white government and the ANC (African National Congress). They are opposed to apartheid but unaligned with "red" movements. The white leaders of South African evangelical groups founded by, or still under the control of, Americans have vigorously opposed the emergence of this "third force" in the black evangelical community.

AMERICAN EVANGELICALS AND APARTHEID

Both white and black evangelicals have a common history of American evangelical influence. From its beginnings, the South African evangelical movement was under the influence of, and sometimes the direction of, American evangelical groups, which have been sending missionaries to South Africa since the early years of this century. In the 1920s American fundamentalists under the auspices of the World's Christian Fundamentals Association, organized a committee to correlate foreign missionary societies with representatives in the South Africa General Mission.[30] Pentecostal missionaries from the United States have worked in South Africa since 1908.[31]

More recently there has been renewed activity on the part of American evangelicals in South Africa. American Pentecostalism, rather than fundamentalism, has had the most success in South Africa. The highly emotional worship of pentecostals, who speak in tongues, lay on hands for healings, and sometimes weep during their meetings, has struck a cord among disaffected white South Africans. Pentecostal styles of worship are also popular among blacks. Jimmy Swaggart, a pentecostal, rather than Jerry Falwell, a representative of an emotionally cooler fundamentalism, has been the most popular evangelist in South Africa (at least until his sex scandal in 1988). In 1987, Swaggart was listed among the top ten in a newspaper poll by the *Sowetan* whom the (mostly black) readers would choose as president of a new South Africa (if they could vote). Even leaders of Concerned Evangelicals, who are among the most critical of American evangelicals, had Swaggart audiotapes in their hands. Swaggart, in fact, financed the purchase of a seminary in Cape Town for his denomination, the Assemblies of God, and maintains a large office and bookstore in Johannesburg. Swaggart's television programs were frequently broadcast on the state-controlled South African Broadcasting Corporation (SABC).

Swaggart was not the only influential American televangelist in South Africa. Trinity Broadcasting Network (TBN), based in southern California, owns and operates the first evangelical station in Africa, in the South African "homeland state" of Ciskei. Pat Robertson's Christian Broadcasting Network (CBN) programming appears on the air in South Africa and in several of the "homelands."

As black evangelicals charge, many American evangelicals and their South African counterparts have chosen to side with the white government in the current political struggle. Comparatively few American evangelicals work against the white government's apartheid policies and side with black groups like the Concerned Evangelicals. One group of American evangelicals that works against apartheid and is allied with Concerned Evangelicals is Evangelicals for Social Action based in Philadelphia. Most popular American televangelists readily denounced apartheid (Botha has done that) and then uncritically accepted the government's claim that apartheid is "dead"—a nonissue—and focused all their attention on the supposed threat of communism.

Jimmy Swaggart probably pleased white evangelicals and the South African government, but he outraged many blacks when he announced at a rally during one of his South African crusades that "apartheid is dead." The government, in what was widely interpreted by blacks as a way of invoking divine approval for its actions, at the onset of the state of emergency in June 1986 televised another Swaggart sermon, which he had given three years earlier in Johannesburg. Swaggart, in that address, said that South Africa was a prime target for the Communist onslaught because it was one of the few countries in Africa "that holds up the Bible and holds up Jesus Christ."

Some American evangelical organizations effectively practice apartheid in their operations. Campus Crusade for Christ, South Africa, is an evangelistic association, transplanted from the United States, which split into two radically segregated ministries in 1983.[32] The black "sister" organization, called Life Ministries, employs about ten black couples in community health evangelism inside the black townships and in the so-called "homeland" states created by the apartheid government. Unlike Campus Crusade in the United States, the organization in South Africa is not primarily a campus ministry. The white branch of Campus Crusade, based in Pretoria, is aimed at the Afrikaans-speaking elite of South African society, especially wealthy businessmen, their wives, and highly placed members of the government. The smaller black branch of Campus Crusade is allotted about 20 percent of the budget, while the white group consumes 80 percent of the organization's total resources.

The whites have American money and ready access to the media empires of evangelicals in the United States. The evangelical media in the United States, dominated by conservatives, has so far ignored progressive black groups like Concerned Evangelicals. Black evangelicals have been effectively cut off from American evangelical money and from access to the evangelical electronic media. Against such money and media power, progressive black evangelical pastors have only their popularity in the black communities and their organizational skills. It is an uneven struggle but the outcome is far from certain.

CONCLUSION

The evangelical movement is the most modernized of all contemporary religious movements. Evangelicals from the United States pioneered religious broadcasting and now literally cover the world with their electronic messages. But evangelicals have also been the most outspoken opponents of "modernism" and upholders of what they considered to be traditional beliefs and values.

White elites in South Africa have always used religion to legitimate white minority rule. The religious anticommunism of rightwing evangelicals from the United States offers the white government religious legitimacy. The old theology of divinely ordained apartheid no longer works. U.S. evangelicals also offer the South Africans valuable airtime on evangelical broadcasting networks in the United States to promote their own propaganda, to claim that white-ruled South Africa was a Christian country under siege by godless Communists, and that sanctions against South Africans mainly hurt poor blacks.

White evangelicals in South Africa have ready access to the money and media empires of evangelicals in the United States, but evangelical media in the United States have so far ignored progressive black groups like Concerned Evangelicals. American religious broadcasting, estimated to be a $1–2.5 billion industry, is dominated by conservative evangelicals who uncritically support the white government of South Africa. Pat Robertson's Christian Broadcasting Corporation, Trinity Broadcasting Network, Jerry Falwell, and Jimmy Swaggart have all provided free air time to representatives of the South African government. Progressive black evangelists in South Africa have been effectively cut off from American evangelical money and from access to their electronic media.

Recent religious revivalism in South Africa seems to be rooted in anxiety, among both blacks and whites, over the political situation in the country. The apocalyptic escapism appeals to an increasingly desperate people. Pentecostal styles of worship provide a kind of psycho-theater where anxious individuals can act out their feelings safely. American pentecostalism offers nervous white and black

South Africans an emotional outlet for their growing anxiety about the situation in their country. Pentecostalism has traditionally been a racially mixed religious movement and provides whites in the suburbs with the gratifying illusion that "apartheid is dead" because their churches are about 20 percent black.

American evangelicals have been popular among striving "middle-class" blacks in the townships. But now the youths are growing up in a revolutionary situation. The townships are under military control. Evangelicalism has always been entrepreneurial and pentecostal theology fairly malleable. The evangelical movement is made up of family businesses, as well as small and large independent churches, and giant broadcasting businesses. There is a great variety of different independent views.

A new kind of evangelical church seems to be emerging in the Transvaal townships of South Africa. As evangelicals the young pastors of Concerned Evangelicals were clearly faced with a crisis of identity and legitimacy. The right-wing diatribes of Jimmy Swaggart and other American evangelicals were no longer compatible with their understanding of Christianity. They began to develop their own theology in the context of growing conflict in South Africa and are creating their own sense of what it means to be an evangelical Christian.

The resurgence of religion around the world is a complex and often contradictory phenomenon. Evangelical Christianity, imported from the United States and easily accessible to anyone with a radio or television receiver, has not created a unified movement in South Africa. Quite the contrary!

Part III.   The Church: An Instrument for Political Protest and Modernization

This part analyzes the political activities of the church and its participation in the protest movement in the Philippines and Latin America. In contrast to the conservative outlook of the Protestants, the Catholic church in the last two decades assumed a liberal orientation in these countries. In chapter 10, Lonnie D. Kliever does not simply agree that the recent successes of the conservative Protestants have eclipsed the liberal religious groups. He points out that there has been a shift in the agenda of the liberal theologians from trying to modernize the Bible to a new political agenda of revolutionizing the gospel in order to promote the interests of the underprivileged.

In chapter 11, C. Neal Tate argues that the church provided a refuge for the political opposition to the dictatorial rule of Ferdinand Marcos. By siding with the opposition, the Catholic clergy delegitimized Marcos's regime. Tate emphasizes that the support of the church was invaluable for the successful outcome of the nonviolent overthrow of the Philippine president in February of 1986.

In chapter 12, Michael Dodson observes that until recently, the Catholic church in Latin America reinforced the authoritarian patriarchal nature of the state. Yet, for a variety of reasons that Dodson explains, the conservative orientation of the Catholic church was replaced by a liberal outlook. The Catholic liberal theologians began to sharply criticize poverty and inequality in Latin America. Dodson concludes that the rise of the "popular church" in some Latin American countries presented a challenge to both the secular authority of the states and the authoritarian structure of the Catholic church.

10

Liberalism in Search of a Political Agenda
Lonnie D. Kliever

In a 1980 survey of contemporary Christian thought, it was argued that the old spectrum of conservative and liberal theology had been shattered by twentieth-century secularism and relativism.[1] The old idea that theologies on the right preserved traditional religious beliefs and social institutions in the name of biblical authority, while theologies on the left challenged traditional religious tenets and social structures in the light of rational knowledge, no longer proved useful. Theological and social agendas could no longer be characterized as "conservative" or "liberal" by the old benchmarks of biblical versus rational authority, of transcendent versus immanent deity, of supernatural versus natural grace, of individual versus social ethics.[2] The old conservative-liberal spectrum was shattered by an explosion of new theologies that were in many ways more biblical and conservative than the conservatives they ignored, in other ways more innovative and radical than the liberals they supplanted.

But, as the old saying goes, "A funny thing happened on the way to the forum." The 1980s saw a revival of the old-time religion as a vital theological and social force that caught many people by surprise. Christian television stations and computer-generated mailing lists succeeded in welding fundamentalist and evangelical Christians together in a common religious and political cause across denominational, class, and sectional lines. The old battle lines between conservatives and liberals were renewed with a vengeance by the emergence of a "New Religious Right."

But, on the face of things, only one end of the old conservative-liberal spectrum has been revived. Put another way, the polarizing rhetoric and strategy of the New Religious Right has not succeeded in generating an opposing New Religious Left. Far from it! Those who are excluded from the circle of evangelical religion and politics seem scattered across a landscape of religious and moral conviction without center or circumference. Indeed, many commentators have insisted that this diffusion of religious sentiments and moral concerns has neutralized the power of the old liberal religious establishment.

Clearly, liberal theologies and denominations have been knocked on their heels by the resurgence of a militant religious Right. Moreover, the diversity and divisiveness of liberal theological experiments and political alignments of the last twenty-five years have deprived liberalism of a single voice in the religious and political arena. But this diversity and divisiveness is a sign of vitality rather than of debility. After all, liberalism has never been a unified and unifying theological or moral perspective. The term *liberalism* became popular during the fundamentalist-modernist controversy at the turn of the century when anyone who was not a fundamentalist was, by definition, a liberal.[3] But there was always enormous variety and often bitter disagreement among those who fell outside fundamentalism's homogeneous circle of faith. Liberalism has never pursued one theological method or pushed one moral message.

This is not to suggest that liberalism is a mere verbal figment of the fundamentalist imagination. Liberal theologians have always shared a common *paradigm* of religious and moral reflection.[4] They have all accepted the eighteenth-century Enlightenment as a critical watershed in the history of Christian thought, calling for new methods of theological reflection and new meanings for religious existence. Moreover, that common paradigm has generated a broad consensus among liberal theologians over the fundamental task of theology. Theology is understood as *interpretation*—as the critical correlation of the Christian tradition with the contemporary situation.

For the most part, this task of correlating Christian symbols with contemporary sensibilities has been directed toward the *crisis of faith* that modern Christians were undergoing. The increasing secularization of modern thought and life has raised serious challenges to traditional Christianity. Liberal theologians from Frederick Schleiermacher, the eighteenth-century German theologian who sought to make sense of Christianity for the "cultured despisers of religion," to John A. T. Robinson, the Anglican bishop who reinterpreted the Christian gospel for secularists in the 1960s, have sought to reconcile biblical religion with modern sensibilities. Not surprisingly, their theologies have always had an air of accommodation about them. The cultural worlds of modern philosophy and science have provided the intellectual framework within which the Christian faith was reinterpreted. Thereby the gospel has been "modernized" by being correlated with the most up-to-date findings of the science, history, and philosophy of the day.

Such theological efforts to "modernize" the gospel still dominate the liberal theological reflection. But a significant shift toward a more political agenda can be seen among a number of recent liberal theological programs. For them, the theological task of correlating Christian symbols and contemporary sensibilities has been redirected toward the *crisis of culture* that the world is undergoing. The increasing fragmentation and privatization of modern thought and life is posing serious threats to human community and even to human survival. Liberal theologians as diverse as James Cone, Mary Daly, and Gustavo Gutiérrez, the new "liberation theologians" whose writings are treated below, are primarily concerned with enlisting Christianity in the struggle to change the suicidal course of human history. Not surprisingly, their theologies have a decidedly revolutionary tone about them. Remaking the cultural worlds of politics and economics is seen as the heart of the Christian faith. The gospel is thus "politicized" by being immersed in the struggles for peace and justice among oppressed races, genders, and classes around the world.

This liberal shift from the crisis of faith to the crisis of culture is more than a matter of theological accent. To be sure, the underlying paradigm of theological and moral reflection remains the same. The fundamental task of theology is still a matter of correlating the Christian tradition with the contemporary situation. But this shift from a *hermeneutical* agenda to a *political* agenda profoundly affects both the context and the content of liberal theological reflection.

THE CONTEXT OF THEOLOGICAL REFLECTION

In the past, the primary context for liberal theological reflection has been the academic community. This location is hardly surprising, given the task of interpreting the Christian tradition in light of the most up-to-date science, history, and philosophy of the day. Where else could the dialogue between science and religion, between philosophy and theology be better pursued than in the academic context? But the inevitable consequence of locating theological reflection in the academic community was its separation from the day-to-day life of the believing community and social order. More and more, theologians owed their fundamental loyalty to the university and to the discipline. More and more, theological reflection lost touch with the religious concerns of ordinary believers and with the moral problems of the wider society.

Theologies for the Oppressed

The newer politicized theologies have broken through the narrow intellectual constraints and institutional loyalties of the academic community. Indeed, these theologians have called the prevailing styles and canons of academic inquiry themselves into question. They believe that the academic community is too heavily invested in the conceits of liberal democratic and socialist solutions to the world's problems. As these solutions have become more and more problematic, the academic community has become increasingly a reactionary rather than a revolutionary community. The university is one among other powerful cultural institutions that must be challenged and changed if peace and justice are to prevail for all humanity.

The church falls under the same kind of criticism as the university. By and large, the church is deemed guilty of the Marxist claim that "religion is the opiate of the people." According to Marx, religion provides a theological justification for the patterns of socioeconomic oppression that give rise to suffering in the first place while simultaneously rechanneling the discontent of the oppressed into other-worldly aspirations for some imagined paradise. While the politicized theologians do not accept the Marxist claim that *all* religion is ideological, they do insist that the established churches are institutions of privilege rather than movements for equality. Like the university, the church must also be challenged and changed if freedom and equality are to prevail for all humanity.

Rather than originating in the university or the church, the newer politicized theologies rise from a growing wave of secular liberation movements the world over. These movements represent a broad range of ethnic, sexual, and socioeconomic concerns. Drives for black, brown, and red power are staking out their own race's claim to full dignity and opportunity. A many-faceted women's movement dealing with everything from equal pay to abortion rights is shaking cultural instincts and male psyches to their foundations. Third World peoples in Latin America, Asia, and Africa are battling their way out from under colonial rule and capitalist domination. The newer political theologians have become militant partners in these secular freedom movements.

According to theologies of liberation, these secular freedom movements present a dual challenge to the Christian faith. Negatively, they offer a sweeping challenge to the church's racism, sexism, and colonialism. They insist that religious ideologies and institutions, which identify with the world's powerful rather than with the world's powerless, are sources of oppression and obstacles to liberation. Echoing the critiques of religion by Marx, Nietzsche, and Freud, they call for a total overthrow of all religions of privilege and all religions of escape. Positively, these secular liberation movements offer the church an opportunity to recover its true faith and recover its true voice. By their opposition to establishment and escapist religion, they direct faith toward where God can be found in this world. The God of the Bible is always at work among the "marginalized"—among those who are left by the social, political, and economic wayside. The God who became incarnate in Jesus preached good news to the poor, release to the captives, and liberty to the oppressed. Thus, both positively and negatively, the world's liberation movements challenge the Church to match their concern with a God and with a gospel of liberation.

Theologies by the Oppressed

As such, the newer politicized theologies differ from earlier forms of social Christianity where advantaged groups sought to express their faith through bettering the lot of disadvantaged groups. The newer "liberation theologies," as they are called, are movements from *within* disadvantaged groups. Indeed, they claim an "epistemological privilege for the oppressed" in theological reflection—that is, only the oppressed can see the world as it really is and as it ideally ought to be. This epistemological claim gives these theologies an unmistakably urgent and authentic tone.

Without question, this intense militancy builds a certain divisiveness into the liberation theologies. Ordinarily, the liberation theologians do not address the problems of oppressed groups *en masse*. Rather, highly partisan theologies of liberation are written from and for distinctive groups. Ethnic, feminist, and Third World partisans address the church and the world primarily in terms of their own perceptions of oppression and programs of liberation. These internal divisions sometimes put the liberation theologies in conflict with one another. Even when they address the problems of *all* the oppressed, as the best of them ultimately do, they see all oppression as an outgrowth of their own group's oppression. For ethnic theologians all oppression is racist; for feminist theologians it is sexist; for Third World theologians it is colonialistic.

This theological partisanship draws even sharper dividing lines between the theologies of the oppressed and the theologies of oppressors. The liberation theologians level their severest criticisms against those Christian beliefs, practices, and institutions that either actively or tacitly sanction oppression in the church and in the world. For liberation theologians, the enemy is not simply white, masculine, capitalist society. It is white theology, masculine religion, and Euramerican ethics that must be overthrown. So strident have been the liberationist internecine polemics that theological counter-charges in kind have been evoked—liberation theologies are charged with being racist, sexist, class theologies! But calmer heads have cautioned that these partisan critiques are interim strategies designed to break down and break through, the structures and sanctions of oppression. Ultimately, freeing the oppressed means freeing the oppressors as well, since being an oppressor is as destructive to one's own humanity as is being oppressed. Thus, whatever else these liberation theologies might mean to their distinctive constituencies, they offer a unique challenge for the whole church to break free from the shackles of white, masculine, middle-class religion.

THE CONTENT OF THEOLOGICAL REFLECTION

On the surface of things, these shifts in the context of theological reflection may not seem all that significant. After all, how different can the Christian message look and sound to theologians of a different race, gender, or class? But the content of theology is profoundly changed when theological reflection occurs "in the world" rather than "in the church," and originates "among the oppressed" rather than "among the oppressors." The extent of these changes becomes obvious in a comparison of the pioneering statements of liberation theology—the "Black Liberation Theology" of James Cone, the "Feminist Liberation Theology" of Mary Daly, and the "Latin American Liberation Theology" of Gustavo Gutiérrez.[5]

Black Liberation Theology

James H. Cone, a professor at New York's Union Theological Seminary, shook the theological world of the 1970s with the publication of his book, *Black Theology and Black Power*, in which he argued that black power even in its most radical expressions is "Christ's central message to twentieth-century America."[6] Worked out in more systematic detail in his book, *A Black Theology of Liberation* and put in historical perspective in *God of the Oppressed*, Cone's theology is an admittedly angry and passionate call for revolution.[7] He calls for the total commitment of Christian thought and action to the black revolution already under way. He leaves no question but that this commitment may include violence since liberation means "the complete emancipation of black people from white oppression by whatever means black people deem necessary."[8]

Cone's revolutionary call rests on two fundamental assumptions—that Christianity has always been a religion of liberation and that theology must always interpret the gospel in the light of the oppressed community's struggle for justice. In light of these assumptions, Christian theology and faith itself have no choice but to become black because oppression and liberation are centered in the black community. Cone is adamant that this black theology is centered in Christ and faithful to Scripture, as all Christian theology must be.[9] The consistent theme of God's election of Israel and his incarnation in Christ is the liberation of God's people from social, political, and economic bondage. Israel prefigures the Christ who, as the Oppressed One, identifies from birth to death with those who suffer and empowers them to overcome through his life and resurrection. But the biblical witness to the living Christ can come alive today only in the company of the oppressed, and in North America that means the black community. Thus, black theology is subject to a single norm that has two aspects—"the liberation of black people and the revelation of Jesus Christ."[10] The kingdom of God is a black kingdom, and the messiah of God is a black Christ. Only the black can truly see and serve God in today's world.

Cone's repeated affirmation of blackness is matched by an unrelenting negation of whiteness. He goes beyond faulting white theology and the white church for ignoring racist oppression and perpetuating racial injustice. Whiteness itself is condemned as the very essence of evil—as antihuman and anti-Christ. Nothing short of a "Black Copernican Revolution" can overthrow whiteness. Only an antiwhite church and antiwhite theology can recover the true meaning and message of the gospel. Daring the razor's edge of heresy and treason, Cone announces that white Christianity and white America must be destroyed before human life and divine love are possible on this earth.

Given his categorical distinction between black and white, Cone's theology is often seen as black racism masquerading as Christian theology. But this assessment misses the subtlety and scope of thought that underlies his sledgehammer language. Cone's analysis of *blackness* and *whiteness* moves on two intersecting levels. Each term has a literal and particular sense and a symbolic and universal meaning. When Cone speaks of black power, black theology, and black liberation, he certainly has in mind the black people of America "whose children are bitten by rats, whose women are raped and whose men are robbed of their manhood." Similarly, when Cone excoriates white values, white theology, and white religion, he is condemning the white people of America who have enslaved, humiliated, and ignored black people for more than two centuries. Cone's comments about black and white America are first and foremost to be taken in their literal and particular sense.

But *blackness* and *whiteness* also have a symbolic and universal meaning in Cone's theology. Those terms describe human attitudes and social structures that bear no essential connection to skin color and racial ancestry. Throughout his writings, he speaks (often coyly) of "black men in white skins" and of "white men in black skins." Being black means being "identified with the victims of humiliation in human society and a participant in the liberation of man."[11] By contrast, "whiteness symbolizes the activity of deranged men intrigued by their own image of themselves, and thus unable to see that they are what is wrong with the world."[12] Ultimately, being black or white has little to do with skin color. "It essentially depends on the color of your heart, soul, and mind."[13]

Having marked that blackness and whiteness are both "visible realities" and "ontological symbols" in Cone's theology, two cautions are in order. First, Cone's literal and particular language must not be too quickly translated into symbolic and universal categories. The priority for defining oppression and undertaking liberation clearly belongs with the community of black-skinned Americans. Hence Cone's ridicule of liberation nostrums by whites, and his refusal of white offers to help in the black cause. White-skinned Americans are too bound by the structures of white racism and too dependent on their rewards to understand racial bondage or to undertake racial liberation. Similarly, Cone makes it clear that the initiative for liberating the oppressors along with the oppressed must come from the community of black-skinned Americans. White-skinned persons can become black—indeed, must become black—

to enter God's kingdom of justice and love. But white-skinned Americans are enslaved and dehumanized by their master's role. Oppressing whites can only be freed from such self-debasing behavior when oppressed blacks refuse to behave according to their master's rules.[14]

Considered as a whole, James Cone's black liberation theology achieves a surprising blend of situational relevance and universal applicability. To the white and nonwhite communities of North America, he proclaims a highly concrete revolutionary gospel calling for the economic, political, and social liberation of blacks, browns, and reds. But, by also universalizing "blackness" and "whiteness" as symbolic modes of existence, Cone recaptures the radical message of biblical religion. He calls the whole Christian community, black and white, back to the prophetic religion of ancient Israel and the iconoclastic faith of primitive Christianity. He calls the church and every Christian to the life of *perpetual* revolution—breaking down all the walls that divide and building in their place one new humanity.

Women's Liberation Theology

Revolutionary ferment in the 1960s also had a sexual dimension. The most newsworthy form this revolution took was in the area of sexual relations, per se. A new sexual candor in the media and the arts and a new sexual freedom in conversation and relationships profoundly altered sexual perceptions and practices. At the same time, on a deeper level, a far more radical revolution in the relations between the sexes was also under way. Spearheaded by Betty Friedan's book *The Feminine Mystique,* and Kate Millet's book *Sexual Politics,* this secular "women's revolt" began to give vision and voice to a whole new way of thinking about women's place in the world.

The church was quickly drawn into the orbit of feminist criticism and activism, thanks in large part to Mary Daly's study of Christianity's sexist attitudes and practices in her book *The Church and the Second Sex.*[15] Compared to her later works, this book was a temperate call for the reform of sexist thinking and action within the Roman Catholic church. Although sharply criticizing the church for perpetuating the subjugation of women through its sexist theology and polity, Daly initially believed that the "personalist strain" in its traditional theology and the inspiring examples of its women saints and religious, opened the way to reform. The time seemed right for the women in the church to pioneer a new level of "democratic" cooperation between the sexes that would in time dissolve hierarchical ideologies and arrangements within the church and the world.

Daly's commitment to gentle and gradual feminist reforms of the church and world was short-lived. Her next book, *Beyond God the Father,* rings of revolution rather than of reform.[16] Many of the same themes of the earlier book are repeated here—the religious roots of sexist oppression, the dehumanizing effects of sexual stereotyping, and the liberation of both men and women from sexual alienation. But all are radicalized in this strident manifesto for a feminist revolution in the church and in the world, to be fought without the help or cooperation of men.

Daly wields the language and logic of feminist revolution with consummate skill and stunning effect. The world is categorically divided into the oppressed (women) and the oppressors (men). Though she looks forward to a time when men and women will live in a human community "beyond sexual caste," Daly leaves no question but that men are to blame for the social arrangements and social systems that "have shortened and crushed the lives of women." As perpetrators and benefactors of a sexual caste system that shapes the whole of personal identity and social reality, men are simply incapable of seeing or solving the problem. Liberation will be achieved only when human life and earth are freed from the "rape" of patriarchy.

Such liberation means far more than men sharing household chores and women gaining equal rights. Liberation from patriarchy finally means "castrating" God.[17] As long as God and God's surrogates are male, then male is God! A world "beyond the death of God the Father" will be a world without the priorities that belong to all the "God-Fathers"—whether biological (the male parent), psychological (the sugar daddy), matrimonial (the man of the household), political (the city fathers) or ecclesiastical (the holy fathers). A world without privileged fathers will be a world without hierarchy and without oppression, a world of equality and fulfillment for all.

Daly's fierce language is more than mere revolutionary rhetoric or empty demagoguery. She understands what all great revolutionary leaders have known intuitively about language, and what recent linguistic studies have made plain to all of us. Human attitudes and actions are formed by a culture's words and images. Personal and social existence are created and maintained by a network of key symbolic constructs—good and evil, mind and matter, church and state, God and world, and male and female. Thus, Daly's concentration on such images and her language of sexual wounding and counterwounding (rape and castration) are deliberate strategies of linguistic confrontation. She seeks to force people into situations requiring new perceptions and values by attacking the language that subliminally builds sexist stereotypes and sexist oppressions into our very minds and muscles.

Daly's "linguistic therapy" goes beyond linguistic confrontation and attack. Beyond her strident "antitheology" lie the makings of a positive theology of women's liberation that promises a new humanity and a new earth for all. She models her feminist theology on the key concepts of classical Christian theology. But each of these doctrines is wrenched out of the traditional context of patriarchy and placed into the contemporary context of sisterhood emerging among feminist "model-breakers" and "model-makers."[18] She reverses the content of these doctrines with masterful irony, beginning with the image of God the Father.[19] Merely changing the color or the class of God will not do. Whether God is white or black, Marxist or capitalist, egalitarian or autocrat, matters little if God remains male. Racial, economic, and political oppression cannot end until sexist oppression is overthrown. Sexual aggression is the "primordial aggression" and women are the "primordial aliens." The oppression of women is the source and the model of all oppression. Thus, only a *women's* liberation theology gets at the root of all oppression because only a women's liberation theology challenges the patriarchal God that symbolizes and legitimates racial, economic, and political repression. Accordingly, Daly summons women to reach "outward and inward toward the God beyond and beneath the gods who have stolen our identity."[20]

Daly is not ready to call this God a person—even a female person. She does acknowledge that a universal matriarchal society and religion preceded patriarchy and that the Virgin Mary in the Christian tradition reflects this ancient religion of the Mother Goddess.[21] But Daly is reluctant to "rename" the deity as the Mother Goddess because feminist experience suggests that neither the Father nor the Mother is God. In their newfound awareness, feminists are moving toward "androgynous being," where all sexual separation and alienation are overcome. But the time for this "diarchal society" has not yet come. Vast changes in sexist psyches and sexist societies must still take place before life beyond sexual caste is possible. These changes cannot happen apart from the breakup of all the symbols and statuses of patriarchy. Because of the risks of challenging the meaning our culture gives to human being and value, only the oppressed who are denied full being and value will have the necessary outrage and courage to begin and complete the journey. Women alone must make the breakthroughs that can alter the course of human evolution. Women alone must write the liberation theologies that will free us all.

Latin American Liberation Theology

Out of the struggles of developing "Third World" countries has come another new theology that clearly belongs to the liberation theology movement. Like black theology, it arises out of a specific context of oppression. Like feminist theology, it contends that the reversal of these oppressive conditions requires a significant revision of Christian belief and practice. Like both, it promises liberation to all the oppressed through deliverance from one particular form of oppression. In this case, however, *class* oppression is seen as the underlying source and model of all other expressions of human bondage. The publication of the book *A Theology of Liberation* by a Peruvian priest named Gustavo Gutiérrez launched the emergence of a distinctive "Latin American Liberation Theology."[22]

Gutiérrez capsules this new way of doing theology in the word, *orthopraxis.*[23] Theology as orthopraxis shifts the burden of faith from right knowledge (ortho-doxy) to right action (orthopraxis). Gutiérrez believes that theology has too long been concerned with formulating truths, and too long unconcerned with changing lives. Not that he totally separates belief and behavior. But he does bend theology to the "historical praxis of liberation." Theology's task is addressing all the forms of class oppression with a word of revelation and a work of revolution.

This concern of rebalancing belief and action is reflected in Gutiérrez's understanding of liberation. He distinguishes three interpenetrating levels of liberation—political, historical, and spiritual.[24] On the political level, liberation involves the struggles of oppressed peoples to escape the domination of wealthy nations and repressive regimes. At a deeper historical level, liberation means assuming responsibility for creating "a new man and a qualitatively different society." Finally, at a still deeper spiritual level, liberation requires a transforming encounter with Jesus Christ that roots out the very basis of oppression in the human heart. Though these three levels of liberation are not the same, one is finally not possible or present without the other two. Political, historical, and spiritual liberation are inseparable parts of a single "salvific process."

These three levels of liberation not only structure Gutiérrez's thought, but they also correspond to three levels of analysis that enter into his theology. Political liberation must be guided by scientific understanding of the structures and functions of oppressive and nonoppressive societies. Gutiérrez draws heavily on Marxist and Freudian accounts of the sources and consequences of class conflict at this level of his theological reflection. But such scientific accounts do not establish the wider historical horizons and the deeper spiritual realities within which liberation occurs. The "Utopian imagination" of historical projection inspires and guides political revolution by furnishing a positive vision of a new kind of person and society that fulfills the needs of "the whole man." In turn, the universal outreach of Christian faith frees such historical projects of Utopian imagination from shallow consumerism and narrow nationalism. Christian faith reveals that every effort to build a more just society finally rests on "the communion of all men with God." Thus does Gutiérrez bring together scientific rationality, historical imagination, and religious perception in his liberation theology.

Addressing theology to the political and historical praxis of liberation means starting with a concrete situation of human oppression and liberation. For Gutiérrez, that concrete situation is a continent dominated externally by the great capitalist countries and riven internally by class differences. Though Latin American social order has always been maintained by the few for their own benefit, the exploited lower classes are beginning to forge a radically different society. In this revolutionary situation, the Christian has no choice but to identify with the marginalized and the impoverished. Such identification means pursuing the construction of a social order where workers are not exploited by owners, and where citizens are not tyrannized by rulers. The Christian in Latin America has the responsibility to participate in the revolutionary creation of that just and free society.

Gutiérrez acknowledges the risks of such involvement, but insists that the Church cannot remain neutral in a revolutionary situation. Refusing to side with the oppressed in Latin America is choosing to side with the oppressors. Indeed, the only way the church can be a "universal sacrament" of Christian love and unity is by taking the side of the poor and alienated. Christian love demands that the oppressed and the oppressors alike be delivered from the social circumstances that destroy the humanity of all. Christian unity requires the destruction of all the walls of separation that divides the human family into the oppressed and the oppressors. Moreover, neither love nor unity precludes conflict or even violence. In a world where conflict and violence are built into the structures of oppressive social order, those structures will not fall without conflict and violence. The church cannot be for universal justice without standing against historical injustice.

Thus does Gutiérrez see theology growing out of the process of liberation in Latin America. He acknowledges that theology is still very much in the process of development. A more in-depth scientific analysis of the social order, more daring historical vision of the human future, and clearer religious understanding of Christian beliefs and practices in the Latin American context are needed. But, for all of these limitations, Gutiérrez believes that Latin American liberation theology addresses the church, both local and universal, with the challenge of the gospel. Latin America is a microcosm of a world and a church being torn apart by social inequity and revolutionary activity. Therefore the meaning of Christianity and the mission of the church are the same for the world as for Latin America. But the courage to address that question, if not the right to answer, may be found only in a church on a continent where misery and upheaval abound. For that reason, a liberation theology of, and for, Latin America, is a liberation theology of, and for, the world.

CONCLUSION

The differences between black, feminist, and Latin American theologies are truly monumental and may seem to preclude all agreements save in their shared concern with liberation. But a more careful reading suggests some important theological agreements both in matter of style and substance. These very different expressions of liberation theology exhibit almost identical patterns of logic and language. They all divide the world into the oppressed and the oppressors and grant to the oppressed alone the responsibility to define oppression and to undertake liberation. They all use language as a weapon of confrontation and as a means of transformation. They all ground the transformation of Christian symbols in a new experiential consciousness born out of oppression. Finally, they all seek a new humanity and a new society for *all* through the particular liberation movement they champion.

Viewed from one angle, these similarities are unexceptional since they are the stock-in-trade of all revolutionary ideologies and messianic movements. But their weight taken together does tell on the very context and content of theological reflection in important ways. Quite apart from the undeniable relevance and power of these liberation theologies for their distinctive constituencies, they have made a remarkable impact on Christian thought and life by addressing a different constituency in a different way for different ends. Unlike most liberal theologies, which address those alienated from the faith by their own powers of mind and body, liberation theologies speak to the powerless—the marginalized that both the world and the church tend to ignore. Rather than seeking a new consensus with the world, as do other contemporary theologies, theologies of liberation set the church against the world in the sense that conflict and contestation become the central demand of faith. Finally, liberation theologies are less concerned with intellectual challenges to belief than with the practical obstacles to life. They are less concerned with understanding the world than with changing it. Consequently, they all bend the substance of theology to the ends of praxis.

Liberalism's search for a political agenda has brought strife into the church as well as into the world. The liberation theologies of recent years have driven the knife of relativity and revolution deep into our settled worlds of religion and politics. But, as suggested earlier, this diversity and divisiveness is a sign of the vitality rather than the debility of liberal Christianity. Perhaps we are on the brink of another "reformation"—not the sort of reformation that would reduce Christianity to what modern consciousness will accept, but that will return Christianity to what biblical faith surely requires. What we see in the present situation is a return of theological liberalism to the *prophetic* task of "comforting the afflicted and afflicting the comfortable."

11

The Revival of Church and State in the Philippines: Churches and Religion in the People Power Revolution and After

C. Neal Tate

There has truly been a revival of Church-state relations in the Philippines as a result of the downfall of the Marcos dictatorship in the relatively bloodless "People Power Revolution" of February 1986. The consequences of that revival are easy to see in the years since the revolution. Its future consequences are less certain.

A number of scenarios are possible. One envisions the churches partners with a reformed and more effective government in the kind of nonviolent democratic revolution that so many Filipinos (and friends of the Philippines) have fervently hoped would be the continuation of the events of February 1986. Another sees the established churches as allying themselves even more firmly with the privileged economic and political elites in an ever more repressive opposition to the forces of radical and even progressive democratic political change. A third scenario depicts the liberal and radical elements of the clergy and laity converting or bypassing church hierarchies to lead the churches to ever stronger support for revolutionary movements that seek the violent overthrow of the established social and political systems in a new Philippine Revolution.

I shall return to these scenarios after providing the necessary background on the role of the churches in Philippine history, society, and politics.

RELIGIOUS COMPOSITION OF THE PHILIPPINES

The Republic of the Philippines is the only nation in Asia whose population professes Christianity as its majority religion. In fact, it has a Muslim minority that consists of about 5 percent of its population, which has been historically, and is still extremely important politically, and an animist minority of 2 percent, the latter concentrated among the country's tribal hill peoples.[1] The political situation of the Muslim minority and, more recently, the position and political power of the mountain peoples, are matters of political significance as pressures for regional autonomy have developed. But these situations are beyond the concerns of this chapter.

As a result of over 300 years of Spanish colonialism, the Philippines is heavily Roman Catholic. About 85 percent of the population professes a Roman Catholic affiliation. Those who are not Muslim or Catholic are divided among two indigenous Philippine churches, the Philippine Independent Church and the Iglesia ni Kristo, and a number of Protestant denominations that have American and European counterparts. Significantly, Robert I. Youngblood points out that the international connections and support of the Protestant churches and "the fact that some congregations draw their membership disproportionately from the middle class, gives the Protestants more influence than their numbers would ordinarily suggest."[2]

HISTORY OF CHURCH-STATE RELATIONS
IN THE PHILIPPINES

The Philippines, like other former Spanish colonies, has a long history of close relationships between church and state. Thus,

> During the Spanish colonial period the powers of the Archbishop of Manila rivalled and sometimes eclipsed those of the Governor-General. The Church operated as one of the two institutions of colonial rule under the terms of the Spanish *patronato real* [royal patronage] which recognized it as an integral part of government.[3]

To continue,

> During the Spanish colonial period . . . religious orders were granted land for their support [and] entrusted with broad re-

sponsibilities for the welfare of the native parishioners, including the provision of their education and the oversight of their elected municipal governments.[4]

The defeat of the Spanish in the Spanish-American War and of the ongoing Philippine Revolution by the United States at the turn of the century, led to nearly fifty years of American colonial governance of the Philippines. Not surprisingly, the political position of the Roman Catholic church changed significantly during the American colonial period. American doctrines of separation of church and state and religious toleration were introduced, the authority of the priests over municipal government was removed, the religious orders were deprived of their landed estates (with compensation), and the dominance of the education of the Filipinos by the religious orders was undercut by the introduction of universal, secular education administered by the colonial government.

The defeat of the Spanish authorities, short-circuiting of the Philippine Revolution, and imposition of a colonial regime by the Americans may have had at least one other important consequence for state-church relations in the Philippines. Because the Philippine Revolution did not run its full course, it never fully confronted the issue of church authority and its close connection with Spanish colonialism. Thus the Philippines never developed a tradition of political anticlericalism like that developed by many other former Spanish colonies in Latin America or the Catholic nations of Western Europe during their nineteenth-century liberal revolutions.

There was little tradition of automatic antipathy to the church, even among democratic radicals, and separation of church and state did not necessarily bar cooperation between the two. Nor did the church find it necessary to move as quickly or as far to embrace progressive or leftist theologies in order to regain its influence on the people.

Still, the Catholic church did not return to its close alliance with the state after the formal end of colonialism. The nationalist leaders who led the Philippines first into commonwealth status and, after the wartime years of Japanese occupation, into "flag independence" from the United States, were not anxious to share secular authority with the prelates of the church. Though "good Catholics," they firmly upheld the principles of separation of church and state and religious toleration, which were written into the 1935 Constitution of the Philippines.[5]

This situation was largely accepted by the Catholic church hierarchy. Carl H. Landé concludes that

> except where the Church found itself under legislative attack, as in the case of measures that conflicted with its doctrines (such as divorce), attacked its reputation, or threatened its economic interests, the Church as an institution sought to avoid involvement in politics.[6]

Dennis Shoesmith characterizes the "political significance" of the church in this period as "indirect" and "harder to evaluate."[7]

Whether a concern with the range of issues Carl H. Landé enumerates constitutes avoiding involvement in politics might be considered a matter of opinion. The church could well have been satisfied with "indirect" influence in other issue areas so long as the traditional, land-based political elite so clearly described by Landé in other works[8] maintained its control of Philippine politics and government. The economic interests of this political elite would normally have been consistent with the traditional interests of the institutional church. And, in the devout Philippines, the electoral necessity of at least appearing to be a religious person would work to maintain the interests of the Catholic church under most circumstances.

THE CHURCHES AND THE MARCOS MARTIAL LAW REGIME

Overall, the Roman Catholic church's political influence decreased during the years of Ferdinand Marcos's authoritarian rule. The president was not inclined to share power with any independent body, and the church was no exception. How to respond to Ferdinand Marcos's declaration of martial law and assumption of one-man rule on September 22, 1972,[9] posed a significant problem for all Philippine churches, which were "left in the unique position—among legal organizations—of still having enough autonomy, authority, and power to question the policies of the government."[10] Their responses to the president's assumption of absolute power were quite varied, and depended upon the ideology and character of the various factions or denominations within the organized church bodies.

Within the dominant Roman Catholic church, the divisions among the conservative, moderate, and progressive elements of the church produced different initial reactions to the martial law regime.[11] The conservatives and, to a large degree, the moderates, as represented by the majority of the members of the Catholic Bishops Conference of the Philippines (Catholic Bishops Conference), did not challenge Marcos. Unlike the conservatives, who favored "avoidance of involvement in temporal affairs" unless "vital church interests" were at stake, the moderates felt that the church should also speak out on social injustices.[12] They adopted a policy of "critical collaboration," which "accepted the necessity of martial law and the legitimacy of the changes made to the political system by the Marcos government."[13]

In contrast, the progressives (including both liberal and fairly radical adherents) condemned martial law as immoral in addition to consistently speaking out against social injustices and the abuses of the regime.[14] Though numerically weak within the Catholic Bishops Conference, progressive sentiment was widespread in influential religious orders among rural parish priests. It was strongly influenced by the progressive doctrines and practices of the Latin American Catholic church. But while it "had its radical heroes, [p]olitically, the Catholic Church in the Philippines was years behind the volatile churches of Latin America . . . [and] the great majority of Filipino clergy were deeply conservative."[15] Conservatives were not inclined to challenge a regime that justified itself in large part through anti-Communist and antileftist rhetoric.

The reaction of the Protestant churches to President Marcos's martial law regime was likewise varied. In contrast to the Catholic Bishops Conference, the most important Protestant coordinating body, the National Council of Churches in the Philippines (National Council) "opposed martial law from the very beginning," adopting a statement in September 1972 that opposed its imposition and continuation.[16] But like their Catholic counterparts, individual mainline Protestant churches, ministers, and lay leaders affiliated with the National Council were divided in their opinions as to whether or how far to oppose Marcos's rule.[17]

The opposition of the National Council of Churches to martial law was not shared by more fundamentalist Philippine Protestants. The position of the Philippine Council of Evangelical Churches (Evangelical Council), representing just less than 1 percent of the population, did not officially move to oppose President Marcos until the outbreak of the February 1986 revolution.[18] And the indigenous *Iglesia ni Kristo*, a tightly organized and controlled fundamentalist church, strongly supported President Marcos to the end of his rule and beyond.[19]

The dominance of conservative and moderate sentiments among the leaders of the Philippine churches meant that religious forces provided only limited opposition to martial law in its early years. For example, the most visible religious leader in the Philippines and the recognized leader of the moderates, Cardinal Jaime Sin, regularly associated with the Marcoses after his appointment as archbishop of Manila in 1974,[20] and even held his peace when a progressive priest was deported in 1976 for his social justice activities.[21]

Cardinal Sin's circumspect approach to criticism of the martial law regime was intended to avoid direct confrontations with Marcos, which might lead to the closing of churches and arrests of priests.[22] Even so, Marcos and his military supporters still

> periodically moved against moderate as well as radical church critics, raiding church organizations, arresting clergy and lay workers, threatening church property and toying with the idea of introducing social legislation condemned by church teaching.[23]

By the late 1970s, it was clear that critical collaboration with the regime was not working to preserve or extend the church's influence or even to protect its progressive and moderate elements (both Catholic and Protestant) from attacks by the regime. To preserve its role as "conscience of the regime," the church emphasized criticism over collaboration in the church-state relationship,[24] and Cardinal Sin began to attack the regime regularly for its corruption and abuses.[25]

After the assassination of Sen. Benigno Aquino on August 21, 1983, the Catholic hierarchy moved even more dramatically and openly to identify with the now-burgeoning opposition to the Marcoses. Cardinal Sin and twelve bishops conducted the funeral mass for Aquino, and Manila's church bells were tolled daily to call for prayer for Aquino and for the oppressed.[26] Aquino's funeral marked a beginning of an open break between the moderate and even the conservative elements of the Catholic leadership and the Marcos regime. Youngblood describes some developments that indicated the growing rejection of the government by the official church.[27]

> Cardinal Sin's castigation of the regime increased. Sin indicated that he felt the government was at least partially responsible for the murder, since Aquino died in the custody of the

military, and Radio Veritas, the church's radio station, provided the most accurate and comprehensive information about the assassination and the subsequent mass demonstrations of anguish and outrage over the murder. He also refused to participate as a member of the commission established by the president to investigate the Aquino killing as he considered that his presence would be little more than a "dissenting voice in the wilderness," and he approved a new newspaper, *Veritas*, in the interests of establishing a free press in the Philippines.

The significance of these events was great. While the churches in general, and the Catholic church in particular, had lost influence with the regime, they retained it with the population. The Catholic hierarchy's move to visible opposition to the Marcos regime

> contributed to a change in the national mood which can only be fully understood in terms of Filipino political culture. Perhaps only half consciously, the hierarchy confirmed in the popular mind that the assassination marked a shift in the moral or even the supernatural order; that the regime had lost all moral authority.[28]

The Aquino assassination led the leaders of the established churches and Manila's business and economic elites to join the long-suffering oppositionists, the progressive Catholic and Protestant clergy and lay persons, and the "cause-oriented groups." With moral leadership now clearly on its side and crucial resources such as mass media now available to it, the opposition began to approach the critical mass that finally produced the February 1986 revolution and the downfall of the Marcoses.

It is worth considering the constellation of factors that led the church hierarchy to openly abandon the Marcos regime. Obviously a major factor was the character of the regime. Over time, it became first difficult, then impossible, for church leaders of any ideological stripe to ignore the evidence of the corrupt and abusive nature of the Marcos regime. The assassination of Aquino at the hands of the regime or its supporters was the final documentation of the regime's character that galvanized moderate and conservative church leaders to action.

In addition to the character of the regime, the opposition of church leaders was stoked by the regime's attacks on church people and programs. To be sure, the targets of the attacks were largely affiliated with the progressive faction within the Catholic church or with liberal Protestant groups. But they were not, for the most part, radical individuals or groups committed to the violent overthrow of the system. They were instead an influential part of the main bodies of the churches with which they were affiliated. Conservatives and moderates might disagree with their doctrines and programs, but they could not remain indifferent to their fates, especially when the policy of avoiding direct confrontation with the regime over such issues failed to stop the attacks.

Finally, it must have become clear to staunchly anti-Communist conservative and moderate church leaders that the continuation of the Marcos regime posed a greater danger of communism than the activities of the progressive and leftist elements being attacked by the regime. The continuation of the regime closed off paths of peaceful change and was forcing the change-oriented to look to the violent revolution promised by the Maoist New People's Army as their only hope.

THE CHURCHES IN THE FEBRUARY 1986 REVOLUTION

The February 1986 Philippine Revolution (the "Edsa Revolution," after Epifanio de los Santos Avenue on and around which its most critical public events took place), was not a complete "revolution" in the sense in which that term is usually understood by political scientists. It did result in the replacement of an entrenched dictatorial regime by another, popularly based government, largely through mass action. But unlike the great revolutions of history (e.g., the French, Russian, Chinese, or Iranian), it did not replace the existing social or economic system with a new one. Had it sought to do so, it almost certainly could not have been essentially nonviolent, and it would not have been strongly supported by established religious institutions.

Just over three years after its occurrence, the Edsa Revolution has no doubt faded from the memory of those who are not regularly concerned with the Philippines. Here is what happened. From the time of Benigno Aquino's assassination, opposition to the Marcos regime became more open and more assertive, while remaining largely nonviolent. An opposition press developed and survived, despite periodic harassment by the regime. Middle-class Filipinos, including the upper middle-class members of the business community of Manila's suburban financial center, Makati, increasingly took part in protest demonstrations and otherwise voiced their displeasure with the regime. Their displeasure mounted as the economic picture became increasingly bleak due, in large part, to the massive rake-offs taken by the Marcoses and their close associates, the "cronies." And, as noted, the hierarchy of the Catholic church identified with the opposition and spoke out ever more critically of President Marcos and his rule in an effort to divert the violent opposition that it felt would otherwise be the inevitable result of the continuation of Marcos's rule.

Foreign journalists began to document abroad the extent of the corruption and economic rape conducted by the Marcoses and the cronies, and even to demonstrate that Marcos had faked his record as the country's most decorated war hero.[29] Their accounts filtered back to the Philippines, shocking into opposition even many who had previously supported the president in spite of doubts about the probity of his regime.

All these developments led to increasing pressure on President Marcos by various politically important elements in the United States, to step down or accept real political opposition in free elections. To divert such pressure and criticism, Marcos announced on U.S. television on November 3, 1985, a "snap" presidential election to be held February 7, 1986. No doubt the president calculated that his opposition would not be able to unite on such short notice behind an effective candidate to oppose him, and that his control of the government budget and offices would insure his victory in any case. A reelection, Marcos must have reasoned, would silence his American and perhaps his domestic opposition. If domestic opposition were not silenced, it could at least be more credibly depicted as antidemocratic and subversive.

Marcos's calculations went awry. The opposition was able to unite, albeit at the last hour, behind the presidential candidacy of Corazon Aquino and to mount an effective counter to government control of the electoral process through a private watchdog movement, NAMFREL (National Movement for Free Elections), which had been active in earlier, less crucial elections. To "win" the election, Marcos had to cheat so visibly that it could not escape the notice of anyone who was watching, including teams of foreign observers from abroad, and to ram through a proclamation of his election in his controlled national assembly.

Aquino and the opposition declared that they had won the election and organized a campaign of nonviolent resistance to the continuation of Marcos's power. The Catholic Bishops Conference announced its agreement that the election had been stolen, supported Aquino, and urged the population to rid itself of Marcos by any nonviolent means, significantly not excluding a coup d'état by reformist military elements. The discovery by Marcos forces of just such a plotted coup led to the defection of his defense minister, Juan Ponce Enrile, and his deputy chief of staff of the armed forces, Fidel V. Ramos. Proclaiming themselves unable to further support Marcos, Enrile and Ramos barricaded themselves in the military camp that serves as the national defense headquarters, announced their support for Aquino, and called for popular support of their rebellion. Such support was forthcoming, as Filipinos ultimately numbering in the hundreds of thousands streamed to Epifanio de los Santos Avenue in front of the Enrile-Ramos headquarters in an exercise of "People Power" that protected the military defectors from counterattack by Marcos-loyal forces, and soon persuaded large segments of the military to switch their support to the rebels.

In three days, the People Power Revolution succeeded in forcing the Marcoses and their close associates from the country. By February 26, 1986, the new government of President Corazon Aquino and Vice President Salvador Laurel was in control of the Philippines.

What was the role played by the churches in all this? In brief, a large one. In the first place, the groundwork for People Power had been going on all through the period of Marcos authoritarianism under the auspices of liberal and progressive elements associated with church-backed community and rural development programs and human rights activist groups. Frequently, church-backed groups were both the targets of the regime's attacks and the sources of information on its human rights depredations. However, the leftist orientations of these groups prevented them from attracting the support of the religious middle class.

Second, as noted, the churches, particularly the moderate leadership of the Roman Catholic church, formed the major institutional opposition to Marcos, especially during the last half of his rule. They increasingly pressured the president on corruption, social justice, and human rights issues. The Catholic church established media resources—a radio station and, later, a newspaper—which were among the few sources of independent information, and that proved absolutely crucial to the success of the People Power Revolution.

Through its reaction to the Aquino assassination the church hierarchy deprived the Marcos regime of its moral legitimacy with the important educated, middle-class, and business communities of

Manila. While the outpouring of rage against the regime that followed Aquino's assassination was probably spontaneous, church leaders took actions that put them in the forefront of that reaction. While still counseling nonviolence, they immediately rejected the regime's theory that Aquino's assassination was a Communist plot, and placed a measure of blame on the Marcos government, even while formal proof of the involvement of government elements was lacking. The church then actively supported the opposition to Marcos in the 1984 legislative elections, and priests and nuns formed a large part of the volunteer labor of NAMFREL in its efforts to monitor the elections, both in 1984 and in the snap presidential election of 1986. Any guise of partisan neutrality was dropped as church leaders assumed the responsibility of helping develop the opposition to the dictator.

The next dramatic involvement of the church in the events leading up to the People Power Revolution occurred as the opposition to Marcos jockeyed to determine its candidates. All opposition elements recognized that it would be difficult enough to defeat the entrenched president under the best of circumstances, but that it would be impossible to do so unless they were all able to unite behind a single effective candidate. The problem was that the two leading candidates, Corazon Aquino and Salvador Laurel, seemed unable to agree on who would step aside to make the unified opposition slate possible.

At the last moment, when filing papers were due, Cardinal Sin stepped in to mediate the differences between Aquino and Laurel. Sin himself was a supporter of Aquino, who was known for her devotion to her religion and her church. But when Sin's conference was over, the opposition was able to announce a unified Aquino-Laurel ticket. Whether because of Sin's influence, his own sense of devotion to country, or a cold calculation that Aquino was the only candidate with sufficient popular support to have a chance of defeating Marcos, the ambitious long-time politician Laurel agreed to run as vice president and to bring his UNIDO (United Nationalist Democratic Organization) political coalition to the support of presidential candidacy of the "simple housewife" and widow of the slain Benigno Aquino.

The involvement of the church in the Aquino campaign and in the activities of NAMFREL was quite obvious. During the election, priests and nuns were everywhere visible working to protect the integrity of the balloting, protecting the ballot boxes with their bodies from the efforts of pro-Marcos goons to steal them or alter their contents. Their efforts were officially in vain, as the national Commission on Elections count showed Marcos the winner, while the unofficial, but incomplete tallies of NAMFREL showed the opposite.

Ballot irregularities and even the criticisms of U.S. observer teams were ignored by the national assembly as it confirmed the reelection of Ferdinand Marcos as president of the Philippines on February 15, eight days after the election. But the proclamation of the Marcos-dominated body was to prove unpersuasive compared to the statement that had already been issued two days earlier by that most establishment of church bodies, the Catholic Bishops Conference. That statement firmly denounced the elections as fraudulent, pronounced the illegitimacy of the continuation of the Marcos government, and urged citizens to use any nonviolent means to bring about its removal. When questioned as to whether the bishops' statement implied the acceptability of even a military coup to topple Marcos, the bishops' spokesman refused to rule out such an action, if essentially consistent with the bishops' emphasis on nonviolence.

It is hard to overestimate the significance of the bishops' statement. It was not only one day earlier, but much stronger than the statement issued by the National Council of Churches, the Protestant coordinating body that was oppositionist, for example.[30] It provided clear moral justification for the large-scale civil disobedience campaign announced by Cory Aquino three days later. It provided respectable support for the efforts of members of the U.S. Congress to officially denounce the election as fraudulent and to cut off military aid to Marcos.[31] And it clearly suggested the probability of official church support for any reform-minded military forces who might wish to move against Marcos.

It is interesting to consider what might have been the consequences of the bishops' statement had Marcos been able to ride out the storm of postelection protest or to quickly put down the Enrile-Ramos coup attempt that produced the outpouring of people power. Certainly it would not have improved the already-strained relationship between church and state. The president might not have been able to attack the hierarchy directly. But it seems likely that, barring a negotiated settlement of his differences with the church, he would have exerted every effort to reduce its influence further and to bring it under his control. The reaction of the church hierarchy might have been to recognize Marcos's *fait accompli* and to work for a reconciliation that would reduce the church's political influence and involvement but protect its policy and economic interests. But it is also possible that the moderate bishops would have moved firmly in the direction of the progressives, adopting a stance of support for social action and intransigent opposition to the regime that they had previously been unwilling to accept. Such a stance would likely have brought them into conflict with the Vatican.

The contribution of the church to the success of the military coup that became the People Power Revolution was great. When, at a 6:45 P.M. news conference on February 22, 1986, Defense Minister Enrile and General Ramos announced their withdrawal of support from Marcos, they were supported in their revolt by a relatively small band of loyal troops, and were quite vulnerable to an attack from the remaining Marcos loyalist forces. In an effort to strengthen their position, and no doubt recalling the bishops' statement, they telephoned Cardinal Sin and asked him to call for popular support of their cause. Sin and Cory Aquino's brother-in-law Butz Aquino soon did so over the church's Radio Veritas. Marcos, in turn, did not attack the rebels immediately, but instead made a television appeal for them to surrender. All this activity produced by midnight a crowd of ten to twenty thousand who surrounded rebel headquarters to fend off a feared Marcos attack.

By morning, no attack had come, but the crowd outside the rebels' gates had dwindled to only a thousand, and the main transmitter of Radio Veritas had been bombed by unknown attackers. Radio Veritas nevertheless stayed on the air, broadcasting from its small emergency transmitter and urging listeners to tune to station FEBC, a Protestant station, that was still on the air, in case it should lose its signal. Renewed appeals started the Edsa crowds growing again. When its emergency transmitter gave out later that evening, Radio Veritas personnel found another radio station from which they once again began to broadcast news about the ongoing rebellion and appeals for popular support. The churches' radio stations thus played a crucial role in stimulating the outbreak and in assuring the success of the People Power Revolution.

As the crowds gathered, the presence of the churches at the forefront of the revolt was obvious. Priests and nuns led worship services and served food to the crowds. They, as well as religious laity, prominently displayed images of the Virgin, crucifixes, and rosaries, and prayed openly for the protection of the rebels and for the conversion of the Marcos loyalist forces, who ultimately came.

Though smaller in number, Protestant clergy, indistinguishable in their clerical mufti, and Protestant lay persons, without visible symbols of their religious commitment, also participated prominently in the People Power movement.[32]

The most dramatic moments of the revolt came when the crowd, with priests and nuns visible in the forefront and lay persons clasping rosaries, blocked the path of tanks and armored personnel carriers finally sent by Marcos to dislodge the rebels. Obviously frightened, those in the front ranks of the crowd prayed and pleaded with the soldiers to join them in their courageous stand. Few did, at first, but their planned attack was stymied, as they were unwilling to harm the crowds in order to achieve their objective of dislodging or capturing the military rebels.

Ultimately, the military revolt which became the People Power Revolution triumphed. Responsibility for the victory was shared among many forces, and each—the "reformist" military, the Catholic church, Protestants, human rights and other cause-oriented groups, Aquino and Laurel's political leaders and supporters, and the middle class and business leaders of Makati—was eager to claim its share of the credit and stake out its position in the new Aquino government. Cardinal Sin described the Edsa revolt a victory for the Virgin Mary.[33]

CHURCH AND STATE RELATIONS
UNDER THE AQUINO REGIME

Given the Roman Catholic church's strong support for Corazon Aquino as a symbol of the anti-Marcos opposition and as a presidential candidate and its role in the snap election and Edsa revolution, one should expect to find church-state relations much warmer under Aquino than under Marcos. One would not be disappointed. One prominent bishop concluded that "[a]t no time in Philippine modern history has the moment been so favourable to the church as now, under Aquino."[34]

The post-Edsa influence of the church in Philippine politics has a number of dimensions. Among the most basic is the influence the church gains as a result of the president's personal religiosity. By all accounts, Aquino is a genuinely devout person who prays and seeks spiritual guidance regularly. She emphasized her faith, and provided fodder for critics of her church-state policies,[35] by instituting a practice of beginning Cabinet meetings with a prayer led by rotating ministers, not all of whom were as devout as the president. While observers are more likely to praise than to fault the president for her personal religiosity, there is *prima facie* evidence that her beliefs have made her especially susceptible to the church's efforts to capitalize on its favorable position and to institutionalize policies favorable to certain church interests.

The coalition that brought Aquino to power—opposition politicians, human rights activists, middle class and business people, the church, the reformist military, and Defense Minister Enrile—was represented in the appointments she made during her first year in office. She did not appoint Church leaders to formal government positions—indeed, under Vatican rules, Catholic priests and nuns could not have accepted such appointments, had they been offered. Rather, the churches were represented by the appointment of lay people well-known for their leadership in church-related organizations, and in Aquino's informal advisers, among whom was Cardinal Sin.

The Aquino regime's economic policies, for example, have been increasingly reflected in the export-oriented approach to economic development espoused by the Center for Research and Communication, a prestigious Makati-based think tank funded by the papal middle-class organization, Opus Dei. Her nationalist critics allege that she is overly influenced by the "Council of Trent," a group of largely Catholic businessmen and scholars, among whose members is Father Joaquin Bernas, a constitutional scholar and columnist who is president of the most important Jesuit educational institution in the country, the Ateneo de Manila, and who has been an important adviser of the president. The church hierarchy has been a consistent supporter of the Aquino regime through the series of military coup attempts it has suffered since February 1986. In the most serious of these, the August 28, 1986 coup led by Gregorio "Gringo" Honasan, Cardinal Sin issued a statement in mid-morning urging a peaceful end to the mutiny, which had already cost a number of lives. My assessment of this statement was that it hardly constituted a ringing endorsement of the Aquino government, although it certainly did not endorse the coup. Perhaps the cardinal was hedging his bets at that early hour, when the outcome of the coup was still uncertain.

After the coup attempt was defeated by loyal troops under the leadership of General Fidel Ramos, members of the church hierarchy and leaders of lay groups strongly endorsed the regime and denounced any attempts to dislodge it by force. For example, Cardinal Sin appeared on television urging the population of Manila to attend an all-night prayer vigil at the national soccer stadium and his public relations officer, Bishop Bacani, wrote a strong letter to the editors of Manila's newspapers appealing to "those who want to dislodge the present Government by an armed rebellion not to attempt to do so." Bacani's letter also stated,

> I can safely predict that even if a coup d'état succeeds, the military men and their collaborators who stage the take-over will meet with opposition coming from the Catholic church that not even Marcos experienced.[36]

There can be little doubt that Bacani was stating the official position of the archbishop of Manila, if not necessarily that of the Catholic Bishops Conference. Certainly it was not surprising that Cardinal Sin strongly supported the incumbent government. He had done so consistently and occasionally controversially since February 1986. For example, after announcing in April 1987, that he would "retire from politics" since it was no longer necessary to be involved, the cardinal strongly and publicly endorsed a list of "ten best" senatorial candidates in the summer, 1987 congressional elections. All the candidates were administration candidates. Cardinal Sin received a significant amount of criticism as a result of this action, and other church leaders suggested that his advisers had acted without proper consultation in associating the church with partisan endorsements. But the endorsements had been made, nonetheless.

POLICY IMPLICATIONS OF THE NEW
CHURCH-STATE RELATIONSHIP

The new warm relationship between church and state has produced some significant changes in the constitutional and policy environments of Philippine politics. The new Constitution drafted by Cory Aquino's hand-picked forty-eight member Constitutional Commission in 1986 and overwhelmingly ratified in a popular referendum in February 1987, clearly shows the influence of this relationship. First, while no religious leaders were appointed to full-time government offices by President Aquino, several were appointed to the Constitutional Commission. These included Bishop Bacani and Father Joaquin Bernas; Christine Tan, a progressive nun known for her work with the poor; Cirilo A. Rigos, a United Church of Christ pastor; and Gregorio Tingson, president of Asian Christian Outreach. Lay members with very close associations with the Catholic church included Maria T. Feria Nieva, a Catholic layman active in NAMFREL and in many church-related groups, including the Family Rights Movement of the Philippines, and Bernardo Villegas, senior vice president of the Center for Research and Communication.

The 1986–1987 Constitution still provides for separation of church and state and religious freedom: Congress is still prohibited from passing laws respecting the establishment of religion or imposing any religious test, and public funds or property may not be used by or for the benefit of any religious institution. In addition, church property used for charitable, religious, or educational purposes may not be taxed. While the latter provision might not seem remarkable to Americans, in the Philippines it is a significant limitation of the government's ability to raise revenue, as well as on its ability to harass churches. At least one reputable critic attributes this tax exemption to the church's influence over the Aquino regime[37] and argues that church-state separation under the new Constitution "means the Church is free to interfere with the affairs of the state, but the state cannot interfere with the church."

Other provisions of the Constitution that reflect the policy views of the Roman Catholic church are more controversial. These include

1. exemption of religious bodies from the constitutional provision that all educational institutions must be Filipino-owned;
2. effective prohibition of divorce and abortion;
3. a provision allowing instruction in a child's chosen religion in the public schools at the option of parents with instruction delivered by teachers approved by the child's religious authorities. Critics fear this will lead to conscription of public school teachers to teach the Catholic religion, since such instruction is to occur "with no additional cost to government," and since the church could hardly staff the required instruction.

Critics of the church's role in creating the new Constitution and in shaping policy under the Aquino regime complain that the church hierarchy has used its newly strengthened position to defend traditional church privileges and property, and to break down the wall of separation of church and state in practice, but not to push the regime toward the social justice activities and economic reforms they think are essential.[38] Not all these critics are secular humanists; some are the priests and nuns associated with the progressive wing of the church.

DIVISIONS WITHIN THE CHURCH AND THE FUTURE OF PHILIPPINE POLITICS

The division of the Catholic church, and to some extent of the Protestant denominations, into ideological groups, has serious implications for the future role of the churches in Philippine politics. These implications can be seen by speculating on what the role of the Catholic church would be in certain scenarios for the future.

The first scenario posits a continuation of the Aquino regime until the end of her constitutional term in 1992 and a "normalization" of the current formally liberal democratic political system without serious socioeconomic reform, or, possibly, even with serious, but nonrevolutionary, socioeconomic reform. Should this be the future of Philippine politics, there will be a growing division between the conservative and moderate wings of the church on the one hand, and the progressives on the other. The nature of this division is already clear. With the establishment of the Aquino government and the restoration of civil liberties, conservative and moderate bishops have concluded that there is no longer a need to challenge the regime. This allows the reemergence of their previously suppressed natural suspicions of their progressive colleagues, who continue to challenge the Aquino government on grounds that the current political system is unresponsive to the poor and to the need for significant social change. The Catholic Bishops Conference has, in fact, already issued statements denouncing those progressive clergy who align themselves with the radical Left, much less with Marxism.

The anticommunism of the majority of the Catholic hierarchy will probably not succeed in reining in all the progressive elements within the church. Instead, it will probably deepen the rift between the progressives and the hierarchy, and strengthen their commitment to radical social action.

The second scenario posits the occurrence of a successful military coup by overtly anti-Communist or rightist elements in the near future. Should such event occur, it is likely that the church hierarchy would indeed oppose the resulting regime, as Bishop Bacani promised. Just how significant the church's opposition would be would probably depend on just how repressive the coup-maker's regime was. In the fairly likely event that such a regime was repressive, especially against non-Communist but leftist elements promoting social change, the moderate and possibly even the conservative elements within the church leadership would find themselves pushed again and quickly, given their experience under Marcos, toward opposition in alliance with their progressive brothers and sisters.

The last scenario is that of a successful takeover by a Marxist revolutionary government as a result of the military triumph of the New People's Army. Such a result would occur probably only after an extremely bitter struggle that would see the nation's wealthy and a large proportion of its middle class emigrate. The bitterness of such a struggle could lead to the establishment of a Marxist regime that had more in common with the Pol Pot regime in Cambodia, than with the Sandinista regime in Nicaragua. Such a regime would not be favorably inclined toward religion in any form, of course, and the divisions within the church would become secondary to the church's survival. Short of such an extreme regime, the relation between church and state in contemporary Nicaragua may have relevance to this scenario and to the future of Philippine church-state relations.

The Sword and the Cross: Church-State Conflict in Latin America

Michael Dodson

Throughout its history, religion and politics have been deeply intertwined on the Latin American continent. For more than a millenium, successive waves of empires have been established, destroyed, and reestablished in the territories reaching from Mexico to Chile. In Mesoamerica, the empire of Teotihuacan was conquered by the Olmecs, who were later overtaken by the Toltecs, only to be conquered themselves by the Aztecs, whose kingdom was destroyed by Spanish *conquistadores* at the beginning of the sixteenth century. Despite their many differences, these varied civilizations shared at least one feature in common: each found in religious dogma a strong source of support for political conquest. Peter Berger has captured this point succinctly. "All over Mesoamerica it was common for each new wave of conquerors to erect their sanctuaries over the ruins of the sanctuaries they destroyed, so that the religious geography of this region has a strange stability."[1] Whether or not the Amerindian civilizations were theocracies is a disputed question and need not be resolved here. What is clear is that religious and political authorities were close partners in the making of American history long before the Spanish conquest.

In European history the close collaboration of church and state was long expressed in the symbolism of the cross and the sword. While this imagery preceded Spanish exploration and conquest in the New World, it was vigorously carried forward in that conquest.

In the Iberian society that gave rise to the *conquistadores,* sword and cross signified the two great powers that ordered everyday life and gave it meaning. The sword symbolized the temporal power of lord, prince, and king. In a sinful world the sword was necessary so as to control the darker impulses of humanity.[2] For its part, the cross symbolized the spiritual power of priest, bishop, and church. The power of the Roman Catholic church derived from its role in mediating grace. In sixteenth-century Iberian society salvation was perhaps the central reference point of human existence. Hence, the Catholic church was an actor of surpassing importance.

It should be noted, however, that as the Spanish conquest was getting under way, the sword was increasingly wielded by monarchs who were consolidating political control over Europe's newly emerging nation-states.[3] As Claudio Véliz has pointed out, this process of political centralization and unification made its earliest advances in the Iberian peninsula. The Catholic monarchs, Ferdinand of Aragon and Isabella of Castile, united their kingdoms through marriage in 1469. Thereafter the two monarchs worked vigorously and successfully to unify the Spanish people under one government, while subjecting the feudal nobility and the military orders to the authority of the crown.[4]

This process of political centralization had a deep and lasting impact on church-state relations in Spain, and consequently in Spain's New World empire. Although they were devout Catholics, Ferdinand and Isabella were determined to control the Spanish church, as well as the secular rivals to their authority. Through a mixture of confrontation and conciliation, they extracted a series of concessions from the papacy over a thirty year period that gave them broad patronage rights over the Spanish church. From the standpoint of Latin American development, the key concession was a papal bull of 1508 in which Pope Julius II granted the monarch of Castile "the privilege of founding and organizing all churches . . . in all overseas territories which they possessed or might acquire in the future."[5]

This grant gave the Spanish crown complete control over religious affairs in the New World and made possible a "union of altar and throne" in Latin America that had no parallel in other instances of European colonization.[6] As J. Lloyd Mecham has written, "It is difficult to conceive of a more absolute jurisdiction than that which the King of Spain exercised over all ecclesiastical affairs in the Indies."[7] Without the monarch's authorization, no church could be founded. He granted permission for the clergy to travel to the New

World, and he appointed all bishops. The Iberian domains in the New World were formally titled, "The Indies of the Crown of Castile," and appropriately so. The historian William L. Schurz expressed the matter this way. "It was a centralized system of government which Spain imposed on her great colonial empire. The king was the source of all power."[8] And this power extended to control over the church and over all religious activity.

It is not surprising, then, that the Roman Catholic church was a reliable partner to the crown in its great project of settlement in the New World, or that it played a multifaceted role in the process of incorporating the peoples of the Indies into the Spanish Empire. In one of its most important dimensions the conquest was a great act of religious conversion. Enormous energy was expended to bring indigenous peoples of the Americas into the Catholic church, which the crown carefully shielded from religious competition. Throughout the early colonial period the church prospered under this arrangement, enjoying such privileges as its own courts, a monopoly in education, and the opportunity to acquire extensive land holdings.[9] Mecham has cogently summarized the result of this close alliance between church and state in colonial Latin America.

> Since Catholicism was indissolubly united with royal authority, the church was quite as effective an instrument in the conquest and domination of the Indies as the army. It was one of the principal agents of the civil power in America for over three centuries. The clerics, being beholden to the king . . . served him without the slightest inclination to rebel. They felt more closely attached to him than to the pope. They were more royalist than papalist.[10]

Roman Catholicism thus played a vital role in the reshaping of Latin American society according to the political and religious values of sixteenth century Spain. The church reinforced a centralized system of authority and broadly justified existing distributions of power, responsibility, and privilege.[11] In this way, Catholicism fostered "ideas and values which [were] clearly antagonistic to various aspects of modernization. An integralist concept of a hierarchical society and a pronounced preference for authoritarian rule [were] prominent components of the Ibero-Catholic heritage."[12] The conservative impact of the church's teachings and religious practices was deepened by its own internal organization. Authority within the church was also centralized and hierarchical, a fact that placed "the believer in a position of extreme dependence upon the clergy."[13]

In sum, Iberian colonization in the New World imposed on the indigenous peoples the political centralism and religious orthodoxy of early sixteenth century Spain. This religio-political model helped to establish a society that was rigidly hierarchical and status conscious, and to preserve that society during three centuries of colonial rule. At the moment of independence Latin American society had changed remarkably little; it continued to exhibit deep and pervasive class inequalities and it remained religiously orthodox. The Roman Catholic church was intimately identified with this social and political order.

The colonial experience had lasting effects on church-state relations after independence, and on the church's capacity to exert influence in the social life of Latin America's new nations. On the surface the formal relationship of Catholicism and the state hardly changed at all. The typical pattern was for the new states to give official recognition to the Catholic church, providing it with a religious monopoly, and guaranteeing it an important role in education and social welfare.

This arrangement had several important consequences. First, it made the church highly dependent on state patronage for its institutional well-being. This dependency compelled the church to devote much of its energies to political strategies aimed at preserving its position. Second, this particular form of politicization allied the church with the old aristocracy and the conservative political parties through which landed elites sought to govern. By the late nineteenth century these parties were losing control to liberal parties that represented a demand for social reform and economic modernization. The liberal movements tended to be anticlerical and hostile to the church. Third, the political strategy adopted by the church competed with, and discouraged, a more strictly religious strategy for influencing society. Pastoral efforts aimed at cultivating lay spirituality were neglected so that in time the church's religious presence among the people atrophied severely. In the words of Ivan Vallier, "the Church became a major political actor on behalf of the forces that promised to protect it as an institution, rather than a differentiated religious system with roots in the spiritual life of autonomous membership groups."[14]

The point of this somewhat schematic survey of the history of church-state relations in Latin America is to demonstrate that the church paid a high price for the state-guaranteed monopoly that it enjoyed for so long. By the midtwentieth century the extensive formal presence of the church in Latin American society was only a facade that belied the church's real weakness and vulnerability to competition from "new value movements."[15] Amid the strong demands for economic and political development that appeared in Latin America after World War II, the church experienced a sudden and profound crisis of identity. Its dominant position in society was threatened from both religious and secular sources. On one hand aggressive Protestant sects with an urgent message of salvation were beginning to make noticeable inroads on the Catholic religious monopoly. Meanwhile, from another direction political movements of the left were beginning to win a hearing among Latin America's intellectuals and within the working classes.

It is important to stress the fact that social teachings, per se, were not necessarily responsible for Roman Catholicism's declining influence. Although religious teachings may often have been used by the clergy to encourage passive resignation among the poor, there was nothing intrinsic to Catholic theology that made such an emphasis necessary. The strong current of prophetic denunciation that runs through both Old and New Testaments was always available as a resource from which to challenge societal injustices. For half a century Catholic social teachings in Europe had condemned the ravages of industrialization among the working class.[16] Similar criticisms might well have been made of Latin America's extremes of poverty and wealth. The church's reluctance to make such criticisms is at least partly explained by pointing to its accustomed reliance on the old landed elite for its institutional welfare. Having made this point, however, it is also important to recognize that by midcentury there was a great restiveness in the Latin American church, a growing desire for renewal and reorientation of religious energies.

THE CHURCH RECOVERS ITS PROPHETIC TRADITION

Two historic events intruded onto this scene, the Cuban Revolution of 1959, and the Second Vatican Council convened by Pope John XXIII in 1962. Each of these events helped to stimulate religious innovation in Latin America. It may seem odd to associate the Cuban Revolution with religious change. The church did not play much of a role in the revolution, although it did not initially oppose Fidel Castro's Twenty-sixth of July Movement, which had a broad appeal in the setting of Fulgencio Batista's repressive and unpopular dictatorship. However, when U.S. relations with Cuba turned sour and Castro began to align Cuba with the Soviet Union, many church people fled the island, leaving the church ill-equipped to play a meaningful social role in the rapidly changing society.[17] This series of events, together with the deep hostility of the United States toward the Cuban Revolution, caused many Latin American Catholics to question their own disposition toward change, and to reflect critically on the church's role in society. In the course of such reflections, many Christians confronted for the first time the manifest and deepening underdevelopment of their societies.[18] This led to a serious rethinking of pastoral commitments, which soon received an unexpected and dramatic imprimatur from Rome through the Second Vatican Council.

The primary aim of Vatican II, a world council in which Latin American representatives played only a minor role, was to open the Roman Catholic church to the modern world. Early in its deliberations an important consensus emerged within the council: it was agreed that while the industrialized countries had produced great wealth, an ethos of unrestrained individualism was encouraging the growth of alarming new inequalities that resulted in unrelieved human misery. To combat this trend, the council called upon the church to change its way of thinking about the world. In lieu of the old deductive (hence dogmatic) approach that merely applied accepted formulas, the Church was encouraged to be more inductive, to gather the facts, to reflect on the reality represented in those facts in light of the gospel message, and then to design appropriate plans of pastoral action.[19]

This subtle change in outlook and methodology had enormous consequences for the Roman Catholic church worldwide. Within the council itself, it led to a strong critique of "the immense inequalities which now exist" in the wealthy societies of the industrialized world.[20] In Latin America this encouragement to "scrutinize the signs of the times" produced an even greater impact than in Europe.[21] In a society where the vast majority was trapped in conditions of extreme poverty and exploitation, the church now set itself to the task of confronting that exploitation. At the meeting of the Latin American Bishops Conference (CELAM) in Medellín, Colombia, in 1968, the Latin American church issued a scathing critique of "systemic poverty."

> The Christian . . . believes that justice is a prerequisite for peace. He recognizes that in many instances Latin America finds itself faced with a situation of injustice that can be called

institutionalized violence. . . . This situation demands all-embracing, courageous, urgent and profoundly renovating transformations.[22]

The specific focus of this call for "profound transformations" was the great mass of the poor, whether *campesinos* trying to eke out a living on ever-shrinking *minifundia*, migrating rural workers who had lost their land altogether, or the growing number of migrants crowding Latin America's cities in search of jobs and security. The church was called to identify and denounce the structural causes of this spreading poverty, to increase its presence among the poor in order to demonstrate its solidarity with them, and to "encourage and favor the efforts of the people to create and develop their own grass-roots organizations for the redress and consolidation of their rights."[23] Thus did the church embrace a new pastoral agenda, an agenda that called for recovery of the church's ancient prophetic tradition, while pointing toward the creation of new religious structures that soon would be known as *comunidades eclesiales de base*, or Christian base communities (CEBs).[24]

One important objective of the church hierarchy at Medellín was to deepen the church's pastoral presence among the poor. It is probably fair to say that most of the bishops present at Medellín also thought these new commitments could serve to stimulate national dialogues that would foster a better integration of diverse groups and social classes. Modernization had deepened the gap between rich and poor in Latin America because economic growth and greater social mobility had not led to increased democratization in the political arena. The bishops assumed, as did many political leaders in the United States and Latin America, that goodwill and dialogue across class lines could lead to reform and greater social harmony. However, it soon became evident that the "preferential option for the poor" would, if pursued vigorously, create serious new dilemmas for the church. In direct proportion to its success in revitalizing religious life at the grass roots, the church weakened or ruptured its venerable alliance with the state, and its close association with the oligarchy. As it identified itself with peasants and workers seeking to mobilize for change, the church found itself at the center of a rising storm of social and political violence. What is more, pursuing the preferential option for the poor raised an unexpected challenge to the institutional church itself, for it gave the poor structural mechanisms for finding their own voice, not only in political society but in the church as well. In the remainder of this chapter I propose to examine some of the changes that took place in the Latin American church during the creative, but violence plagued, decade that separated the bishops' meeting at Medellín from the outbreak of the Nicaraguan Revolution in 1978. I will focus on the particular form that recovery of the prophetic tradition took in Central America, and will sketch out some of its more important repercussions in both religious and political life.

PROPHETIC CRITICISM AND POPULAR MOBILIZATION

All across Latin America the following initiatives were implemented in the wake of Vatican II and Medellín. The church authorized the saying of mass in vernacular languages and encouraged translation of the Bible to make it more accessible to the laity, even in poor communities. One implication of this initiative was the need for literacy programs, which the church undertook at local levels. (Teaching the poor to read and write had significant long-term political implications, which soon became apparent. Authoritarian control is more easily maintained over a populace that is ignorant of its rights and unable to determine what those rights are, due to illiteracy.) At the same time, the church explicitly acknowledged the importance of the laity to the fulfillment of its spiritual mission and sought to mobilize the laity more fully.[25] This initiative became a great innovation through the widespread creation of CEBs.

The typical CEB might draw together between twenty and thirty people from the same *barrio* or, in rural areas, from a collection of adjacent farms. In this respect, the CEB organized people who had always been united by common life experiences and problems, but who had been disaggregated by migratory labor patterns, political repression, and neglect by the church. The CEB brought such people together for the express purpose of worship, but the way in which it did so, especially in Central America, enabled a new kind of learning to take place.

If a priest could be present he was apt to sit in a circle and conduct a study session of biblical texts with the members. Part of the study would consist of a dialogue that would show the relevance of the Bible to the members' own lives. In this way CEB activities were more and more participatory. Very often CEBs had to make do without the priest. To make this possible a program to train lay leaders who could guide CEBs and, as it were, stand in for the priest, was established. These lay leaders, called Delegates of the Word, multiplied profusely in the early 1970s, creating a network of individuals who could potentially offer political as well as religious leadership.[26]

The impact of the CEBs on religious life was almost immediate, and it continued to gather momentum throughout the 1970s. It revitalized religious life at the grass roots dramatically, by giving it coherence and relevance in the milieu of the poor, and by mobilizing a popular participation that had been dwindling for generations. Among people whose opinions had never mattered before, either in the church or in the wider society, the CEB offered a means of building up their sense of self-worth, dignity, and power. The political repercussions were not far behind. It should be noted that the rise of CEBs corresponded to a period of widespread militarization in Latin America and to the advent of repressive authoritarian rule in many countries.[27] In a setting where little or no opposition was tolerated, and where the economic system visited extreme hardship and misery on the poor, the CEB created a space within which the poor could generate a sense of group or class consciousness and begin to organize themselves for collective action. In short, the CEB facilitated an integration of spiritual motive and social class interest that yielded a powerful stimulus to popular demand-making in Latin America. The CEB was a potentially potent instrument for democratization in societies that were, at that moment, deeply resistant to it.

Our analysis suggests, then, that in some areas of Latin America the Roman Catholic church was as likely as any Marxist movement to be the catalyst behind impulses toward popular rebellion. The primary source of this energy was the prophetic current latent in Christian faith, which Latin Americans now began to recover through study of the Bible. By gaining direct access to the Bible (a point developed later), Latin America's marginalized poor came into contact with a radical, and radicalizing message. The Bible insisted that God loved justice and that to know God was to do justice. A characteristic expression of this attitude is found in Lev. 25:10. "You shall proclaim liberty throughout the land to all its inhabitants; it shall be a jubilee for you." This jubilee promise spoke directly to the situation of growing landlessness that afflicted more and more *campesinos* throughout the continent. Growing landlessness, together with harsh, almost slavelike working conditions, led them irresistibly to an identification with Moses and the Egyptian bondage. As H. Mark Roeloffs has put it, "What they recover is Moses as the founder of a tradition that besides being religious is at once political and radical and that stretches through the whole Bible to the

Messiahship of Jesus himself."[28] The hermeneutical perspective developed for biblical interpretation at the grass roots confronted the peoples' exploited condition and denounced it passionately. Nor was there anything new in such a stance for it reflected a notable continuity with earlier rebellions stretching "back through the Levelers and Diggers, the Anabaptists and Lollards, all the way back to the first century Christian communities before the time of Constantine," and on to the Hebrew liberation led by Moses.[29] What represented a revolutionary attitude in Latin America now had been a revolutionary perspective within the biblical tradition for well over two thousand years.

In this brief chapter we may sketch only a general outline of the transformation that took place at the grass roots in the Latin American church. For purposes of comparison I wish to comment on two cases in particular, those of Nicaragua and Brazil. On the face of it, these two countries are vastly different. Brazil is one of the largest and fastest-growing countries in the Third World, with the tenth largest gross national product (GNP) in the entire world at the beginning of the 1980s.[30] Nicaragua is a "ministate" the size of Iowa, with a total population of only about three million.

The Catholic churches of these two countries vividly reflect the differences in size and scale. There are more bishops in the Brazilian church than there are priests in Nicaragua. Although the number of clergy per capita in Brazil is low compared to European countries, the Brazilian church is relatively resource rich and institutionally sophisticated compared to Nicaragua. To carry out its pastoral mission the Brazilian church can draw upon a multitude of seminaries, research centers, and lay organizations under its sponsorship. Coherence and direction is given to this overall picture by the National Conference of Brazilian Bishops (CNBB), which was created in 1952.[31] These resources enable the Brazilian church to have a considerable impact across the society when it chooses to do so. In contrast, the Nicaraguan church has long been institutionally weak, with little capacity to generate sophisticated theological reflection or to mount effective pastoral or educational programs that could reach a large number of Nicaraguans. The Nicaraguan church was as underdeveloped as the host society.[32]

Despite these broad differences, the Brazilian and Nicaraguan cases do invite comparison. For one thing, in the years immediately following Medellín each of these countries experienced deep political turmoil and widespread political violence associated with authoritarian rule. Church renewal took place in this setting of extraordinary political violence. Secondly, in each country post-conciliar religious change took the form of systematic efforts to reach out to peasants and other marginalized groups at a moment when the logic of the political system was turning even more explicitly against their interests. Thus, the church opted to demonstrate its solidarity with the poor at a point in time when exploitation of the poor was increasing. As a result, in both countries the church itself became a target of repression. Finally, in both Brazil and Nicaragua the option for the poor led to the creation of a grass-roots "popular church" movement that gave hearing to a prophetic new voice in the church at the same time that it mobilized sectors of the poor and challenged the structures of elite domination. Let us now examine some of the details of each case, taking Nicaragua first.

EMERGENCE OF A PROPHETIC CHURCH IN NICARAGUA AND BRAZIL

Nicaragua was ruled virtually without interruption by the Somoza family dynasty from 1936 until 1979. We may pick up the story of Somoza rule in 1967, the year Luis Somoza died of a heart attack and his younger brother, Anastasio Somoza Debayle, who was director of the National Guard, had himself "elected" president. Although scandal and popular discontent led Somoza Debayle to turn power over to a three-person junta in 1971, the earthquake that destroyed the nation's capital city of Managua in December 1972 gave him the opportunity to seize control of the country once again. Somoza was named president of the National Emergency Commission, which managed the large amount of relief aid flowing into the country.[33] Ruling by decree until he could be elected to the presidency in 1974, Somoza initiated a period of increasingly corrupt and despotic rule that isolated his regime internationally and set the stage for the successful popular insurrection of 1979.

Meanwhile, as these political developments were taking place, the Nicaraguan Catholic church was beginning to evince those changes that would give it such a remarkable presence in the popular insurrection that toppled Somoza from power. In 1967, the first year of Somoza Debayle's rule, one Nicaraguan bishop publicly defended his bloody repression of a demonstration by opposition groups, reflecting the ancient pattern of a dependent church apologizing for the actions of its patron. However, in a sharp departure from this pattern, another bishop refused to receive a visit from Somoza because there were so many political prisoners in Nicaraguan jails.[34] Over the next several years other bishops began to speak out against repressive actions by the government. At the same time Catholic university and high school students engaged in a variety of public protests reminiscent of the civil rights movement in the United States a few years earlier. Perhaps most importantly, clergy inspired by Medellín began organizing the country's first CEBs, both in the poorest *barrios* of Managua and in the countryside.

Focusing on the countryside we can discuss two specific programs that had long-term consequences for change in the church and for church-state relations in Nicaragua. These programs were the Evangelical Committee for Agrarian Advancement (CEPA), and the Delegates of the Word. CEPA was set up in 1969 by Nicaraguan Jesuits in order to train peasant leaders. Originally based in coffee-growing areas south of Managua, the program gradually spread northward to León and Estelí. (Each of these areas played a vital role in the insurrection ten years later.) While a primary intent of the program in its early stages was to see to the Christian formation of *campesino* leaders, CEPA gradually concentrated more and more of its energies on helping these leaders build viable organizations that could defend peasant interests. In other words, in Somocista Nicaragua the program took on a political hue. As the government sought to control the peasant movement through violence, clergy involved with CEPA were pushed by actions of the regime to defend the rights of peasants, which were being violated with marked brutality.

Repression led many Christians associated with CEPA to sympathize with the Sandinista Front of National Liberations (FSLN) long before the insurrection actually broke out. For its part, the FSLN showed unusual flexibility for an armed opposition movement with Marxist leadership, by carefully cultivating ties with CEPA, and with other Christian organizations such as the Revolutionary Christian Movement based in the universities.[35] Out of CEPA programs emerged key peasant leaders of the FSLN-sponsored Association of Rural Workers (ATC), established in 1977.[36]

In Nicaragua, programs such as CEPA were associated with the broader church program called Delegates of the Word, which had counterparts in all the countries of Central America. Delegates were lay leaders trained to promote worship activities in rural areas who also encouraged the spread of basic literacy and rudimentary health care. Delegates were taught to lead Bible study classes. As an integral element of that study, they fostered an ongoing dialogue among CEB members "that dealt with the immediate economic and social problems of the community."[37] Such dialogues were strongly influenced by the perception that social conflict grew out of class differences and economic exploitation. In this sense they had a broadly "Marxist" aspect. Nevertheless, these dialogues were driven not by Marxist ideology, but by reading the gospel with a prophetic frame of mind. In this way delegates emerged as principal leaders in rural Nicaragua and, with the growing repression after 1972, became a primary target of political repression. Even though neither CEPA nor the broader delegate movement had much direct oversight from the Nicaraguan church hierarchy, political violence directed at these Christians was soon seen as an attack on the church itself.

Somoza wanted, and indeed tried, to avoid conflict with the church. However, these postconciliar developments, which brought the political interests of his regime into direct and violent conflict with groups that the church now cultivated, made this impossible. Regime violence, carried out by the hated National Guard that was so intimately associated with the Somoza family, "served to push the institutional church into opposition to Somoza, while pushing the delegates and the CEBs they represented into support of the FSLN."[38] In this manner, Nicaragua's emerging popular church became an important element in the broad coalition of forces which, under Sandinista leadership, came together in the late 1970s to overthrow the Somoza dictatorship. Following the lead of this prophetic element, which was strategically located among the popular sectors of society, the Nicaraguan Catholic church initiated a profound rupture in church-state relations. In the prerevolutionary setting of the 1970s the church changed sides, as it were, lending its support to an emerging popular rebellion. A unique feature of this period of concentrated religious change was the relative autonomy enjoyed by the popular church vis-à-vis the formal hierarchy of the institution.

This will be a good place to introduce the Brazilian case. A brief summary of the historical background to postconciliar religious change in Brazil can begin by focusing on the military coup of 1964. This coup marked an important turning point in the nation's political development. Postwar Brazil had been experiencing rapid social change and economic growth, which had the effect of destabilizing the traditional political system. A series of ineffective or unfulfilled presidencies from 1950 onward had culminated in the presidency of João Goulart in August 1961. As Rollie Poppino has written, "[F]or the next sixteen months . . . all economic questions

were subordinated to politics as Goulart engaged in an uninter-
rupted demagogic campaign to build a popular following."[39] The
demagogic populism of Goulart, which both the military and the
church saw as opening Brazil to dangerous Communist influence,
led eventually to a military coup in March 1964.

Initially, the Catholic church praised the coup and expressed
confidence that the new military rulers would restore needed stability to the country. In the ensuing years however, the policies of Brazil's military government, formed as they were in the context of a
national security ideology that anathematized popular democratic
demand-making, brought greater and greater suffering to rural and
urban poor. When the church began in earnest to mobilize these
sectors, not only Christian *campesinos*, but clergy and even bishops,
were subjected to government, or government-instigated violence.
In 1968 the regime suspended the right of *habeas corpus*, sharply cur-
tailed the independence of the judiciary, and unleashed the security
forces to quell political dissent. Brazil entered into a period of severe political repression.[40]

Several examples can illustrate the changing nature of church-
state relations in Brazil between the coup of 1964 and the end of the
1970s. Let us first discuss the vast Amazon region, which the new
military government sought vigorously to open up for economic exploitation and development through a program called Operation
Amazon.[41] This program provided government incentives to Brazilian landowners and foreign agribusinesses willing to expand agricultural production for export. The consequences in Brazil's
Amazon were similar to those in Central America, where comparable development policies were pursued at the same time. The concentration of land increased dramatically, generating a growing
landlessness among the peasantry.[42] Government policies displaced
peasants who had cleared land and brought it under cultivation.
When Indians and peasant settlers sought redress, they were subject to arrest, beatings, or other violent forms of intimidation.

Gradually, church workers in direct contact with *campesinos*,
began to focus their pastoral work on defending these peoples'
rights. As they did so, they increasingly called upon the church hierarchy to support them, and to denounce abuses perpetrated by
large landowners or the government. Here we have a variation of
the Nicaraguan experience, at least in degree. In the Nicaraguan
countryside, church work with *campesinos* was carried out almost
entirely at the grass roots, and found its organizational expression
opening more and more to the emerging Sandinista political revolu-

tion as the 1970s wore on. The Somocista regime did suppress much of the political opposition at this time, but was unable to suppress *campesino* organizing through CEBs and such related structures as CEPA. The regime's increasing isolation, both at home and abroad (the Carter administration suspended aid to Nicaragua in 1977, calling Somoza a serious violator of human rights), was a major factor. The Catholic church hierarchy played a relatively low profile role until the insurrection had already begun. In Brazil, by contrast, the CNBB responded vigorously to the plea for support from the grass roots.

Throughout the early 1970s bishops and clergy, acting in concert, sought to respond pastorally to the situation of deepening conflict in the Amazon. In May 1972 the church established a Pastoral Land Commission to assist in defending the economic interests of peasants and Indians. The church tried to provide some of the sustaining infrastructure, such as schools and health clinics, that was needed to preserve the integrity of rural communities in the Amazon. In response to these and other actions, violence was increasingly directed at the church itself. Lay leaders were imprisoned, tortured, or murdered. Nor were priests immune; several were arrested, tried, and convicted under state security laws while others were tortured in police custody. In Mato Grosso, Bishop Pedro Casaldáliga's house was ransacked by police, who later placed the bishop himself under house arrest.

In Brazil's huge and impoverished northeast, a similar pattern of church activism and government repression evolved. If anything, the violence against church personnel was even more extreme and widespread than in the Amazon. At least one priest was assassinated and numerous others were arrested and tortured.[43] Typically their crime was in organizing workers or peasants.

In the Brazilian setting these attacks on a church that saw itself as carrying out its prophetic mission had the effect of pushing the entire church in a progressive direction. Being the voice of the poor meant being a defender of human rights. This was a mission consciously embraced at all levels of the institution, from CEBs (which grew to number more than eighty thousand by the late 1970s) to regional encounter groups of bishops and pastoral agents, to the CNBB. The initial commitments of solidarity and the great bulk of the suffering took place at the grass-roots level, as was true in Nicaragua also. But in Brazil a significant portion of the church at all levels eventually took up this challenge in a conscious fashion. In that regard, the popular church evolved its prophetic commitment in concert with the hierarchy. In practice the impact of that prophetic commitment was to render the church the major voice speaking out in the political arena against authoritarianism and the abuse of human rights. As Scott Mainwaring has concluded, the exercise of its prophetic voice during the 1970s made the Brazilian church "the most progressive Catholic Church in the world. It has been at the forefront of some of the most significant changes the Church has undergone in recent centuries."[44]

CONCLUSION

The argument advanced in this chapter is that the Second Vatican Council provoked a radical rethinking of religious faith in Latin America. At its meeting in Medellín in 1968, CELAM furthered this process by establishing a framework of teachings within which both theological and pastoral experimentation could take place. In the setting of economic exploitation and political repression that so marked Latin America in the 1960s and 1970s such experimentation led to a dramatic recovery of the prophetic tradition. Efforts to pursue that tradition culminated in a radical reordering of priorities within the church that sharply altered church-state relations.

The original initiatives for a prophetic renewal came from the Roman Catholic hierarchy. But the real impact in society and politics came through implementation at the grass roots. It was the reorganization of pastoral work through the creation of such structures as Christian base communities, that really altered the church's role in society and reshaped its relationship to the state. CEBs and other similar grass-roots structures proved to be far more dynamic than anyone in the church hierarchy expected. The environment of political repression and economic hardship in which CEBs developed proved to be exceptionally fertile for the spread of a prophetic perspective and conducive to a vigorous growth of religious activism. CEBs fostered a dynamic sense of community among the most marginalized peoples of Latin America. That sense of community, and the renewed sense of religious purpose associated with it, gave strength and direction to prophetic denunciation.

Thus, led by a grass-roots element that had traditionally been passive and subordinate, the church became the principal critic of political authoritarianism and societal injustice. In Nicaragua such a posture led to the church's incorporation into a process of popular rebellion that overthrew a brutal dictatorship. In Brazil it helped to check the excesses of military rule and provided strong encouragement to the "democratic opening" that began at the end of the 1970s by nurturing both the spirit and the practice of popular participation. In this way a key result of prophetic renewal was the drive for greater democratization in society and politics.

Part IV. Religious Resurgence: A Mechanism for Social Discontent and Political Change

This part of the book discusses religious resurgence in the Middle East and India. In chapter 13, Louis J. Cantori points out that liberal pluralism and Marxism do not adequately explain Islamic resurgence in Egypt. He proposes a third way of looking at the resurgence of Islam that emphasizes morality rather than reason, tradition rather than idealism, and the collective interests of the community rather than the individual.

In chapter 14, Jamal Sanad and Mark Tessler examine the relationship between Islamic orientations on the one hand, and attitudes about the status of women on the other. Although they use Kuwait as a case study, presenting findings from an original public opinion survey carried out among five hundred and fifty Kuwaiti women in 1984, Sanad and Tessler deal with issues and processes relevant to all contemporary Muslim societies and incorporate information from pertinent research conducted in other Islamic countries.

In his discussion of religious resurgence in Iran (chap. 15), Gregory F. Rose dismisses the utility of fundamentalism as an approach for the understanding of the political revitalization of Shi'a Islam. He contends that the collective action model is a more appropriate explanatory variable for the phenomenon of religious resurgence. In his opinion, Shi'a Islam offers an efficient mechanism for collective action and political mobilization. Shi'a Islam is not opposed to modernization; on the contrary, Rose concludes that it is a powerful vehicle for the mobilization of the resources of the government and the mass public alike for economic development.

Augustus Richard Norton, in chapter 16, traces the emergence of the Shi'i political movement in Lebanon. Utterly ignored before the late 1970s, he argues that the Shi'a have traded quietism and irrelevance for a leading role in shaping the future of that country. Initially mobilized by the secular parties of the reformist and revolutionary Left, which still maintain a Shi'i following, many of the Shi'a have been drawn—over the last decade—by the powerful symbolism of their religion into distinctively Shi'i organizations. Norton also discusses the role of the charismatic religious leaders and the influence of the modernization process upon the Shi'a.

Karandeep Singh (chap. 17) attributes Indian fundamentalism to the role of the new agrarian technology that led to more economic power in the hands of the rural Jat Sikh elite of Punjab, the machinations of the various factions within the Akali and the Congress parties, and the specific political line adopted by Indira Gandhi in the late 1970s to pander to Hindu majority communalism to win political success. All of these factors are reinforced by the background of Sikh cultural ethos and history.

In chapter 18, Mark Tessler focuses on the relationship between religion and politics in Israel and analyzes the major ideological trends dealing with the place of religion in the Jewish state. Tessler places special emphasis on the rise of Jewish fundamentalism after the 1967 Arab-Israeli War.

The Islamic Revival as Conservatism and as Progress in Contemporary Egypt

Louis J. Cantori

The Islamic revival is part of a global process of religious revival.[1] As great as is the importance of its religious meaning and its societal impact, it is also in danger of being misunderstood and misinterpreted. The reason for this is a basic lack of correspondence between the widespread mass societal nature of the phenomenon on the one hand, and the often narrowness of intellectual efforts at understanding it on the other. The Islamic revival is both an expression of religious recommitment that emanates upward from the base and lower middle ranges of society, and one that combines with initiatives from the top and the state to intensify religious sentiment on a large-scale basis. The intellectual effort to understand the vastness of the phenomenon, however, is generally one of a narrow focus upon what is called its fundamentalism or its radicalism. The empirical preoccupation with fundamentalist and radical fringe groups on the margin of Islamic society are limited in their significance for the understanding of that society. As a result, the impreciseness of the conceptual labels of radicalism and fundamentalism combine with the misplaced emphasis upon the violence of marginal groups to produce an inadequate and misleading understanding of the truly historic nature of the phenomenon.[2] What is missing is both a sense of the historical context of Islamic revivalism and a larger conceptual context within which it might be located. The discussion of the historical context of the Islamic revival in order to capture its societal as opposed to commonly characterized conspiratorial qualities can be postponed for the moment in order to concentrate at the outset upon the conceptual challenge.

THE CONSERVATIVE CORPORATIST PARADIGM AND THE STUDY OF RELIGION

There exist two dominant analytical research paradigms in the social sciences: liberal pluralism and Marxist radicalism.[3] It can be argued that neither of them is adequate to the task of comprehending religion as a dynamic modern phenomenon. Liberal pluralism in its guise as modernization or development theory explicitly premises the achievement of modernity with the decline of religion under the label of secularization. Marxist radicalism has a similar but more pronounced inability to deal with religion as an expanding rather than declining process. Dialectical materialism after all posits that all belief, including religion, is the product of the material economic conditions of society and that religion especially operates to obscure this "scientific" fact.

Conservative corporatism is an approach that is explicitly sympathetic to religion and sees no contradiction between a commitment to it and the ability of society to progress.[4] Conservative corporatism, like its preceding companions of liberal pluralism and Marxist radicalism, consists of two elements: the normative one of conservatism, and the structural one of corporatism. It is the normative dimension of conservatism that has the obvious directness of relationship to religion. The conservatism referred to here is one that primarily has its origins in nineteenth-century Germany, but that also figured quite prominently in France as well. In Germany this conservatism, with its correlate of structural corporatism, was to become the dominant mode of thought until eclipsed by liberalism at the end of the century. In France, liberalism was to take center ideological stage but conservatism was to remain an important ideological competitor well into the present century.[5]

What is striking about the development of this thought was the explicitness of its formulation in rejection of the egalitarian and rationalistic tenets of the Enlightenment and its preference via Hegel and others for classical philosophy and medieval Christianity. Its rejection of the Enlightenment focused upon the condemnation of what it termed *Manchester individualism*, i.e., liberalism on the one hand, and Marxist materialistic class conflict on the other. Both were rejected as responses to the political, social, and economic injustices of the Industrial Revolution. Conservatism was developed explicitly as an alternative and superior approach to these problems. Not only was this to be a theoretical exercise in conservative progressivism directed to remedying injustice, but its leading proponents made contributions to the astonishingly progressive social welfare legislation of the conservative Bismarck in Germany in 1881, and the Papal Encyclical, *Nova Rerum* ("On the Condition of the Working Class") in 1891 as a further, progressive conservative statement. In fact, social Catholicism was important to this body of thought in both countries.

A perusal of the writings of the more important German and French theorists yields the following definition of conservatism with three distinct emphases: (1) the existence of a real or imagined past that is employed as the criterion or "blueprint" for the future; (2) the precedence of the welfare of the community over the individual and the latter's subordination to the needs of the community; and (3) the primacy of moral principles over competing political, social and economic ones.[6] The manner in which religion and Islam figure in this formulation will be addressed shortly, but it is important to note the explicitness with which the definition differs from the ideal utopias of Enlightenment individualism and rationalism.[7] It is its aversion to the Enlightenment, along with other factors, which suggests its possible relevancy to an Islamic world largely devoid of an historical experience with the Enlightenment except derivatively via the impact of liberal and Marxist thought.

RELIGION AND CONSERVATISM

Religion can be viewed as traditional and therefore as an expression of conservatism. It is the prism through which the past as tradition is viewed. Religion as revealed truth also is an alternative to Enlightenment rationalism. It is an authoritative way of knowing. Religion therefore works to conserve the past and adapts to change in terms of the criteria of the past. The past, however, is celebrated in terms of its assumed superiority. This superiority consists of its moral principles. Furthermore, these moral principles are related to the welfare of a community of believers. Intrinsic to this welfare is its spiritual content and sense of political, social, and economic justice. The intensity of feeling and commitment to these moral principles in the nature of things, waxes and wanes. This process represents the characteristic cyclical nature of the historical rising and falling of the world's great religions. Presently, we live in a time of the waxing of religious sentiment and hence the intensity of

concern about the community in terms of standards of morality
drawn from the past. It is the dynamism of this projection and its
concern with both things spiritual and just that gives the religious
revival its progressivism and adaptability to modern change. Religious revivalism is not to be confused with religious extremism. The
latter is extreme in the narrowness and sometimes heterodoxy of its
vision of the religious past and it is extreme in that it often represents a minority point of view that is imposed on a majority. It
therefore is inclined to work outside the mainstream of institutions
and processes and to challenge them and often to attempt to sub-
vert them. Most often, however, it is religious extremism that gains
the headlines of the world and works to distract attention from the
mainstream character and even the positive accomplishments of the
religious revival.

Islam is reflective of these qualities of tradition and conservatism. Its past is defined by the message of God as revealed to his
prophet Muhammad and as preserved in *al-Qur'an*. The nature of
this revealed truth is such that while having been revealed in the
historical past (600–632 A.D.) in Mecca and Medina, in fact the revelations are timeless in their truth. As such, therefore, they are always of the present and the future. These truths of *al-Kitab (The Book*
or *al-Qur'an)* are the hallmark of Islam. This hallmark is embellished
at a minimum by the religious practices of the prophet Muhammad
(the Sunna) and the examples of the four successor leaders (Khalifa
or Caliph) of the community of believers (the Umma), known collectively by the label of the Divinely Guided Ones (Rashidun). The
practices of the prophet and the examples of the Rashidun are more
technically historical in the sense that they represent concrete people and events. It is also true, however, that in speech and in
thought Muslims often speak of them in the present tense as sub-
jective fellow contemporaries. Thus they, as well as the *Qur'an* itself, represent a past that simultaneously collectively constitutes
knowing and the criterion of behavior as well as a blueprint for the
future.[8] It is the *Qur'an*, the Sunna, and the Rashidun taken together, which constitute the theological cornerstone of the Islamic
revival. Reformers and fundamentalists alike are in essential agreement that the astonishingly compressed period of sixty years (from
the approximate beginning of the revelations in the adulthood of
the prophet in 600 A.D. and the death of the last of the Rashidun,
Ali, the son-in-law of the prophet in 661 A.D.) contains the essential
meaning of Islam.[9] Among the differences between reformer and
fundamentalist, however, is that the former expands its theological

horizons to include the interpretation (*tafsir*) of the *Qur'an*, the sayings of the prophet and his companions (the Traditions or Hadith) and the schools (*madhab*) of Islamic law (the *sharia*), while the latter is more restrictive and more selective in the choice of these additional "sources" of Islam.

The emphasis upon morality in Islam is self-evident. The fundamental commitment of the believer to belief in the oneness of God (*tawhid*) and Mohammad as his messenger, has added to it prescriptions of behavior that center on obeying God and thereby gaining salvation. Islam has always placed this adherence to morality as the primary expectation of the Muslim in society, and in so doing places economic and social goals and ambitions in a secondary position. It is this primary insistence upon morality that represents the historical nature of Islam as a total belief system. Revitalization has meant a renewed emphasis upon morality whose effect has been to raise this point from its implicitness and lesser prominence in the recent modern Egyptian experience to its present prominence. This prominence consists of wider participation in worship, more media attention to issues of belief and behavior, and the adoption of Islamic styles of dress. For men this might involve growing a beard, and for women, donning the *Hegab* or *zay al-Islam* ("veil"), a scarf-like covering for the face and a gownlike dress. What is interesting as illustrative of the compatibility of modernity and tradition, is that having defined the problem of the desirability of increased modesty, the solution is not to adopt older, veiled styles or even the *milayya* (black shawl) of contemporary peasant women, but rather to invent head gear and body covering that have couturelike style and eye-catching colors. In short, the purpose is traditional; the solution is modern.

Increased attention to the past and emphasis upon morality bears directly on the importance and precedence of community over the individual. This is evident in the emphasis of the *Qur'an* upon the community of believers. For the reformer, revitalization has meant, among other things, an enhanced sense of religiously inspired social responsibility. The evidence of this has been the increased number of Islamic charitable societies (*jamiyyat al-khayri al-Islami*), undertaking social welfare responsibilities; and operating health clinics, day-care centers, and adult literacy programs often independent of the government and often totally beyond its control.[10]

The importance of community for the fundamentalist is dramatically evident in two respects. There is first the importance of the concept of *hegira* or migration, in defining their subgroupings. *Hegira* refers to migration from the larger society on the model of the prophets' migration from Mecca to Medina in 622 A.D. This migration is, however, a symbolic way of separating and establishing its own society and rules while remaining physically within the larger society. Unlike the increased sense of social responsibility of the reformist that is an expanding and inclusive dynamic, the fundamentalist is involved in contraction, exclusion, and opposition to the larger society. The conception of the larger society as constituting a *jahilyya* ("barbarism") allows the conduct of a *jihad* ("religious struggle") against it, and martyrdom in the *jihad* is embraced as the ultimate evidence of sacrifice for the community of believers.[11] Religious revitalization therefore has resulted also in the revitalization of the conservative tenets of Egyptian society as well.

THE DYNAMIC OF ISLAMIC REVITALIZATION

Revitalization in Egypt has had both an ideological and structural dynamic. Ideologically, it has been recognized that revitalization begins with the societal trauma of the Egyptian defeat by the Israelis in 1967. The defeat was not perceived as the result of the prowess of the Israeli army or American assistance of the Israeli effort. Instead, the perception was the traditional one that such a monumental disaster was God's work. He had decided to punish the Egyptians for their inattention to their religious duties.[12] It is clear that cultural introversion and introspection was to date from this event. This was the case of majority reformist Islam, as well as fundamentalist minority Islam. But like all such milestone dates in history there were additional complexities as well.

Egypt, prior to 1967, had passed through two ideological phases that interacted with the emergence of modern nationalism. The first was that of a Western-inspired liberalism that took significant roots in Egypt from 1890 until 1952. This liberalism embraced the ideals of democracy and successfully rid Egypt of its British colonial occupiers. By 1952, however, it had partly exhausted itself in a rearguard conflict throughout the 1940s to attempt to more definitively rid Egypt of continued British interference.[13] In addition, Egypt also was saddled by an ineffective but interfering monarchy. Adding to these defects was the fact that an effective corruption-free second generation of liberal leaders failed to emerge, and parliamentary democracy ground to a halt by early 1952. An exhausted liberalism was succeeded by appending to Egyptian nationalism first the anti-imperialism of Nasser, and then Arab socialism. Nasser succeeded in conclusively ridding Egypt of the British and the monarchy and he significantly addressed the problems of economic and social injustice in Egypt. By 1967, however, the economy was depleted and near bankruptcy and corruption and an unpopular war in Yemen had exhausted Arab socialism as an ideological driving force. The 1967 defeat drove a stake through its heart.[14]

It is against this backdrop then that Islamic revitalization begins in Egypt. As a process, it has been a very complex phenomenon. Crucial to its understanding have been the elements of a religiously aware mass public, a new president (Sadat) who succeeded Nasser upon the latter's death in 1970 and reached out for religious support and legitimacy, and Islamic fundamentalists who are the heirs of pre-1967 religious protest against the state. The process in which religious self-consciousness develops in the mass population as renewal and reformism is complex and takes on the vestiges of a movement (*haraka*), i.e., a semiformalized and structured process with varying stimuli and leaders but with a definable direction and a palpable energy. It is the movement quality of the phenomenon that makes efforts to understand and analyze it so difficult, and conclusions regarding it so elusive and tentative.

Perhaps the most difficult intellectual challenge is understanding Islamic revitalization as a mass popular movement. The devastation of the Egyptian armed forces, the military casualties, and the destruction and evacuation of the Suez Canal cities of Port Said, Ismailiya, and Suez, all had a depressing effect on the popular mind. Evacuees from the Canal cities were distributed throughout Egypt and were visible war victims in countless towns and villages. It is important at the outset to appreciate the role of popular Islam as a dynamic force whose emergence was to be brought into the revitalization process.

The texture and dynamics of popular Islam may vary over time, but what is constant is the way in which saint worship, and saint birthday celebrations (*mawlid*), mystical religious rituals (e.g., Sufist *zikr* line dances in mosques), and magic-like rituals of exorcisms (e.g., *zar* ceremonies) operate to enthuse the worshiper and to cement his ties to Islam on an effective and ecstatic basis.[15] This religious "energy" of mass commitment to Islam seems always intrinsic to the dynamic of the faith, but there is evidence that this sentiment was intensifying during the 1970s. The most dramatic evidence of this that both validates the point and reinforces the phenomenon, is the observation by soldier and officer alike in the assault force on the BarLev Line on the Suez Canal on October 6, 1973, that angels were seen dancing on the Israeli parapets.[16] The cry of Allahu Akbar ("God is great") shouted by the attackers, was thus deeply felt and religiously expressive. The military success in capturing the positions represented an important vindication and reinforcement of the nation's recommitment to religious values.

This popular sentiment has been expressed in books, articles, and television discussion programs. In fact, popular Islam, which had always been spurned and considered religiously suspect, now has been made more legitimate by the process of sympathetic public discussion. Expressive of the foregoing is the popularity of Shaykh Kishk, who has become a leading spokesman on the issues and concerns of ordinary people about Islam.[17] As an *alim*, or "learned man of Islam," he legitimizes popular Islam in the process. This is especially the case because he frequently idealizes the sincerity of what might also be called populist Islam over against the alleged insincerity of the official Islam of al-Azhar University.

The state has been in a dialectical relationship to this mass sentiment. Sadat had sought religious support from the time he took power in September 1970 onwards. He did this in three ways in reference to mass-based popular Islam. The first was by initiating a vigorous program of new mosque construction. The second was by claiming the popular benefits of releasing thousands of imprisoned members of the Muslim Brethren. In addition, he allowed the publication of its banned newspaper, *al-Dawa*, even while legally the Muslim Brethren remained proscribed. In fact, however, its members became increasingly active as intermediaries between the regime and the mass public.[18]

What Sadat had improvised, Mubarak has routinized. He, for example, moved to release the large number of religionists whom Sadat had arrested in September 1981. At the same time he loosened restrictions of television programming of religious topics and created an atmosphere of almost total religious freedom of opinion. He also began to allow the official Islamic newspaper, *al Liwa al-Islami*, to publish articles and letters to the editor on a range of religious topics. The circulation of what had been a very modest publication expanded explosively.[19] What emerges is a dialectical relationship between state and religious forces in which the state co-opts and/or tolerates the overwhelming majority of religious matters, while filtering out and repressing those that are subversive.

ISLAMIC FUNDAMENTALISM

It is only against the background of the preceding discussion of the majority experience with reformist religion that the minority fundamentalist experience can be considered. If this perspective is not adopted, then what is in fact religious extremism is permitted to be presented as if it was the norm of Islam in contemporary Egypt. The argument that minority radical and fundamentalist Islam is somehow synonymous with majority reformist revivalism stems from the fact that the vision and use of the past of both is similar.[20] The vision is one of the same narrow 600–661 A.D. year period. Both seek to use the past as a criterion for the establishment of an Islamic society. Similarly, both have a prime concern with a stricter standard of morality. It is the case, however, that the fundamentalists have a more literal view of that standard. But perhaps the greatest and most distinguishing difference between revivalist reformist and radical fundamentalist is in respect to the means adapted to secure these ends on Muslim society. What is striking about radical fundamentalism in Egypt is that it is frequently connected to at least the historical Muslim Brethren founded by Hassan al-Banna in 1928. Each decade of protest from the 1930s onward has found members of the Muslim Brethren in especially the 1940s, 1950s, and 1960s in the front ranks of militant protest and violent acts.[21] Beginning in the 1970s, however, the older generation of the Muslim Brethren left the violent periphery and joined the reformist center where their willingness to compromise now finds them in elected public positions and in the media where they attempt to effect change by persuasion. A younger generation, however, has split off from the Muslim Brethren and has sustained violent means throughout the 1970s and 1980s. Some of the dates and events that have punctuated their efforts, have been the 1974 attack upon the Egyptian College of Military Arts, the kidnapping and killing of ex-minister Muhammad al-Dhahabi in 1977, and the assassination of President Sadat in October 1981, as well as other events.[22] The important point is that programmatically, they have had little or no popular support and their repression by the state has until now been successful. They are therefore definitionally marginalized and unless their leadership changes or the regime miscalculates by employing disproportionate force against them and thereby arousing public sympathy, they are likely to remain of lesser overall importance. Perhaps most important to keeping them on the margins is the continued movement of Egypt toward a more accommodationist Islamic state.

ISLAMIC PROGRESSIVISM

Reformist revivalist Islam in Egypt also displays evidence of its progressivism. Progressivism is used here in the broadest meaning to indicate a basic acceptance and accommodation to modernity. An argument can be made that the ascendancy of Islamic culture to replace more Western derived ones of liberalism and socialism is creating a cultural context that is possibly more receptive to modern social, economic, scientific, and technological innovation primarily because their "Western" overtones are now filtered through an indigenous cultural screen.

In the area of social behavior, for example, it is possible to argue that "veiling" for women is an issue of acute concern to educated middle-class women whose mothers and grandmothers fought to be free from it in the 1920s. On the other hand, an increased practice of wearing Islamic dress perhaps gives lower-class women more social confidence to undertake modern office and other tasks. There is anecdotal evidence to support this logical proposition, but perhaps the real issue is not so much the heavy symbolism of the veil, as it is accessibility to modern occupations themselves. This accessibility does not seem to be causing a decline in, for example, the 30–40 percent student enrollment rates in the prestigious fields of medicine and engineering.

Much of the activism of Islam in contemporary Egypt occurs privately and separate from the government. Thus, for example, there exists an estimated nine thousand private voluntary Islamic charitable organizations. Their activities range from social welfare to the indigent, to day-care centers, to health clinics, and now even elementary education as an alternative to a vastly inferior and underfunded public school system.[23] What is extraordinary about such organizations is that these functions are carried out by government mosques as well as by those that are privately built and maintained. The mosques become complementary organs for the dissemination of social services for which government aptitude and funding is inadequate. These functions of the mosques are also important because they express neighborhood solidarity, thus bringing this additional tie of community into play. What appears to be at work is a complex matrix of private organizations, mosque social functions, and government social welfare services. In short, there exists in Egypt an Islamic infrastructure protecting and educating the mass public.

A similar Islamic accommodation to modernity can be seen in the capitalist economy. The long-observed point that Islam and capitalism are natural to one another and complementary is dramatically evident in Egypt today as it is in the Islamic world as a whole. Reference here is to both Islamic banking and financial investment. The issue of usury is being addressed at least partially by interest free banking and by a return on loans by declarations of fluctuating earning. More dramatic has been the ability of Islamic investment companies to cause Muslims to invest billions of dollars. This has erupted into controversy because until legislation was passed in the spring of 1988, these were unregulated and did not have to reveal their financial affairs to the public. Seemingly unrealistic rates of return of 20 percent or more have created suspicions of mismanagement. Nonetheless, what is striking is the willingness of thousands of Muslims to undertake investment risks under the auspices of Islam.[24]

In the area of science and technology, an important research conclusion by those who have studied the educational characteristics of radical fundamentalists is that the majority come from student and occupational areas that are in science, engineering, agricultural engineering, and commerce.[25] Furthermore, their activism is not so much a denial of their education as a statement of its spiritual imcompleteness. As Egypt continues its recommitment to Islamic values it can be anticipated that the reason for this spiritual emptiness will decline even while a continued commitment to science and technology advances. Perhaps the most dramatic evidence of this general point can be seen in that persons espousing self-conscious religious viewpoints have come to dominate the executive committees of the important professional associations of medicine, pharmacology, and engineering.[26] These associations have long histories in advancing the modern knowledge of their respective fields. Their more Islamic cast does not suggest any reversal or discontinuance of their professional advances.

CONCLUSION

There are several conclusions that can be made regarding the foregoing analysis.

1. It is important to redirect scholarly attention away from the distracting subject of Islamic radical fundamentalism toward the mainstream belief, which in the case of Egypt, seems to express itself as reformist revitalization.

2. It is important, in the case of Egypt and perhaps elsewhere in the Muslim world, to understand Islamic revitalization as an expression of cultural authenticity, which is an affirming phe-

nomenon. Its positive qualities need recognition rather than a pre-occupation with its criticisms and reservations, especially about Western culture.

3.   It is possible that religion operates in Egypt as both a conservatizing and progressive modernizing force.

4.   It is possible to recognize conservatism as a set of assumptions and categories representing an alternative research paradigm to those of liberalism and Marxism.

Finally, an observation can be made that is even more speculative than the preceding ones, but that seems to be tentatively suggested by the analysis and the data. It is possible that what the Islamic state longed for, however, ultimately and vaguely by fundamentalist and reformist alike, has in fact already significantly developed in Egypt. What is striking about Islam in Egypt today is not only its theological, ritual, and cultural pervasiveness, but also its equally pervasive institutionalization. From mosque, to private voluntary organization, to newspapers and regular television discussion, to parliamentary representation, Islam has come to dominate Egyptian society in a fascinating fashion. The fascination is that it is largely a societal phenomenon with relatively little connection to government. As such, the policy of the Mubarak government resembles very much the classical Islamic theory of the state and politics, namely the ruler's responsibility to carry out taxation (hence its apprehension regarding the economic independence of Islamic investment companies as directing money away from government control) and to maintain order (hence the repression of fundamentalism and its encouragement of Islamic reformism). One possible consequence of this is an explanation for the stability of the Mubarak government due to the manner in which a sense of heightened religious values diminishes pressures for material advances and the Islamic "sector" of society assumed developmental burdens the state is not able to bear. While one should not be too optimistic in one's conclusions on a subject so volatile as religion, it may be that this "traditional" arrangement has a potential for stability and even democratic progress as some scholars have recently argued.[27]

14

Women and Religion in a Modern Islamic Society: The Case of Kuwait
Jamal Sanad and Mark Tessler

Kuwait is a small, oil-rich nation on the Arabian Gulf. It is unique in that its small population and massive wealth combine to give citizens and many other inhabitants one of the highest standards of living in the world. So far as issues of development are concerned, the problems confronting Kuwait are accordingly somewhat unusual, having to do primarily with a shortage of labor, bottlenecks in the absorption of income from petroleum exports, and the productive investment of surplus revenue that is not needed for development. Located in a turbulent region and surrounded by powerful neighbors, Kuwait must also seek political and diplomatic strategies that will protect it from the pressures that buffet the Gulf region.

In other respects, however, particularly those bearing on matters of religion, the Kuwaiti case is much more typical. Like most other states in the Middle East, and some elsewhere, Kuwait strongly identifies with Islam at both the popular and governmental level. Virtually all Kuwaitis are Muslim, and many are deeply religious. Even more important, only a tiny handful would welcome the separation of religion and politics, as it exists in the West. Indeed, a significant, though undetermined number support militant Muslim groups that advocate a deepening of Islamic influence over all aspects of political and social life. So far as the government is concerned, the state is officially Islamic, with the legal system and public policy explicitly linked to religion in many areas. Indeed, a formal rejection of secularism is set forth in the country's Constitution, which proclaims that "the religion of the state is Islam, and the Islamic shari'a ("law") should be a main source of legislation." In addition, mosques and other Muslim institutions are administered by the state, and numerous religious officials are accordingly government employees. In all of these respects, Kuwait is not only typical of the sheikhdoms of the Gulf, or even of the conservative monarchies of the Arab Middle East more generally; it accords social and political roles to Islam in a manner that is replicated throughout the Arab and Islamic world.

Not surprisingly, under these circumstances, Islam plays a major role in the socialization of young Kuwaitis and in the life of most adults. The transmission of Islamic values starts early in life and continues through adolescence. Parents begin to teach Muslim values and principles to children as young as three years old and religious education, in the form of a mandatory course entitled "The Islamic Religion," is part of the school curriculum in every grade from kindergarten through high school. Even at the university level, there is a seminar on "Islamic Civilization" that all students are required to take.[1] In addition, Islamic institutions influence the attitudes and behavior of many adults, there being mosques in every urban neighborhood and village and a widespread expectation of respect for numerous religious practices, such as Islamic dress for women and fasting during the holy month of Ramadan. As a result, Islamic values and ideas are extremely influential in Kuwait. Even individuals who do not practice Islam strictly in their personal behavior for the most part believe that the religion should play a leading role in shaping the social and cultural environment within which Kuwaitis and other Muslims live.

WOMEN IN ISLAM

This situation derives its social and political significance in large measure from the fact that Islam is a comprehensive system of beliefs, values, and legal codes, and that it accordingly addresses itself to an extremely wide range of societal concerns. Among such concerns are matters of personal status and, of particular concern in the present chapter, questions bearing on the proper relationship between men and women and on the public and private roles deemed appropriate for women.[2] The rights and duties of women are set forth in many Quranic verses (suras), which, upon interpretation, are the bases for Islamic codes governing marriage, divorce, notions of modesty and proper dress for women, women's rights in matters of inheritance, the relative weight of male and female witnesses in a court of law, and much more. Given the influence of Islam on public law, to say nothing of the religion's influence on custom and public morality more generally, the circumstances of women cannot be properly understood without attention to Islam. This is the situation in Kuwait and in most other Muslim countries as well.

It is frequently asserted that Islam denies to women rights that are granted to men, and otherwise restricts the opportunities and choices available to women, and in some areas Islam does indeed impose an inferior status upon women. For instance, a woman's testimony is worth only half that of a man's in a Muslim court of law. Similarly, in matters of inheritance, Islam grants a daughter only half the share of a son. Yet another example concerns marriage; a man but not a woman may marry a non-Muslim, and Islam permits a man to take up to four wives. Moreover, in addition to the specific inequalities imposed in these and other behavioral domains, it is often argued that Islam subordinates women in even more fundamental ways. On the one hand, the cumulative impact of numerous individual *suras* dealing with women is said to be the inculcation of cultural norms that view women as weak, dependent, untrustworthy, and less capable than men. On the other, the religion has provided a legal and institutional foundation for the broad application of such views, even in areas about which Islamic law is in fact silent.[3] As a result, in Kuwait and in most other Muslim societies, the seclusion of women, a belief that education is less important for women than for men, opposition to women's entry into the salaried labor force, and other aspects of gender-based discrimination are often justified in the name of Islam. Even though there is nothing in the Quran about any of these common practices, those who oppose them are often condemned for anti-Islamic sentiments.

This is not the whole story, however. When seen within the Islamic context, at least some regulations are not as discriminatory as they at first appear. With respect to inheritance, for example, men are given a larger share because they are required by Islam to assume a disproportionate burden in meeting the financial needs of the family. Such considerations do not pertain to all Islamic codes that place women in a subordinate position, and even when they do, Muslims sometimes disagree among themselves about whether this justifies the differential treatment of men and women. But most

Muslims who ponder these issues, including most of the women among them, would object to any critical discussion of Islam that does not consider the intent as well as the text of a particular *sura* and that does not recognize that knowledge of this intent requires the analytical juxtaposition of competing Islamic prescriptions and the careful review of relevant historic precedents.

For many Muslims, then, questions should be asked not about the rightness, fairness, or modern day relevance of Islam but, rather, about the proper interpretation of specific Islamic prescriptions. Furthermore, both so far as the status of women is concerned and more generally, there has long existed within the Muslim world a school of thought which argues that the letter rather than the spirit of Islam has usually prevailed, and that many practices carried out in the name of Islam are actually antithetical to the religion.

Arguments of this sort were put forward in the nineteenth century by such Arab and Islamic modernists as Jamal al-Din al-Afghani and Muhammad Abduh, both of whom argued that Islamic practice had been corrupted over the centuries as a result of the misguided and self-serving interpretations advanced by many Muslim jurists and other religious authorities (*ulama*). Al-Afghani and Abduh were concerned with the general stagnation of the contemporary Muslim world and, in this connection, they denounced the *ulama* and the conservative mosque universities that trained them. Al-Afghani, Abduh, and other modernists proclaimed a need to rediscover the "true spirit" of Islam, the openness and tolerance that had produced the brilliant Muslim civilization that flourished during the early Islamic centuries, and in order to accomplish this task they called for educational reforms that would enable the mosque universities to produce competent jurists and scholars.[4] The application of these arguments to questions about the status of women in Islam was taken up with particular force by Qasim Amin, one of Abduh's pupils. In a book published in 1899, Amin challenged the validity of many established interpretations of Muslim law pertaining to women and asserted that Islam, properly understood, actually encourages women's emancipation and equality between the sexes.[5]

The analysis of these early modernists continues to be put forward by some present-day Muslims. Calling attention to the central issue of interpretation, these men and women argue that the problem is with Muslims, not with Islam, by which they mean, so far as women's issues are concerned, that Islam legitimates sexual inequality and restricts opportunities for women only in the minds of those Muslims who do not understand their religion properly. In support of this view, Islamic advocates of women's emancipation usually make two interrelated points: first, there can be no doubt that the Quran grants women numerous specific rights, in such areas as marriage, divorce, economic independence, and education;[6] and second, since most of these rights were absent in the pre-Islamic period, it is clear that the intent of Islamic doctrine is to foster movement in the direction of improving women's status.[7] It is in this connection that Qasim Amin declared that Islamic law was the first law to provide for the equality of women and argued that this historic impulse must be borne in mind by those striving for the proper interpretation of particular Quranic edicts. Even with respect to the controversial and oft-cited issue of polygamy, Islamic modernists point out that the clear intent of Islam is to discourage the practice and to increase the rights of women, not to institutionalize and legitimize special privileges for men. Noting that Islam requires a man to take only one wife if there is any chance that treatment will not be equitable, modernists insist that Islam not only improved the conditions of women at the time of its introduction, but imposed restrictions which, properly interpreted, virtually prohibit the taking of a second wife.

In the face of such arguments, one must ask why a more conservative and restrictive version of Islam became dominant over the centuries, and why even today, although it is by now quite familiar, the reasoning of Islamic modernists is still resisted by many Muslims. One consideration, as noted by al-Afghani and Abduh over a century ago, is the orientation and training of many of the jurists and scholars who have traditionally had responsibility for instructing the Muslim masses in the meaning of their religion. With respect to the status of women, as in many other areas, restrictive practices carried out in the name of Islam are, to a significant degree, a result of the *ulama*'s narrow interpretation of *shari'a* law (Muslim legal codes) and associated local traditions, an interpretation that reifies continuity and order and works to discourage "deviation," rather than seeking to discover and apply the reasoning behind the law. Thus, while one scholar writes that the *ulama* have historically constituted "a powerful and respected body of men with considerable sources of personal and corporate wealth and a large influence in the shaping of Muslim societies,"[8] another reports, based on his own research in Egypt and on a number of additional studies, that most "have not been able to shed the oppressive burden of medievalism . . . [and that as a result] modernization has been successfully delayed in Egypt by the *ulama*."[9] Conservatism in the interpretation of Islamic law has for the most part characterized both Muslim scholars at prestigious Islamic universities, such as al-Azhar in Cairo, and Islamic jurists and teachers working in villages and rural communities.[10]

A second factor that has historically contributed to the dominance of conservative interpretations of Islam has to do with tribal traditions and practices. While the origins of such traditions and practices are actually pre-Islamic in many cases, they persisted after the introduction of Islam and created a strong predisposition in favor of those interpretations of *shari'a* law that stress the subordination and seclusion of women. Moreover, tribal customs and values are still important in Kuwait and in other states of the Arabian Gulf,[11] as well as in a number of additional Arab and Islamic countries. Most men from tribal backgrounds are strongly in favor of seclusion, limited education for women, and other customs that reduce contact between the sexes and, more generally, limit the roles of a woman to that of wife and mother. Consequently, especially with respect to gender-based segregation, the values and practices of tribal society have played, and continue to play, a major role in promoting interpretations of Islamic law that narrow the opportunities available to women and perpetuate established patterns of male dominance. Although a more in-depth treatment is beyond the scope of the present inquiry, the analytical lesson of these observations is that a proper understanding of the position of women in Islam cannot be obtained from a simple reading of the Quran. Such an understanding also requires attention to the political and cultural context within which Islam is comprehended and practiced, and in particular to factors that shape the pronouncements and actions of those in a position to determine how Quranic verses are interpreted and applied to real life situations.

THE ISLAMIC RESURGENCE AND VIEWS ABOUT WOMEN

The Islamic resurgence that has been taking place in recent years raises additional questions about the status of women in Islam. Furthermore, while it is often asserted that this resurgence is strengthening conservative or fundamentalist interpretations of Islam with respect to the circumstances of women and other social issues, in reality this is only part of a much more complex situation. First, there are important ideological differences among the various Islamic-tendency movements that have been thrown up by the current religious resurgence, not only from country to country, but within many countries as well.[12] Second, despite significant differences among them, these groups disapprove of many established practices carried out in the name of Islam and, in particular, they have in common a strong antipathy to conservative *ulama* who give religious legitimacy to Quranic interpretations deemed at variance with the true meaning of Islam. Running through the literature of most militant Islamic groups, and through the statements of their leaders, are the themes of purification and the rediscovery of an Islam from which distortions and corruptions have been removed. Drawing a distinction between their own normative platforms and the decadent Islam of the political and religious establishment, a call for "renewal" is the common denominator of the Islamic resurgence.

Some militant Islamic groups see the problems of the contemporary Muslim world as derived first and foremost from the decadence of the individual. Muslims have wandered away from the lifestyle called for by Islam and this has produced an inner weakness in Muslim society, from which all other problems flow. One group whose thinking runs along these lines is the Liberation party, which has followers in Kuwait and in a number of other countries in the Arab Middle East.[13] Liberationists are more concerned with proper personal behavior than political reform, although they see the former as leading to the latter in the Islamic context, and their main call is thus for greater piety among Muslims. Prayer and mosque attendance are stressed, as is the faithful performance of other Islamic obligations. So far as questions about women are concerned, Liberationists and like-minded groups tend to be conservative, calling for strict separation of the sexes. They also strongly advocate Muslim dress for women, not only because they believe modesty is required by Islam but also as a symbol of their rejection of Western cultural and political influences. For these groups, purification and renewal involve the removal of foreign, non-Islamic practices from Muslim society.

Larger and more influential are groups that reverse the relationship between the individual and society and see the problem of the Muslim world as essentially one of social and political, not individual, decadence. Individual Muslims cannot be blamed for inappropriate behavior since the society in which they live, and that shapes their patterns of thought and action, itself is not organized in an appropriate fashion. In this connection, the values and behavior patterns of the modern era are often compared to those of Arabian society before the introduction of Islam, which Muslims regard as devoid of spiritual enlightenment and social purpose and which they refer to as *jahiliyya*. As stated by Sayyid Qutb (1906–1966), a radical Muslim theorist from Egypt whose writings have been very influential among some Islamic-tendency groups, "Nowadays the entire world lives in a state of jahiliyya so far as the source from which it draws the rules of its mode of existence is concerned, a jahiliyya that is not changed one whit by material comfort and scientific inventions, no matter how remarkable."[14] The Muslim Brotherhood, which has adherents in Kuwait and in many other Arab countries, is the most important of the movements putting forth this sort of analysis, and for the Brotherhood, therefore, the first priority is the struggle to establish a just social and political order, one that is based on a proper understanding of Islam. The Jami'at al-Islah al-Ijtimai, or Association for Social Reform, is an increasingly popular organization in Kuwait that takes a similar position.

The Muslim Brotherhood and similar groups are sometimes vague in their definition of the proper understanding of Islam, both in general and with respect to the status of women. Their leaders usually articulate a desire to return to the principles of the "model" Islamic society, which was the community established at Madina by the prophet Muhammad. To this extent, their view of Islam tends to be idealized and monolithic—the one true Muslim path is that followed in Madina, where the Quran was the living Constitution of the political community led by God's Messenger. Yet among those who take this view are many who see the prophet's community as dynamic, not stagnant, and who recognize that the true essence of Islam is revealed not by the practices of Madina alone, but by the differences between that community and pre-Islamic Arabian society. Finally, there is no coherent consensus on the proper balance between the letter and the spirit of the legal system that governed Madina, or on the meaning of that balance, whatever it may be, so far as numerous details of modern social and political organization are concerned.

This diversity and vagueness to an extent characterize judgments about the Islamic view of women, although supporters of the Muslim Brotherhood and similar groups are for the most part strongly opposed to contemporary notions of women's emancipation and hostile to the analyses of Islamic modernists who write in the tradition of Qasim Amin. The Brotherhood thus favors Islamic dress for women and opposes any contact between the sexes with the potential to lead to intimacy outside of marriage. It is also strongly opposed to the personal status codes that some Muslim countries have enacted to ban polygamy or otherwise replace Quranic laws pertaining to women with statutes that treat men and women more equitably. Furthermore, it appears that all of these views are widely held by the women, as well as by the men, who support the Brotherhood.

Perhaps most important, many who identify with groups like the Muslim Brotherhood tend to believe that women's roles should be confined to those of wife and mother, or, at the very least, that a married woman should be permitted to work outside the home only if this does not interfere with her primary obligation, which is to care for her husband and to bear and raise Muslim children.[15] These duties are required by Islam, which puts the interest of the Islamic community above the personal advancement of the woman as an individual. They also recognize the physical and emotional differences between men and women, which are, of course, divinely ordained. Thus, although they do not deem it a violation of Islam for women to join the salaried labor force, Muslim Brothers, and Muslim Sisters, usually insist that Islam prefers women to make their contributions within the home. As expressed by one leader of the Brotherhood, "A woman's mission is to be a good wife and a compassionate mother . . . [and so] an ignorant rural woman is better for the nation than one thousand female lawyers."[16]

Another powerful example of the view that a woman's rightful place is in the home is provided by the writings of Abu al-Ala al-Mawdudi (1903–1979), a contemporary Muslim theorist whose ideas are very influential among supporters of the Muslim Brotherhood and like-minded groups. Though al-Mawdudi is of Pakistani origin, his writings on Islamic questions have had an impact throughout the Muslim world. For example, he contributed to the thinking of Sayyid Qutb, who was a leading ideologue of the Muslim Brotherhood, and similarities have also been noted between his ideas and those of Hasan al-Banna (1906–1949), the founder of the Brotherhood in Egypt.[17] So far as the circumstances of women are concerned, Al-Mawdudi argues that justice for women, as well as the interest of society as a whole, requires that they be discouraged from working outside the home; since women are not fit to carry out the work of men, in part due to a lack of physical strength, it would be unfair to expect them to enter the labor force. Al-Mawdudi extends this analysis by suggesting that chaos would result if women were permitted to become soldiers. "Imagine that there are women soldiers trying to enter the battlefield; a quarter of the soldiers cannot work because of menses and one-sixth have no energy because of pregnancy, and some of them are bedridden after childbirth. Therefore, imagine what these soldiers would do in the battlefield."[18]

At the same time, at least some who support militant Islamic groups like the Muslim Brotherhood stress the rights as well as the obligations of women. Some also concede that men have neglected women's rights and have been excessive in extracting obligations, although they add that this is the result of the overall corruption and spiritual emptiness of the present-day social order.[19] Thus, the Brotherhood encourages education for women, even at the highest level. Indeed, the founder of the Brotherhood in Egypt, Hasan al-Banna, established private schools for the education of women in the 1930s. Al-Banna also favored women's participation in public life, and many within the Brotherhood today would agree that women should be politically conscious. In this connection, the battle for a just society is not seen as one in which only men are warriors.[20]

Reflecting this belief that women should be politically conscious and socially active, female supporters of the Muslim Brotherhood have formed their own organizations in a number of countries. Commonly known as the Muslim Sisters, these groups carry out activities similar to those of their male counterparts, undertaking simultaneously to deepen their appreciation and love of the religion and to advance the cause of Islam more generally. They are particularly active on university campuses, in Kuwait, Egypt, and in many other Arab and Muslim countries, and they are often heavily involved in efforts to mobilize student opinion on behalf of the Brotherhood or other Islamic movements. An important model for women's organizations of this type is the Society of Muslim Women that was formed in Egypt in the 1950s. Led by Zaynab al-Ghazzali, the society undertook charitable work in a number of areas, including the provision of assistance to the families of Muslim Brothers who had been jailed by Egyptian authorities. Al-Ghazzali and the society also carried out underground political work on behalf of the Muslim Brotherhood during the 1950s and 1960s, especially after the organization was declared illegal. As one scholar has written of Zaynab al-Ghazzali, "Her network of relations among Brotherhood sympathizers enabled the leader of the Muslim ladies to act as a link to the secret reconstruction of the organization that had been formally dissolved in 1954."[21]

These examples make it clear that many associated with the Muslim Brotherhood do not believe that Islam desires women to be ignorant or uninvolved in public life. On the contrary, Muslim Brothers and others usually argue passionately that Islam, properly understood, is a force for the advancement of women and for equality between the sexes. This view of what Islam intends is also relevant to the thinking of Muslim Brothers and Muslim Sisters about matters of personal status, most notably marriage and divorce. As noted, they are opposed to legal reforms that outlaw practices tolerated by Islam. Man cannot prohibit what God and Islam allow. Yet most nonetheless disapprove of practices like polygamy and unilateral divorce. Pointing out that these are pre-Islamic traditions that the religion seeks to regulate and restrict, and that the civil and legal rights of Arabian women were thus vastly improved by the introduction of the Muslim religion, they insist that Islam strongly discourages actions that deny equal treatment to women. While these views are not accompanied by a rejection of the belief that a woman's primary responsibilities lie within the family, or that authority in the Muslim family flows from the man to the woman, they do add up, in the minds of many, to a view of Islam that places as much emphasis on the rights as on the duties of women. Many add, moreover, that the protection of these rights is in the interest of all Muslims, men as well as women.

At the other end of the ideological spectrum, in addition to those who share the thinking of either the Liberation party or the Muslim Brotherhood, are groups and individuals who stress the decadence of neither the individual nor the society but rather of Islamic thought. Tracing their intellectual origins to early modernists, like al-Afghani and Abduh, these progressive Muslims stress the spirit rather than the letter of Muslim law. They place emphasis on reason, rather than text, and they call for new interpretations of religious codes in light of modern needs. The relevance of Islam is passionately affirmed by these men and women; problems confronting the Muslim world can best be solved by applying the teachings of the religion, and meaningful participation in this critical task is impossible without a thorough grounding in Islam. Yet progressive Muslims are clear that there can be no return to the past, to the social and political order that existed in Madina. Some even assert that it is inappropriate to speak of a single Muslim path. Though the divinely revealed wisdom of Islam is unchanging, the circumstances to which this wisdom applies vary widely over space and time and the result may be several different kinds of societies, each of which, potentially, is properly and genuinely Islamic. As expressed by the leader of a progressive Muslim group in North Africa, Islam is not a "cookie-cutter" which, when applied, always reproduces the same form.[22] Indeed, those who hold such views often add that tolerance and pluralism are important strengths of Islam and are prominent among the reasons for its rapid expansion, both in the past and at present. Finally, with reference to questions about the status of women, progressive Muslims reiterate the analysis of Qasim Amin and other modernists, to the effect that Islam, properly understood, stands for expanded opportunities for women and equality between the sexes.

All of these ideological tendencies are visible in Kuwait, although that associated with the Muslim Brotherhood and the Jami'at al-Islah al-Ijtimai is the most widespread. Moreover, women as well as men figure prominently among the supporters of various Islamic-tendency movements associated with the Islamic resurgence. Kuwaitis, particularly the young, have begun to join these groups in large numbers, and student unions and associations with an Islamic focus are now dominant at both the high school and university level, having largely eclipsed the more secular Arab nationalist movements that predominated fifteen or twenty years ago. Other signs of the Islamic resurgence are also in evidence. Mosque attendance has increased dramatically and Islamic dress for women has become much more widespread as well. The sale of magazines and audiocassettes devoted to religious themes has also grown markedly. In these and in other areas, the pattern is similar to that observed in many other Arab and Islamic countries.

THE ORIGINS OF THE ISLAMIC RESURGENCE

As in most other Muslim societies, a major factor contributing to the Islamic resurgence in Kuwait is a search for identity and familiar values in the midst of rapid social and economic change. Dislocations associated with social change are considerable in most Middle Eastern countries; but in Kuwait and in several other petroleum-exporting states, the availability of resources for accelerated development has meant that the life-styles that most individuals maintained as little as a generation ago are rapidly disappearing. Moreover, given the country's high standard of living and the high level of personal consumption enjoyed by most Kuwaitis, renewed interest in Islam may not only be a mechanism for seeking continuity in the midst of rapid change, it may also be a way to find meaning in a society where there is increasingly little concern for material needs.

Gains in education are one aspect of the rapid transformation taking place in Kuwait. Literacy rates have jumped from roughly 10 percent in 1960 to about 55 percent in 1975 and almost 83 percent in 1985, when the last census was conducted. Moreover, literacy rates have climbed rapidly for women as well as for men, reaching 76 percent among women in 1985. Transformations associated with life-style and social environment constitute another critical dimension of contemporary social change. Thousands of individuals have abandoned the bedouin life-style of the desert and the fishing and pearl-diving cultures of the coast to become residents of a sprawling urban complex. Changes in employment and economic activity are major elements of this transformation, too, and particularly important in this respect is the disappearance of economic patterns based on subsistence and barter and the elimination of traditional modes of production in fields where manufactured products are now available. Many women, especially nomadic and other traditional women, have lost their productive roles as a result of these changes. Whether viewed as positive or detrimental, the cumulative effect of these and other life-style changes is that people sometimes feel like strangers in their own society, and they are accordingly drawn to Islam in order to deal with the disorientation produced by rapid modernization.[23]

The origins of the Islamic resurgence are also to be found in the political circumstances of the Arab and Islamic world.[24] Many citizens have a vivid sense of the failure of government in the countries where they reside and support for anti-establishment Islamic groups is an important expression of the growing frustration and anger that has resulted from this crisis of leadership. Continuing Arab powerlessness vis-à-vis Israel is frequently seen as a manifestation of this crisis. Even more important are the corruption and authoritarianism that characterize the domestic behavior of so many governments in the Arab and Islamic world. Many of these governments have also shown themselves capable of considerable brutality when citizens voice complaints or speak out in favor of political reform. Finally, deteriorating living conditions in many countries, coupled with elite privilege and an increasingly unequal distribution of the burdens of underdevelopment, have fueled public outrage in many societies. Indeed, the last decade has witnessed major outbreaks of public unrest in at least seven or eight Middle Eastern countries in response to this constellation of grievances. Not all of these grievances are felt with such intensity in Kuwait, and in particular there is no popular discontent fueled by poverty or a gap between rich and poor. Nevertheless, the discontent and even rage felt in many Middle Eastern countries has spilled over into Kuwait, where to a degree it is reinforced by local complaints about the absence of movement toward a democratic political system.

This crisis of leadership has produced a loss of faith not only in particular governmental regimes but, more broadly, in the strategies of political development pursued in the 1950s and 1960s, and herein lies the connection to the Islamic resurgence that began to take form in the 1970s. Some regimes were allied with the United States and were guided in their development efforts by capitalist economic principles, whereas others allied themselves with the Soviet Union and sought progress through socialism. In almost all cases, however, the result was the same, or at least that is how it is widely perceived: international impotence and growing dependence on foreign powers concerned only with their own interests, continuing or even increasing poverty at home, the squandering of resources through corruption and elite privilege, and a rise in authoritarianism and the brutal suppression of dissent. A logical conclusion drawn by many who view their political world in these terms is that Arabs and Muslims must cease to be guided by ideologies imported from the West, for these ideologies obviously do more harm than good when applied to the conditions that exist in the Middle East. Instead, the Middle East must look to its own traditions, and especially to Islam, to find solutions to its problems. A young member of the Kuwaiti Muslim Brotherhood articulates this logic in the following terms, using language that is at present heard frequently in many Muslim societies: "We tried everything . . . pan-Arabism, Socialism, Marxism, and Ba'athism. All these ideologies have failed us. We have not tried Islam . . . why don't we follow Islam? It is the religion which unites our history and future."[25]

It is worth noting that the current Islamic resurgence challenges some established theories about modernization and development. Social scientists have often predicted a decline in religious attachments as a result of modernization, hypothesizing that urbanization, education, increased opportunities for modern employment, and similar life-style changes would lead to the adoption of new values that conflict with religious teachings. In fact, however, the opposite appears to be the case; in Kuwait and in other Arab and Muslim societies, social change and modernization have created strains and dislocations that lead to greater, not diminished, interest in Islam. The religion has become increasingly important to many men and women because it provides a sense of direction and continuity in the midst of a potentially disorienting societal transformation. Islam is also increasingly valued because it appears to offer an effective strategy for realizing the goals to which the possibility of development has led people to aspire, especially since these goals were not achieved when pursued through development efforts based on "foreign" ideologies. Although not all or even a majority of the Middle East's Muslim citizens identify with militant Islamic groups, the intensity, scope, and persistence of the Islamic resurgence suggest that theories of modernization that posit a decline in the influence of religion are clearly in need of modification. Islamic values and institutions appear fully capable of accommodating themselves to the conditions of modern life. Indeed, the case of Kuwait, as well as that of other Arab and Islamic societies, indicates that social change can not only coexist with, but may actually strengthen, traditional religious values.

WOMEN'S ATTITUDES TOWARD ISLAM

It is against this background that a survey of Kuwaiti women was conducted in 1984. With important and long-standing differences of opinion about the proper interpretation of Muslim codes pertaining to women, and with a religious resurgence challenging established Islamic interpretations and practices and impinging upon debates about the place of women in Muslim society, empirical research was conducted with a view toward charting the nature and distribution of Kuwaiti women's attitudes on salient issues. In the present analysis, attention will be focused on degrees of religiosity and the strength of Islamic attachments. It will also be focused on levels of support for women's emancipation, including expanded opportunities for women and equality and contact between the sexes. The methodology of the survey need not be discussed here since a detailed account is readily available.[26] It is necessary only to report that interviews were conducted with a random and largely representative sample of 553 women above the age of 17, that the survey instrument was administered by trained interviewers, and that tests of measurement validity and reliability were employed to establish the appropriateness of survey items included in the analysis.

Indicative of degrees of religiosity and the strength of Islamic attachments are responses to the following four questions. The percentage of women answering in a manner indicative of higher, as opposed to lower, levels of religiosity is given in parentheses.

1. Do you pray regularly? (yes: 84%)
2. Do you refer to religious teachings when making important decisions concerning your life? (always: 51%)
3. Do you approve of raising Kuwaiti children according to the teachings of Islam? (yes: 93%)
4. Do you approve of the Islamic resurgence taking place in contemporary society? (yes: 68%)

The data show that attachments to Islam are strong and widespread among Kuwaiti women. Eighty-four percent of the respondents report praying regularly and a majority, 51 percent, state that they always refer to religious teachings when making important decisions concerning their lives. In the latter connection, moreover, whereas it might appear that nearly half of the respondents consider Islam irrelevant for their personal lives, 42 percent refer to religious teaching at least sometimes. Only 7 percent say they rarely or never consider Islam when making important decisions.

The data also show that most respondents welcome the influence of Islam beyond their personal circumstances, throughout the society as a whole. In other words, they embrace the view that Islamic laws and values are intended as guides not just for individual Muslims, but for the political communities of which these individuals are a part. Thus, 93 percent of those interviewed believe that Kuwaiti children should be raised in accordance with the teachings of Islam. Furthermore, there is support for the political as well as the religious dimension of Islam's role in society, including support for the current Islamic resurgence. Even though most respondents are not directly involved in any of the Muslim groups that have emerged or grown stronger as a result of this resurgence, a substantial majority, 68 percent, look with favor on the religious revival taking place in Kuwait and in other Arab and Islamic countries. Moreover, only 18 percent declare themselves opposed to the resurgence of Islam, with the remainder stating that they are uncertain. These findings reflect and give greater specificity to the general conclusion presented earlier: historically and at the present time more than ever, Kuwait strongly identifies with Islam at both the popular and societal level.

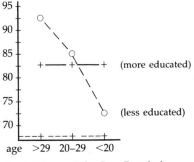

Fig. 1. Women Who Pray Regularly

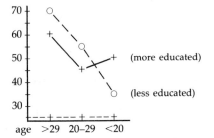

Fig. 2. Women Who Refer to Religion When Making Important Decisions

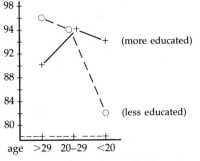

Fig. 3. Women Who Raise Children According to the Teachings of Islam

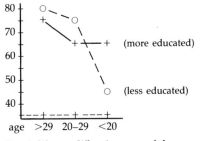

Fig. 4. Women Who Approve of the Islamic Resurgence

As shown in figures 1–4, there are attitudinal differences associated with age and education among Kuwaiti women. Respondents are divided into three groups based on age: older than 29, between 29 and 20, and less than 20 years of age. They are also categorized as either more or less well educated, depending on whether they have completed high school. Finally, the variables of age and education are considered in combination, with the mean response to each of the survey items given for each combination of age and education. Thus, in figure 1, for example, it can be seen that among less well-educated respondents older than 29, 93 percent of the respondents say they pray regularly. Among better-educated respondents in this age bracket, the figure is about 83 percent, and so on.

The pattern in all four figures is strikingly similar. In each case, high levels of religiosity and a strong attachment to Islam are most widespread among older and poorly educated respondents, and least widespread among younger and poorly educated respondents. Thus, there are substantial attitudinal differences associated with age among women who are at least relatively poorly educated. By contrast, attitudinal differences between older and younger respondents are not very great among women who have completed high school or had university training.

It is not surprising that religiosity is high among those who are older and less well educated. These women are drawn from the more traditional and conservative sectors of society, where Islamic attachments have historically been strong. What is surprising, however, are the lower levels of religiosity found among many younger women with comparatively little education. Few of these women are totally opposed to Islamic influences, of course. For example, 73 percent pray regularly, and 82 percent believe that Kuwaiti children should be raised according to the principles of Islam. Nevertheless, these levels are noticeably lower than those of women in all other respondent categories based on age and education, and only 36 percent of these women consistently refer to religious teachings when making important decisions.

At least part of the explanation for this pattern is probably that younger and less well-educated women see themselves as disadvantaged and marginalized in a society where educational and other development-related gains are being made rapidly and, for this reason, they identify less strongly with the value system that predominates in that society. It might be argued that poorly educated older women are marginalized as well, but in fact, women in the latter category are for the most part married and established in their personal lives. Moreover, they reached adulthood at a time when secondary and higher education for women was much less common, placing them within the mainstream of their demographic cohort. Thus it is the younger and poorly educated women who have the most serious doubts about their future and who are most likely to be alienated from the social mainstream. If this explanation is correct, it suggests an important conclusion about the relationship between modernization and cultural change: just as social and political alienation in a modernizing society can lead to a rejection of the "foreign" ideologies championed by national leaders, it can also reduce support for "indigenous" values and institutions when these are seen as the normative orientation of the dominant political class. This important proposition, for which the evidence presented here is admittedly limited, deserves to be the subject of additional research.

The most important findings from figures 1–4 are probably that religiosity levels and attachments to Islam are relatively high among well-educated women and, furthermore, that there are no significant attitudinal differences associated with age among women with a high school or university education. On the one hand, this is consistent with the general critique of modernization theory offered earlier; contrary to what some prominent theorists have asserted, education and social mobilization do not necessarily lead to diminished religiosity or the rejection of traditional values in other areas. On the other, so far as Kuwait is concerned, it appears highly likely that Islam will retain its central place in national life for the foreseeable future. An identification with religious values is not being eroded by the important educational advances taking place in Kuwait, and the views of well-educated young women who are only now reaching adulthood suggest that this will remain the case for at least another generation. Thus, to the extent that well-educated women become more numerous and play an important role in defining and transmitting Kuwaiti culture, the country's identification with Islam is unlikely to diminish and will perhaps grow even stronger.

ATTITUDES ABOUT THE STATUS OF WOMEN

The survey also focused on levels of support for women's emancipation, including expanded opportunities for women and greater equality and contact between the sexes. Indicative of attitudes toward these issues are responses to the following nine questions. The percentage of women answering each item in a manner indicative of higher, as opposed to lower, levels of support for equality between the sexes is given in parentheses.

1. Should a woman be required to cease working after marriage in order to devote full time to her family? (no: 47%)
2. Should opportunities to work in commercial, industrial, and specialized technical positions be available to women? (yes: 46%)
3. Should there be equality between men and women in jobs, wages, and promotions? (yes: 63%)
4. Do you approve of men and women working together in the same job setting? (yes: 57%)
5. Do you approve of coeducation in high schools and universities? (yes: 47%)

6. Should women have the right to vote in elections for the National Assembly? (yes: 48%)
7. Should laws be passed that punish men who take more than one wife or that give women the right of separation in such cases (yes: 59%)
8. Do you believe it is mandatory to wear the veil? (no: 26%)
9. Do you believe that women should have the same rights as men with respect to divorce? (yes: 39%)

In contrast to levels of religiosity and attachments to Islam, issues having to do with the status and roles of women are the subject of considerable disagreement. On many of the items examined, the women surveyed are approximately equally divided between those who favor and those who oppose greater opportunities for women and greater equality and contact between the sexes. Furthermore, on almost all of the remaining items, only about 60 percent of those interviewed hold the same view, meaning that in each case the dissenting position has considerable support as well. Finally, within these limits, there are some items on which a majority favors equality for women and other items on which a majority is opposed to women's emancipation. All of this suggests that debates and disagreements are likely to continue with respect to the position of women in society, and with respect to the meaning and proper interpretation of Islamic codes pertaining to women in particular.

These conclusions apply both to issues about which there are specific Muslim legal codes and to patterns of behavior governed by religious and other traditions of a more general nature. The former include questions about marriage and divorce, and it is particularly notable in this respect that 59 percent of those surveyed favor laws that would nullify Islam's explicit tolerance of polygamy. With respect to divorce, where Muslim legal codes again give superior rights to men, 39 percent call for equality despite Quranic edicts to the contrary. The latter include questions about married women working outside the home and about expanded professional opportunities for women. Although there has long existed a strong predisposition against equality for women in these areas, established practice is not mandated by specific Islamic statutes that deny to women the rights granted to men. Thus, whether specifically governed by Islam or not, issues having to do with the behavior of women are seriously divisive, not only between men and women, but among women themselves.

TABLE 1

Attitudes about the Status of Women by Levels of Religiosity

	All respondents ($N = 551$)	More religious respondents ($N = 281$)	Less religious respondents ($N = 270$)
Women not required to cease working after marriage to devote full time to the family	47	46	49
Acceptable for women to work in commercial, industrial, and specialized technical positions	46	36	55
Favor equality between men and women in jobs, wages, and promotions	63	58	67
Acceptable for men and women to work together	57	47	65
Approve of co-education in high schools and universities	47	40	55
Women should be able to vote	48	41	55
Favor laws against polygamy	59	51	67
Veil not mandatory for women	26	17	35
Women should have same rights as men in the area of divorce	39	33	44

The survey data may be analyzed to examine further the relationship between attitudes toward the status of women on the one hand and Islamic influences on the other. This is of interest for two reasons. First, it will provide information about the degree to which levels of religiosity and Islamic attachments at the individual level help to shape specific attitudes about the circumstances and behavior of women. Second, it will suggest whether and how any intensification or waning of the Islamic resurgence is likely to modify the aggregate distribution of views about the status of women. Toward this end, Table 1 contrasts the responses of more and less religious respondents to each of the nine survey items just presented. More religious respondents are those who report that they always refer to Islamic teachings when making important decisions, whereas those who refer to such teachings less frequently are classified as less religious. This item was selected as an indicator of religiosity because statistical analysis showed it to be very highly correlated with an index based on all of the survey items measuring strength of attachments to Islam.

Table 1 shows that there are some attitudinal differences between more religious and less religious Kuwaiti women. Moreover, these differences are in the same direction on all items. Less religious respondents are consistently more likely than more religious respondents to favor greater opportunities for women and greater equality and contact between the sexes. For example, while only 36 percent of the more religious women surveyed consider it acceptable for women to work in commercial, industrial, and specialized technical professions, fields women have traditionally been discouraged from entering, 55 percent of the less religious respondents deem it acceptable for women to hold jobs in these areas. Similarly, while only 51 percent of the more religious women interviewed favor the enactment of laws against polygamy, such laws are favored by 67 percent of those who are less religious. These findings suggest that the level of personal religiosity and strength of attachment to Islam is related to views about the status of women and, more specifically, that greater religiosity is associated with, and is presumably a factor that contributes to, opposition to women's emancipation in contemporary Kuwait.

On the other hand, the magnitude of differences between more and less religious women are for the most part quite limited, suggesting that this relationship is a weak one at best. In both categories, the proportion of respondents favoring women's emancipation is never more than 10 percent above or below that of all respondents, and in many cases it is considerably less. For example, although Islamic law is quite clear in giving superior rights to men in the area of divorce, more and less religious respondents do not have very different opinions on the subject. Thirty-nine percent of all respondents favor equal rights for women in this area, and among more religious women this figure only drops to 33 percent, and among less religious women it only rises to 44 percent, making the attitudinal differences between the two groups much smaller than might have been expected. The important conclusion to be drawn is that, among women in Kuwait, personal religiosity and level of attachment to Islam is no more than a secondary factor in shaping attitudes about the status of women. At the level of the society as a whole, Muslim influences are undeniably critical: Islam plays a leading role in shaping the cultural context within which attitudes and opinions are formed, and it is the foundation of the normative framework that organizes most debates about important social issues, including issues concerned with the status of women. But what is true at the societal level apparently does not hold at the individual level of analysis. Strength of Islamic attachment at the individual level is only weakly associated with attitudes about the roles and behavior patterns appropriate for women.

Given the clear overall differences of opinion on questions about the status of women and the fact that these differences are only weakly correlated with levels of personal religiosity, it follows that there is significant attitudinal variation within each respondent category based on religiosity. Both more religious respondents and less religious respondents, like the sample as a whole, are characterized by important attitudinal differences about the circumstances of women. Furthermore, this also means that there is considerable support for women's emancipation among more religious respondents and considerable opposition to women's emancipation among less religious respondents. In the former category, for example, among women who say that they always refer to religious teachings when making important decisions, 46 percent do not believe married women should be required to cease working in order to devote full time to their families, 47 percent see nothing wrong with men and women working together, and 51 percent favor the enactment of laws against polygamy. Similarly, among less religious women, those who report that they do not always refer to the teachings of Islam when making important decisions, 56 percent do not believe that men and women should have equal rights in the area of divorce, 51 percent believe that women should be required to cease working after marriage, and 45 percent oppose both coeducation and voting rights for women.

These and other responses indicate that neither more religious women nor less religious women constitute a homogeneous demographic category and, accordingly, that a woman's level of religiosity is not necessarily indicative of her attitude on issues pertaining to women's status. A high level of personal religiosity and a strong attachment to Islam are not necessarily associated with a conservative interpretation of Muslim codes or with other traditions pertaining to women, just as a lower level of personal religiosity and a weaker attachment to Islam are not necessarily associated with a progressive interpretation of these codes and traditions. These findings offer important empirical evidence that the impact of Islam on the status of women is not monolithic and depends, ultimately, on the way that Muslims choose to interpret and apply their religion and associated cultural norms. Opposition to women's emancipation is no more inherently Islamic than is support for women's emancipation, and to only a limited degree do individuals who are more religious identify with the former orientation more frequently than those who are less religious.

Finally, so far as Kuwait is concerned, all of this reinforces the earlier conclusion that questions about the status of women are likely to remain both salient and divisive for the foreseeable future. With development gains and increasing education among women, it seems inevitable that concern about the circumstances and behavior of women will remain intense, and perhaps even increase. Yet, even among women themselves, there is no consensus on any of the pertinent issues examined, issues whose preoccupations include economic life, marriage and divorce, political participation, and contact between the sexes. Furthermore, since attitudes toward these issues are only weakly related to religiosity, it is unlikely that either an intensification or a waning of the current Islamic resurgence will change this situation very much. For the foreseeable future, as in the past, some will claim that Islamic codes require denying women at least some of the rights and opportunities enjoyed by men, whereas others will argue with equal conviction that the emancipation of women is encouraged by Islam and that fidelity to the religion therefore demands an end to laws and practices that discriminate in favor of men.

15

Shi'i Islam: Bonyadgiri or Fundamentalism?
Gregory F. Rose

The concept of "fundamentalism" has gained currency in analysis of the resurgence of Islam, occasioned by the Islamic Revolution in Iran and increasing, explicitly Islamic, political activism throughout the Muslim world. It is not clear how this category has much advanced our understanding of these political processes and, indeed, there is much evidence that it has led to systematic misinterpretation of these events and their causes. This chapter will lay out a critique of the concept of "fundamentalism" as it is applied to Shi'i Islam and present an alternative explanation for the Islamic resurgence in Iran, based on collective action theory. Finally, it will apply this alternative framework to the cases of Islamic attitudes toward economic modernization and contemporary Iranian political development.

PARSONS AND THE CONCEPT OF FUNDAMENTALISM

The basic problem with the concept of fundamentalism is that it is an ethnocentric, militantly secularist sociological categorization based on specious cross-cultural analogies. The problem is not one of semantics, but of a misconceptualization that makes meaningful analysis of Islamic resurgence difficult, if not impossible. While the notion of fundamentalism first gained currency in discussions of nineteenth-century American religious movements, it was Talcott Parsons's study of the "fundamentalist reaction" (1942a, 1942b, 1947)—an attempt to explain the rise of European Fascist movements—which has come to color use of the term, particularly when it was extended to the sociology of religion. For Parsons, the fundamentalist reaction—what he regarded as the core motivation in adherence to fascism—was a pathological, authoritarian reconstruction of an idealized social *status quo ante* in response to increasingly high levels of dysfunction in the existing social *status quo*. Purely a deviant, retrograde consequence of the failure to discover strategies for integrating the *status quo* and eliminating dysfunction, fundamentalism was seen as either pathological—as when it achieved state power—or residual/marginal, as when it is observed on the fringes of social and political life in the Western democracies.

The leap from Nazism to religious belief systems seems, retrospectively, breathtaking. However, it rests on the assumption that religious belief structures serve the same pathological dysfunction as fascism for those who are unable to resolve general social dysfunction. While this is surely an assumption of a militantly secularist framework, it seems inappropriate to bias the theoretical and empirical questions involved in analyzing the role of a non-Western religion (Islam) in a non-Western cultural milieu (the Middle East) with a theoretical proposition that rests on an undemonstrated analogy to a particularly gruesome episode in European political culture. However, the influence of this Parsonian schema is evident in terms of modernization and development theory's attitude toward role of religion as residual/marginal.[1]

The problem in Parsons's framework rests on what Rolf Dahrendorf (1958), C. Wright Mills (1959), Lewis Coser (1956), and David Lockwood (1950) have identified as functionalism's normative commitment to a particular notion of stability and social integration— Parsons's "first law of social inertia." In such a framework, all challenges to the *status quo* are deviant, regardless of their source. The problem with the modernization and development theory treatment of religion as residual/marginal is, first, its uncritical acceptance of Parsonian functionalism and its assumptions and, second, its related insistence that the Western model of economic and political development—albeit with greater social disruption—would be replicated in non-Western settings.[2]

IS THE RESURGENCE OF SHI'I ISLAM "FUNDAMENTALIST"

In asking this question, three questions are being posed:

1. Is this resurgence a reaction to social dysfunction?
2. Is this resurgence a result of the failure to develop strategies to eliminate dysfunction?
3. Is this resurgence "pathological"?

The answer to the first question is almost certainly yes. First, a considerable literature has emerged that locates the origin of much of the late Pahlavi period's social dysfunction to the role of Western and Eastern imperialism in encouraging what Homa Katouzian (1981) has termed "petrolic despotism." While petrolic despotism is the particular form that political-economic dysfunction has historically taken in Iran, it is related to the socioeconomic dysfunctions associated with other authoritarian-monarchical systems, as well as those common to capitalist development in general. Second, examination of the rhetoric of the revolution reveals explicitly, recognition by the revolutionary movement and its adumbrations of the extent of social dysfunction in Iranian society (Khomeini, 1981; Ahl-e Ahmad, 1983).

The second question must be answered in the negative. If one concedes that much of the social dysfunction of the late Pahlavi period arose from the interface between the Iranian political-economy and the international political-economy (particularly Western imperialism), then it is difficult to see how advocacy of a strategy of Islamic cultural, political, and economic authenticity—in contradistinction to the perceived "foreign" sources of dysfunction—is a failure to develop strategies to eliminate dysfunction. This is particularly so when this strategy is seen in terms of the efficiencies it introduces to political and economic mobilization, as we shall see when dealing with this question from a collective action viewpoint. Such a strategy may not be much to the liking of those who believe that social dysfunction can only be eliminated by pursuing strategies modeled on the experience of the Western liberal democracies, but that merely highlights the ethnocentricity of the fundamentalist category.

The question of this resurgence's "pathology" is directly related to the second question. If it is not an example of a failure to develop strategies for eliminating social dysfunction, then it is clearly not pathological in Parsons's terms. However, demonstration of this requires elaboration of an explanatory framework, which elucidates the potential of such a strategy for success.

AN ALTERNATIVE FRAMEWORK: COLLECTIVE ACTION THEORY

The starting point for an alternative perspective is the realization that correction of the macroeconomic and macropolitical inefficiencies, which result in crises of economic distribution and political legitimacy—precisely the form that social-political-economic dysfunction took in prerevolutionary Iran—requires collective action. Thus, the strategies for resolving dysfunction must be collective action strategies. However, before evaluating the Islamic revolutionary alternative as such a strategy, we should review the theoretical insights that underlie collective action theory generally.

Mancur Olson outlined the basis for collective action theory in terms of resolving the problem of free ridership. Assuming the rationality of political actors (i.e., that they are able to discern open alternatives and are capable of rank-ordering alternative courses of action in terms of maximizing some preferred utility) and their egoism (i.e., that they most prefer that utility that most realizes their self-interest), and that the good under consideration is a collective good (i.e., exhibits the properties of nonexcludability and jointness of supply), then the problem arises that "unless there is coercion or some other special device to make individuals act in their common interest, rational, self-interested individuals will not act to achieve their common or group interest." [1971:5]. That is, rational, self-interested actors will not contribute to obtaining a collective good if the collective action of others produces that good from which they cannot be excluded, despite their non-contribution. Olson argues that obviation of this free-ridership problem can be accomplished either by coercion or the provision of excludable, private goods as a "by-product" of provision of the collective good.

Samuel Popkin, in his masterful study of revolutionary mobilization in Vietnam, extended Olson's analysis to include additional conditions under which free ridership can be obviated:

> Contributions can occur (1) because persons contribute for reasons of ethics, conscience, or altruism; (2) because it pays to contribute on a pure cost-benefit basis; (3) because of selective incentives (excludable benefits), which can be either positive or negative; or (4) because it pays to contribute, given that the contributions of others are contingent on one's own contribution [1979:254].

Most useful to our discussion are Popkin's identifications of the effects of culture on the formation of an actor's utility function (e.g., ethics, conscience, and altruism as potential values over which self-interested maximization can occur); the role of positive and negative special incentives; and the role of Bayesian calculations over the probability that the collective goodwill be obtained absent the actor's contribution.

Norman Frölich, Joe Oppenheimer, and Oran Young have made the further contribution of identifying the crucial role of political entrepreneurship in the provision of collective goods. They define a political entrepreneur as "any individual who acts to supply a collective good without providing all of the resources himself" [1971:6] and argue that such an entrepreneur's ability to collect resources in excess of his costs leads to his assumption of this role. The existence of widespread political entrepreneurship establishes institutional structures that reduce the transaction costs associated with the provision of collective goods.

Thus, collective action theory provides a set of decision rules for evaluating the efficacy and rationality of strategies aimed at resolving social dysfunction through collective action. Briefly, effective and rational strategies will

1. provide selective, excludable positive and negative benefits;
2. take advantage of cultural predispositions exhibited in actors' utility functions that facilitate collective action;
3. employ networks of political entrepreneurship to reduce the transaction costs associated with providing collective goods.

BONYADGIRI: SHI'I ISLAM AND COLLECTIVE ACTION

The term most often used by Islamic activists in Iran to characterize their enterprise is *bonyadgiri*. It literally means "seizing the foundations." The semantic field within which it operates, however, is quite broad. Essentially, it refers to a strategy for eliminating social-political-economic dysfunction occasioned by the interface of the political-economy of the Muslim world with Western and Eastern imperialism by employing the ideology and institutional structures of Islam as a means of engendering independence, cultural authenticity, and social welfare. Such objectives are, surely, collective goods and it is for this reason that a collective action theory framework seems apt for evaluation of the strategy underlying Islamic resurgence.

Shi'i Islam is an exquisite engine for producing collective action outcomes. The institution of *marja'iyaat* is an excellent case in point. This institution grew out of the obligation that any Shi'i believer who is not himself an expert in Islamic jurisprudence, emulate in religious practice someone who is such an expert. In addition to establishing normatively sanctioned patterns of behavior, this institution has facilitated the emergence of a popularly based religious leadership (one becomes an Ayatollah or Hojjatolislam by accumulating emulators) which is funded by the obligatory charitable contributions (*sadaqat* and *khums*) of emulator-followers (*moqallidin*). Thus, the existence of the institution of *marja'iyyat* has led to the emergence of a class of political entrepreneurs—the senior religious leadership—who are able to facilitate collective action outcomes through institutionalization of their political and financial resources.

Marja'iyyat is, however, by no means the only contributor to the efficient realization of collective goods in Shi'i Islam. Equally important is the cultural milieu shaped by Islam that imposes an ethical system in which the provision of collective goods, particularly those associated with justice, economic egalitarianism, and the like, is encouraged. The Islamic cultural milieu contributes directly to the formation of actors' utility functions by conditioning those actors to specific notions of self-interest that posit a direct connection between self-interest and collective-interest. In Islamic society the individual's sense of identity is lodged in the *ommat*—the "believing community"—and it is from his membership in this community that the Muslim actor derives the notion of self that underlies his conception of self-interest. It is in this context that what appears to be absolute self-abnegation, for example, martyrdom, can become absolute self-interest. An additional consequence of this cultural milieu is to increasingly homogenize the utility functions of actors.

The provision of selective, excludable benefits, both positive and negative, also characterizes *bonyadgiri*. These benefits include, ultimately, salvation, for participation in the struggle to realize an Islamic social-economic-political order is intimately, doctrinally tied to personal salvation and the Islamic revolutionary movement attempted to make this connection as direct as possible in the public's perception. Among the other positive, excludable benefits were the provision of foodstuffs and money to the unemployed in Iran's urban centers as the Iranian economy contracted from 1975 onward. These benefits were accompanied by political education and served not merely as selective benefits encouraging mobilization for collective action, but called into question the ability of the government to deliver such private goods in the absence of a social insurance system and, thus, degraded the government's efficacy in the eyes of many while elevating their perception of the Islamic movement's efficacy. Nor were these benefits exclusively positive. In a cultural milieu wherein "encouraging the good and forbidding the reprehensible" is a normatively sanctioned activity, the negative benefits—participate or you will be shunned by the community, for example—powerfully reinforced the positive benefits.

Thus, in light of the failure of secular, nationalist ideologies, and institutions to provide mechanisms for facilitating collective action and for obtaining collective goods outcomes consistent with the preferences of the majority of individual participants, it should not be surprising that Shi'i Islam is so appealing as a vehicle for social, political, and economic change. Indeed, by the criteria of collective action theory, the resurgence of Shi'i Islam is neither a failed strategy nor pathological, but the most efficient means of obviating the collective action problems that impede the elimination of social dysfunction.

ISLAM AND MODERNIZATION

As Ziauddin Sardar perceptively suggests,

"Development is far from being a simple, anodyne, economic process of raising living standards or increasing the rate of growth. As currently understood it is a cultural process which inevitably leads to occidentalization." [1977:39].

It is precisely athwart the path to occidentalization that *bonyadgiri* stands. In its rejection of non-Islamic cultural, social, political, and economic values, it is absolute. However, this is not to say that it opposes economic modernization, rather that it seeks to focus modernization along paths compatible with Islamic values and to avoid those social, political, and economic consequences of economic modernization that intrude most painfully on Islamic notions of justice.

The Constitution of the Islamic Republic of Iran places economic modernization among its chief objectives and, while the costs of the war with Iraq have impeded pursuit of this objective, considerable strides, particularly in the area of industrialization, have taken place. As a recent study of the Iranian economy suggests, industrial policy in the Islamic Republic is geared toward economic modernization while seeking to ameliorate the relations of dependency, that industrialization has traditionally implied for Iran.

Their efforts have, therefore, been concentrated on

- Importing technology and reducing the technological dependency on industrialized nations.

  To achieve this aim, self-sufficiency study groups have been formed to study and research in the methods of manufacturing the parts and basic materials required by the Iranian industries.

  Moreover, manufacturing technology has been imported along with importing the required machinery. The industrial policy making bodies have been conditioning conclusion of contracts with foreign companies to importation of technology as much as possible. . . .

- Drawing up a plan to suit the present circumstances and the pertinent problems. This plan has given priority to establishment of industrial plants creating larger numbers of jobs, producing for export, manufacturing the machinery required by industry, and independence from foreign basic materials [*Iran Yearbook 88*, 1988:404–405].

At the same time, increasing government regulation aimed at ensuring observance of Islamic standards in labor relations, income distribution, and social welfare has been enacted. Similar policies are being pursued with respect to the mechanization of agriculture and rationalization of the distribution of goods.

Indeed, the relative success of the Islamic Republic in economic modernization serves as a counterexample to the predictions arising from a fundamentalist framework. These successes are, however, entirely comprehensible as the outcome of a successful mobilization system that is increasingly being turned from revolutionary mobilization to economic modernization. The efficiencies that Shi'i Islam introduces to the realization of collective goods—and economic modernization consists of both collective and private goods—lie at the basis of the effective mobilization of Iran not merely for revolution, but for development, both fundamentally Islamic in character.

The Islamic Republic adduces other difficulties for secularly minded theorizing about the impact of economic modernization on political development. James Coleman, one of the most adept and insightful of the modernization theorists, has derived the notion of political development from Parsons's category of an "evolutionary universal" and defined it as

> . . . an integrative, responsive, adaptive, and innovative capacity. It is a capacity not only to overcome the divisions and tensions created by increased differentiation, but to respond to or contain the participatory and distributive demands generated by the imperatives of equality. It is also a capacity to innovate and to manage continuous change [1971:78–79].[3]

Following Weiner's quite broad definition of political participation—

> . . . any voluntary action, successful or unsuccessful, organized or unorganized, episodic or continuous, employing legitimate or illegitimate methods intended to influence the choice of public policies, the administration of public affairs, or the choice of political leaders at any level of government, local or national [1971:164]

—it is difficult to conclude that the Islamic Republic is anything but a relatively highly politically developed system. This certainly runs contrary to the expectations engendered by the fundamentalism category and by the attitude of modernization toward religion. However, the empirical evidence is considerable.

The level of political participation in revolutionary regimes is almost always quite high as such regimes achieve state power (a consequence, no doubt, of the need for high levels of political mobilization to successfully seize the state apparatus). However, there is ample evidence that, in the absence of a concerted effort at building institutions for popular interest articulation and participation, such initially high levels of participation do not routinely persist. It is precisely the case in the Islamic Republic that the collective action efficiencies afforded by Shi'i Islam have abetted the regime's effort to build such institutions. The proliferation of Islamic committees and associations at every level of Iranian political life and the seriousness with which both executive and parliamentary political actors respond to these popular interest articulation institutions argue powerfully for regarding the degree of political participation in the Islamic Republic as rather high. While to speak of Western-style democracy in these cases is misleading at best, they represent culturally authentic vehicles of popular participation. Furthermore, suggestions that the proliferation of such institutions is strictly a means of imposing control by the central state apparatus are belied not merely by the extent to which modifications in public policy have arisen as a result of the intervention of these institutions (this has been particularly true in matters of economic distribution), but also in the ability of electoral participants in these institutions to defeat a majority of incumbent *majlis* (parliament) deputies in the 1988 parliamentary elections. A careful reading of official debates in the *majlis* cannot escape the conclusion that both the executive and legislative branches of the Iranian government are rigorously attentive to the interests articulated through these Islamic institutions. All of this argues mightily for the Islamic Republican polity possessing "a capacity not only to overcome the divisions and tensions created by increased differentiation, but to respond to or contain the participatory and distributive demands generated by the imperatives of equality," as Coleman suggests that developed polities do.

Thus, one is led almost inescapably to the conclusion that Shi'i Islam is not the impediment to modernization that the category of fundamentalism would suggest, but is rather a facilitator of modernization and development as a direct result of the efficiency that Shi'ism imparts to the resolution of the problem of collective action.

16

Religious Resurgence and Political Mobilization of the Shi'a in Lebanon

Augustus Richard Norton

The Shi'a of Lebanon have emerged as major political actors on the Lebanese scene against a background of social exclusion and economic deprivation. Well into the twentieth century the Shi'a were only bit players in Lebanon. They were unnoticed by their countrymen, given scant or no attention by scholars, and presumed insignificant by Lebanese politicians. Socialized into a religious tradition that extolled sacrifice and presumed temporal injustice, the Shi'a found ready confirmation for their beliefs in their mundane surroundings. Lebanon's confessional political equation—in which privilege, office, and political rights were allocated according to sect—operated to the disadvantage of the Shi'a, and increasingly so as the population share of the Shi'a grew disproportionately to the country's other major sects. In a political system in which Maronite and Sunni politicians called many of the shots, the Shi'a were trapped by their sectarian identity.

Although they lagged behind their non-Shi'i countrymen, the Shi'a were still very much affected by the rapid modernization that had marked Lebanon since independence in 1943. Access to education produced a growing pool of individuals who were no longer content to confine their horizons to subsistence farming. Improved transportation eroded the geographic isolation of the community. A rapidly growing communications network, both within and without Lebanon, brought the outside world—with its political ideologies and its "modern" ideas and technologies—into even the most remote village.[1]

Modernization of the agricultural sector, including an increasing emphasis on cash crops and farm mechanization, led to underemployment and unemployment. Many of the Shi'a were forced to move off the land in order to survive. As the modernization process began to have its effects, and as the Shi'a gained an exposure to horizons wider than the village, they became more aware of the disparities that distinguished them from their relatively affluent countrymen. Fleeing the poverty of the village and the drudgery of farm labor, many Shi'a took work where they could find it in Beirut, usually as petty laborers or peddlers. The resultant migration led to the swelling of the Lebanese capital by the 1960s. The Shi'a made their homes in the squalid suburbs; while some actually escaped from poverty, most remained dreadfully poor. Not surprisingly, these migrants from the country became a fertile pool for recruitment by radical parties who claimed to have answers.

More important, the dearth of economic opportunities within Lebanon was an important factor that prompted the movement of many Shi'i men overseas, where the rich opportunities of the Gulf, and especially West Africa, provided a clear means with which to break the bonds of poverty. Some made their fortunes and thereby gained the wherewithal to support political movements in their image. Indeed, the fruits of West African labors are readily observable in southern towns (e.g., Jwayya and Shaqrah) where impressive homes stand as testaments to the money that has been earned in Abidjan and in other African locales. Later, the money earned by these Shi'i migrants would play a crucial role in financing the growth of Shi'i political activism within Lebanon.

Though the Shi'a as a whole are still relatively impoverished, many Shi'a have done quite well as merchants, as building contractors, and as professionals. Yet, even among the affluent, there is an ethos of deprivation—a lingering memory imparted by a lifetime of accumulated grievances and slights.

As the Shi'a began to break the bindings of underdevelopment, their needs became more complex and numerous, and the traditional "political bosses" (zu'ama') who had dominated the sect's politics for so long, grew increasingly irrelevant. Moreover, there was little incentive for the zu'ama' to meet the demands of their formerly pliant clients, for doing so would further loosen their grip. Clientelism, though, is a socially sanctioned institution in Lebanon, and the decline of one set of patrons only opened the field for aspiring zu'ama' to take their places. Thus, it should not be surprising that the tumultuous recent history of Lebanon has produced a new class of *zu'ama'*—men who have made their way in the rough and tumble of internal warfare, but whose stock-in-trade is still a timely loan, or a good word.[2]

In addition, the 1950s—and especially the 1960s and 1970s— saw a growth in alternative social, political, and economic organization. Government-chartered family associations organized for business purposes, grew at a disproportionately high rate among the Shi'a.[3] The 'Amiliyah Islamic Benevolent Society, mimicking the Maqasid Benevolent Society of the Sunni Muslims, sponsored schools in the Beirut area.[4] Previously grossly underrepresented in the bureaucracy, the Shi'a began to receive a larger share of senior civil service appointments as the Lebanese government began to respond to their demands during the tenure of President Fuad Chehab (1958–1964).

THE STAGES OF POLITICAL MOBILIZATION

Religion is an ascriptive fact in Lebanon. The Lebanese is born into a religion, which conditions his cultural realm and that decisively defines his social and political identity. Thus, religion as a label is an inescapable fact, both because of Lebanon's natural history and her political system that only takes account of citizens as members of one or another religion (the term *confession* is actually used). However, to be born a Lebanese-Shi'i or a Lebanese-Maronite or a Lebanese-Druze, obviously does not signify a genetically defined predisposition to paroxysms of religiosity. This is important to remember, because too often the confessional label of a Lebanese is taken to signify too much. In the case of the Shi'a, the Shi'i label is only an accident of birth and it may tell us very little about the political directions that a person will follow.

Despite empirical evidence to the contrary, some scholars have been tempted to give the recent history of the Lebanese Shi'a a deterministic slant, to describe Shi'i activism and anger as an inevitable by-product of an anti-establishment religious tradition.[5] Others have simplified this history, so as to treat the Shi'a as an undifferentiated whole, a community of crazed flagellants intent on martyrdom. These perspectives deny individuality to the Shi'i and ignore the diversity of motives and perspectives that have defined the political mobilization of the Shi'a.

The Shi'i resurgence in Lebanon has not been a simple reflection of Shi'ism's supposed rejection of secular authority. It is not generally true that the Shi'a have rejected all temporal authority as illegitimate, though some Shi'a have interpreted their dogma in this way.[6] History is replete with examples of accommodation, and most Lebanese Shi'a do not reject the legitimacy of all temporal states, though they find the Lebanese state, as it has functioned, illegitimate.

It is also a gross oversimplification to explain their activism as a reflection of Iranian moves, or Israeli missteps, though the actions of Iran and Israel have had significant consequences to be sure. As we have seen already, the Shi'a did not magically appear on the scene. Indeed, it is possible to identify a series of steps in the still unfolding story of the political mobilization of the Shi'a of Lebanon. It is a longer and more complex history than many presume.

In fact, like most political events, this saga is a complex one that played out in stages. Only in the last stage, when intersectarian alliances evaporated and confessionally heterogeneous political organizations lost favor, was the political recruitment of the Shi'a largely conducted in terms of contending variants of Shi'ism, and even then there were many exceptions. The important fact is that the political mobilization of the Shi'a as a community of assertive, aware, and active people, preceded the emergence of a minoritarian Shi'i extremism by a margin of decades. For more than thirty years the Shi'i Muslims of Lebanon had been searching for their place in Lebanese politics and society. After centuries of impoverishment and subservience to Maronite, Druze, and Sunni masters and Shi'i political bosses, the Shi'a began to find their political footing in the early 1960s. In the remainder of this section, the four stages of the political mobilization of the Shi'a are surveyed.

STAGE I, PRE-1975

As just indicated, the decades preceding the onset of civil war (in 1975) were marked by a proliferation of radical and reformist parties successfully recruiting among the economically and politically disenfranchised Shi'a. The increasingly politicized Shi'is began to participate in a wide range of secular political parties. Indeed, the 1960s and the early 1970s were a period marked by a swelling of antiestablishment parties like the Ba'ath (Arab Renaissance party), the Lebanese Communist party (LCP), and the Organization for Communist Labor Action (OCAL), with Shi'i recruits who were attracted by the appeal of ideologies that promised radical social, economic, and political reform in Lebanon. Even the predominantly Maronite Christian Kata'ib (or Phalangist) party attracted a modest number of Shi'is as members. Simultaneously, the Palestinian guerrilla organizations attracted large numbers of Shi'i recruits who saw in their own plight a parallel with that of the Palestinians. It is a measure of the level of Shi'i membership in the revisionist, radical, and revolutionary parties (and their militias) that far more Shi'is were to fall during the civil war of 1975–1976 than members of any other group in Lebanon. The Shi'a were the cannon fodder and the foot soldiers of the war.

The 1960s and 1970s also exposed the Lebanese Shi'a to the vibrant and dynamic leadership of al-Sayyid Musa al-Sadr.[7] Al-Sadr, though born in Iran, traced his ancestry back to southern Lebanon. He moved to Lebanon in 1960 from Najaf in Iraq, where he had been studying Islamic jurisprudence (*fiqh*), under the sponsorship of several of the most important *ayatullahs* of the day. He was a looming presence in the pre–civil war period, and it was under his direction and leadership that the Harakat al-Mahrumin (Movement of the Deprived)—the forerunner of the Amal movement—emerged in 1974. Al-Sadr was a populist leader with an agenda of reform, not destruction and revolution.

While the Movement of the Deprived claimed to represent all of the politically dispossessed Lebanese, regardless of confession, it was transparently a party of the Shi'a. The charismatic Sayyid Musa al-Sadr skillfully exploited Shi'ism's potent symbolism to remind his followers that they were a people with a heritage of resistance and sacrifice. He revitalized the epic martyrdom of Imam Husain (the grandson of the prophet Muhammad) at Karbala in 61 Higara (680 A.D.) and he inspired his followers to emulate the bravery of Husain.

Yet, despite his magnetic appeal for many Shi'a, al-Sadr's movement was only one in a field of organizations that successfully mediated the entry of the Shi'a into political action. Only later, and under bizarre circumstances, did al-Sadr's movement assume center stage for the Shi'a.

STAGE II, THE CIVIL WAR AND IMMEDIATE AFTERMATH
(1975–1978)

The two-year civil war of 1975–1976 ended inconclusively, and with the Lebanese political system no closer to reform as the fighting ended than it had been when the bloodshed began. As noted, initially many of the Shi'a flocked to the parties of the Left, which gave voice to their demands for social equity and radical change in the Lebanese political system. But, the Left failed to deliver on its promises, and the alliance of the Left with the Palestine Liberation Organization (PLO) helped to buttress the Palestinian quasi-state, which dominated West Beirut and major portions of South Lebanon.

Significantly, in 1976, Musa al-Sadr broke with his erstwhile allies in the Lebanese National Movement (LNM) and the PLO. He was especially maddened by the all-or-nothing attitude of Kemal Joumblatt, the Druze prince who led the LNM, and who had rejected a reasonable political solution to his civil war in early 1976. When the Syrian army intervened in Lebanon against the PLO and its allies, during late May and early June 1976, in order to prevent the defeat of the Maronite militias, al-Sadr supported Syria. In doing so, he signaled the profound disenchantment with the Left felt by many of the Shi'a.

Increasingly, throughout 1977 and 1978, the Shi'a often found themselves in the cross-fire between the PLO and Israel. This was a period of heightened suffering, especially in southern Lebanon where a heavy price was paid for the armed Palestinian presence.

STAGE III, THE EMERGENCE OF AMAL AS A VIBRANT FORCE (1978–1982)

By the late 1970s, many—but by no means all—of the politicized Shi'a, deserted the Left and joined or supported the rejuvenated Amal Movement, the populist reform movement that first emerged in the early 1970s under Musa al-Sadr's leadership as the Movement of the Deprived.[8] In 1978 the Israelis increased their military pressure on South Lebanon, and thereby helped to stoke the tensions between the Shi'a and the PLO, although subsequent Israeli errors would indicate that they had only a very incomplete understanding of what was taking place among the Shi'a. Amal began to take shape as a loose grouping of village home-guards, intent on circumscribing the influence of the PLO and thereby reducing the exposure of the Shi'a to Israeli preemptive and retaliatory strikes.

With the revolution in Iran gathering momentum by 1978, many Lebanese Shi'a took inspiration from the actions of their Iranian coreligionists. If the "Islamic Revolution" was not a precise model for Lebanon, it was still an exemplar for action, and Amal, as an authentically Shi'i movement, was the momentary beneficiary of this moment of enthusiasm. Al-Sadr was known to be a key supporter of Ayatullah Ruhollah Khomeini, and an adversary of the

Shah (although his opposition had been tempered by a good dose of realism). Moreover, several key Amal officials, including the Iranian Mustafa Chamran, took up key positions in the new regime.

Ironically, it was also Musa al-Sadr's disappearance in 1978 that helped to retrieve the promise of his earlier efforts. In August 1978 he visited Libya with two companions, the Sheikh Muhammad Shahhadih Ya'qub and journalist 'Abbas Badr al-Din. The party has not been heard from since. While his fate is not known, it is widely suspected that he was killed by the henchmen of the Libyan leader, Colonel Mu'ammar Qadhdafi, for reasons that remain obscure. The Libyans did attempt a clumsy cover-up, sending a trio of impersonators, armed with doctored passports and the luggage of the ill-fated group to Rome, but good evidence suggests that the group never left Libya. It is clear that the disappearance of Musa al-Sadr has been of enormous importance to the Shi'a of Lebanon. (The anniversary of his disappearance, August 31, is celebrated annually with a national strike.)

Musa al-Sadr became a hero to his followers, who revere his memory and take inspiration from his works and his plight. The symbol of a missing *imam* (Islamic religious leader)—reminiscent as it is of the central dogma of Shi'ism—is hard to assail, and even blood enemies were heard to utter words of praise for the missing leader. The movement al-Sadr founded has—since his still unresolved disappearance—become the largest Shi'i organization in Lebanon. By 1982, when Israel launched its star-crossed invasion of Lebanon, Amal was arguably the most dynamic force in Lebanese politics.

STAGE IV, POSTINVASION PERIOD (1982 TO PRESENT)

Unfortunately, Amal's justified and reasonable calls for the reformation of the Lebanese political system went unheeded in 1982. The Maronite Christians, who have enjoyed the dominant role in the politics of modern Lebanon, were intent to preserve their power, not to share it. The Sunni Muslims, the Maronites' junior partner, were also little interested in seeing the diminishment of their privileges to the advantage of the Shi'a. Thus, the answer to Amal's demands was calculated intransigence. The predictable result has been increased anger and frustration among the Shi'a.

The last six years have been witness to a marked radicalization and fractionation of Lebanon's Shi'i community. Amal, which promised in the early 1980s to become the dominant organizational voice for the Shi'a, has faced a serious erosion in its following. Ineffective and even incompetent leadership, corruption, and more than a modicum of arrogance have undermined its support, especially in the environs of Beirut.

Hizballah (or the Party of God), the Iranian-funded alternative to Amal, has emerged as a competent, dedicated, and well-led challenger. Though young Shi'i clerics dominate the leadership of Hizballah, it is noteworthy that Hizballah has been especially effective in recruiting among well-educated Shi'a from secular professions, many of whom have lost confidence in Amal. The May 1988 fighting in the Beirut suburbs, which saw Hizballahis triumph over Amal militiamen, underlined Hizballah's steady success in enlisting the Shi'a, many of whom are ex-Amal members. Symptomatic of Amal's decline in the suburbs were the widely circulating rumors that Hizballah conquered some of the Amal positions through the simple expediency of paying off the local Amal defenders. Whatever the truth of such rumors, it is reliably reported that many Amal defenders simply deserted their posts, rather than fight. Amal's support was further reduced when it reflexively shelled the quarters from which it had been displaced.

As the overall situation has grown worse, Hizballah has gained supporters, though Amal remains a force with which to be reckoned. The persistent insecurity, the stalling of political reform, and the near total collapse of the Lebanese economy, has made religion a refuge—skillfully manipulated to be sure—in a situation where there were no other answers. Taking its cue from Iran, Hizballah has exploited the symbolism of Shi'ism to enlist support. For instance, 'Ashura, the day upon which the Shi'a commemorate the martyrdom of Imam Husain over thirteen hundred years ago, and certainly the most significant day of the Shi'i calendar, has become not just a plea for intercession or an act of piety, but a revolutionary statement.

Hizballah has enjoyed much less success in south Lebanon, where about one-third of the Shi'a live (the total population of Shi'a in Lebanon is usually estimated to be at least one million, or 30–35 percent of the total Lebanese population, though it may even be higher). Anti-PLO animosity runs deep in the south, and Amal's staunch stance against the restoration of an armed PLO presence in the area accurately reflects popular sentiment and distinguishes Amal from Hizballah. Amal forcefully demonstrated its supremacy in April 1988, when it eliminated Hizballah as an organized military presence in the south, following the kidnapping of U.S. Marine Lt.

Col. William R. Higgins. Amal saw the Higgins kidnapping as not just a blow against the U.N. Interim Force in Lebanon, which Higgins served as an unarmed observer, but a direct challenge to Amal's authority. Both shi'i organizations are riven by local animosities and conflicts over turf.

POLITICAL DIVERSITY AMONG THE SHI'A

It is important to stress that the political loyalties of the Shi'a span a wider organizational and ideological breadth than that represented by the Amal-Hizballah spectrum. It is not simply a question of whether a Shi'i adheres to Hizballah's vision of an Islamic Republic of Lebanon versus Amal's quest for a reformed political system in which the political share of the Shi'a matches their status as the plurality in Lebanon. Not only are there a multitude of trends within Amal and Hizballah, but by no means are all of the Shi'a active either in Amal or Hizballah. The Lebanese Communist party (LCP) and the Syrian Social Nationalist party (SSNP) continue to count many Shi'a as members, and, of course, numerous Shi'a have managed to avoid any organizational affiliation whatsoever.

In an interesting survey of 400 Shi'i college students (273 men and 127 women), conducted in 1987 at the Lebanese University in Beirut, Prof. Hilal Kashan of the American University of Beirut found that only 1 in 5 men (as opposed to 1 in 3 women) acknowledged involvement in Hizballah, and a little less than 1 in 3 males (vs. 1 in 14 women) acknowledged involvement in Amal.[9] (As might be expected, Hizballah members reported a higher level of religiosity, as measured by fasting during Ramadan, reading the Qur'an, or the frequency of praying.) Twelve percent of the male and female respondents acknowledged involvement in the LCP, and 8 percent in the SSNP. Over one-quarter of all men, and more than 40 percent of the women claimed no political affiliation at all. While Professor Kashan's findings do not purport to represent definitive proportions for the Shi'a in general, they do illustrate that among a significant segment of Shi'i youth, there is much more political diversity than may often be presumed.

IRAN'S ROLE

Since 1982, Iran has put a very significant amount of resources into Lebanon—including impressive sums that some estimates indicate have reached as high as $30 million per month in the first half of 1988—to promote Iranian influence among the Shi'a and to spread the Islamic revolution. These funds have been used not only to underwrite Hizballah, but to run an array of social services, including hospitals, schools, and sanitation services.[10] A contingent of Pasdaran (or Revolutionary Guards), deployed to Ba'albak in 1982, has provided military training and arms to Hizballah. The Iranian Embassy in Damascus has had a direct role in guiding Hizballah's activities, and, according to published accounts, also has been the nodal point for planning and executing sensational acts of political violence, such as the 1983 attacks on the American Embassy in Beirut and the U.S. Marine contingent of the Multinational Force.[11] Thus, Iran has erected an impressive infrastructure with which to ply its influence in Lebanon. Yet, most of the Shi'a, including several of the most senior and influential Shi'i 'ulama, remain convinced that the Iranian model is inappropriate for culturally diverse Lebanon where the majority of citizens are non-Shi'a.

In general, the Iranian revolution has not traveled nearly as well as some observers anticipated it would. There is no denying the emotive appeal of the revolution—its capacity to inspire young men and women—but the prospects for the establishment of an Iranian-style Islamic republic in Lebanon are slim at best. The special circumstances of prerevolutionary Iran, in which the Iranian people were united in their hatred of the shah, if not in their political prescriptions for post-Pahlavi Iran, are hardly replicated in Lebanon where the Shi'a are divided against themselves. Moreover, even leading Lebanese Shi'i clerics are equivocal and often skeptical about the applicability of Ayatollah Khomeini's innovative dogma of the *wilayat al-faqih* (the rule of the jurisconsult) for Lebanon.[12]

Though numbers of poor Shi'is stuck in the misery of Beirut's suburban slums may see an Islamic republic as the road to salvation, there is little support for the idea among the young men and women who have escaped poverty. In his 1985 dissertation, which studied the attitudes of 400 Lebanese college students studying in the United States, Dr. Ahmad Nizar Hamzah found that when asked which political system they favored, only about 3.4 percent of the Shi'i respondents (16.2 percent of the sample) named Iran.[13] (About 63 percent of the Shi'i students reported that their fathers were illiterate, and almost 68 percent identified themselves as members of the lower social class, so the Shi'i respondents were reasonably representative.) Dr. Hamzah produced similar results in a survey of 150 students at the American University of Beirut. In contrast, about one-third of the students, irrespective of confession, named the United States, while over 41 percent of the total sample (and almost 52 percent of the Shi'a) preferred Switzerland, notable for its system of culturally homogeneous cantons, as the best political system.

Despite the significant recent successes that Hizballah has enjoyed in the suburbs of Beirut, Iran has not succeeded in persuading a majority of the Lebanese Shi'a that Iranian answers are appropriate for Lebanon. In fact, the Hizballah victory seems to have had much more to do with the failings of Amal and a general sense of exasperation, than the attraction of Iran. Many Shi'a resent Iran's campaign to extend the Islamic revolution to Lebanon, and this resentment has been openly voiced. With the end of the Gulf War in the summer of 1988, there has been a discernible decline in Iranian material and financial support for Hizballah. Some reports indicate that funding may have declined by as much as 90 percent, though such estimates are always suspect and seldom definitive.[14] One expert observer refers to the "Lebanonization" of Hizballah, surely an incipient phenomenon, but nonetheless an interesting one—should it gain further force.

THE SYRIAN AND ISRAELI ROLES

Notwithstanding the role to which Iran has been inspired in Lebanon, Syria and Israel remain the two major regional players in the country. Since 1982, both states have seen grand ambitions thwarted in Lebanon, and, as a result, Damascus and Tel Aviv have separately resolved to cope tactically with Lebanon, rather than engage in ambitious strategies to reshape Lebanon to their tastes. Yet both have also continued to play an influential, if not always intentional, role in mobilizing the Shi'a.

Damascus had a major role in permitting the Iranians to establish themselves in 1982, at a time when Syria was weak and was anxious to undermine those elements—like Amal—that were playing a moderate hand and striving to improve relations with the United States. Since 1982, Syria's most delicate balancing act has been to maintain its strategic relationship with Iran, while simultaneously keeping the pro-Iranian Hizballah under control. As early as 1984, Damascus turned the screws on Hizballah, since Hizballah had outlived its usefulness as a counterbalance to Amal, which from 1982 to 1984 had tried to keep Syria at arms' length. After the withdrawal of the Multinational Force from Beirut, in early 1984, Amal rushed into Syria's arms, but, by then, Hizballah was well entrenched among the Shi'a.

There is little sympathy in Damascus for Hizballah's or Iran's declared goal of establishing an Islamic republic in Lebanon, but Syria has resolutely avoided a decisive head-on clash with Hizballah. Syria has walked to the edge of the precipice, but it has refused to jump, time after time. The June 1988 Syrian army deployment into the Beirut suburbs has precisely this tentative character. Although Hizballah was not permitted to fully consolidate its victory over Amal, it was not disarmed and has continued all of its political activities. In other words, it remains a very potent force, the Syrian army notwithstanding.

In 1982 and 1983 Israel placed most of its chips on the Maronite Christians, and discovered, to its pain, that the Lebanese Forces militia was incapable of playing the role that was envisaged for it. One of the most significant effects of the invasion was the enlivening of resistance among the Shi'a, who, in the end, succeeded in forcing the vaunted Israeli army to withdraw from most of the territory it had seized. For most Israelis, the 1982 war is a very bad memory and while there are reports of a steady flow of Israeli armament to the predominantly Maronite Lebanese Forces militia, the real action is in south Lebanon, where Israel is entrenched in the self-proclaimed "security zone."

In league with her Lebanese proxy force, the 2,600-man South Lebanon Army (SLA) led by Gen. Antoine Lahad—which is described by the Israeli journalist Ze'ev Schiff as "absolutely dependent on Israel,"[15]—struggles to control the region just north of her border. The task is a difficult one, since the security zone acts as a magnet for attacks by an admixture of resistance fighters from groups as varied as the LCP and Hizballah. In addition, the PLO is anxious to reestablish its front in Lebanon and some Palestinian guerilla groups have been quietly cooperating with Hizballah to that end. In the short term, the security zone has been judged a success by Israeli officials, who are loathe to trust their security to UNIFIL (United Nations Interim Forces in Lebanon) soldiers, or to the relatively moderate pragmatists of Amal. (Since Israel created the security zone in 1985, 36 IDF (Israeli Defense Force) soldiers have been killed, 64 wounded, and 3 are missing in Lebanon.)

It is certainly true that Israel has become much more sensitive to the possibility that disproportionate military actions can create more enemies than they destroy. But though it has become more deft in the use of military force, reckless shooting by Israeli and SLA soldiers still kills innocent Lebanese all too regularly and only helps to make new enemies. In summary, the effect of the continuing Israeli occupation of Lebanese territory is the discrediting of moderation. Or, as one astute Lebanese observer puts it, the security zone is "the major enemy of moderation" in Lebanon. So long as the security zone is maintained, Shi'i politicians will continue to try to outbid one another in their vociferous opposition to the Israeli occupation.

CONCLUSION

The battle for supremacy, which now rages in Lebanon among the Shi'a, is in large measure over who is the rightful heir to the legacy of Musa al-Sadr. On the one side is Hizballah, with its admixture of firebrand clerics and strong influence of Sheikh Muhammad Husain Fadlallah, the charismatic Shi'i scholar who transparently desires to supplant Musa al-Sadr. On the other side is Amal, still a reform movement, but an angrier, more vengeful one than it was under al-Sadr's leadership. Both organizations can only be viewed as corruption of al-Sadr's reformist designs. It is doubtful that he would have been very proud of either one.

The Shi'a are certainly not on the verge of casting down their arms, and the contending loyalties of the Shi'a to family, Islam, Arab and Lebanese nationalism will not miraculously coalesce into a unified political organization. Contrary to the expectations of some strategists, the Shi'a evince no desire to be enfolded by Iran, Syria, or Israel. Meanwhile, there is still a vast gulf separating the disparate claims of the Shi'a from their many opponents in Lebanon. Without an end in sight to the continuing conflicts within Lebanon, it is a safe bet that Shi'i politics will continue to be disputatious and dangerous, but also important for shaping the future of Lebanon, for better or worse.

17

The Politics of Religious Resurgence and Religious Terrorism: The Case of the Sikhs of India
Karandeep Singh

Little rigorous effort has been expended so far by social scientists toward the understanding of the rise of Sikh resurgence and terrorism in the Indian state of Punjab. A 1987 survey of the prevalent explanations cites unclear definitions, insufficient empirical evidence, and inadequate attention to the question of the level of analysis and concludes that there remains a need for "rigorous analysis."[1] This chapter examines the case of Sikh resurgence in the Punjab province of India. It employs a "political" model of the situation based on the works of R. Aya, L. A. Tilly and C. Tilly, and Barrington Moore, Jr.[2]

Religious resurgence movements are one of the many "repertoires of collective action" available to groups to protest against perceived grievances or injustices. Collective action here is defined as "when sets of people commit pooled resources, including their own, to common ends."[3] Such movements are one of the many forms of political conflicts in society over resources and public policy. And in the case of religious terrorism, however abhorrent some of the acts of the aggrieved groups in the drama might appear to the ordinary person, they are nevertheless guided by a sense of legitimacy and perceived injustice.

One must begin with the birth of grievances of specific groups and classes, for little analytical advantage accrues from a study of generalized frustration. This, however, is not enough. One must also focus on the "pathways from arousal to action."[4] Indeed, in the case of the protestors, for example, the analyst must go beyond their grievances to the amount of power resources of the aggrieved. Power resources can include ideology, economic and social status, culture, and organizational strength of the protestors.

These variables indicate the level at which perceived injustice is reacted to, and also determine the nature and form of this reaction. Careful observation often reveals that it may not be the really deserving who are able to fight political battles but those who already have a significant status in society. One must also consider the space in the political structure that is available for the protest movement. A state structure weakened by serious internal conflict within the ruling class or by international military or economic pressure[5] can provide significant political space to the aggrieved groups and classes to make their voices heard in an effective manner.

The response of power holders to protest is another factor very often neglected in social research. This interactive process lends the situation its own dynamic apart from the other factors just mentioned. The Tillys argue that many of the forms of collective action are determined precisely by the response of the power holders to the protest movement, that the movement learns and very often practices the methods used on it by the state. This point is very pertinent in the context of contemporary Sikh terrorism. Terrorism emerges after the demands that are perceived as legitimate by the aggrieved groups are denied for a prolonged period by power holders and after repressive measures are unleashed. This produces among some sections of the aggrieved populace, especially the youth, a total lack of faith in the political process and hatred and contempt for the state.

Terrorism is the response of the weak, the young, and the proud to structural violence and perceived injustice.[6] Culture and history, in addition to state violence, also have a role to play in the selection of this form of protest. In the case of the Sikhs one can find instances of terrorist acts against oppressive and bigoted state officials who had been persecuting the Sikhs and destroying their religious places and shrines.

Religious values and politics also interact. Religion provides one element of "the nexus of established rights and obligations in which groups of ordinary people are embedded and which, once violated, make for grievances."[7] In addition it is a powerful mobilizing force with a generally strong organizational network. But above all, in certain contexts and cases, it enables a mass political movement to circumvent the problem of "free ridership."[8] The belief in individual salvation via martyrdom in certain religions, Islam and Sikhism, for example, needs to be explored. The possibility of salvation through martyrdom constitutes a powerful individual "noncollective" benefit available to religious-based mass protests. It can motivate participants to accept risks not otherwise justifiable in pursuit of a collective good, like justice. The preceding theoretical perspective serves as a guide to the complex problem of the resurgence of religion among the Sikhs of Punjab, where everyday terrorism and violence are taking a great toll in human lives.

The present analysis traces events from the middle and late 1970s till the attack by the Indian army on the Golden Temple, the holiest of the Sikh shrines, in June 1984, and the consequent assassination of Mrs. Gandhi six months later. This desecration and the killing of the leader of the resurgence movement, Sant Jarnail Singh Bhindranwale, and his lieutenants, gave religious fundamentalism and terrorism a very powerful impulse. These events were the most important factors in the rise of religious terrorism in the state of Punjab. They not only inflamed the general mass of the Sikhs, who till this period were not very sympathetic to the terrorists, but gave an increasing legitimacy to terrorist actions and pronouncements. Bhindranwale had repeatedly stated that he would die rather than have the holiest of Sikh shrines desecrated by the entrance of the army or the police. By living up to his word, he heightened the credibility of his pronouncements and ensured a legacy marked by assassinations and increased terrorism.

The anti-Sikh pogrom organized under government auspices[9] after the assassination of Mrs. Gandhi was another crucial event in the inflammation of Sikh anger. According to the government's own estimate, 2,897 people were killed in riots; most of them were Sikhs.[10] This is not to mention the thousands rendered homeless and fear stricken by the brutality of the violence. Not only were the riots following Mrs. Gandhi's death inspired by the government, but subsequently, and till 1989, no major effort has been made to punish the guilty. This has vindicated Sikh claims of government sponsorship of these riots.

After months of procrastination, the government appointed the Misra Commission to investigate the matter. Subsequently, its terms were amended so that the report could not be made public.[11] Commenting on the report in its August 31, 1987 issue, *India Today* noted that the Commission basically evaded its job by asking for two more committees to finish the task it began. Indeed, many of those identified as the perpetrators of these riots by independent civil rights bodies have been elevated to ministerial positions. The pogrom and its aftermath was a major factor in developing the perception of structural injustice among the Sikhs. The hanging of the two persons accused of killing Mrs. Gandhi in 1989 further inflamed the Sikhs.

GEOPOLITICS AND THE CULTURE OF THE CASTE

The territory and cultural region of Punjab lies on the main invasion route to the Indian subcontinent and has played an important role in the history and politics of the area. The intermittent breakdown over the centuries of central rule, and frequent plunder and invasion from the northwest helped to create a situation of uncertainty and chaos that shaped the distribution of land in the region. The necessary political stability to possess large estates simply did not exist, so that landholding evolved into predominantly smaller holdings with the bulk of agrarian land being controlled by the middle and rich peasants. Agrarian stratification is based on ownership/non-ownership of land and the quantum of such ownership as well as the manner of land cultivation—by family, hired labor, or tenant labor.[12]

According to the 1970–71 agricultural census, the rich peasants (households with landholdings generally above 20 acres, cultivated with hired labor and mechanized farm operations) and middle peasants (with landholdings between 10 and 20 acres, cultivated with both family and hired labor) comprise 23.36 percent of the total peasant households in the state and control 64.97 percent of the total cultivated area in the state, while the poor peasants, with operational holdings below 5 acres, comprise 20 percent of the total peasant households and farm a like amount of the total cultivated area in the state.[13] Any categorization can never be neat and is bound to violate empirical reality. Thus, depending on the area within the region, a developed one like the Doab, or a relatively underdeveloped one like the Malwa, these categories may be somewhat inappropriate and arbitrary. Nevertheless, the general point being made is that the amount of land and wealth in peasant hands today constitutes key power resources for a protest movement to be launched.[14]

From the social angle, the bulk of the agrarian population in Punjab comprised of the Jats, an agricultural caste, generally accepted to be of Aryan stock.[15] The Jats were "mainly small proprietors and tenants, and a few were landowners."[16] Being on the main invasion route, they developed private armies and bands for protection. J. Pettigrew states:

> political circumstances—the frequent changes of political rule in which an individual could create his power, make the utmost use of, or augment the power he had, fostered a particular cultural tradition among the Jats: they did not regard themselves as subordinate to any other person.

In this context, the eminent historian of the Sikhs, Khuswant Singh, states in *A History of the Sikhs:*

> The Jat was born the worker and the warrior. He tilled his land with his sword girded round his waist. He fought more battles for the defence of his homestead than the Kshatriya, for unlike the martial Kshatriya the Jat seldom fled from his village when the invaders came. And if the Jat was maltreated or if his women were molested by the conqueror on his way to Hindustan, he settled his score by looting the invaders' caravan on their return journey and freeing the women he was taking back. The Punjabi Jat developed an attitude of indifference to worldly possessions and an instinct for gambling with his life against odds. At the same time he became conscious of his role in the defence of Hindustan. His brand of patriotism was at once hostile towards the foreigner and benign, even comtemptuous, towards his own countrymen whose fate depended so much on his courage and fortitude (pp. 15–16).

The word *Punjabi Jat* needs to be stressed in this quote, for the characteristics referred to, cut across the prevailing religions of the period. The subsequent conversion of some of these sections of Jats, a distinct identity with its own history, to Sikhism, gave the converts a higher degree of militancy relative to the unconverted Jats. A perusal of historical evidence, reveals that the Jat caste has a sense of pride and a propensity to react to perceived injustice quickly and rather vigorously. Moreover, the threshold at which such reaction occurs tends to be rather low.

CASTE AND RELIGION

When it was founded in the early part of the sixteenth century, Sikhism was an eclectic, simple religion based on monotheism and social equality. It opposed idol worship and ritual and was peace loving. Sikh religion developed its "aggressive credo" from the influx of Jats to its fold.[17] In this connection Pettigrew mentions that even the present-day symbols of the Sikh faith evolved with this influx.

This process began at the time of the sixth guru of the Sikhs, Guru Hargobind, and reached its culmination with the founding of the Khalsa (the Pure) by the tenth and the last guru, Gobind Singh, in 1699. Guru Hargobind fused the temporal and the spiritual for the community, an important task. He constructed the Akal Takht (seat of the Immortal) opposite the Harimandir Sahib in the Golden Temple at Amritsar. Harimandir Sahib represents the seat of spiritual authority for the Sikhs, and to this was added the Akal Takht, the center to guide the Sikhs in their temporal affairs. The Golden Temple, the most sacred shrine for the Sikhs, carries within its precincts the twin centers of Sikh spiritualism and temporalism.

Guru Gobind Singh baptized the Sikhs and made the carrying of weapons obligatory. It was also stressed that the use of violence for a sacred and a righteous cause, when all other methods had failed, was justified. In his words,

> Lord, these boons of Thee I ask,
> Let me never shun a righteous task,
> Let me be fearless when I go to battle,
> Give me faith that victory will be mine,
> And when comes the time to end my life,
> Let me fall in mighty strife.[18]

The influx of the Jat social identity gave a degree of militancy to the Sikh religion and the latter, in turn, strengthened this militancy by evolving the concept of martyrdom. Two of the ten Sikh gurus became martyrs in the eyes of the members of their faith. These developments also led to a change of leadership among the Sikhs from the nonmilitant and urban Khatri caste, to the militant Jat. Sikhism became a vehicle for the expression of peasant grievances against the Muslim rulers of the day and also helped in the fight against invaders. How much of the resistance comprised peasant grievances and how much religious persecution need not detain us here. Indeed, the thesis of exclusive religious persecution has not been free from challenge.[19]

For our purposes, it is sufficient to state that the Sikh ethos reflects a belief that the Sikhs were the subject of brutal persecution at the hands of the Mughal rulers and that their ancestors did not

let the prestige and glory of their religion suffer. They were prepared to, and did, sacrifice even their lives toward this end. In fact
the daily *ardas* (the prayer of the Sikhs) recounts the heroic deeds of
their martyred ancestors who suffered torture and brutality but did
not give up their faith. Any situation today that might expose Sikhs
to perceived religious and political persecution would in all likeli-
hood meet stiff resistance from the community, especially from
the Jats.

 Gurudwaras (places of worship) were built to commemorate
such occasions and are places of pilgrimage for the devout. In modern Punjab these *gurudwaras* number approximately twenty thousand. Not all of them are historical shrines. The Sikh masses
congregate here on the anniversaries of martyrdom of their gurus,
their birthdays, and on other such special occasions connected with
the history and culture of Punjab and the Sikh religion. In addition,
the more devout visit the *gurudwaras* on a more regular basis for the
recitation of the holy book of the Sikhs, the Guru Granth Sahib.
These *gurudwaras* provide a well-established organizational network
for the Sikh community to mobilize in times of need. The Sikh *gurudwaras* are not simply places of worship and commemoration of
historical events in the history of Sikh religion. They are also places
where members of the community as well as others can rest and
stay. They represent the ideal of salvation via service to the community. In fact, the Sikh slogan of Degh, Tegh, Fateh represents this in
a nutshell. Degh is the cauldron in which the community food is
cooked; Tegh is sword, and Fateh means victory. They serve as a
constant reminder to the community of the sacrifices of the Sikh
ancestors.

 Commenting on the Sikh tradition in Punjab, Pettigrew, in her
book *Robber Noblemen*, goes on to say that the Sikhs had

> fought and died for their community. The Sikh heritage was a
> past of 400 years of Muslim persecution: and these 400 years
> were packed with legends of brave actions. Sikh mythology
> consisted of accounts and tales of ancestors and heroes who in
> a very recent past fought and died for "community" (p. 80).

With this went a strong legitimation for violence in the culture.

> But for men, young and old, death was excitement, drama, a
> proof of their daring, their bravery, as true sons of the Khalsa.
> The legitimation of killing and violence was historical and cul-

tural. Courage, the willingness to take risks, the absence in the ideology of any concept of defeat and submission and the capacity to impose oneself on others, were major values of the culture (p. 59).

In contemporary Punjab, the terrorists who have been killed by the security forces are considered martyrs of the Sikh faith. It has been reported that the entire stretch of border villages in the Amritsar, Gurdaspur, and Ferozepur districts of Punjab is dotted with memorials to slain terrorists.[20] Most of these people were shot by the security forces in false "encounters"—that is, the security forces reported to the public that terrorist(s) of the following name(s) were killed while trying to escape from custody or while they attacked the security forces. Most often only one side ended up dead. Amnesty International, in its recent report on India, has charged the Indian government with the illegal killings of scores of Sikh militants since 1987.[21] Culture and religion may not by themselves help to bring about a situation marked by political violence. But both have the tendency to heighten the impact, and even condition the response of groups who have perceptions of injustice. There is a dialectical relationship between the various elements of a social situation and it may be very difficult, and perhaps impossible at times, to analyze them separately. The slicing of reality into segments, for the purpose of analysis, does, of necessity, injustice to its holistic and dialectical nature. Keeping this in mind, it is worthwhile to consider now the long-term changes in the social structure of Punjab in the context of new agrarian technology introduced in the mid-1960s.

THE POLITICS OF THE GREEN REVOLUTION

In India, the kulak (if we may use that word) has marched boldly through the door of politics and is very much a force to be reckoned with in Indian polity.[22]

The national level Congress party and the regional and the Jat Sikh-dominated Akali Dal are the two main contenders for political power in the state of Punjab. The Akali Dal came into existence in the early part of this century in the context of a protest movement against British rule for the reform of Sikh religious places. It has had an anti-imperialist tradition and after independence it was the main force that initiated, and eventually got in 1967, the demand for the creation of a state of Punjab, based on linguistic considerations. In its struggles, the Akali Dal has had not only to contend with Congress, but also the Punjabi Hindu-dominated Jana Sangh (today called Bharatiya Janata party). The latter party, though sharing a common language and culture, nevertheless took little initiative to side with the Akali Dal for fear of domination by the Sikhs in a state where the Sikhs would be in a majority. The history of this relationship is rather intricate and need not detain us here, but it has generally been the case that the Akali party has had to launch agitations for demands that a number of enlightened Hindus and even the Indian Left thought were in the interests of the state of Punjab.

During Congress rule in Punjab (1972–1977), the Akali Dal demanded control by the Sikhs, of Sikh religious places all over the country; the return to Punjab of some Punjabi-speaking areas from the neighboring states of Haryana and Rajasthan, originally left out when the state was formed in 1967; decentralization of power in center-state relations; better terms of trade for agriculture; and the recognition by the Center of Punjab's rights as the sole riparian state over the waters of the rivers Ravi and Beas. The Anandpur Sahib Resolution (1973) is a formal document embodying these demands.

When Congress was replaced by the Akali-Janata coalition (the Punjabi Hindu-dominated Jan Sangh was the main component of the Janata party in Punjab) in 1977, the Akali government did little to press for these demands apart from filing a case on the river waters dispute in the Supreme Court in 1978. When Congress regained power nationally and in the state in 1980, it was time for the Akalis to resume their agitation for the implementation of the Anandpur Sahib Resolution.

This is best appreciated in the context of the Green Revolution and of its impact on regional and national politics. The Green Revolution was introduced in some regions of India in the mid-1960s, including the Punjab, and it led to the introduction of high-yielding varieties of seeds, better farm management techniques, and other inputs required for a vibrant agriculture. It had significant impact on the prosperity of the agricultural sector in general, and more particularly on those who owned larger units of land. According to one estimate, the widespread prevalence of irrigation across all sizes of landholdings—a distinctive feature of the Punjab agrarian economy—enabled the Green Revolution to bring all-round general prosperity to the peasantry. The gains, however, came in proportion to the initial landholdings; in other words, those with initially larger landholdings got more out of this revolution than those with less. This resulted in a significant rise of inequality in the agricultural sector in the state.[23]

The Jats among the Sikhs, who are primarily an agricultural landholding caste, were the main beneficiaries of this revolution. According to one estimate, the Jat Sikhs are approximately 20 percent of the Sikh population and they own 60 percent of the agricultural land in the state. Another study estimates that 35 to 66 percent is the proportion of the Jat Sikhs to the total Sikh population in the different districts of Punjab. The 1931 census mentioned that 50 percent of the total Sikh population were Jats.[24]

The number and proportion of landless has increased in the state due to the impact of the transformation in agrarian technology. In the years 1961–1981, the landless nearly doubled in number from approximately 17 percent of the total agricultural work force in 1961, to 38 percent in 1981.[25] In terms of wage increases this segment of the rural population has not benefited very much.

> Inspection of the figures shows that in the Punjab as a whole, in the period 1966–77, for all operations, the index of real wages reached a peak in 1970 and showed a downward trend thereafter, although output has proceeded ever upwards. In all cases the 1977 figure is below the 1970 one, and for the seven years after 1970 in ploughing, sowing, seeding and harvesting real wages fell in five of the years.[26]

In the absence of a specifically "political" model, one should expect from the aforementioned, that the landless and the poor peasants should be the spearhead of unrest in the state. Indeed, some have expected that the Green Revolution would be a "prelude" to a red one.[27] Given our model, however, this is not the case. As Eric Wolf mentions, "Ultimately, the decisive factor in making a peasant rebellion possible lies in the relation of the peasantry to the field of power which surrounds it. A rebellion cannot start from a situation of complete impotence; the powerless are easy victims."[28]

Most of the landless in the state are the Sikh untouchables (an anomaly for a religion that believes in a casteless society and whose sacred book, the *Guru Granth Sahib*, includes hymns written by some of the untouchable saints of the times) who hardly have had any sympathy for the Jat Sikh-dominated Akali Dal, which was the spearhead of the initial movement for the implementation of the Anandpur Sahib resolution. The Sikh lower- and even the upper-urban castes have been more or less opposed to the Akali Dal and have long voted either for the Communists or the Congress party. This was well established till recently, when the desecration of the Golden Temple by Mrs. Gandhi in June 1984 swung these sections to vote for the Akali party in 1985.

The poor peasantry has in the past aligned itself politically with the upper Jat castes, and therefore the Akali party, because it shares a similar social status with them despite its economic inferiority to its allies. Besides, in some respects the Green Revolution has benefited the poor peasantry also, though far less than it has the upper classes in the agrarian sector of Punjab, as already seen. Thus, reasons embedded in the history and the caste structure of the region account for a "mystification" of rural class consciousness, especially for the lack of an alliance between the poor peasantry and the landless in the state.

Structural changes in the agricultural proletariat also have had a contributory role in this mystification.[29] This has occurred because of the increased demand for permanent labor by the rich households because of the time-bound operations that are required by the new technology. It appears that many of the local landless have gotten better deals from this development. They have managed to get better wages, longer contracts, and advance payments. The demand for casual labor is mainly fulfilled by migration from the neighboring states that are more impoverished, like Uttar Pradesh and Bihar. A full-blooded contradiction of these migrants with the indigenous landless has perhaps not emerged because of the above-mentioned fact, for in the absence of a structural change in the agrarian proletariat, migration would certainly help bring down the wages of the landless. But nevertheless, a recent survey documented the hostility of the local labor to the migratory workers and the positive attitude toward the migratory trend of the rich and middle peasants. Bhushan Kapoor also demonstrates in an empirical manner, the discrimination faced by the migratory labor in Punjab.[30]

The distribution among castes of ministers in the Punjab state government from 1952 to 1980 is a good indicator of the rising clout of the Jat Sikhs in Punjab. In the period 1952–1956, they constituted 25 percent of the total ministers in the state, in 1957–1966, they were 29.2 percent, and in the period 1967–1980, they constituted 48.7 percent. The latter period is the one that felt the effect of the Green Revolution.[31]

Not only in Punjab, but in the entire country, a new elite has emerged from the agrarian areas where the impact of the Green Revolution was felt, and has come into a clash with the industrial interests insofar as it demands cheaper agricultural inputs and higher prices for agricultural products.[32] To demand a better deal for the farm sector, it is not necessary to have had a decline in terms of trade. But this has happened. As A. Ray mentions:

> Since 1975–76, the price index of agricultural products has lagged behind that of manufactured products. Under pressures from urban industrial and professional interests, the national government has disturbed parity between the prices of agricultural and industrial products by attempting to siphon surpluses from agriculture to industry. (p. 162).

Even in the absence of a shift in terms of trade, protests could have emanated from the rural elite. All that is required is a discrepancy between perceived needs and perceived want satisfaction. Generally, want satisfaction and income increase does generate the appetite for more. A. de Tocqueville, in the context of protest, mentions very pertinently that

> patiently endured so long as it seemed beyond redress, a grievance comes to appear intolerable once the possibility of removing it crosses men's minds. For the mere fact that certain abuses have been remedied draws attention to the others and they now appear more galling; people may suffer less, but their sensibility is exacerbated.[33]

It is this basic idea that has subsequently evolved into theories of relative deprivation, J curve, and the like. A decline in the terms of trade to the detriment of the rural sector is hence not a necessary condition for rural protest to emerge The rural elite, primarily because of its rise of expectations and given the power resources at its command, could have indulged in protests for a still better deal. But here, in this concrete instance, we witness a combination of a rise of expectations and deteriorating terms of trade for agricultural products. The situation so to say, has a double-edged character to it.

It was in this context that the Jat Sikh-dominated Akali Dal launched an agitation for the implementation of the Anandpur Resolution in the early 1980s. Relying on religion to mobilize its constituencies, the Akali Dal also expanded its economic demands with some religious issues. It calls the agitation a "Dharma Yudh Morcha," or a struggle for the protection of religion. In this context, we can now better appreciate the inputs from the elite power groups into the Punjab situation.

ELITE INPUT

Analysts of the Indian scene have discerned a process of change in the culture of Indian elite since the mid-1960s. Amal Ray and John Kincaid mention the "tradition of elite accommodation" prior to the struggle for the office of prime ministership between Mrs. Gandhi and her Congress rival Morarji Desai. This was the "first time in free India, the tradition of elite accommodation and consensus in the Congress party suffered a serious fracture." This was again made very obvious in 1974, when Mrs. Gandhi broke the rules of the political game and imposed internal emergency in the country and put the entire opposition behind bars. Another dynamic in the rise of religious resurgence in Punjab came from various elite factions and political party rivalries both at the local and national level.

In an interesting study, Pettigrew points out that the faction is a traditional form of organization for the Jat Sikhs and has represented "a relatively persistent and typical mode of organization."[34] With factionalism among the Jats, who are primarily in the Akali party, went the rivalry at the party level between the two main contenders for political power in the state, the Akali Dal and the Congress party, and also the rivalry between various Congress factions. All of this led to a significant boost to fundamentalism in the state embodied in the rise of the fundamentalist leader Bhindranwale.

After losing the 1977 national elections, Mrs. Gandhi initiated a change in her strategy—a greater reliance on majority, that is, Hindu communalism—to win power.[35] In Punjab this facilitated fundamentalism as Congress sought to embarrass their moderate Akali rivals who mobilized their constituencies on religious appeals on the one hand,[36] and to stoke Hindu communal fears on the other. This effort found fertile demographic and economic soil in the state because Hindus lived primarily in the urban areas and were traders, while the Sikhs lived and worked predominantly in the rural areas.[37] The growing nexus between trade and agriculture as a result of the Green Revolution, had already sharpened the conflict between the two communities, to which now were added the machinations of Congress.

The clash between the Akalis and Nirankaris (a heterodox Sikh sect according to many Sikhs) in April 1978, was used by Congress, then in opposition in the country and in the state, to whip up Sikh fundmentalism in Punjab[38] and to embarrass the moderate Akali government that was in power. In the March 1979 elections of the Shiromani Gurudwara Prabhandak Committee (SGPC) (an elected body of the Sikhs that controlled the Sikh shrines), Congress supported the fundamentalist religious leader Bhindranwale against the Akali Dal.[39] After its accession to power in 1980 at the center and the state, Congress kept on building Bhindranwale up, for example, in the way he was arrested for the murder of the journalist Lala Jagat Narain and then released.[40] In consonance with its policy of boosting majority communalism in the state, in the 1980 assembly elections, the Congress leadership drastically changed the religious composition of the Congress Legislature party to the detriment of the Sikhs.[41]

In the course of events, however, Bhindranwale fell out with Congress but "by surrendering justice to petty political gains the government itself created the ogre who was to dominate the last years of Mrs. Gandhi and to shadow her until her death."[42] Not to be left behind in its political rivalry with Congress, the moderate Akali Dal, according to Tully and Jacob, now started wooing the fundamentalist Sant Bhindranwale to side with them with regard to the demands with which they had launched the agitation. Soon there was a joint agitation of the fundamentalist and the moderate sections of the Akalis for a mixture of religious, economic, and political demands.

The various moderate Akali factions, in their rivalry, also adopted fundamentalist postures depending on the circumstances. Thus, to embarrass the Akali chief minister, Badal, his rival Akalis inflamed a clash with the heterodox sect of the Nirankaris in April 1978.[43] This was a major boost to fundamentalism in the state from within the moderate Akali ranks apart from the Congress party as seen earlier. This process also ultimately resulted in Bhindranwale taking refuge in the holiest shrine of the Sikhs, the Golden Temple, with the connivance and perhaps the encouragement of Tohra, one of the faction leaders and the head of the SGPC. This dynamic is still being witnessed after so much tragedy that has occurred in the state and with the Sikhs in particular. In November 1986, Tohra, who "had allowed militant groups to use the shrines as headquarters," got reelected to this body, "and upon his re-election he set about dismantling the safeguards intended to keep extremists from seizing the sites."[44]

These developments also went hand in hand with the rivalry within Congress, between the state chief minister Darbara Singh and the union home minister Giani Zail Singh, both of whom were Congress members, belonged to the state of Punjab, and were archrivals. On returning to power Mrs. Gandhi had made these appointments knowing full well that they were archrivals. "It was just because Mrs. Gandhi did not want politicians to be able to command any independent influence that she did her best to prevent any of her colleagues from becoming too powerful in their home states." While the chief minister wanted a hard line on Bhindranwale and on the fundamentalists, the home minister, to embarrass him, undermined his efforts. In fact, Giani Zail Singh and Mrs. Gandhi's son originally devised the plan of stirring up fundamentalism in order to embarrass their Akali rivals. Darbara Singh was known to be secular-minded.[45]

The scenario of an administration at odds with itself, one wing supporting and the other opposing fundamentalism, the moderate Akalis vying with each other, and the political rivalry between the two leading contenders for power in the state, Akali Dal and Congress, provided the necessary space in the political structure for fundamentalism to gain strength.

In the wake of this, the specter of fundamentalism grew and ultimately Mrs. Gandhi, pursuing her strategy of majority communalism, sent in the army to the Golden Temple in June of 1984, killing Bhindranwale and many of his lieutenants. This incensed the vast Sikh masses, the bulk of whom still were not yet sympathetic to extremist and fundamentalist slogans. Given the ethos and culture of the community just outlined, it was not surprising that Mrs. Gandhi was assassinated a short while after this attack on the holiest of the Sikh shrines. Sikh grievances mounted still further when under the nose of the Congress administration and with its encouragement, Sikhs were brutally massacred in various parts of India.

THE PAKISTAN FACTOR

The state of Punjab has a 342.86 mile border with Pakistan, which is marked by ravines and elephant grass. It is relatively easy to cross the border for smuggling and for other such activities. Pakistan is a country with which India has fought three wars and, from the security standpoint, the Indo-Pakistan relationship has been a predominant concern for the Indian government. Without naming anyone but in an obvious reference to Pakistan's support of Sikh terrorists, a White Paper released by the Indian government in July of 1984 mentioned "active support from certain foreign sources with deep rooted interest in the disintegration of India." In August 1986, legislation was passed to create a 3 mile militarized zone on the Indian side of the border with Pakistan, and in January 1987 the Indian army and air force were placed on maximum alert following tensions between the two countries arising out of border maneuvers. At this time the army also sealed the Punjab border with Pakistan.[46]

The international dimension is another power resource with the fundamentalists and terrorists today; India has witnessed a number of hijackings of their aircraft to Pakistan and many arrested terrorists have also confessed to being trained in Pakistan. *India Today* (February 15, 1987) described in detail the various terrorist training camps set up in Pakistan.

While the resurgence of Sikh fundamentalism in Punjab can be attributed primarily to internal factors in the country, the international dimension came to play a part after fundamentalism and subsequently terrorism had grown significantly and had become a problem for the leadership. Once nurtured by the factors mentioned previously, Sikh fundamentalism and terrorism have been supported and encouraged by India's traditional enemy.

Interestingly and paradoxically, Sikh ethos and history, as mentioned earlier, have been built on a past that consists of Muslim persecution and the brave resistance of Sikh ancestors. Politics indeed makes strange bedfellows for the state of Pakistan does indeed glorify that period in Indian history that the Sikhs and Hindus both condemn as bigoted and sectarian. This said, all the same, Punjab's status as a border state and the historical animosity of the two neighbors, India and Pakistan, should not be overlooked in an analysis that seeks to explain the politics of Sikh resurgence and terrorism in the contemporary epoch.

CONCLUSION

In recent years several specifically politico-economic and contextual factors have boosted Sikh religious fundamentalism and terrorism in the Punjab province of India: the history, culture, and social structure of the region; the characteristics of the Sikh religion and the Jat Sikh caste; long-term changes in the agrarian social structure; elite and governmental inputs; and the machinations of political parties, factions, and politicians to win and maintain power. There are some similarities evidenced with the contemporary resurgence of Islam, Christianity, and Judaism.[47] In the Sikh case too, we see the characteristics of activism, identity assertion, and participation by the relatively well-off.

While not denying the role of factors like anomie and the social dislocation and psychological vacuum caused by modernization, I believe that these factors need to be treated as hypotheses that are complementary and not rival to my analysis. This is one point of departure from analysts like Hegland who stress that anomie and the motivating factors behind the involvement of religious resurgence movements in politics (e.g., the emergence to power of an economic group) are competing explanations for the emergence of religious resurgence in the world today. In rural Punjab for example, the appeal of fundamentalism on women, in the context of a male-dominated society and the high consumption of liquor by men, cannot be underestimated. According to one estimate (*India Today*, April 30, 1987), the state of Punjab alone collects about 200 crore rupees ($125,000,000) (roughly 30 percent of the total state revenue) every year from the liquor trade. Surely, only a naive analysis will overlook these support factors. This, however, is the task of the respective disciplines within whose purview the subject falls. Our concern is only on the adjacency of these factors to the explanation just given, and not to their rivalry.

The prevailing political economy determines, to a significant extent, the social color of a situation. Thus today in the Sikh religion, little emphasis is given to Sikhism's strong traditional belief in social equality, opposition to the caste system, and belief in a ritual free and simple life. Indeed, the holy book of the Sikhs, as mentioned before, is adorned with verses from saints who belonged to the untouchable castes. The overwhelming stress, on the other hand, is today placed on struggle and sacrifice for a righteous cause. The historian Khuswant Singh mentions that the evils associated with caste entered Sikhism at the time of Ranjit Singh.[48] The above is better explained in the context of the political economy just outlined, though it also needs to be mentioned that even today the virulence of caste is relatively less in Sikhism as compared to orthodox Brahmanical Hinduism, for example.

The Indian government continues to place political gain above principle and essentially relies on repressive measures for a solution that requires political acumen and willingness to take risks. In July 1985 it signed an agreement with the Akali Dal that led to a cessation of agitation by the Akali Dal for the implementation of the Anandpur Sahib Resolution, and a considerable decrease in terrorism. In May 1987, it dismissed the popularly elected Akali Dal led Barnala state government ostensibly for its failure to bring peace and communal harmony to the state, but actually to win political gains in the forthcoming state election in the neighboring state of Haryana. The Akali moderates have a no less enviable record. Recently, all of their legislators were accommodated in powerful ministerial and/or high official positions. None of the legislators wanted to be left behind in the race for power and the chief minister, in order to keep everyone happy, gave every legislator some important position or the other. One is reminded of Pettigrew's remark in *Robber Noblemen.*

> Throughout history the [Sikh] community has been broken into various political coalitions and never represented by any single political allegiance or alliance. Unwittingly, the effect of this pattern has always been that it has been pregnant with the possibilities of guarding the community on all fronts or of betraying it on all fronts (p. 33).

With all of this, there is nevertheless a hard-core Sikh element that has lost its faith in the political structure, legitimacy of government, the various parties including the Akali moderates, and is demanding an independent state of Khalistan. One source has listed eight Sikh extremist organizations.[49] These groups indulge in terrorist activities like killing innocent Hindu bus passengers in the state and outside, and planting bombs at public places. Additionally, they also kill police officers and prominent politicians. Basically, the terrorists want to have a Hindu backlash on the Sikhs outside Punjab, thereby facilitating Sikh migration into Punjab, and a migration of the Hindus from Punjab to other parts of India. In this way they hope to drastically alter the population composition of the state. This in turn should be a step toward the founding of an independent Sikh state. The border status of the state is another crucial element to be considered here.

The increasingly repressive measures of government rather than serving to crush the terrorists, gives them stronger grounds for the beliefs that they already possess. The government in this respect does not even take minimal steps to woo these elements back into the mainstream by implementing its own accord of July 1985 with the Sikh moderates thereby providing a somewhat conducive atmosphere in the state. It, in its wisdom, does not recognize the implications of the legend of the region at the time of the brutal persecution of the Sikhs by the Mughal governor of Punjab, Mir Mannu.

> Mir Mannu is our sickle
> We the fodder for him to mow
> The more he reaps, the more we grow.[50]

Postscript (December 1989)

The extent of the present-day alienation of the state of Punjab, and especially the Sikhs, is evident from the results of the recent parliamentary elections held in India. Simranjit Singh Mann, the head of an Akali faction and accused in a conspiracy to kill Mrs. Gandhi, won the Tarn Taran constituency (in which the Golden Temple is located) with the second highest vote margin in all of India. Also elected from the state were the widow of one of the assassins of Mrs. Gandhi and a supporter of an independent Sikh state (*New York Times,* November 29, 1989, p. 4).

18

Religion and Politics in the Jewish State of Israel
Mark Tessler

This chapter examines the relationship between religion and politics in the Jewish state of Israel, focusing both on the relationship between Zionism and Judaism and on major political and ideological trends relating to the place of religion in affairs of the state. The first section reviews the ways in which religious and nonreligious Jews responded to the emergence and evolution of the modern Zionist movement in the nineteenth and twentieth centuries, providing a foundation for the discussion of religion and politics in present-day Israel. The second section focuses on the period between 1948 and 1967 and devotes attention to issues associated with Israel's desire to be both a modern and a Jewish political community. The third section examines the emergence of Jewish fundamentalism in Israel in the years after 1967.

JUDAISM AND ZIONISM IN THE PRESTATE PERIOD

Modern political Zionism arose in Europe in the middle and latter part of the nineteenth century and had as its objective the construction of a Jewish national home in Palestine, a territory that the Jews considered Eretz Israel, the Land of Israel, and from which the Jewish people had been driven out almost two millennia earlier. The modern Zionist movement was vigorously denounced by most orthodox Jews, however, who regarded it as heretical and who insisted that it was based on flawed principles and fatal internal contradictions. Consistent with traditional Jewish beliefs, with what is sometimes called classical, religious Zionism, these pious Jews believed that their people's return of the Holy Land must await the coming of the Messiah. According to the logic of the orthodox, only a Jew who had lost faith in the biblical prophecy of a Day of Redemption would undertake to work on his own for an ingathering of Jewish exiles; and yet, without such faith, the idea of a return to Zion was meaningless. The Jews had remained a nation despite their long centuries in the Diaspora, and as a nation they had retained an unbreakable bond to the land of their ancestors, precisely and solely because of the historic covenant between themselves and their Creator.

Since the destruction of the second Jewish commonwealth in Palestine in the first century of the Christian era, believing Jews had lamented and regarded as temporary their sojourn in the Diaspora. Their daily prayers contained passages that affirmed their faith in the promise God had made to the Jewish people at the time they were chosen to receive His law, a promise that He would send a Messiah as part of His plan for the Jews and for humanity and that the coming of the Messiah would be accompanied by the establishment for all time of a Jewish dominion in the land of Israel. This faith even prompted messianic speculation among some Jews, with zealots and mystics using numerology and other forms of calculation in a vain attempt to discover in the Hebrew Bible a hidden message that would tell when the messianic era and the return to Zion would begin.[1]

Beyond reaffirming their faith in the divine plan, Jews were expected to be passive before God. Some believed they might hasten the coming of the Messiah by living righteous lives and by observing God's commandments scrupulously. Others, by contrast, asserted that the Day of Redemption was fixed. Nevertheless, whether preordained or amenable to modification, the unfolding of God's plan and the onset of the messianic era were matters the Creator alone could determine. Until the arrival of the Messiah, therefore, faith, patience, and obedience to God's law were what was required of the Jewish people.

This situation gave credibility to those orthodox Jews who saw contradictions in modern Zionism. Without a belief in the covenant between God and the Jewish people, on what basis could it be claimed that the Jewish citizens of various states were actually members of a single Jewish nation living in exile? Similarly, without faith in this covenant, by what right could that Jewish nation advance claims to a dominion in the land of Zion, a territory that for hundreds of years had for the most part been inhabited by others? Modern political Zionism made no sense, in other words, unless one trusted in God; and what man or woman trusting in God could possibly be unwilling to wait for the Creator's plan to unfold in its own divinely ordained fashion? The activist posture of modern political Zionism was thus denounced as heretical by orthodox Jews. By acting in God's stead to return the Jews to the land of their ancestors, modern Zionists betrayed their lack of faith and, thereby, made illogical and illegitimate their own proclamations of Jewish nationhood and the Jewish people's right to a national home in Eretz Israel. So strongly held were the convictions of these orthodox Jews that their leaders eventually contacted Britain and the League of Nations in order to denounce the Zionist Organization and to insist that its program was at variance with the wishes of the Jewish masses.

Pious Jews of the old school not only opposed political Zionism, which at the time was a new movement with a limited following, but they were also strongly opposed to the currents of secularism and assimilation that for several decades had been expanding rapidly among middle-class Jews in Western Europe. By the late nineteenth century, these currents were also making themselves felt in some Jewish communities of Eastern Europe. To the consternation of traditional Jewish leaders, there had grown up a class of European Jews who embraced a new definition of Judaism. To these Jews, modern concepts of citizenship were more important than historic religious attachments, and religion itself was increasingly seen as an exclusively personal matter. A man or woman might remain a Jew at home, of course, but political and national identity were expressed through loyalty to a modern European state and thus, from a purely political point of view, the distinction between Jew and non-Jew was regarded as having no legitimate importance. Moreover, among Jews who ceased to regard themselves as part of a Hebrew nation living in exile, even personal life-styles of an identifiably Jewish character were increasingly seen as anachronistic, suggesting that intermarriage and even conversion might not be long in coming.

The spread of such secularist and assimilationist currents, and the debates these currents produced among Jews of differing philosophical and religious inclinations, were undermined by the waves of anti-Semitism that broke out in Eastern Europe in the 1870s, and by the subsequent rise of serious, though less widespread or violent, anti-Jewish outbursts in Western Europe toward the end of the century. The upheavals of this period provided the impetus for the birth of modern Zionism, transforming what had been an intellectual movement with a limited following into an international network of steadily growing proportions that was organized for the specific purpose of establishing a Jewish homeland in Palestine. In response to pogroms in czarist Russia, the first organized Jewish migrations to Palestine began in 1882. Roughly twenty thousand Jews immigrated to Palestine in the ensuing two decades, almost doubling the size of the Jewish community in the country. Other developments included the first World Zionist Congress in 1896, the formation of the World Zionist Organization in 1897, and the establishment of the Jewish National Fund (JNF) in 1901. The purpose of the JNF was to raise money for Jewish settlement in Palestine.

The emergence and evolution of modern political Zionism made it necessary to address questions about the relationship between Judaism and Zionism and, in particular, to respond to the charges of heresy that continued to be issued by pious Jews of the old school. Religious Jews within the Zionist movement took the lead in articulating this response, advancing the argument that there was no contradiction between ancient Jewish beliefs about the coming of the Messiah and the founding of a modern political movement dedicated to the reconstruction of a Jewish homeland in Eretz Israel. Many religious Zionists were members of Mizrahi, a political party whose name was an abbreviation for Merkaz Ruhani, meaning spiritual center. Mizrahi's origins lie in the Hovevei Zion (Lovers of Zion) movement of Eastern Europe, whose pious members had initiated and sustained the wave of Jewish immigration to the Holy Land beginning in 1882. To distinguish themselves from nonreligious Zionists, these devout Jews established a separate office in 1893. They called this office the spiritual center and used it to organize orthodox Jews oriented toward Zionism, and within a decade Mizrahi was an important partner within the coalition of political parties governing the Zionist organization.

Mizrahi's response to the criticism of Zionism articulated in most orthodox Jewish circles was to deny that Zionists had lost faith in God and in His plan for the Jewish people and to insist that they had no thought whatsoever of acting in God's stead to return the Jews to Zion. On the contrary, it was Mizrahi's conviction that modern political Zionism, however secular and temporal a movement it might appear, was actually the instrument God had chosen to carry out the divine promise on which classical, religious Zionism is based. Thus, to religious Zionists, the messianic era had in fact begun and they, far from acting independently and without regard for the Creator, were actually, knowingly or not, responding to His will and serving His purpose. How could it be otherwise, they added, affirming their belief in the omnipotence of the Almighty and suggesting that it was their orthodox critics whose faith must logically be in doubt.

This view was articulated most forcefully by Rabbi Avraham Yitzhak Hacohen Kook (1865–1935), who immigrated to Palestine in 1904 and first became head rabbi of Jaffa and then Ashkenazi chief rabbi of Palestine. Kook insisted that God, not the Jews, had created the Zionist movement, as indeed He created all things. For a believing Jew, this could mean only that the messianic age was at hand, and proof of this observation lay in the fact that the Jews had begun to return to Palestine. The breakup of thousand-year-old Jewish communities in Eastern Europe was also, in Kook's view, evidence that the history of the Jews had entered a new era. Finally, Kook expressed confidence that the Jewish community in Palestine, the *yishuv*, would ultimately turn to religious law for governance. The modern Zionist movement was an instrument designed for returning the Jews to the Holy Land, but once in Eretz Israel the Jews would be reunited with their divine law by another instrument of God's design.[2]

Religious Zionists were actually but one of three major "streams" that crystallized within the movement, each of which eventually came to have several political parties within its ranks. In the early years of the twentieth century, a socialist stream, associated with Labor Zionism, emerged and became increasingly important. In addition to Religious Zionism and Labor Zionism, there was also a heterogeneous stream spanning the political center and right of the Zionist movement. It included a nonideological "General Zionist" wing and the militant but nonetheless secular revisionist faction. By the 1930s, Labor had established itself as the dominant faction and Mizrahi represented about 15 percent of all Zionists.

As the notion of "streams" suggests, there were important normative differences within the Zionist movement and some bore directly on the relationship between Zionism and Judaism. One particularly significant early issue, which also had implications for the debates between pro- and anti-Zionist Jews, concerned the degree to which the Zionist community in Palestine should have an identifiably Jewish character or, alternatively, should be a political community like any other, one that just happened to have a Jewish majority. In the early years of the movement, dissimilar answers to this question were articulated by men who called themselves political Zionists and cultural Zionists, respectively. The former argued that European nation-states provided the model for the development of the *yishuv* and championed what they sometimes called Jewish "normalcy." The state of the Jews should resemble other progressive polities and become an inconspicuous member of the modern world's community of nations. The latter, by contrast, called for the construction of a political community that was uniquely and identifiably Jewish, one that would be based on the laws and ethics God had given to the Jewish people and would also, in some important respect, fulfill the sacred mission for which God had chosen the Hebrews. For these Zionists, the Jewish state was not to be a state like any other.

While there soon emerged a consensus that the national home under construction in Palestine should have a meaningful Jewish identity, there continued to be disagreement about the practical implications of this consensus, about what should be the character and structure of a polity that declared itself to be Jewish. Religious Zionists were committed to the construction of a national home that was Jewish from a religious and spiritual, as well as from a sociological and demographic, point of view; they sought the establishment of a political community that would make no distinction between religion and politics and that would have as its mission service not only to the Jewish people but to Judaism as well. Members of Mizrahi and its sister party, Hapoel Hamizrahi (the Mizrahi Worker), accordingly argued that the *yishuv* should be governed by Jewish rather than secular law. As expressed by Rabbi Samuel Mohilever (1824–1898), a founder of the Mizrahi movement, "the Torah, which is the source of our life, must be the foundation of our regeneration in the land of our fathers."[3]

Labor Zionists and others, who constituted a substantial majority, saw things differently. They argued that worship and religious observance were essentially private matters and that the Jewish identity both of the *yishuv* and of the state to which it would eventually give rise could be adequately expressed in cultural and nationalist terms. While nonreligious Zionists did not advocate secularism, if secularism is defined as the absence of any formal tie between the institutions of government and the religious identity of individual citizens, neither did they favor theocracy. Their conception of a Jewish political community placed emphasis on the revival of Hebrew as a national language; on ties to the land of Eretz Israel, including a rejection of early proposals to establish a Jewish national home somewhere other than Palestine; on an institutionalized connection between the *yishuv* and Jewish citizens of other countries; and on the use of names and symbols that established an affinity between the modern Zionist polity and the ancient Hebrew commonwealths.

This debate within the ranks of Zionism has never been fully resolved. Although more and more of the world's Jews became ardent supporters of Zionism during the first half of the twentieth century, strongly held differences of opinion continued to exist about the proper relationship between religion and politics. On the eve of Israel's independence in 1948, there was widespread agreement that the goal of Zionism was the creation of a Jewish state in Palestine, not just *a* state and not even "a state for Jews." But there continued to be profound disagreement about the proper definition of a Jewish state. This disagreement, moreover, is the principal reason why Israelis failed to produce a Constitution to govern their newly independent polity. Israelis were simply too deeply divided about how to give specific meaning to the idea of a Jewish state to be able to agree on the provisions of a national Constitution.

As modern Zionism matured, the views of many previously anti-Zionist religious Jews began to change, and the experience of the Holocaust intensified this process greatly. While some of these pious Jews continued to reject all worldly political activity, the more moderate mainstream of this community organized itself into Agudat Yisrael, the Federation of Israel. Aguda remained outside the Zionist organization, which was headquartered in Europe until the 1930s. It also placed itself apart from the political institutions of the *yishuv*; although initially prepared to cooperate with other factions in order to meet the needs of Palestine's growing Jewish population, the party soon abandoned this policy, arguing that it would not help to govern a community that sanctioned Jews living in violation of *halacha* (orthodox Jewish law). Nevertheless, Aguda moved toward cooperation with Zionists as the circumstances of European Jewry deteriorated. Tragically, this came too late to save many of the orthodox Jews trapped in the ghettos of Eastern Europe. According to one scholar, most would have followed their rabbis to Palestine, had the latter not continued to oppose the construction of the *yishuv* until it was no longer possible to escape.[4] Be this as it may, many members of Aguda in the *yishuv* now displayed a willingness to cooperate with Zionist political parties; and in 1947, on the eve of Israeli independence, a formal agreement was reached whereby Aguda would take part in the political life of the new Jewish state.

To remove Aguda's refusal to join a Jewish polity whose laws were not based on *halacha*, the executive of the Jewish Agency agreed in a letter to the Aguda World Union that in four critical areas the circumstances of Jews in Israel would be governed by orthodox Jewish law. These areas were public observance of the sabbath and other Jewish holidays through the closure of government offices and the suspension of government operations; respect for Jewish dietary regulations, meaning that only kosher food would be served in state-run kitchens; observance of Jewish law in matters of marriage and divorce, with the added provision that no civil marriages would be permitted in Israel; and public financing for religious educational institutions. A few extremely orthodox elements, most notably the Neturei Karta, rejected this accommodation with Zionism and refused to recognize the State of Israel. Aguda accepted the arrangement, however, clearing the way for the party's participation in elections and enabling its members to accept Israeli citizenship. Aguda did not recognize Israel as *the* Jewish state. Rejecting Mizrahi's belief that the creation of the modern state of Israel reflects the beginning of the messianic era, Aguda continued to see modern Zionism as irrelevant from a religious point of view. On the other hand, since the majority of its citizens are Jewish, Aguda accepted Israel as *a* Jewish state and agreed that its fortunes are important for the temporal if not the spiritual well-being of Jewish people.

RELIGION AND PUBLIC POLICY FROM 1948 TO 1967

The achievement of Israeli independence in 1948 offered powerful evidence to Mizrahi and to other religious Zionists that the messianic era had indeed begun and that God's plan for the return of the Jews to Zion was continuing to unfold. On the other hand, Jews who subscribed to these views were a distinct minority in the new Jewish state. Moreover, not only did most Israelis pay little attention to Mizrahi's proclamations about the spiritual significance of Israel's modern existence, but they also displayed little enthusiasm for the more temporal aspects of the party's platform, namely that the country should be governed by orthodox Jewish law. In the first elections to the Israeli Knesset, or Parliament, which took place in 1948, a religious bloc including not only Mizrahi and Hapoel Mizrahi, but also several parties associated with Aguda, received only 12 percent of the vote. Three years later, Mizrahi and Hapoel Hamizrahi formed the National Religious party (NRP; also Mafdal), which ran its own slate of candidates in the parliamentary election of that year. The NRP captured 8.3 percent of the votes and was awarded 10 seats in the 120-member Knesset. Aguda received 3.6 percent of the vote and received 5 seats. Although the NRP was the fourth largest political party in Israel, it was far behind the principal Labor party, Mapai, which won 46 seats, and the party of the General Zionism, which won 23 seats in 1951.

Although most Israelis did not support the platform of religious political parties, the vast majority favored a meaningful Jewish identity for their state. They wanted a state that was both modern *and* Jewish. Thus, even as they disagreed with orthodox Jews about the degree to which their political community should be governed by religious law, and even as they remained divided about other issues bearing on the relationship between religion and politics, they reaffirmed a consensus reached by Zionists decades earlier and declared that Israel should be, and was, a Jewish as well as a modern polity. These sentiments were stated forcefully in the country's Declaration of Independence, which proclaimed that "it is the natural right of the Jewish people, like any other people, to control their own destiny in their sovereign state." Affirming also the ancient and historic rights of the Jewish people in Eretz Israel, the preamble declared that "the Land of Israel was the birthplace of the Jewish people. Here their spiritual, religious and national identity was formed. Here they achieved independence and created a culture of national and universal significance. Here they wrote and gave the Bible to the world." Thus, the document continued, "WE DO HEREBY PROCLAIM the establishment of the Jewish State in Palestine, to be called Medinath Yisrael," the State of Israel. Interestingly, the name "Israel" was selected at the last minute by the Jewish Agency, which had for a time been inclined to call the new nation the "State of the Jews" or "The Jewish State."[5]

The Declaration of Independence of course provided little specific information about the character of the Jewish state. It left unanswered what one Israeli scholar has called the "ever unsolved question" that had long preoccupied Zionist theoreticians: "Will the new Hebrew nation, on regaining sovereignty in its land, forsake all claims to Jewish exclusivist tradition and become a nation like every other nation?" Will the Jews eventually "differ from other peoples only as the French differ from the English, or will they retain some universal message, some uniqueness, some 'otherness'—the heirlooms of their past—in the world they seek to join?"[6] On the other hand, now that the State of Israel was a reality, questions about the relationship between religion and politics in the Jewish state would no longer, and could no longer, be debated in the abstract. With or without a consensus in vital areas, Israel's government would make decisions, allocate resources, and implement policies, all of which would shape the country's character and evolution and, in so doing, give empirical meaning to the idea of a modern Jewish state.

Early actions by Israeli leaders reflected self-conscious efforts to move in this direction and one such action was the enactment in 1950 of the Law of Return, which declares that every Jew has a right to immigrate to Israel and become a citizen. Only in the case of "acts against the Jewish nation" or of a threat to public health or state security may citizenship be withheld. Helping to define what it means to be a Jewish state, the Law of Return made clear Israel's conception of itself as the state of the entire Jewish people, not only of Jews in Palestine but of those in the Diaspora as well. While it does not address the more theological aspects of Jewish statehood, and also leaves unresolved many specific questions about the relationship between Israeli and Diaspora Jews, the Law of Return constitutes a major decision about a critical aspect of the connection between Judaism and Zionism. Jews throughout the world are seen as having a claim on the State of Israel, to which they may immigrate at any time either to find religious fulfillment or to escape persecution. And Israel will serve them even while they remain in the Diaspora, as the spiritual and cultural center of the nation of which they are a part.

Efforts to give substance to Israel's desire for a Jewish identity not only provided the context within which religious political parties could pursue their objectives, they also added to the legitimacy of these parties' activities. Indeed, in the view of some, religious parties were an indispensable element in a political system whose agenda included debates designed to produce an acceptable definition of what it means to be a Jewish state and actions designed to build a living polity based on that emerging definition. It is in this connection that Israel's first prime minister, David Ben Gurion of Mapai, asked Mizrahi leaders to join his cabinet, even though he did not need their votes to form a ruling coalition.

The National Religious party became a perennial coalition partner of Mapai and other Labor Zionist parties, and religious Zionists thereby participated on a regular basis in the governing of the country. Mapai received an average of about one-third of the votes in elections during the 1950s and 1960s, with another 13–14 percent usually going to smaller and more left-leaning Labor Zionist factions. Aided by a proportional representation system of balloting that treated the entire country as a single electoral district, the NRP regularly obtained 8–10 percent of the votes during this period, enough, when combined with the votes obtained by Labor, to provide the parliamentary majority necessary for a ruling coalition. From the viewpoint of the dominant Labor Zionist parties, the NRP was an attractive coalition partner not only because its participation in the government constituted the kind of political symbol that had been of concern to Ben Gurion, but also, and in all probability even more, because of the narrowness of its political platform. In return for concessions on religious questions, the NRP gave the government a relatively free hand in matters of defense, foreign policy, and economic development.

Through judicious and effective political bargaining, the NRP traded its support on nonreligious issues for the passage of laws and for the allocation of resources that responded to the priorities of its religious constituency. Thus, the new state adopted a number of measures that were unpopular among the nonorthodox majority but that were the result of compromises forged in the political arena. One such measure forbade buses from running on the sabbath in most cities and towns, the mixed Jewish-Arab city of Haifa being the only major exception. Another, adopted in 1962 after years of NRP lobbying, made it illegal for Jewish agricultural settlements to raise pigs, although in practice this regulation was not uniformly enforced. Many measures favored by the orthodox were not adopted, of course. For example, the NRP and other religious parties failed to secure passage of a law requiring interurban "service" taxis to suspend operations on the sabbath. Nevertheless, with both victories and defeats, the lobbying efforts of the NRP and other religious parties became a familiar and accepted part of the political scene. In a country that rejected definitions of secularism involving a complete separation of religion and politics, political debates and activities designed to resolve questions about the proper relationship between religion and state were seen as legitimate, perhaps even necessary. Even Israelis strongly opposed to the views of the orthodox, who sometimes complained bitterly that religious parties sought to impose on the entire nation the will of a small minority, for the most part shared this judgment.

The case of Brother Daniel illustrates the perplexing issues that sometimes arose as Israel struggled to determine what it means to be a modern Jewish state. Born of Jewish parents in Poland during World War II, Brother Daniel was hidden in a monastery during the Holocaust and subsequently converted to Catholicism, later becoming a monk. Then, in 1962, he decided to live in the Holy Land and, since Jewish law defines a Jew as anyone born of a Jewish mother, he applied for Israeli citizenship under the Law of Return. A decision in this case depended on whether the question of "Who is a Jew" should be answered with reference to *halacha*, as orthodox Jews insisted it logically must be, or in accordance with the commonsense principle that a Jew who converts to Christianity is no longer a Jew. The matter was ultimately referred to the Israeli High Court, which, despite opposition from the orthodox, made a distinction between Israeli and Jewish law and ruled that the definition of a Jew for purposes of the Law of Return is a "secular" rather than a religious matter. As a result, Brother Daniel was denied automatic citizenship, although he eventually became an Israeli through naturalization procedures. The question of "Who is a Jew" has also arisen on other occasions and, adding to confusion, the result has sometimes been a determination that *halachic* criteria *are* applicable.

To report that debates about the relationship between religion and politics are widely regarded as both legitimate and inevitable is not to suggest that they have been devoid of passion. On the contrary, disagreements about whether secular or religious authority should prevail in matters of Jewish self-definition, as well as about many other questions bearing on the application of religious law, have often been highly emotional. Moreover, political competition and conflicts have not always been confined to the Knesset and the courts. Taking their lobbying efforts into the streets, as it were, religious Jews have frequently staged marches and demonstrations in protest of business establishments that violate the sabbath, sometimes harassing patrons in an attempt to force the closure of shops, cinemas, and coffeehouses and sometimes seeking to put pressure on municipal councils to enact ordinances that will bring about the desired result. There have also been counterdemonstrations, organized by groups opposed to such ordinances.

In opposing the extended application of *halacha*, nonreligious Jews have frequently charged the orthodox with a failure to recognize that Judaism must accommodate itself to a world characterized by choice and change or be condemned to irrelevancy. "They would have us turn our back on present-day realities, they would plunge us back into the dark ages," it is often asserted; and, as an example, critics point to a conflict between modern medicine and the orthodox insistence that autopsies and organ transplants are prohibited by *halacha*. In other words, critics accuse the orthodox of wishing to make Israel a society that is Jewish alone, not Jewish *and* modern. Furthermore, accusing religious Jews of emphasizing the letter rather than the spirit of the religion, many add that a rejection of modernity and change is not required by a proper definition of Judaism. Some go so far as to label religious parties "anti-Judaic," stating that it is up to progressive Jews to differentiate between "a pagan degeneration of Judaism and its true substantive and creative vocation and development."[7] Similar views have also been expressed by some liberal-minded orthodox scholars, who criticize nonreligious as well as religious Jews and chide the former for failing to participate in debates about the true nature of Judaism. As expressed by one analyst, nonreligious Jews must recognize that Judaism "belongs to them as well as to those who officially represent religion."[8] If they do not assume responsibility for articulating a view of religion that can accommodate itself to present-day realities, adds another, "modern Zionists . . . will be left with a Judaism that repudiates modernity and will, in the end, undermine the whole Zionist structure that has been built here."[9]

While many nonreligious Israelis complained that orthodox Jews had influence disproportionate to their numbers, in the years following independence the NRP was in fact accused by some pious Jews of being too moderate and too ready to compromise on fundamental principles. This criticism was put forward by Agudat Yisrael, for example, whose followers are often described as "ultraorthodox." Aguda left the ruling coalition led by Ben Gurion in 1951 over the issue of women's service in the army. While the government agreed to exempt religious women from military service, Aguda at the time refused to support a government that made service compulsory for any Jewish women. It also stated, more generally, that it did not wish to lend legitimacy to an administration that disregarded *halacha* in many areas and that governed largely on the basis of secular law. So far as the NRP is concerned, Aguda complained about its "go-slow" approach, which pressed for particular bills extending the application of religious law but preferred not to push for comprehensive legislation, such as a national sabbath observance law. In addition, Aguda charged the NRP with putting its own interests above the defense of Jewish principles.

The NRP rejected these charges, of course, pointing out that Aguda's pronouncements were largely symbolic and asserting that far less religious legislation would have been passed were it not for its own pragmatism. It added that since Aguda had no governmental responsibilities, its Knesset members had the luxury of introducing any bill they might wish, but that such bills had nothing more than symbolic value. Some NRP spokesmen also suggested that Aguda knew its legislative proposals had no chance of passing and introduced them primarily for the purpose of embarrassing the NRP, which would frequently be required to abstain because of its position in a Labor-led coalition.[10] Finally, the NRP quite correctly observed that Aguda itself often cooperated with the government and frequently did so in pursuit of its own interests. Despite its denunciations of partisan politics, it was not unusual for Aguda to vote with the government and receive concessions in return.

This is the situation that crystallized during the two decades following Israeli independence, as the country struggled to discover what it means to be a Jewish state and to fashion a political process that would permit the formulation of public policy bearing on this critical issue. Between 1948 and 1967, there were important actions that gave substance to Israel's efforts to construct a society and a polity that are Jewish as well as modern. These include the agreement reached with the Aguda World Union on the eve of independence; the passage of the Law of Return in 1950; and a series of Knesset bills, court decisions, and local ordinances appearing in subsequent years. Moreover, the pattern of partisan politics that emerged in the years before 1967, characterized by the NRP's place in the government's parliamentary coalition and by loud debates and vigorous behind-the-scenes bargaining among orthodox, ultraorthodox, and nonreligious Israelis, describes the way that public policy dealing with religious issues was, and to a considerable extent still is, formulated.

Missing from this account is any consideration of Israel's non-Jewish population, a subject that is largely beyond the scope of the present inquiry and which, in any event, has not figured prominently in debates among Israeli Jews about the proper definition of a Jewish state. Nevertheless, it should be noted that Christian and Muslim Arabs constitute approximately 18 percent of the country's citizenry and that the presence of these non-Jews has important implications for Israel's search for a meaningful and modern Jewish identity. In particular, Israel must struggle to resolve, or at least to minimize, any potential contradiction between its desire to be a Jewish state and, since it wishes to be democratic as well, the need to treat all of its citizens equally. While Israel's Arab citizens do possess full and legally guaranteed political rights, equal under the law to those of Jewish Israelis, they are inevitably second-class citizens in important respects since they are not served by the country's declared political mission, which is to be the state of the Jewish people, and perhaps even of Judaism, as well as the state of all Israeli citizens.

Such concerns have thus far figured only peripherally in Israel's efforts to define and give substance to the Jewish national identity that is desired by the country's majority. They could become more important in the future, however, as Israel's Arab population becomes larger and more politically conscious and, also, if peace in the Middle East removes some of the tension associated with relations between Jews and Arabs in Israel. Under these conditions, Israeli Jews will become more aware of the need to define the identity of their state in ways that respond to Arab as well as to Jewish desires, and non-Jews in Israel will become a more potent force in the national and local political arenas where decisions regarding such matters are taken.

JEWISH FUNDAMENTALISM AFTER 1967

The war of June 1967, the so-called Six Day War, had a profound effect on Israeli politics and foreign policy. One particularly important consequence was the territorial modifications that resulted from Israel's stunning victory. Israel captured the Sinai Peninsula of Egypt; the Gaza Strip, which is inhabited by Palestinians but had been under Egyptian control; and the Golan Heights, which had been a part of Syria. Israel also captured the West Bank, and with it East Jerusalem, which had been part of Jordan prior to the war. While Israel's capture of these territories constituted a major turning point in the Arab-Israeli conflict more generally, it was also important because of the meaning it held for many orthodox Jews in Israel. Specifically, since these Jews consider the West Bank to be part of Eretz Israel, the historic and sacred Land of Israel, many of them saw Israel's victory as yet additional proof that the messianic age had begun. The return of the Jewish people to its land was continuing, they asserted, some professing also to find meaning in the fact that the war had lasted precisely six days. And of special significance to these Jews was the recapture of the Temple Mount in East Jerusalem. This was the political and religious center of the ancient Israelite kingdoms and its recapture by the Jews, an emotional experience for almost all Jewish Israelis, was taken as a particularly clear sign that Israel's fortunes in the war must have been bound up with God's plan.[11] A leading role in articulating this orthodox interpretation of Israel's victory in the June War was played by Rabbi Zvi Yehuda Kook, who succeeded his father, Avraham Y. H. Hook, as the most influential theoretician of religious Zionism. The younger Kook defined the State of Israel as the

"Kingdom of Heaven on Earth" and asserted that every Jew living in Israel is holy.[12]

It is interesting to note that some of Israel's Arab enemies also attached religious significance to the Jewish state's decisive victory. Some Arab and Muslim analysts noted that while the regimes in Syria and Egypt had been pursuing developmental strategies inspired by Arab socialism and secular nationalism, these countries were, if anything, weaker in 1967 than they had been when defeated by Israel in 1948. Israel, on the other hand, which was perceived as comfortable with its Jewish national identity, had grown stronger militarily and had been able simultaneously to provide for the welfare of its citizens. A rejection of secularism had not been injurious to Israeli development, these Arab and Muslim intellectuals pointed out, and perhaps Israel's Jewish character had actually contributed to its accomplishments. Whether or not these views reflected an accurate understanding of Israeli strength and Arab weakness, they gained currency in some Arab and Islamic circles and gave encouragement to the Islamic tendency political movements that began to appear in the early 1970s.

The future of the territories Israel had occupied in the war soon became a major issue in Israeli political life. By the end of 1967 there had emerged an international consensus that the Arabs and Israelis should seek to resolve their long-standing conflict through the application of a formula based on an exchange of land for peace. Specifically, Israel was to withdraw from territories captured in the June War and the Arabs were to recognize the Jewish state's right to exist. But while Israel's Labor-led government endorsed this formula in principle, it did not accept the interpretation offered by the Arabs, and by most outside observers as well, that Israel should relinquish all the territory it now occupied. Moreover, and even more important for the present analysis, there was no agreement inside Israel about the amount of territorial withdrawal that was appropriate. The future of much of the disputed territory was debated in terms of implications for national security. In addition, however, Israelis who advocated territorial compromise in the West Bank or East Jerusalem found themselves opposed not only by those concerned about the country's ability to defend itself in future wars, but by religious Zionists who attached spiritual significance to Israel's retention of these territories.

Most religious Zionists insisted that withdrawal from any part of Eretz Israel was unthinkable, even if the territory had no strategic value. Likening withdrawal to the human body's loss of a limb, these Jews insisted that the West Bank and East Jerusalem were not captured Arab territories at all but, on the contrary, liberated portions of the indivisible Land of Israel. Religious Zionists also claimed that withdrawal was prohibited by Jewish law, which, in their view, disallowed the surrender of Jewish sovereignty over any part of Eretz Israel. Indeed, this assertion was later given official sanction by one of Israel's two chief rabbis, who ruled in 1979 that "according to our holy Torah and unequivocal and decisive *halachic* rulings, there exists a severe prohibition to pass to foreigners the ownership of any piece of the Land of Israel, since it was made sacred by the *brit bein ha betarim* [Abraham's Covenant]."[13] Finally, taking their lead from Rabbi Kook, many orthodox Jews asserted that the retention of these territories would hasten the coming of the Messiah and, in the meantime, deepen Israel's spiritual character.

For all these reasons, many orthodox Jews in Israel were profoundly disturbed that some of their country's leaders were considering a withdrawal from part or all of the West Bank, and they denounced with special bitterness the small number of Israelis who advocated compromise with respect to East Jerusalem as well. The more militant and activist elements within the ranks of religious Zionism, including some younger individuals within the NRP, were committed not only to expressing the religious point of view on territorial issues but, if necessary, to taking action to prevent Israel from relinquishing the West Bank. Anything less would be a betrayal of their faith, they declared, since they were guided not by political calculations or even by philosophical principles but by a fundamental, God-given moral obligation. As expressed more recently by one orthodox leader, "Those who even discuss territorial concessions are committing the sin of 'Profanation of the Name of God.'"[14]

A high priority for Israelis holding these views was the construction of civilian Jewish settlements in the West Bank, which religious Jews and some others now called by the biblical designations of Judea and Samaria. Use of these terms was designed to call attention to the religious significance of the West Bank, to indicate that Jewish territorial claims are legitimate and predate those of the Arabs, and, finally, to create a subtle but politically important distinction between East Jerusalem and the rest of the West Bank. In seeking to establish settlements in the West Bank, religious Jews aspired to make tangible the Hebrew people's return to what they regarded as liberated portions of the Land of Israel. Many saw this as a religious duty with significant theological implications. In addition, however, addressing themselves to temporal concerns, they self-consciously sought to create a demographic presence and a network of Jewish interests that would make it difficult for the Israeli government ever to return the territory to the Arabs. This policy, supported by militant secular nationalists as well as by religious Zionists with a fundamentalist orientation, was often described as "creating facts" and was pursued with the explicit objective of making permanent Israel's control of the West Bank.

Qiryat Arba, adjacent to the West Bank Arab town of Hebron, was the first and most important settlement that religious Jews undertook to construct in the immediate postwar period. Work on the new settlement began in the spring of 1968 but was technically illegal, since the government had refused to authorize its construction. Then, in an important victory for religious militants, Qiryat Arba was given official recognition in February 1970 and continued construction of the new town was approved. This action followed repeated confrontations between the government and would-be settlers and was part of a compromise by which the former sought to prevent the latter from settling *inside* Hebron.[15]

Religious Jews committed to the retention of Judea and Samaria, whom nonreligious Israelis increasingly described as Jewish fundamentalists,[16] in 1974 formed Gush Emunim, or Bloc of the Faithful, a political movement composed of nongovernmental groups that had been working for some time to intensify Jewish settlement in the West Bank and in other territories occupied in the June War.[17] Although perhaps 20 percent of Gush's membership was not orthodox, the movement made no distinction between its religious and political objectives and, basing its arguments on Mizrahi's traditional views about the beginning of the messianic era, it regarded territorial issues as having deep spiritual significance. The movement was committed to Torah and well as to territory, in other words, insisting that there was no way to think about one without the other: fidelity to *halacha* and love of God required an attachment to all of Eretz Israel and, simultaneously, involvement in Judea and Samaria could not but promote devotion to Jewish law and hasten the Day of Redemption. Thus, in its own eyes at least, Gush is far more than a settler lobby making common cause with secular nationalist movements on the political right. It is a vanguard movement doing the work of the Almighty, pressing the government and fellow Jews to understand what God expects of them and to strive in the way He has chosen.

Gush's militancy and organizational effectiveness enabled it to exert considerable pressure on the Labor-led Israeli government, contributing to a significant increase in the number of West Bank settlements authorized by the cabinet between 1975 and the parliamentary elections of May 1977. Later, as the movement matured and gained adherents, it established its own settlement-construction organization, Amana, or Covenant; its own settlement administration, Yesha, or Salvation, which stands for the Association of Local Councils in Judea, Samaria, and the Gaza District; several more focused organizational structures, such as the Qiryat Arba-based Committee for the Jewish Return to Hebron; and its own monthly periodical, *Nekuda*. Thus, as one analyst has written with reference to Yesha, Gush Emunim's institutional foundation gave it "a semi-official governing body, elaborate economic and administrative resources, and direct involvement in implementing government policies in the occupied territories."[18]

Gush attempted to achieve its objectives not only through lobbying efforts designed to influence the government, but also, on occasion, by engaging in illegal activities. Such actions included the founding and transfer of Jewish residents to settler communities that had not been authorized. For example, Gush activists tried on eight separate occasions in 1974 and 1975 to establish a new West Bank settlement in the region of Nablus-Sebastia; and, though their construction efforts were dismantled by the army in each instance, the government was eventually forced to negotiate with Gush Emunim and accept a compromise. Still another important dimension of Gush's program of direct action was the harassment of Palestinian Arabs who refused to sell their land to Jewish settlements seeking to expand.

There were important affinities between Gush Emunim and the National Religious party, despite the absence of any formal connection between the two organizations. Indeed, Gush began as a faction of the NRP. The initial ideological and organizational thrust out of which the movement emerged took place within the party's educational institutions, and the NRP's B'nai Akiva's religious school network has remained one of the most important vehicles for the recruitment of Gush cadres. The National Religious party had become somewhat heterogeneous in the years since independence and not all of its leaders shared Gush's attitude toward the West Bank. Some, after years of participation in Labor-led governments, had become sympathetic to the need for territorial compromise. Furthermore, some NRP leaders who did favor retention of the occupied territories were nonetheless embarrassed by Gush's frequent lawlessness and by the aura of vigilantism that characterized many of its actions. Nevertheless, the shared spiritual and theological assumptions of the two movements were too important to ignore; and, in any event, a new generation of NRP leaders had begun to emerge by the mid- and late 1970s, and this "young guard" faction articulated a platform of religious militancy and territorial maximalism that placed it squarely in the camp of Gush Emunim. Under the influence of its young guard wing, the party became more ideological and began moving away from its established role as a compromise-oriented lobby for orthodox Jewish interests.

The elections of 1977 were a turning point in Israeli political life. The right side of the political spectrum was led by Menachem Begin and the Likud Union, which was descended from the militant revisionist wing of the Zionist movement and whose competition with Labor Zionism dated back to the British Mandate. In 1977, in what some analysts call Israel's "earthquake" election,[19] Likud scored a decisive victory over Labor and Begin then assumed the premiership and formed a government led by his party. This was the first time the country had not been led by Labor, and the change constituted a revolution that few would have thought possible a decade earlier. Begin, heir to revisionist Zionism's tradition of territorial maximalism and former leader of the irregular and illegal Jewish underground, had become prime minister.

Although Likud does not share Gush Emunim's views about the religious significance of the West Bank, the party is strongly committed to Israel's permanent retention of the territory. Moreover, its motivation is not based on considerations of security and defense but, rather, on what it considers to be the legitimate national rights of the Jewish people. Likud emphasizes considerations of history rather than spiritual fulfillment or the coming of the Messiah. Nevertheless, like Gush Emunim and the NRP, it regards the West Bank as part of Eretz Israel, the ancestral homeland of the Jews, and believes it essential that the territory be retained and developed for the benefit of its rightful owners. The newly elected Likud government thus promised a significant increase in settlement activity in the West Bank and in other occupied territories and almost immediately took steps to translate this promise into action. Whereas there had been about thirty Jewish settlements in the West Bank when Likud came to power in mid-1977, the number had more than doubled by the end of 1979. The number of Jewish settlers in the West Bank increased more than 300 percent during the same period, reaching 13,000 in early 1980.

The NRP, which won 9 percent of the vote in the 1977 elections and obtained twelve seats in the Knesset, joined Likud in forming a government coalition and used its influence inside the cabinet and the Parliament, just as Gush Emunim continued to exert pressure from without, on behalf of Israel's expanded settlement drive. Although a few senior NRP leaders had reservations about the wisdom of the government's approach to territorial issues and argued that compromise was necessary to achieve peace with the Arabs, the party's center of gravity continued to shift toward younger, more militant men who were eager to form a right-wing alliance of secular and religious nationalists opposed to any concession on questions of territory and settlement.

Israeli opponents of the right-wing alliance of Likud, Gush Emunim, and the NRP frequently argued that retention of the West Bank and other occupied territories threatened rather than enhanced Israel's Jewish character. Thus, quite apart from the question of peace with the Arabs, they asserted that Gush Emunim and secular advocates of territorial maximalism were actually undermining the very cause to which they claimed devotion. For the most part, this argument involved what Labor and parties further to the left called the "demographic" issue: should Israel retain the occupied territories, it would add more than a million Arabs to its population and threaten the country's Jewish majority. Indeed, given the higher birth rate of the Arabs inside Israel and in the occupied territories, it was probable that there would be more Arabs than Jews living under Israeli rule within a generation. Not only would this threaten Israel's Jewish character, moreover, it would also pose a significant challenge to the country's democratic political system. If granted citizenship, West Bank Arabs would help to vote the Jewish state out of existence, whereas the denial of citizenship would debase Israeli democracy and lead to governance on the model of South Africa. Likud, the NRP, and Gush Emunim rejected these arguments, of course, asserting that retention of the territories would stimulate Jewish immigration to Israel and encourage Arab emigration and, as a result, that critics of the settler movement were presenting not a demographic issue but a "demographic lie." Many in the NRP and Gush stated further that there was no need to address such questions since retention of the West Bank was divinely ordained.

The political orientation of Aguda also experienced some changes in the wake of the 1977 elections. The party joined the Likud-led ruling coalition and increased its efforts to extend the application of orthodox Jewish law. Moreover, in a manner that resembled the posture that the NRP had assumed in its early alliance with Labor, Aguda extracted promises of Likud support for religious legislation before agreeing to enter the latter party's coalition. Aguda's position became stronger as some centrist parties originally aligned with Likud defected from the coalition, and it grew stronger still following the 1981 elections, in which Likud repeated its victory over Labor but by a much smaller margin than in 1977.

In the coalition agreement which Aguda and other parties negotiated with Likud following the 1981 elections, fifty of the eighty-three provisions pertained to matters of religious law. The agreement called for the closure of Haifa and Ashdod ports on sabbath, for example, and for the suspension of sabbath flights by the national airline, El Al. A particularly controversial provision, raising again the question of "Who is a Jew?" called for amending the Law of Return so that among individuals converted to Judaism the law would apply only if the conversion had been carried out by an orthodox rabbi in strict accordance with *halacha*. The coalition agreement did not promise immediate action on all provisions. With respect to the Law of Return, for instance, it specified only that the prime minister felt that an amendment was needed. What is important, however, is the renewed emphasis on questions about the application of religious law and the fact that this emphasis was emerging primarily in response to political pressure exerted by religious parties, including Aguda.

So far as the occupied territories are concerned, some elements associated with Aguda took a hard-line position approaching that of Gush Emunim, but the mainstream of the party continued to oppose the highly nationalistic orientation of Gush and the settler movement. Indeed, leaders of the party severely criticized Gush and the NRP for "having two flags, one of nationalism and another of Torah," whereas "we have only one flag: the Torah."[20] Consistent with its traditional attitude toward Zionism, Aguda maintains that the territories are of no spiritual significance, since the messianic era has not begun and Israel is not *the* Jewish state, and that from a religious point of view it thus makes no difference whether the West Bank is retained by Israel or returned to the Arabs. The future of the territory should be determined by the temporal needs of the Jewish people, with the added provision that its return would actually be desirable should this save Jewish (and other) lives or otherwise enhance the well-being of the Jewish people. Aguda has participated in settlement activity in the West Bank; but the party insists that its followers would be willing either to withdraw from the territory or live under Arab rule should Israel someday relinquish the land on which ultraorthodox settlements are built.

Beginning in the late 1970s, encouraged by the policies of the Likud government, Gush Emunim and other Jewish fundamentalists intensified their settlement-related activities in the West Bank and elsewhere. Furthermore, seeing itself as the vanguard of the settler movement, Gush argued that it must lead rather than follow the government in establishing and populating new settlements, and in fact it often criticized Likud for inadequate support of its efforts to deepen Israel's control of the occupied territories. The movement organized numerous seminars, field trips, and programs for youths in an effort to win converts. It also mounted direct action campaigns to embarrass the government or force its hand. Finally, as noted, Gush more or less deliberately encouraged the harassment of Palestinians in the West Bank, in order to create tension and increase Israeli reluctance to withdraw from the area. Although the use of violence is strongly condemned by some Gush supporters, the movement has contributed, not altogether unconsciously, to the creation of an atmosphere in which lawlessness and vigilantism are defended as expressions of Jewish patriotism.

In May 1984, Israeli authorities arrested thirty-seven settler-activists on charges of membership in a Jewish terrorist network. The network called itself Terror Against Terror (TNT) and the charges against its members included bombings that maimed two West Bank mayors in 1980 and a shooting and handgrenade attack on the Islamic University of Hebron in 1982. In the verdicts handed down in 1985, twenty-eight of the accused were found guilty and several were sentenced to life imprisonment. Others received lesser punishments, some as little as a few months.[21] Evidence that the accused terrorists were operating within the framework of Gush Emunim was provided by statements of the defendants themselves, and their actions were in fact defended by many Gush leaders.[22] Some condemned the government for prosecuting members of TNT, saying that terrorist activities would be unnecessary if the government gave adequate support to Jewish settlers and was more vigorous in suppressing Palestinian political activities. On the other hand, at least some Gush supporters were genuinely dismayed by the revelations about Jewish terrorism. For example, Shubert Spero, holder of the Stone chair of Jewish thought at Bar Ilan University, wrote that "grim foreboding took hold of many of us who saw ourselves in the ideological camp of Gush Emunim. . . . The discovery [of terrorist activities] has posed a very serious challenge to Gush Emunim and those who identify with its philosophy."[23]

The political climate prevailing in the early and mid-1980s encouraged the emergence of new religious parties with a fundamentalist orientation, parties that cooperated with Gush Emunim and that occupied the political space to the right of the NRP. One such party was Morasha, which won two Knesset seats in the elections of 1984. The party was formed by Rabbi Chaim Druckman, a former NRP Member of Knesset and Gush Emunim activist who criticized the government for lethargy in the expansion of West Bank settlements.

Kach is an even more militant party that won a Knesset seat in 1984. The movement is headed by Meir Kahane, an American-born rabbi who founded the Jewish Defense League in the United States and who retained his American citizenship until September 1985.[24] Kach has as its objective the breakdown of communication between Jews and Arabs and the exacerbation of hostility and violence to the point where all prospects for peace, or capitulation from Kach's point of view, will be destroyed. Asserting that Judaism and democracy are incompatible, Kahane and Kach also seek to rescind the rights of citizenship currently enjoyed by Arabs living inside Israel. As Kahane has declared, "No non-Jews can be citizens of Israel." If they nonetheless chose "to live there in tribute and servitude, then they must be treated charitably. Never as equals, though." And if they refuse to accept this situation, "We'll put them on trucks and send them over the Allenby Bridge."[25] Although Kach is often dismissed as a group of the "lunatic fringe," public opinion polls conducted in 1985 and 1986 suggested that support for Kahane and his movement was growing.

In addition to the growth of fundamentalism in orthodox Jewish circles, fragmentation on the right side of the Israeli political spectrum also had an important effect on religious parties in the 1980s. Much of this fragmentation was the result of increased political consciousness among religious Jews of Afro-Asian origin, those whose parents migrated to Israel after 1948 from Muslim countries in the Middle East and North Africa and who adhere to the Sephardi (rather than the Ashkenazi) Jewish tradition. Like their nonreligious counterparts, orthodox Afro-Asian Jews complained that they had been taken for granted and neglected by established political parties; and, in the case of the NRP, this included charges that the party's schools and programs had consistently slighted Sephardi personnel and practices. A bloc of Afro-Asian Jews thus defected from the NRP prior to the 1984 elections, forming a new party, Tami, that captured three Knesset seats.

The NRP also lost some votes because of the changing character of its ideological appeal. On the one hand, as the party became more militant and nationalistic, some of its longtime supporters defected to centrist parties. On the other, since the party was now campaigning on a platform of territorial maximalism, it was in competition with other right-wing parties supporting the settler movement. As a result of these various challenges, the NRP captured only six Knesset seats in the elections of 1981 and, with the successful performance of Morasha and Kach, this dropped to only four seats in the balloting three years later.

Similar developments affected Aguda, which experienced some defections from ultraorthodox Jews who were acquiring a more nationalistic orientation and, even more, like the NRP, was plagued by the disaffection of its own Afro-Asian supporters. As one Israeli scholar explained, Sephardi Jews belonging to Aguda came to the realization that "they had been used as vote-getters, rather than accepted as genuine participants in the party's leadership."[26] The emergence of this attitude among Afro-Asian Jews supporting Aguda resulted in the creation of a new party, the Sephardi Torah Guardians, or Shas, in time for the 1984 elections. The consequences for Aguda were severe. Whereas the party had won four Knesset seats in 1981, it was left with only two after the 1984 elections. Shas, by contrast, captured four seats in the balloting of the latter year.

While these developments placed in doubt the future of Israel's two oldest and most established religious parties, the NRP and Aguda, they did not lead to a diminution of support for the settler movement. The electoral successes of Morasha and Kach, as well as those of nonreligious factions on the far right, meant that parties which identified with Gush Emunim and which criticized Likud from the right side of the political spectrum now made up fully 10 percent of the Israeli Parliament. Furthermore, as noted, public opinion polls in 1985, 1986, and 1987 indicated that these extremist factions were continuing to gain strength and might do even better in the elections scheduled for 1988.

Looking to the future, there are some factors that could limit the growth of Jewish fundamentalism and others that may contribute to its further development. On the one hand, many Israelis are deeply disturbed by the activities of the settler movement, and particularly by those of Gush Emunim and Kach. The number of

Israelis who have participated in demonstrations protesting fundamentalist goals and tactics probably totals several hundred thousand. Furthermore, since Gush represents a fusion of religious
orthodoxy and territorial maximalism, it is important to note that
criticism of the movement has sometimes come from religious Jews.
For example, in a 1984 address to Oz VeShalom and Netivot Sha-
lom, two religious peace organizations, the president of the Israel
Academy of Sciences and Humanities told his audience that "what
provokes my deepest opposition is their totalitarian orientation.
This derives from a pronouncedly chauvinistic approach which has
the effrontery to wrap itself in a religious mantle. They [Gush mem-
bers] talk as if they alone know the intentions of Divine Providence,
whose instruments they are."[27]

On the other hand, public tolerance of the settler movement
and associated fundamentalist tendencies should not be underestimated. It is not unusual to hear Israelis who oppose both their
methods and goals express grudging admiration for the idealism
and self-sacrifice of Gush Emunim's members. Many Israelis claim
to be unhappy about present-day materialism and, looking with
nostalgia to the pioneer spirit and sense of purpose that brought
their parents to Palestine, they may accord the settler movement a
certain respect on the grounds that its members are motivated by
considerations of principle, rather than by the pursuit of wealth or
status.

An opportunity to gauge the degree to which fanaticism on
the far right is tolerated was provided by the trial of Jewish terrorists in 1985. Though vigorously denounced by many Israelis,[28] the
accused were also defended by Israelis having no connection with
the settler movement. Some prominent Israelis even testified on behalf of the defendants, among them a Member of Knesset affiliated
with the Labor Alignment.[29] The light sentences given to many defendants may be a further indication of public tolerance. Indeed, although it did emphasize the gravity of the crimes the terrorists had
committed, the three-judge panel deciding the case specifically declared that it was influenced by "humanitarian and extraordinary
personal" considerations. One judge stated of the defendants, for
example, that "they are mostly men of Torah and labor, who left
behind them an easy way of life and went, with their families . . .
[to contribute] to the causes of state, security, settlement and
welfare."[30] Finally, after serving short terms in prison, at least
seven of the convicted Jewish terrorists had their sentences com-
muted by Israel's president, Chaim Herzog. Twenty of the twenty-

eight convicted terrorists were thus out of jail in three years or less and, following their release, some assumed important positions in West Bank settlement organizations.

CONCLUSION

Israel's expanding presence in the West Bank and Gaza Strip has led to mounting anger among the Palestinian inhabitants of these territories; and, although this has brought protests and clashes with Israelis on numerous occasions, the most sustained and significant expression of Palestinian discontent was the general uprising, or *intifada*, that began in December 1987 and was still under way in mid-1989. The elections of November 1988 were held against the backdrop of the *intifada* and, not surprisingly, given both the violence and worldwide attention that the Palestinian uprising had produced, the disposition of the occupied territories was the overriding issue in the elections. Labor campaigned on a platform of territorial compromise, Likud advocated sterner measures to suppress the uprising, and parties associated with Gush Emunim and the settler movement issued familiar calls for the enlarging of Israel's demographic and political presence in all parts of Eretz Israel.

Labor and Likud won almost the same number of Knesset seats and both also fared more poorly than they had in 1984. To the surprise of most observers, however, and in contrast to what had been predicted by the most public opinion polls, the big winners were not the religious and secular nationalist parties of the far right, those in the ideological camp of Gush Emunim, but the ultraorthodox, non-Zionist parties that stood apart from the settler movement. Aguda gained three Knesset seats, bringing its total to five; Shas gained two seats, giving it a total of six; and a new ultraorthodox party, Degel Torah, won two seats. Thus, the ultraorthodox, non-Zionist parties, which together had won six seats in 1984, more than doubled their representation in the Knesset that was elected in 1988. One factor that contributed to these developments is the rapid demographic growth of Israel's ultraorthodox community, as a result of both natural increase and immigration. Equally important, in all probability, is the increasing political consciousness of non-Zionist religious voters. It appears that voter turnout among the ultraorthodox was higher in 1988 than it had been in the past. Also, perhaps dissatisfied with the diminished attention to religious issues paid by the national unity government formed in 1984, there may have been some ultraorthodox Jews who voted for either Labor or Likud in previous elections but decided to give their votes to a religious party in 1988.

As a result of their electoral success, religious parties were aggressively courted by both Likud and Labor representatives seeking to establish the basis for a ruling parliamentary coalition. The ultraorthodox made extensive demands of both Labor and Likud, moreover, suggesting that the price of their support would be high and raising fears among the country's nonreligious majority that the new government would extend the application of religious law to many aspects of public life. Jews in other countries were concerned as well, especially when Likud promised the ultraorthodox parties that it would support an amendment to the Law of Return. In response to growing fears of undue religious influence, thousands of Israelis sent letters and telegrams to the president of the country, urging that he try to persuade Labor and Likud to establish another national unity government and thereby prevent the formation of a coalition which, irrespective of whether it was led by Labor or Likud, would be dependent on religious elements for survival. In the end, reluctantly, Labor and Likud did form such a coalition. On the other hand, the success of ultraorthodox parties in the 1988 election suggests that religious issues may nonetheless emerge with renewed intensity in the years ahead and that Israel will be forced to address with more urgency and self-awareness than it has for some time the nature of the modern and Jewish society it wishes to become.

The future of Jewish fundamentalism and the settler movement also remains to be determined. Although the religious and secular parties of the nationalist right did not fare as well as did ultraorthodox parties, or as had been expected by many Israeli analysts, they captured as many seats in 1988 as they had in 1984 and remain a potent force in Israeli political life. The NRP gained one seat in the election, bringing its total to five. Moreover, a new centrist religious party, Meimad, which sought to appeal to orthodox voters who disapproved of the NRP's drift toward fundamentalism, did not win a single seat in the new Parliament. Both Kach and Morasha lost the seats they had won in 1984, with the former party having been banned by the elections commission on the grounds that Kahane's proposals and rhetoric exceeded what could be tolerated in a democratic society. On the other hand, two seats were won by Moledet, a militant new party that campaigned openly on a platform advocating action to drive Palestinians out of the West Bank and Gaza. Moledet, which means homeland, called this the "transfer" option. Five other Knesset seats went to secular parties of the far right, the same number these ultranationalists had captured in 1984. Thus, the strength of those parties associated with Gush Emunim and like-minded factions was not diminished by the election of 1988, and this in turn suggests that Israel can expect continuing debates and political confrontations about the future of the West Bank and its relationship to Judaism, Zionism, and to the will of the Almighty.

Part V. Afterword

In the following chapter, Emile Sahliyeh uses the case studies in this volume as the foundation for advancing some potentially generalizable analytical conclusions about the relationship between religious resurgence and politics.

19

Concluding Remarks
Emile Sahliyeh

As we enter the last decade of the twentieth century, it seems certain that the political role of religion has been more enduring and resilient than originally thought in the 1950s and 1960s. Earlier expectations that urbanization and social mobilization would diminish the role of religion in public life have not been fully realized in many Third World countries. In these societies, religion and politics have remained closely intertwined despite modernization literature's prediction about the inevitable triumph of secularism. Rather than disappearing from the political scene, the traditional religions of Judaism, Islam, and Christianity have proven to be adaptive and accommodating to the requirements of modernization.

Based upon the essays in this volume, as well as other existing literature,[1] four broad conclusions seem warranted. First, in an increasing number of societies religion serves as a vehicle for social and political change. Many of the chapters have pointed to the need to recognize religion as a modern dynamic political force rather than as an archaic and reactionary phenomenon. Second, the causes of religious resurgence are too complex and diverse to be explained by a single approach. Third, the majority of the politically revitalized religious groups in the West do not constitute a threat to democracy, civil liberties, or political stability, while in the Third World some of the religious groups advocate democratic ideals in an effort to consolidate their political support. However, many others are authoritarian in their approach to politics. Finally, despite the challenges to secularism emanating from the politicization of traditional religions, the effects of religious resurgence should not be overexaggerated.

RELIGION AS A DYNAMIC POLITICAL FORCE

Notwithstanding religion's opposition to aspects of modernization that clash sharply with established moral and social values as
well as religious absolutes, many of the revitalized religious groups
are not against the benefits of modernization and scientific advancement. They want such advances to take place in a "proper" cultural
setting. In view of the rapid social and economic change that is taking place in many parts of the world, such religious groups do not
want to be left behind. This explains why they constantly try to
adapt themselves to the requirements and needs of modern life.
Such a process of adjustment is inescapable if these traditional religions wish to remain relevant and appealing to their followers. This
has been evident in their pursuit of higher education, their engagement in diverse occupations, and their widespread use of radio and
television and other means of communication to disseminate their
message and broaden their recruitment potential.

One of the most important modernizing roles of religion lies in
its opposition to authoritarianism in different parts of the Third
World. Despite religion's traditional role of support of the status
quo and advocacy of the simple life, the phenomenon of religious
resurgence has been accompanied by calls of several contemporary
religious movements (Islamic groups in Egypt, Lebanon, and Iran
together with the Catholic church in Latin America) to go beyond
their "renewal of the prophetic tradition." They call for social, economic, and political equality and offer social-welfare-related services
to the underprivileged. In addition, religion provides the rising
classes with a tool for collective action. A unifying ideology, symbolism, leadership, organizational structure, and communication
networks are among the resources that religions can make available
for the aggrieved persons. In this connection, Islamic symbolism—
in the form of Shi'a doctrine and Shi'a clerics—has been valuable in
the efforts of the Lebanese and Iranian Shi'a to resist foreign domination and oppressive rule, and to demand the redistribution of
available resources more equitably. Likewise, the organizational
structure of the Catholic church in Poland, the Philippines, and
Latin America and the availability of a sophisticated communication
network to the conservative Protestants in the United States, increased the mobilization and recruitment potential of these religious
groups in their respective societies.

Also, the revitalization of traditional religions widened the circle of political participation and made politics relevant to many tra-

ditional societies. Moreover, in places where secular political structures and ideologies have not been allowed to operate freely, religion served as a mechanism for the articulation of popular demands for socioeconomic equality and political freedom. The sanctity of the places of worship makes the political cost of clamping down upon religious institutions and leaders prohibitive.

As Michael Dodson has indicated in his chapter, after abandoning its former allies (the ruling classes and the landed gentry) the Latin American Catholic church joined the ranks of the popular opposition to protest the military dictatorships and the widespread poverty. The church's sponsorship of the Christian base communities fostered a strong sense of class consciousness, communal solidarity, and popular participation among the Latin American poor. In Egypt, Poland, and the Philippines the clergy supported the process of democratization. Religion also offers itself as a mechanism for the lobbying activities of pressure groups. In the United States and Israel, among others, conservative interest groups use religious symbolism to apply pressure upon their respective governments to be more accommodating and responsive to their needs and interests.

In the aforementioned cases, self-interest lay behind the religious support of the process of democratization and opposition to authoritarianism. Such self-interest includes coping with the challenge of modernization, neutralizing rival ideologies and groups, and gaining political legitimacy to operate in the open. Irrespective of the true motives of these revitalized religious groups' support of democratic principles, two points are noteworthy. First, the new patterns for popular political participation will affect the authoritarian organizational structure of traditional religions. Second, it would be wrong to conclude from the preceding analysis that the phenomenon of religious resurgence can always be expected to be associated with the quest for a greater degree of popular participation. As the two chapters by Laura O'Shaughnessy and Lawrence Jones have pointed out, the antidemocratic stands of the conservative Protestants in Central America and South Africa will not support such a conclusion. Most evangelicals in Central America support the right-wing authoritarian regimes and accept the conditions of social marginality of the Latin American poor. Similarly, evangelicals in South Africa have been vehemently opposed to the extension of equal political rights to the Afrikaans.

Finally, despite the transnational and global character and orientation of religions, religious resurgence has been associated with a strong nationalist overtone. In the Middle East, for instance, Islamic revivalism has assumed an anti-Western and anticolonial orientation and manifested a strong desire for political and economic independence. These nationalist orientations have also been revealed in the drive of Islamic modernists to replace Western values and life-styles with Islamic ones and to rid imported science and technology of their Western overtones. Nationalist sentiments have also been visible in the attitudes of the Catholic church in Poland, the Philippines, and Latin America. In the United States and Israel the revitalized religious groups exhibited strong patriotic sentiments and support for a viable defense program.

EXPLAINING RELIGIOUS RESURGENCE

A second primary undertaking for this study has been to advance a more sophisticated explanation to the phenomenon of religious resurgence. Such an explanation would go beyond viewing religious renewal as being primarily a response to grievances and deprivations. In fact, many of the essays went beyond viewing religion as a refuge to which alienated individuals and groups retreat. Instead, religious precepts are invoked to promote political demands and socioeconomic interests of newly emerging classes and social groups.

The combination of the following four factors have served as a catalyst for the political revitalization of traditional religions. First, the failure of secular ideologies to provide solutions to pending socioeconomic and political problems have prompted the aggrieved to look to their religion for an answer. More to the point, given the inconclusive presence of the political, social, and economic modernization programs in several parts of the Third World, the secular ideologies lost much of their glamour and appeal. The political elite themselves could no longer provide their adherents with the same kind of excitement and energy they did a few decades ago.

By contrast, religion seems to provide its adherents with well-defined answers and a clear vision for the future. The success of religious groups in addressing some of these grievances may convince others of the utility of the religious model.

Second, the political revitalization of traditional religions depends upon the prevailing socioeconomic and cultural conditions. The uneven economic modernization within and among Third World states provides a proper environment for religious resurgence. The prevailing poor living conditions in these countries;

mounting unemployment; and the scarcity of social, educational, and health services, would certainly make the underprivileged susceptible to the appeal of religion—especially one that emphasizes themes of equality or personal development. In an effort to force the government to redistribute available resources and to have a greater share of economic prosperity, the politicized poor may very well invoke religion. Clergy in Islam and in the Latin American popular church have been important agents of political mobilization. The renewed interest in religion may also occur in response to upheaval resulting from a rapid process of social and economic change, the disruption of habitual life-styles, and the perceived spiritual and moral emptiness of modernization. In such a case, religion will give the individual a sense of continuity and direction.

Religious resurgence is also likely to occur in those societies whose culture does not distinguish between religion and politics. For instance, in both Israel and the Arab world, religion is an essential component of secular nationalism and an important source for individual personal identity. In fact, Islam and Judaism have provided a congenial environment for the revitalization of traditional religious groups.

In some cases, religion may provide its adherents with strong ideological justifications to undertake political risks that otherwise may not be contemplated. The exaltation of personal sacrifice and martyrdom by the Sikh and Shiite cultural and religious traditions have in part been responsible for the emergence of a militant religious movement in both communities. The recent history of Lebanon, Iran, and India provides numerous examples of men and women who sacrificed their lives in the name of achieving higher religious and communal goals.

Third, outside threats to group ethnic identity and political integrity may lead to the restoration of past traditions as a mechanism for national self-preservation and cultural purity. Exposure to the "alien" Western culture or subjugation to foreign control are held in many Third World countries to be responsible for the decline of indigenous social and economic institutions and for the erosion of traditional political values.

The threats to group ethnic identity do not have to always be externally generated. Minorities like the Sikhs in India and the Christians in southern Sudan may reinvoke their traditional religion in order to resist the efforts of their governments who in the name of national unity may impose the culture of the majority upon the rest of the society. In such a situation, the distinctive religious backgrounds may be used by these minorities to buttress their demands for autonomy for the central government or even complete independence. In the West, by contrast, the threat to group morality and spiritual identity emanates from the excesses of the new permissive culture. The high divorce rate, homosexuality, frequent use of drugs, increase in the crime rate, decline in traditional family values and unity, and legalization of abortion are some of the reasons behind the crisis of morality and spiritual identity in the industrialized West.

Fourth, the availability of economic assets, leadership resources, organizational structures, and political opportunities are crucial factors for the political mobilization of traditional religious groups and movements. As the chapters on the United States and Egypt demonstrated, the improvement in the quality of life, the access to advanced education, occupational flexibility, and the availability of more leisure time and mass media have enabled the socially marginal groups to be increasingly politically active. Being aware of their newly acquired power, members of those groups go beyond seeking the improvement in their standard of living to demand a greater degree of political influence.

The emergence of a charismatic religious leadership is another factor that may accelerate the process of religious resurgence. This leadership can give hope to their followers for a better future and represent their interests before the incumbent regimes. Television, radio, and other means of communication enable the leaders to spread their message and recruit new followers.

Finally, political backing of the secular elite is crucial for the political activation of traditional religious groups. In their effort to widen their popular support and political legitimacy, secular politicians often use religious symbols and form alliances with traditional religious groups. Indeed, religion's increasing appeal has compelled many of the Third World leaders to give religious overtones to their rule. In the United States, the conservative Republican politicians formed political coalitions with the new Christian Right in the 1980s in order to widen their base of popular support. Despite the expedient nature of such secular-religious alliances, the support of the incumbent regimes would give the followers of these religious movements political legitimacy and credibility and would enable them to operate with fewer political restrictions.

The opportunities for the political revitalization of traditional religions need not be confined to domestic political support. Outside governmental or private help can be also crucial in sustaining the politicized religious movements. In this regard, the Islamic re-vivalist religious movements in individual Arab countries benefited significantly from the financial and political support of neighboring rival regimes. Both Jordan and Iraq backed the Muslim Brotherhood rebellion against the Syrian regime in the early 1980s. Similarly, the Sikh separatist movement in India and the United States-supported Islamic opposition to the Soviet invasion of Afghanistan received generous aid from Pakistan. Finally, private aid was also extended by evangelicals in the United States to their conservative counter-parts in South Africa and Central America.

THE LIMITS OF RELIGIOUS RESURGENCE

Before bringing this book to an end, two additional crucial is-sues need to be addressed: the violence associated with some ex-tremist religious groups and the future of religious resurgence. These issues continue to generate heated debate among scholars and politicians alike. Terrorism by some extremist religious groups and the militant rhetoric of others have left a negative imprint on the general phenomenon of religious resurgence. Critics often argue that religious resurgence constitutes a threat to civil liberties, de-mocracy, political stability, and national integration. There is no doubt that the terrorist activities of some of these extremist religious groups have been despicable and abhorrent and that other religious movements are authoritarian in nature. Yet it is wrong to generalize from this to the whole phenomenon of religious resurgence. To do so would lead to misleading conclusions about the causes and the nature of religious revivalism.

Religious resurgence is not a cohesive or monolithic movement in either individual countries or across national boundaries. It man-ifests itself differently throughout the world, reflecting diverse cul-tural settings, tactics, strategies, and programs. One would err to group together those extremist religious movements that engage in violence and terrorism with those that demand the reinstitution of the prophetic tradition and the observance of a strict social and moral code of behavior. It is also a mistake to try to equate either of these two groups with those who advocate the introduction of far-reaching socioeconomic and political reforms in their societies.

Those religious groups that practice violence and terrorism constitute only a small fraction within the larger religious resur-gence movement. The majority of these religious groups are re-formist. Despite their publicly expressed desire to fundamentally transform the society, many of the revitalized religious groups accept incrementalism and compromise and use peaceful tactics to achieve their objectives. In an effort to widen their political appeal they also address issues of wider secular interests, form political parties, and contest parliamentary elections. Still others lobby their governments to serve their respective interests.

It is difficult to imagine that the contemporary religious movement of the new Christian Right and liberal Catholicism in Latin America, the Philippines, and Poland would seriously threaten the prevailing secular values and political institutions. Most elements within each of these religious tendencies accept the separation of religion and the state, the freedom of religion, and the equality of the individual. It is only when their grievances are left unanswered and unattended or they are repressed that some of these religious groups may embark upon the use of violent tactics to advance their goals.

THE FUTURE OF RELIGIOUS RESURGENCE

Two decades after the prediction of the modernization literature about the eventual demise of traditional religions, a number of religious movements emerged and religion and politics remained closely connected in many societies. The resilience of traditional religions and their adaptation to requirements of modernization present a challenge to the unilinear deterministic orientation of the secularization model.

Given these challenges, can we conclude that the current wave of religious political activism is ushering in the onset of a new dawn of a worldwide religious resurgence? A far-reaching conclusion of this sort is certainly unwarranted. There is no doubt that the role of religion in public life is more enduring and extensive than the literature of modernization expected. The strength and the influence of the politicized religious groups should not, however, be exaggerated. Despite the emergence of several of these religious groups and movements during the 1970s and 1980s, there is no wide-scale cooperation among them or coordination of activities across state boundaries. Religious resurgence is not sweeping across the world at a rapid pace nor is the secularization model threatened by an eminent religious paradigm takeover. There is no automatic spillover effect of religious resurgence to other societies. After all, religio-cultural boundaries between nations are not easily penetrable.

As Donald Eugene Smith argues, religious resurgence is not a unique phenomenon to the 1980s despite its importance among Third World countries; it is a cyclical and recurring phenomenon. In the Middle East, for instance, Islamic revivalist movements emerged in the 1920s and 1930s to oppose Western colonialism. Likewise, conservative Protestant groups surfaced in the United States during the nineteenth and early twentieth centuries. It may well be then, that in the 1970s and 1980s several recurring cycles of resurgent religious activism—in the United States, the Catholic world, and Islam—have occurred simultaneously.

Almost one decade after the emergence of many of the politicized religious groups, their political gains have been modest. With the exception of the Islamic Revolution in Iran no other religious state has come into existence. Most of the activities of these religious groups and movements have been confined to the realm of political opposition to the authoritarian regimes and to the unequal distribution of resources.

Despite the militant rhetoric of several of these religious groups and the publicity surrounding their activities, the secular trend remains strong—not only in Western Europe, the United States, and the Communist countries, but also among Third World societies. With regard to Western Europe and the United States, several powerful secular forces would work to prevent a large-scale wave of religious resurgence from taking place. The formal separation between religion and politics, the widespread public belief in secularism, the pervasiveness of secular education, and the presence of powerful advertisement and entertainment industries would continue to constitute formidable barriers in the path of any overall religious revival.

The prospect of sustaining impressive political gains for the revitalized religious groups among the Communist countries are equally dismal. Such Communist regimes would certainly not allow the politicization of traditional religions to function on a large scale. Similarly, despite the continuing utility of religion as a legitimizing tool for Third World governments, their support toward the religious groups is tactical and not strategic in nature. Past experience demonstrates that any significant increase in the strength of these religious groups would lead to a drop in governmental support for them. Indeed, these very same regimes would not hesitate to suppress their religious allies should they seriously threaten the existing political order.

Aside from such legal and political constraints the longevity and the persuasiveness of the politicized religious movements would depend upon the ability of such groups to realize some of the dreams of their followers. The long-term challenge for the leadership of the revitalized religious movements would be to translate their political rhetoric and support of their followers into long-term sustainable political gains. The failure of these religious movements to bring about social, economic, and political equality to their members would undermine the credibility of these movements, dampen the morale of their followers, and compel them to search for alternative secular ideologies. The appeal of religion can hardly be maintained if religion fails to provide adequate answers for the grievances of its adherents.

As noted in the preceding section, the revitalized religious groups are not monolithic or homogeneous. Contemporary religious movements advocate differing views and assumptions concerning the organization of society and the exercise of political authority. No unified leadership has yet to exist that would speak in the name of the entire revitalized religious movements within individual societies or across state boundaries. The fact that those leaders appeal to the same audience may exacerbate tension within their ranks and create divisions among their followers.

In conclusion, one should exercise caution when making sweeping generalizations about a large-scale spread of religious resurgence and a simultaneous retreat of secularism. However, the role of religion in public life, its relevance to modern society, and its capacity to adapt to the requirements of modernization do need to be acknowledged. Traditional religions are not simply fading away. Their political roles seem to be a lasting feature in many contemporary political systems.

At the same time, no far-reaching conclusions should be drawn from the current wave of religious resurgence in different parts of the world. Though the unilinear deterministic outlook of secularism has been recently challenged, secularism remains widespread and powerful in many societies. Numerous factors work together to limit any substantial gain for religious resurgence. Religion and secularism ought not to be mutually exclusive. Both would remain relevant for our complex modern societies.

Contributors

Joe Barnhart is Professor of Philosophy at the University of North Texas. He is the author or coauthor of books on the philosophy of religion, including *The Study of Religion and Its Meaning* (1977) and *Religion and the Challenge of Philosophy* (1975). A novelist, he has published articles in such journals as *The American Philosophical Quarterly, Harvard Theological Review,* and *Free Inquiry.*

Louis J. Cantori is Professor of Political Science at the University of Maryland, Baltimore County, and Adjunct Professor, the Center for Contemporary Arab Studies and the Department of Government, Georgetown University. He is the author or editor of such books as *Local Politics and Development in the Middle East* (1984). He is presently the editor for *Political Development Reconsidered: Political Change in the Middle East* and *Democratization in Egypt.*

Michael Dodson is Professor of Political Science at Texas Christian University. In 1984 he was a member of the Latin American Studies Association observer delegation for the Nicaraguan elections, and in 1985 he was a Fulbright Senior Lecturer in the United Kingdom. He is coauthor of *Let My People Live: Faith and Struggle in Central America* (1988) and of the forthcoming book *Nicaragua's Other Revolution,* in addition to many articles on religion and social change in Latin America.

Allen D. Hertzke is Assistant Director of the Carl Albert Congressional Research and Studies Center and Assistant Professor of Political Science at the University of Oklahoma. He is the author of *Representing God in Washington: The Role of Religious Lobbies in the American Polity* (1988). His current work focuses on the role of churches as "precincts" in presidential campaign mobilization.

Lawrence P. Jones received his Ph.D. from Union Theological Seminary in 1988. His most recent research deals with Reagan and nuclear war. He has published articles in *Old Westbury Review,* the *Journal of American Culture,* and *Theological Students Fellowship Bulletin.*

Lonnie D. Kliever is Professor of Religious Studies at Southern Methodist University. His major publications include *H. Richard Niebuhr* (1977), *The Shattered Spectrum* (1981), *The Terrible Meek* (1987), and *Dax's Case* (1989).

Ronald H. Nash is Professor of Philosophy at Western Kentucky University. He is the author or editor of *Faith and Reason* (1988), *Evangelicals in America* (1987), *Poverty and Wealth* (1986), *Process Theology* (1986), *Liberation Theology* (1985), *Christianity and the Hellenistic World* (1984), *Christian Faith and Historical Understanding* (1984), and *The Concept of God* (1983). Nash is a Fellow of the Christianity Today Institute and an advisor to the U.S. Civil Rights Commission.

Augustus Richard Norton is Associate Professor of Comparative Politics at the U.S. Military Academy, West Point, New York, where he has taught since 1981. In 1989 he was a Fulbright Scholar at the Norwegian Institute of International Affairs, where he wrote about peace-keeping, particularly in the Middle East. He was a featured commentator on the Emmy Award-winning television documentary, "Sword of Islam," and his research on the Middle East has been supported by the National Endowment for the Humanities and the MacArthur Foundation. His most recent books are *Amal and the Shi'a: Struggle for the Soul of Lebanon* (1987), and *The International Relations of the PLO* (1989).

Laura Nuzzi O'Shaughnessy (former Associate Dean of Faculty Affairs) is Associate Professor of Government at St. Lawrence University. She is coauthor (with Luis Serra) of *The Church and Revolution in Nicaragua* (1986) and coauthor (with Michael Dodson) of *Nicaragua's Other Revolution: Religious Faith and Political Struggle* (1990).

Gregory F. Rose is Assistant Professor of Political Science at the University of North Texas. He is the author of several articles on Iran, Middle Eastern politics, and mathematical modeling, which have appeared in volumes and journals such as *Iranian Studies* and the *Journal of Political Science*. He is co-author (with Emerson Niou and Peter Ordeshook) of *The Balance of Power: Stability in International Systems* (1989).

Emile F. Sahliyeh is Associate Professor of International Relations and Middle East Politics at the University of North Texas. His most recent publications are *The PLO After the Lebanon War* (1986), and *In Search of Leadership: West Bank Politics Since 1967* (1988), in addition to several articles.

Jamal Sanad is Assistant Professor of Political Science. He received his Ph.D. from the University of Wisconsin-Milwaukee in 1989. He has also taught courses in political science and international relations at UW-Milwaukee. Mr. Sanad has recently published an article about the economic orientations of Kuwaiti women in the *International Journal of Middle East Studies*. His Ph.D. dissertation, based on opinion surveys among Kuwaitis, Egyptians, and Palestinians in Kuwait, is a comparative study of the relationship between political culture and Islam.

Anson Shupe is Professor of Sociology and Chair of the Department of Sociology and Anthropology at Indiana University-Purdue University at Fort Wayne, Indiana. He is the author of books on family violence and social movements as well as professional and popular articles. His most recent publications are *Televangelism: Power and Politics on God's Frontier* (1988, coauthored with Jeff K. Hadden) and *The Politics of Religion and Social Change* (1989, also coedited with Hadden).

Karandeep Singh is Assistant Professor of Political Science at Punjabi University, Patiala, Punjab, and a Ph.D. candidate in Political Science at the University of North Texas. His dissertation is based on a time-series analysis of religious terrorism in the state of Punjab, more specifically, the impact of state interventions and the rise of terrorism.

Donald E. Smith is Professor of Political Science at the University of Pennsylvania. His publications include *India as a Secular State* (1963), *Religion and Politics in Burma* (1965), *South Asian Politics and Religion* (1966), *Religion and Political Development* (1970), *Religion and Political Modernization* (1974), and *Anti-Americanism in the Third World* (1985, with A. Z. Rubinstein).

C. Neal Tate is Regents Professor of Political Science at the University of North Texas. During 1987 he was a Fulbright Senior Research Fellow to the Philippines, where he conducted a National Science Foundation-funded project on the long-term decision-making process of the Philippine Supreme Court. He is the coauthor of *Using Microcomputers in Research* (1985), *Your TI Professional Computer* (1984), *The Supreme Court in American Politics* (1980, 2d ed.), and author or coauthor of articles on comparative judicial politics and political behavior.

Mark Tessler is Professor of Political Science at the University of Wisconsin-Milwaukee. He received his Ph.D. from Northwestern University in 1969, having previously studied at the Hebrew University of Jerusalem and the University of Tunis in Tunisia. Professor Tessler has conducted research in Israel, Tunisia, Morocco, Egypt, and the West Bank. He is the author or coauthor of six books, the most recent being *The Evaluation and Application of Survey Research in the Arab World* (1987) and *Israel, Egypt and the Palestinians: From Camp David to Intifada* (1989). Professor Tessler has served on many national and international panels concerned with foreign area studies. In addition, he was recently elected President of the Association for Israel Studies.

Kenneth D. Wald is Professor of Political Science at the University of Florida. The recipient of research grants from the National Science Foundation and the National Endowment for the Humanities, he is the author of *Religion and Politics in the United States* (1987) and *Crosses on the Ballot* (1983). He has written extensively about the public role of religion in the United States and the United Kingdom. His research on the Christian Right has been published in the *American Political Science Review*, the *Journal of Politics*, and the *Journal for the Scientific Study of Religion*. Wald has served as a member of the executive committee and newsletter editor for the Religion and Politics Section of the American Political Science Association.

Notes

CHAPTER 1. RELIGIOUS RESURGENCE AND POLITICAL MODERNIZATION

AUTHOR'S NOTE: I would like to thank Professors John A. Booth, C. Neal Tate, and Mark Tessler, as well as JoAnn Lutz, a Ph.D. candidate in Political Science at the University of North Texas, for their comments.

1. For a survey of the literature on modernization, see, among others, Frank Sutton, "Social Theory and Comparative Politics," *Comparative Politics: A Reader,* eds. Harry Eckstein and David Apter (New York: Free Press of Glencoe, 1963); Daniel Lerner, "Modernization: Social Aspects," *International Encyclopedia of the Social Sciences,* ed. David L. Sills (New York: Macmillan, 1968); Gabriel Almond, "Introduction: A Functional Approach to Comparative Politics," *The Politics of the Developing Areas,* eds. Almond and James S. Coleman (Princeton, N.J.: Princeton University Press, 1960); Donald Eugene Smith, *Religion and Political Development* (Boston, Mass.: Little, Brown, 1970); Smith, ed., *Religion, Politics, and Social Change in the Third World* (New York: Free Press, 1971); Manfred Halpern, "Toward Further Modernization of the Study of New Nations," *World Politics* 17 (October 1964): 157–181; and Lucien W. Pye, *Aspects of Political Development* (Boston, Mass.: Little, Brown, 1966).

2. See Smith, *Religion and Political Development.*

3. See Howard J. Wiarda, ed., *New Directions in Comparative Politics* (Boulder, Col.: Westview, 1985), chap.7.

4. See Myron J. Aronoff, "Introduction," *Political Anthropology,* vol. 3, *Religion and Politics,* ed. Myron J. Aronoff (New Brunswick, N.J.: Transaction, 1984), pp. 1–3; and Irving Louis Horowitz, "Religion, and State, and Politics," *Religion and Politics,* ed. Aronoff (New Brunswick, N.J.: Transaction, 1984), pp. 5–11. See also, Raimundo Panikkar, "Religion or Politics: The Western Dilemma," *Religion and Politics in the Modern World,* eds. Peter H. Merkl and Ninian Smart (New York: New York University Press, 1983), pp. 44–60.

5. For an additional discussion of the crisis milieu, see R. Hrair Dekmejian, "Islamic Revival: Catalysts, Categories, and Consequences," *The Politics of Islamic Revivalism*, ed. Shireen T. Hunter (Bloomington: Indiana University Press, 1988), pp. 3–23.

6. See Hunter, "Introduction," *The Politics of Islamic Revivalism*, pp. ix–xv.

7. See Emile Sahliyeh, "The West Bank and the Gaza Strip," *The Politics of Islamic Revivalism*, pp. 88–103.

8. For an explanation of the resource mobilization model, see Charles Tilly, *From Mobilization to Revolution* (Reading, Mass.: Addison-Wesley, 1978); Louise A. Tilly and Charles Tilly, eds., *Class Conflict and Collective Action* (Beverly Hills, Calif.: Sage, 1981); and R. Aya, "Theories of Revolution Reconsidered: Contrasting Models of Collective Violence," *Theory and Society* 8 (1979): 39–99.

CHAPTER 2. THE STUBBORN PERSISTENCE OF RELIGION IN THE GLOBAL ARENA

1. Anthony F. C. Wallace, *Religion: An Anthropological View* (New York: Random, 1966), pp. 264–265.

2. Harvey Cox, *The Secular City* (New York: Macmillan, 1965), pp. 1–4.

3. John Naisbitt, *Megatrends* (New York: Warner Books, 1982).

4. Anson Shupe and Jeffrey K. Hadden, "Sociology of Religion," *The Future of Sociology*, eds. Edgar F. Borgata and Karen S. Cook (Newbury Park, Calif.: Sage, 1988), pp. 120–137; Hadden and Shupe, eds., *Prophetic Religions and Politics* (New York: Paragon House, 1986).

5. Phillip E. Hammond, "Introduction," *The Sacred in a Secular Age*, ed. Hammond (Berkeley: University of California Press, 1985), pp. 1–6.

6. Hadden, "Towards Desacralizing Secularization Theory," *Social Forces* 65 (1987): 587–611.

7. See, for example, David G. Bromley and Hammond, eds., *The Future of New Religious Movements* (Macon, Ga.: Mercer University Press, 1987); Hammond, *Sacred in a Secular Age*; B. L. Smith, ed., *Religion and Social Conflict in South East Asia* (Leiden, The Netherlands: E. J. Brill, 1976); Gunther Lewy, *Religion and Political Modernization* (New York: Oxford University Press, 1974); Donald E. Smith, *South Asian Politics and Religion* (Princeton, N.J.: Princeton University Press, 1966); D. E. Smith, *Religion and Social Con-*

flict in Political Development (Boston: Little, Brown, 1970); and D. E. Smith, *Religion and Political Modernization* (New Haven, Conn.: Yale University Press, 1974).

8. Andrew M. Greeley, *Unsecular Man* (New York: Dell, 1972), p. 1.

9. Richard John Neuhaus, "Foreword," *Unsecular America*, ed. Neuhaus (Grand Rapids, Mich.: Erdmans, 1986), p. 1.

10. See Hadden and Shupe, eds., *Secularization and Fundamentalism Reconsidered* (New York: Paragon House, 1989).

11. The most outstanding proponent of this school of theory is unquestionably Immanuel Wallerstein. See Wallerstein, "Crisis: The World Economy, the Movements, and the Ideologies," *Crisis in the World System*, ed. Albert Bergesen (Beverly Hills, Calif.: Sage, 1983), pp. 21–36; Wallerstein, *The Modern World System* (New York: Academic, 1974); and Wallerstein, "The Rise and Future Demise of the World Capitalist System: Concepts for Comparative Analysis," *Comparative Studies in Society and History* 16 (1974): 387–415.

12. Roland Robertson, "The Sacred and the World System," *The Sacred in a Secular Age*, pp. 347–358.

13. Marshall M. McLuhan and Quenten Fiore, *War and Peace in the Global Village* (New York: Bantam Books, 1968).

14. Ben H. Bagdikian, *The Information Machines* (New York: Harper, 1971).

15. Hadden and Shupe, *Televangelism: Power and Politics on God's Frontier* (New York: Henry Holt and Co., 1988).

16. Robertson, "Sacred and the World System," *Sacred in a Secular Age*, p. 348.

17. Talcott Parsons, *Action Theory and the Human Condition* (New York: Free Press, 1978), pp. 352–443.

18. Robertson and Joann Chirico, "Humanity, Globalization, and Worldwide Religious Resurgence: A Theoretical Explanation," *Sociological Analysis* 46 (1985): 225.

19. Ibid., 239

20. Rodney Stark, "Must All Religions Be Supernatural?" *The Social Impact of New Religious Movements*, ed. Bryan Wilson (New York: The Rose of Sharon Press, 1981), pp. 159–177.

21. Robertson, "Toward a New Perspective on Religion and Secularization in the Global Community," *Secularization and Fundamentalism Reconsidered*.

22. See Stark and William Sims Bainbridge, *The Future of Religion* (Berkeley: University of California Press), pp. 190–195.

23. Greeley, *Unsecular Man*.

24. See Hadden and Shupe, *Televangelism*; David G. Bromley and Shupe, eds., *New Christian Politics* (Macon, Ga.: Mercer University Press, 1984); and Robert C. Liebman and Robert Wuthnow, eds., *The New Christian Right* (New York: Aldine, 1983).

25. See Hadden and Shupe, *Televangelism*, pp. 38–54; and Hadden and Charles E. Swann, *Prime Time Preachers: The Rising Power of Televangelism* (Reading, Mass.: Addison-Wesley, 1981), pp. 125–174.

CHAPTER 3. THE INCURABLY RELIGIOUS ANIMAL

1. See Karl Popper, *Conjectures and Refutations: The Growth of Scientific Knowledge* (New York: Harper, 1963), pp. 5–30, 373–376.

2. See Joe E. Barnhart, *The Southern Baptist Holy War* (Austin: Texas Monthly Press, 1986), pp. 163–174.

3. On technology mingled with magic, see Gerard Thomas Straub, *Salvation for Sale: An Insider's View of Pat Robertson* (Buffalo, N.Y.: Prometheus Books, 1988); and the seminal Edmund D. Cohen, *The Mind of the Bible-Believer* (Buffalo, N.Y.: Prometheus Books, 1986), pp. 48, 398–400, 405.

4. On distinctions between science and magic as diverse ways of approaching problems, see Robin Horton, "African Traditional Thought and Western Science," *Africa* 37 (January, April 1967): 50–71, 155–187.

5. See Popper, *Objective Knowledge: An Evolutionary Approach* (New York: Oxford University Press, 1972), pp. 192–198.

6. Francis L. K. Hsu, *Exercising the Trouble Makers: Magic, Science, and Culture* (Westport, Conn.: Greenwood, 1983), p. 149.

CHAPTER 4. THE LIMITS OF RELIGIOUS RESURGENCE

1. For an elaboration of this model of the traditional religio-political system, see Donald E. Smith, *Religion and Political Development* (Boston, Mass.: Little, Brown, 1970), pp. 57–84.

2. See Fred R. von der Mehden, *Religion and Nationalism in Southeast Asia* (Madison: University of Wisconsin Press, 1963). For an analysis of Gandhi's reinterpretation of Hindu tradition, see Joan V. Bondurant, *Conquest of Violence: The Gandhian Philosophy of Conflict* (Princeton, N.Y.: Princeton University Press, 1958).

3. Edward J. Williams, *Latin American Christian Democratic Parties* (Knoxville: University of Tennessee Press, 1967).

4. See Daniel H. Levine, ed., *Religion and Political Conflict in Latin America* (Chapel Hill: University of North Carolina Press, 1986); and Philip Berryman, *Liberation Theology* (Philadelphia: Temple University Press, 1987).

5. See Urmila Phadnis, *Religion and Politics in Sri Lanka* (New Delhi, India: Manohar, 1976); and D. E. Smith, *Religion and Politics in Burma* (Princeton, N.J.: Princeton University Press, 1965).

6. V. K. Sinha, ed., *Secularism in India* (Bombay, India: Lalvani, 1968); D. E. Smith, *India as a Secular State* (Princeton, N.J.: Princeton University Press, 1963).

7. Michael M. J. Fischer, *Iran: From Religious Dispute to Revolution* (Cambridge, Mass.: Harvard University Press, 1980); Said Amir Arjomand, *The Turban for the Crown: The Islamic Revolution in Iran* (New York: Oxford University Press, 1988).

CHAPTER 5. THE NEW CHRISTIAN RIGHT IN AMERICAN POLITICS: MOBILIZATION AMID MODERNIZATION

1. For a summary of research trends and emerging themes, see James Guth et al., "The Politics of Religion in America: Issues for Investigation," *American Politics Quarterly* 16 (July 1988): 357–397.

2. The theme of cultural conflict has been explored by Aaron Wildavsky in "Choosing Preferences by Constructing Institutions: A Cultural Theory of Preference Formation," *American Political Science Review* 81 (March 1987): 3–21.

3. William G. McLoughlin, *Revivals, Awakenings and Reform: An Essay on Religion and Social Change in America, 1607–1977* (Chicago: University of Chicago Press, 1978).

4. These data have been summarized in Kenneth D. Wald, "Social Change and Political Response: The Silent Religious Cleavage in North American Politics," *Politics and Religion Since 1945*, ed. George Moyser (London: Routledge, forthcoming). That essay also contains a discussion about

how modernization has affected the general pattern of religious expression in politics.

5. Tom W. Smith, "General Liberalism and Social Change in Post–World War II America: A Summary of Trends," *Social Indicators Research* 10 (July 1982): 1–28; Carole Mueller, "In Search of a Constituency for the 'New Religious Right,' " *Public Opinion Quarterly* 47 (Summer 1983): 213–229.

6. I have summarized this evidence in chaps. 4 and 6 in Kenneth D. Wald, *Religion and Politics in the United States* (New York: St. Martin's, 1987). In characterizing the NCR as the creation and agent of traditionalist Protestants, I do not wish to suggest that it enjoys exclusive support from that community. On selected issues, the movement has received support from a variety of religious groups including mainline Protestants, orthodox Jews, Mormons, and Catholics. Sizable segments of the evangelical community also dissent from a number of the core positions of the Christian Right. All I mean to suggest is that the movement's center of gravity is clearly within the most traditionalist Protestant denominations, not that it has a monopoly of that group or totally excludes others from its range. The distinctive social profile means that explanations for the movement must be keyed to examining its core constituency.

7. John C. Green, James L. Guth, and Kevin Hill, "Faith and Election: The Christian Right in House Races, 1978–1986" (Paper presented to the Citadel Conference on Southern Politics, Charleston, S.C., 1988).

8. For example, the early data broke down the large Baptist category only by race. Thus defined, Baptists included the relatively affluent adherents of the northern wing as well as the Southern Baptist Convention. The net effect is to overstate the relative economic standing of Baptists in the 1950s. When this inclusive group is compared with Southern Baptists of the 1970s, it will seem as if Baptists have gained less ground than a comparison of strictly comparable populations would surely reveal.

9. Sidney Verba and Norman H. Nie, *Participation in America* (New York: Harper, 1972); Raymond E. Wolfinger and Steven J. Rosenstone, *Who Votes?* (New Haven, Conn.: Yale University Press, 1980).

10. Raymond E. Wolfinger, "The Development and Persistence of Ethnic Voting," *American Political Science Review* 59 (December 1965): 896–908.

11. See the data on church growth rates in Dean M. Kelley, *Why Conservative Churches Are Growing* (rev. ed.; San Francisco, Calif.: Harper, 1977).

12. Frances Fitzgerald, "A Disciplined, Charging Army," *New Yorker*, May 18, 1981, p. 73.

13. Wald, *Religion and Politics*, p. 25.

14. Wald, Dennis E. Owen, and Samuel S. Hill, Jr., "Churches as Political Communities," *American Political Science Review* 82 (June 1988): 531–548.

15. Aldon Morris, *The Origins of the Civil Rights Movement* (New York: Free Press, 1984).

16. Robert C. Liebman, "Mobilizing the Moral Majority," *The New Christian Right*, eds. Robert C. Liebman and Robert Wuthnow (New York: Aldine, 1983), pp. 50–73.

17. The discussion draws heavily upon Jeffrey K. Hadden and Anson Shupe, *Televangelism: Power and Politics on God's Frontier* (New York: Henry Holt, 1988), esp. chaps. 2–3.

18. Allen Crawford, *Thunder on the Right* (New York: Pantheon, 1980).

19. I do not, however, agree that the values represented by the NCR have been overthrown by a conspiracy of secular humanists. Nor do I take at face value a large number of the other claims made by supporters of the movement. Nonetheless, the evidence supports the notion that NCR supporters are motivated by resentment toward the inadequate public respect accorded to them and to groups that represent what they regard as traditional social values. See Wald, Owen, and Hill, "Evangelical Politics and Status Issues," *Journal for the Scientific Study of Religion* 28 (March 1989): 1–16.

20. David Fairbanks, "Religious Forces and 'Morality' Policies in the American States," *Western Political Quarterly* 30 (September 1977): 411–417.

21. For a good example of the cultural conflict, see Timothy K. Smith, "Dirty Dancing Is Another Hot Topic in Atlanta Just Now," *Wall Street Journal*, July 15, 1988, pp. 1, 12.

CHAPTER 6. CHRISTIAN FUNDAMENTALISTS AND THE IMPERATIVES OF AMERICAN POLITICS

1. See Robert Booth Fowler, *A New Engagement: Evangelical Political Thought, 1966–1976* (Grand Rapids, Mich.: Erdmans, 1982); Fowler, *Religion and Politics in America* (Metuchen, N.J.: Scarecrow, 1985); Kenneth Wald, *Religion and Politics in the United States* (New York: St. Martins, 1987); Robert Zwier, *Born Again Politics* (Downer's Grove, Ill.: Inter-Varsity, 1982); A. James Reichley, *Religion in American Public Life* (Washington, D.C.: Brookings, 1985); Richard John Neuhaus, *The Naked Public Square* (Grand Rapids, Mich.: Erdmans, 1984); Robert C. Liebman and Robert Wuthnow, eds., *The New Christian Right* (New York: Aldine, 1983); Matthew Moen, "The New Christian Right and the Legislative Agenda." (Ph.D. Diss., University of

Oklahoma, 1986); Corwin Smidt, "Evangelicals in the 1984 Election: Continuity or Change," *American Politics Quarterly* 15 (October 1987): 419–444; James Guth, "Political Converts: Partisan Realignment among Southern Baptist Ministers," *Election Politics* 3 (1986); David G. Bromley and Anson Shupe, eds., *New Christian Politics* (Macon, Ga.: Mercer University Press, 1984); and Guth and John Green, "Faith and Politics: Religion and Ideology Among Political Contributors," *American Politics Quarterly* 14 (July 1986).

2. See, esp., Seymour Martin Lipset and Earl Raab, "The Election and the Evangelicals," *Commentary* 71 (March 1981): 25–31; Emmett Buell and Lee Sigelman, "An Army that Meets Every Sunday? Popular Support for the Moral Majority in 1980," *Social Science Quarterly* 66 (June 1985): 427–434; Lee Sigelman, Clyde Wilcox, and Emmett Buell, "An Unchanging Minority: Popular Support for the Moral Majority, 1980 and 1984," *Social Science Quarterly* 68 (December 1987): 876–884; Shupe and William Stacey, "The Moral Majority Constituency," *The New Christian Right*; Guth and Green, "The Moralizing Minority: Christian Right Support Among Political Contributors," *Social Science Quarterly* 68 (September 1987); and Clyde Wilcox, "Popular Support for the Moral Majority in 1980: A Second Look," *Social Science Quarterly* 68 (March 1987): 157–169.

3. Conservative Christians are represented by a diverse set of groups, including Concerned Women for America, Christian Voice, Eagle Forum, and the more moderate National Association of Evangelicals. The newest group is the Family Research Council, a division of Focus on the Family. James Dobson's popular syndicated radio program aired 8,000 times a day on 1,600 radio stations. When Dobson asked his listeners to register their objection to the "intrusiveness" of the Civil Rights Restoration Act, circuits at the capitol were overloaded and the flood of calls continued for days.

4. See Lipset and Raab, *The Politics of Unreason* (Chicago: University of Chicago Press, 1978); Karl Patel, Denny Pilant, and Gary Rose, "Christian Conservatism: A Study in Alienation and Life Style Concerns," *Journal of Political Science* 12 (Spring 1985): 17–30; Wilcox, "Evangelicals and Political Tolerance" (Paper presented at the annual meeting of the American Political Science Association, Chicago, 1987).

5. Kathleen Beatty and Oliver Walter, "Religious Preference and Practice: Reevaluating Their Impact on Political Tolerance," *Public Opinion Quarterly* 48 (1984): 318–329; Wilcox, "Evangelicals and Political Tolerance."

6. Allen D. Hertzke, *Representing God in Washington: The Role of Religious Lobbies in the American Polity* (Knoxville: University of Tennessee Press, 1988).

7. Interview, December 1984.

8. This theme is developed more fully in Hertzke, *Representing God in Washington.*

9. Thomas Edsall, "Will Feuds Sink the GOP?" *Washington Post Weekly Edition,* June 15, 1987, p. 29.

10. Interview, June 10, 1988.

11. Ibid.

12. Jane Mansbridge, *Why We Lost the Era* (Chicago: University of Chicago Press, 1986).

13. Sylvia Ann Hewlett, *A Lesser Life: The Myth of Women's Liberation in America* (New York: Morrow, 1986).

14. It is interesting that in an issue of *PS: Political Science and Politics,* vol. 21 (Winter 1988) devoted to censorship in education, none of the articles mentioned the mounting evidence of secular and liberal censorship of textbooks, but instead attacked the usual suspects, Bible thumpers and right-wingers.

15. Paul C. Vitz, *Censorship: Evidence of Bias in Our Children's Textbooks* (Ann Arbor, Mich.: Servant Press, 1986).

16. Barbara Vobejda, "History Books: One Nation Under Whom?" *The Washington Post National Weekly Edition,* May 4, 1987, pp. 23–24.

17. See Hertzke, *Representing God in Washington.*

18. Walt Harrington, "The Good Book versus the Textbooks," *Washington Post Weekly Edition,* August 3, 1987, pp. 8–11; Richard John Neuhaus, ed., "Oops, Wrong Witness," *Religion and Society Report* (August 1987).

19. Nat Hentoff, "A Liberal Journalist Reflects on His Involvement in the Pro-Life Movement," *Moral Majority Report* (February 1988): 12–13.

20. Richard A. Baer, "Teaching Values in the Schools: Clarification or Indoctrination?" *Principal* (January 1982).

21. See "The War Against Pornography: Feminists, Free Speech, and the Law," *Newsweek,* cover story, March 18, 1985; "Is One Woman's Sexuality Another Woman's Pornography?" *MS.,* cover story, April 1985. Two of the most active feminists in this area are Andrea Dwarkin and Catherine MacKinnon, authors of a controversial Minneapolis ordinance against pornography. See Kaye Schultz, "Feminists Label Pornography as a Woman-Killer," *Capital Times* (Madison, Wisc.), September 14, 1984. Edward Donnerstein's research is summarized extensively in these articles, and by the Associated Press religion writer George W. Cornell, "Council of

Churches Committee Links Aggressiveness, TV Violence," *Wisconsin State Journal*, October 13, 1984.

22. As cited by Walter Benjamin, "Church and State: The Case for Benevolent Neutrality," *Religion and Politics: Is the Relationship Changing?* ed. Thomas Scism (Proceedings of the Eleventh Political Studies Conference, Eastern Illinois University, April 1987).

23. James S. Coleman and Thomas Hoffer, *Public and Private High Schools: The Impact of Communities* (New York: Basic, 1987).

24. In spite of the evidence that easy divorce has tended to liberate men from sexual and financial responsibility more than women from suffocating marriages, some feminists continue to claim that marriage and the family are the root of oppression of women. See William L. O'Neill, *Feminism in America: A History* (2d rev. ed.; New Brunswick, N.J.: Transaction Books, 1989).

25. John Chodes, "Mutiny in Paradise," *Chronicles* (February 1988): 10–13.

26. Daniel Bell, *The Cultural Contradictions of Capitalism* (New York: Basic, 1976).

27. As reported on "ABC Nightline," August 10, 1988.

CHAPTER 7. WHAT DO THE EVANGELICALS WANT?

1. Nathan Glazer, "Fundamentalism: A Defensive Offensive," *Piety and Politics*, eds. Richard John Neuhaus and Michael Cromartie (Washington, D.C.: Ethics and Public Policy Center, 1987), p. 247. Glazer disagrees with the position he describes.

2. Neuhaus, "What the Fundamentalists Want," ibid., p. 5.

3. Ibid.

4. For an explanation of how the meaning of *evangelical* evolved, see Ronald Nash, *Evangelicals in America* (Nashville, Tenn.: Abingdon, 1987), chaps. 3–4.

5. See Nash, ed., *Evangelical Renewal in the Mainline Churches* (Westchester, Ill.: Crossway Books, 1987).

6. Some insist on making a distinction between pentecostals and charismatics, but that is a subject for another time.

7. See the discussion of the split within fundamentalism that has led hyperfundamentalists to denounce Falwell for being too liberal! See Nash, *Evangelicals in America*, chap. 5.

8. Stuart Rothenberg, "Evangelicals Are Politically Diverse," *Piety and Politics*, p. 232.

9. Clifford G. Kossel, "The Moral Majority and Christian Politics," *Communio* 9 (1982): 340. Of course, the organization known as the Moral Majority ceased to exist midway through 1989. But since the term continues to be used of people who still share its goals, Kossel's comments can apply to them.

10. Ibid.

11. Robert Zwier, *Born-Again Politics* (Downers Grove, Ill.: InterVarsity Press, 1982), p. 99. Zwier's book testifies again to the remarkable political diversity of the evangelical movement. Unfortunately, it also demonstrates how easily political ideology can prevent one evangelical from understanding another.

12. Neuhaus, "What the Fundamentalists Want," *Piety and Politics*, p. 12. In case it needs saying, Neuhaus himself is certainly not a fundamentalist. And, to repeat, while I myself am interested in more than fundamentalism, Neuhaus's observation could also be made about the word *evangelical*.

13. See Glazer, "Fundamentalism," ibid., p. 247.

14. See Neuhaus, "What the Fundamentalists Want," ibid., p. 6.

15. For example, see Ed Dobson, "The Bible, Politics and Democracy," *The Bible, Politics and Democracy*, ed. Neuhaus (Grand Rapids, Mich.: Erdmans, 1987), pp. 1–18. Dobson was for years closely associated with the Moral Majority and with Jerry Falwell's Liberty University.

16. Glazer, "Fundamentalism," *Piety and Politics*, p. 250.

17. Ibid.

18. Ibid., p. 251.

19. Ibid., p. 245.

20. Neuhaus, *The Naked Public Square* (Grand Rapids, Mich.: Erdmans, 1984), p. vii.

21. Ibid.

22. Ibid., p. 86.

23. Neuhaus, "The Post-Secular Task of the Churches," *Christianity and Politics*, ed. Carol Friedley Griffith (Washington, D.C.: Ethics and Public Policy Center, 1981), p. 14.

24. See Neuhaus, *Naked Public Square*, pp. 36ff.

25. For examples of such efforts in the areas of social theory, political theory, and economics, see Nash, *Poverty and Wealth* (Westchester, Ill.: Crossway Books, 1986); and Nash, *Social Justice and the Christian Church* (Grand Rapids, Mich.: Baker, 1983).

26. Dobson reprinted his 1985 editorial in his chapter, "The Bible, Politics and Democracy"; the following quotations appear on p. 17 of that book.

27. Jerry Falwell, Ed Dobson, and Ed Hindson, *The Fundamentalist Phenomenon* (Garden City, N.Y.: Doubleday-Galilee, 1980), p. 191.

28. This quote comes from Dobson's 1985 editorial.

29. Neuhaus, *Piety and Politics*, p. 3.

30. Ibid., p. 18.

CHAPTER 8. ONWARD CHRISTIAN SOLDIERS: THE CASE OF PROTESTANTISM IN CENTRAL AMERICA

1. Calvin Center for Christian Studies, interview, January 5, 1987, author present.

2. Christian Lalive D'Espinay, *Haven of the Masses* (London: Butterworth Press, 1969), as quoted in Miguez Bonino, "Protestantism in Latin America."

3. Wilton M. Nelson, *Protestantism in Central America* (Grand Rapids, Mich.: Erdmans, 1984), p. 11.

4. Ibid., p. 13.

5. Ibid., pp. 30–33.

6. James C. Dekker, "North American Protestant Theology: Impact on Central America," *Occasional Essays of CELEP* (San Jose, Costa Rica: 1984), p. 65.

7. Guatemalan Presbyterian missionary Dennis Smith, interview, January 12, 1987.

8. John Stam, "Missions and U.S. Foreign Policy—A Case Study from the 1920's," *Evangelical Missions Quarterly* 15 (July 1979): 167–175.

9. Nelson, *Protestantism in Central America*, p. 56. According to Nelson, "To calculate the 'Protestant community' it is customary to multiply the number of communicant members by three."

10. More than a century later, Herman Melville again captured the American self-image when he said, "We Americans are a peculiar, chosen people, the Israel of our times: we bear the ark of the liberties of this world." Both quotations are cited in Russell B. Nye, *This Almost Chosen People* (East Lansing: Michigan State University Press, 1966), chap. 4.

11. Ibid., p. 197.

12. Exact figures, which include all major denominations and faith missions, are difficult to obtain, but this statement is based on a reading of Nelson, *Protestantism in Central America*, as well as documents on the history of the Presbyterian church.

13. For a recent and detailed discussion of this period see John F. Findling, *Close Neighbors, Distant Friends: United States-Central American Relations* (Westport, Conn.: Greenwood, 1987), chaps. 1–4.

14. For a more complete discussion of this Congress see Michael Dodson and Laura N. O'Shaughnessy, *Nicaragua's Other Revolution: Religious Faith and Political Struggle* (Chapel Hill: University of North Carolina Press, 1990).

15. Juan Kessler and Wilton M. Nelson, "Panama 1916 y Su Impacto Sobre el Protestantismo Latinoamericano," *De Panamá a Oaxtepec: El Protestantismo Latinoamericano en Busca de Unidad-Pastoralia*, Año 1, no. 2 (San Jose, Costa Rica: CELEP, 1978), p. 7.

16. Ibid., p. 13.

17. This theme is discussed in G. William Carlson, "The Theme of 'Anti-Communism' in the Shaping of Contemporary Evangelical Responses on American Policy: 1953–1988" (Paper presented at the Conference on Evangelicals and American Foreign Policy, Calvin College, Grand Rapids, Michigan, October 7–8, 1988).

18. Michael Dodson has discussed this in his chapter in this book.

19. The casting off of foreign garments, a phrase with clear biblical reference, became a phrase associated with CELA III in 1969, which will be discussed later.

20. For a more complete discussion of the CELA conferences see Dodson and O'Shaughnessy, *Nicaragua's Other Revolution*.

21. See the discussion in T. S. Montgomery, "Latin American Evangelicals: Oaxtepec and Beyond," *Churches and Politics in Latin America*, ed. Daniel Levine, vol. 14 (Sage Focus Editions, 1980).

22. As discussed in Orlando Costas, *Crossroads Theology: Latin America* (Amsterdam: Editions Rodopi N.V., 1976).

23. Ibid.

24. Ibid.

25. Montgomery, "Evangelicals at Oaxtepec," *Churches and Politics*, p. 96.

26. Costas, *Crossroads Theology*, p. 107.

27. For a thorough and basic presentation of these differences see Nash, *Evangelicals in America Who they Are, What they Believe* (Nashville, Tenn.: Abingdon Press, 1987).

28. I must say frequently but not always, because evangelical groups like the Sojourner community, have clear policy differences from other evangelical groups.

29. Numerous interviews with Christians in Nicaragua who identify themselves as fundamentalists, when asked about their participation in government-sponsored projects, responded that they want nothing to do with any government.

30. An interesting case in terms of regime support is that of Nicaragua where progressive evangelical groups, such as CEPAD, support the regime and more conservative evangelical groups, such as CNPEN, challenge the Sandinista regime.

31. General Ríos Montt interview with the Calvin Center for Christian Studies team, January 5, 1987, author present.

32. Church attendance at the Elim Church in Guatemala City was a joyful experience shared with at least 3,000 others who sang with their arms raised and moving in unison, while an elevated TV platform transmitted the service to 2,000 other people whom the main santuary could not accommodate.

33. Enrique Domínguez and Deborah Huntington, *The Salvation Brokers: Conservative Evangelicals in Central America*, NACLA 18 (January-February 1984). See also, Merrill Collett, "The Cross and the Flag: Right-Wing Evangelicals Invade Latin America," *The Progressive* (December 1987).

34. Collett, "The Cross and the Flag," pp. 18–21.

35. Domínguez and Huntington, *The Salvation Brokers*.

36. See, for example, Deborah Barry, "U.S. 'New Right' Plays Pivotal Role in Reagan's Central American Strategy," *Latinamerica Press*, March 27, 1986, pp. 5–6; "The Rise of the Religious Right in Central America," *The Resource Center Bulletin*. no. 10 (Summer-Fall 1987); Ana María Ezcurra, "Neo-Conservative and Ideological Struggle Toward Central America in the USA," *Social Compass* 30 (1983): 349–362.

37. Penny Lernoux, "The Fundamentalist Surge in Latin America," *The Christian Century*, January 20, 1988, pp. 51–54.

38. A classic work in this regard is H. Richard Niebuhr, *The Social Sources of Denominationalism* (New York: Henry Holt, 1929).

39. By comparison, one wonders whether the nineteenth-century Protestant missionaries considered themselves to be "above politics," or did they realize that they were part of the modernization project of liberalism?

40. María Gallardo and José Roberto López, *Centroamérica: La Crísis en Cifras* (San José, Costa Rica: Flacso, 1986).

41. *La situación*, or the situation, is the most common euphemism used by Salvadorans to describe the violent conditions of life that have prevailed in their nation since 1980. The use of this neutral term is an attempt not to reveal their political preferences, and is a measure of the degree of civic trust that exists.

CHAPTER 9. DIVIDED EVANGELICALS IN SOUTH AFRICA

AUTHOR'S NOTE: This research was made possible by the assistance of the Phelps Stokes Fund and the Ford Foundation. I would also like to thank David Bonbright, Gail Gerhardt, Enid Gort, and Tom Karis for their kind help.

1. See *Christianity Today*, October 21, 1988, for an interview with Caesar Molebatsi, chairman of Concerned Evangelicals, p. 45.

2. A number derived from the census statistics in Marjorie Froise, ed., *South African Christian Handbook, 1986/87* (Florida, South Africa: World Vision of South Africa, 1986), pp. 2–3. The overall percentage of Pentecostals/Charismatics is small (1.1 percent in 1970, and 3.3 percent in 1980), but the rapid growth in their numbers seems to have taken place largely within the minority white community and the growth rate of the new churches has been quite high.

3. About 80 percent of the congregations of the new Pentecostal churches in the Durban area are white. See Elda Susan Morran and

Lawrence Schlemmer, *Faith for the Fearful?: An Investigation into New Churches in the Greater Durban Area* (Durban, South Africa: Centre for Applied Social Sciences, 1984), p. 56.

4. See Ron Steele, *Ray McCauley: Destined to Win* (Cape Town, South Africa: Conquest Publishing, 1986).

5. Each cell group is comprised of about twenty families.

6. Jerry Falwell, for example, entitled a 1983 "prophecy packet" and a television broadcast, "Nuclear War and the Second Coming of Jesus Christ." In the text of the accompanying pamphlet, Falwell remarked that nuclear war and the Second Coming "are indelibly intertwined." Falwell used the "prophecy packet" as propaganda against the "Nuclear Freeze Movement." See Falwell, "Nuclear War and the Second Coming of Christ" (Lynchburg, Va.: Old-Time Gospel Hour, 1983).

7. From a sermon called "The Great Escape" (Rhema Ministries South Africa, P.O. Box 50574, Randburg 2125, South Africa: Tape Department). McCauley then went on to comment on 1 Thess. 4:13–18, a favorite dispensationalist proof-text for the Rapture.

8. Morran and Schlemmer, *Faith for the Fearful?*, pp. 76ff.

9. The date of the deacon's remark was April 3, 1987. The strike later became violent. The police shot dead a number of strikers and black workers burned trains. Soldiers and police patroled the railroad stations with automatic weapons, shotguns, and sjamboks and raided the COSATU headquarters, a mostly black labor federation with a membership of about eight hundred thousand. Less than a year later, on February 24, 1988, the government banned sixteen antiapartheid groups and barred COSATU from all political activity.

10. A useful compendium of information on various right-wing church groups was compiled by Harald E. Winkler of the University of Cape Town, "Final Report on Pilot Study on Right Wing Church Groups for Department of Religious Studies, University of Cape Town," January 1988. The report is available only for research purposes and has not been published. Also see Paul Gifford, *The Religious Right in Southern Africa* (Harare, Zimbabwe: Baobab Books and University of Zimbabwe Publications, 1988); and L. Jones, "Right-Wing Evangelicals and South Africa," *Moto* (Zimbabwe) 64 (April 1988): 12ff.

11. See Larry Kickham, "How U.S. Evangelicals Bless Apartheid," *Penthouse* (March 1988): 43–44, 118, 120. Later in 1988, Mokoena was accused by a former associate of being a police agent.

12. "Bishop 'talking nonsense'," *The Star*, December 11, 1984. Prof. G. C. Oosthuizen, head of the Research Institute on Black Independent

Churches at the University of Zululand, stated that Mokoena's following was only a few thousand.

13. *The Kairos Document: Challenge to the Church* (Braamfontein, South Africa: Skotaville Publishers, 1986).

14. Terry Valentine, an American who works as the personnel director of Campus Crusade of South Africa, told me that Campus Crusade circulated Cain's speech without indicating where it came from in order to preserve their appearance of political neutrality. They marked Cain's speech "*Urgent*: To be read by every Christian in South Africa!" and added a postscript urging readers to send copies to every committed Christian they knew, to pray for the government, and to "build a chain that will reach *every* Christian in South Africa within 6 months." It was dated July 25, 1986.

15. See Derrick Knight, *Beyond the Pale: The Christian Political Fringe* (Lancashire, United Kingdom: Caraf Publications, 1982), pp. 110ff.

16. Fred Shaw, the leader of the Church League, admitted to receiving financial support from the South African government in this manner during an interview with me on June 17, 1983, while he was attending the annual convention of the International Council of Christian Churches in New Jersey, a right-wing association of fundamentalist churches led by Carl McIntyre. Shaw said that he did not at first know that the money came from the South African government.

17. The groups involved in UCA are Bet-El, one of the new pentecostal churches in the Pretoria area; Christians for Partnership Association, Foerdergesellschaft Africa; Frontline Fellowship; German South African Friendship Association; Gospel Defence League; Reformed Independent Churches Association; Rhodesia Christian Group; SA Catholic Defence League, Signposts; the Aida Parker Newsletter; Victims Against Terrorism; and Vox Africana. Of these, Frontline Fellowship, Gospel Defence League, Vox Africana, Signposts, and the Aida Parker Newsletter, the groups whose leaders I was able to interview, receive much of their funding from a small group of businessmen. Most of these operations are very small, just cottage industries run out of suburban homes. Vox Africana and Gospel Defence League, for example, like Cain's UCA and Signposts, operate from one individual's home.

18. "Church Condemns SA Sanctions Lobby," *The Star* (Johannesburg), June 13, 1988.

19. Quoted from "Statement by Full Gospel Church Members, Soweto," September 1988.

20. M. L. Badenhorst, interview, January 30, 1989. Badenhorst was a

member of the South African delegation to the 1989 National Religious Broadcasters convention in Washington, D.C.

21. "Forum Disagrees with Archbishop," *The Star*, January 17, 1988.

22. Concerned Evangelicals, *Evangelical Witness in South Africa (Evangelicals Critique Their Own Theology and Practice)* (Dobsonville, South Africa: Concerned Evangelicals, 1986).

23. The course taught the students, among other things, how to properly eat a hamburger and French fries in an automobile.

24. Concerned Evangelicals, *Evangelical Witness in South Africa*, p. 16.

25. There has been a rent boycott in the Vaal townships since September 1984.

26. Concerned Evangelicals, *A Call for Relevant Evangelical Witness: A Critical Response to the Mission of Evangelist Nicky van der Westhuizen to Sebokeng on 19–23 October 1987* (Dobsonville, South Africa: Concerned Evangelicals, 1987).

27. Ibid., p. 13.

28. Concerned Evangelicals, *Evangelical Witness in South Africa*, p. 24.

29. Ibid., p. 25.

30. Ernest Sandeen, *The Roots of Fundamentalism* (Grand Rapids, Mich.: Baker Book House, 1978), p. 245.

31. A small group including John G. Lake, an elder of the Zion Apostolic Church, arrived in South Africa in 1908. Lake preached in South Africa for five years, mostly in the Johannesburg area. Lake cast out demons, spoke in tongues, and practiced faith healing. See Gordon Lindsay, *John G. Lake—Apostle to Africa* (Dallas, Tex.: Christ for the Nations, 1981).

32. See Larry Kickham, "How U.S. Evangelicals Bless Apartheid."

CHAPTER 10. LIBERALISM IN SEARCH OF A POLITICAL AGENDA

1. Lonnie D. Kliever, *The Shattered Spectrum* (Atlanta, Ga.: John Knox Press, 1981).

2. For a useful summary of characteristics that ordinarily distinguished religious liberals and conservatives from each other, see George C. Bedell, Leon Sandon, Jr., and Charles T. Wellborn, eds., *Religion In America*

(New York: Macmillan, 1975), pp. 208–209. *Conservatives* are described as theocentric, otherworldly, revelational, traditional, and dogmatic. *Liberals* are described as anthropocentric, naturalistic, rationalistic, revisionist, and pragmatic.

3. William E. Hordern, *A Layman's Guide to Protestant Theology* (rev. ed.; New York: Macmillan, 1958), p. 73.

4. Peter C. Hodgson and Robert H. King, eds., *Christian Theology* (2d ed.; Philadelphia: Fortress Press, 1985), p. x.

5. The following discussion of James H. Cone, Mary Daly, and Gustavo Gutiérrez is condensed from Kliever, *Shattered Spectrum*, pp. 69–94.

6. Cone, *Black Theology and Black Power* (New York: Seabury Press, 1969), p. 1.

7. Cone, *A Black Theology of Liberation* (Philadelphia: Lippincott, 1970); and Cone, *God of the Oppressed* (New York: Seabury Press, 1975).

8. Cone, *Black Theology of Liberation*, p. 6.

9. Ibid., p. 18.

10. Ibid., pp. 79–80.

11. Ibid., p. 183.

12. Ibid., p. 29.

13. Cone, *Black Theology and Black Power*, p. 151.

14. Ibid., p. 41.

15. Daly, *The Church and the Second Sex* (New York: Harper, 1968).

16. Daly, *Beyond God the Father* (Boston: Beacon, 1973). Daly clearly moved beyond the circle of "Christian theologian" with the publication of *Gyn/ecology: The Metaethics of Radical Feminism* (Boston: Beacon, 1978), but her first two books clearly belonged to women's liberation theology and continue to exercise enormous influence in that movement.

17. Daly, *Beyond God the Father*, p. 19.

18. Ibid., pp. 83–87.

19. Ibid., pp. 13–45.

20. Ibid., p. 29.

21. Ibid., pp. 82–97.

22. Gutiérrez, *A Theology of Liberation* (Maryknoll, N.Y.: Orbis Books, 1973).

23. Ibid., p. 10.

24. Ibid., pp. 25–37.

CHAPTER 11. THE REVIVAL OF CHURCH AND STATE IN THE PHILIPPINES: CHURCHES AND RELIGION IN THE PEOPLE POWER REVOLUTION AND AFTER

AUTHOR'S NOTE: Many of the materials and insights used in this paper were gathered during my stint as a Fulbright Research Scholar and Visiting Research Associate at the Institute of Philippine Culture (IPC), Ateneo de Manila University, August 16, 1987—January 17, 1988. I am grateful to the Fulbright program and to the IPC and Ateneo for their support. However, they should not be held accountable for the statements and conclusions of this analysis.

1. Chester L. Hunt et al., *Sociology in the Philippine Setting: A Modular Approach* (Quezon City, Philippines: Phoenix Publishing House, Inc., 1987), p. 259.

2. Robert L. Youngblood, "Church and State in the Philippines: Some Implications for United States Policy," *Rebuilding a Nation: Philippine Challenges and American Policy*, ed. Carl H. Landé (Washington, D.C.: Washington Institute Press, 1987), p. 354.

3. Dennis Shoesmith, "The Church," *The Philippines After Marcos*, eds. R. L. May and Francisco Nemenzo (New York: St. Martin's , 1985), p. 71.

4. Landé, "The Political Crisis," *Crisis in the Philippines: The Marcos Era and Beyond*, ed. John Bresnan (Princeton, N.J.: Princeton University Press, 1986), pp. 118–119.

5. See Renato Constantino, Jr., *Renato Constantino and the Aquino Watch*, compiled and ed. Renato Constantino, Jr. (Quezon City, Philippines: Karrel, Inc., 1987), pp. 156–157.

6. Landé, "Political Crisis," *Crisis in the Philippines*, p. 119.

7. Shoesmith, "Church," *The Philippines After Marcos*, p. 71.

8. Especially his *Leaders, Factions and Parties: The Structure of Philippine Politics* (New Haven, Conn.: Yale University Southeast Asia Studies Monograph Series, no. 6, 1985).

9. While the official date of Marcos's martial law declaration is September 21, martial law was actually implemented on September 22, and not announced until September 23. The president backdated the official proclamation so that it would occur on a date that was a multiple of his lucky number 7.

10. Youngblood, "Church and State in the Philippines," *Rebuilding a Nation*, p. 354.

11. For the authoritative discussion of the divisions within the Roman Catholic church and the Catholic Bishops Conference of the Philippines, see Youngblood, "Structural Imperialism: An Analysis of the Catholic Bishops Conference of the Philippines," *Comparative Political Studies* 15 (April 1982).

12. Ibid., 35–36.

13. Shoesmith, "Church," *The Philippines After Marcos*, p. 72.

14. Youngblood, "Structural Imperialism," 36.

15. Lewis M. Simons, *Worth Dying For* (New York: Morrow, 1987), p. 90.

16. Richard L. Schwenk, *Onward Christians! Protestants in the Philippine Revolution* (Quezon City, Philippines: New Day Publishers, 1986), p. 9.

17. Youngblood, "Church and State in the Philippines," *Rebuilding a Nation*, p. 361.

18. See Schwenk, *Onward Christians!*

19. See James Clad, "Politics of the Cloth: Priests of 'Peaceful Revolution' Committed to New Role," *Far Eastern Economic Review*, June 18, 1987, p. 42.

20. Simons, *Worth Dying For*, p. 91.

21. Youngblood, "Church and State in the Philippines," *Rebuilding a Nation*, p. 356.

22. Ibid.

23. Shoesmith, "Church," *Philippines After Marcos*, citing Youngblood, "Church-Military Relations in the Philippines," *Australian Outlook* 35 (1981): 250–261.

24. Shoesmith, "Church," *Philippines After Marcos*, p. 72.

25. Youngblood, "Church and State in the Philippines," *Rebuilding a Nation*, pp. 356–357.

26. Shoesmith, "Church," *Philippines After Marcos*, p. 73.

27. Youngblood, "Church and State in the Philippines," *Rebuilding a Nation*, p. 357.

28. Shoesmith, "Church," *Philippines After Marcos*, p. 73.

29. Lewis Simons and his coauthors won a Pulitzer Prize for their account of the "hidden wealth" of the Marcoses and their cronies. Simons, *Worth Dying For*, contains an abbreviated account. Another account is Belinda A. Aquino, *The Politics of Plunder: The Philippines Under Marcos* (Quezon City, Philippines: Great Books Trading and University of the Philippines College of Public Administration, 1987). Raymond Bonner, *Waltzing with a Dictator: The Marcoses and the Making of American Policy* (New York: Times Books, 1987) contains accounts of both the Marcos's hidden wealth, based largely on Simons's work, and of the faked medals controversy.

30. See Schwenk, *Onward Christians!*, p. 94.

31. The Senate formally condemned the election of February 19, the same day that a House subcommittee voted to cut off military aid to the Philippines (ibid., p. 95).

32. Ibid.

33. Clad, "Politics of the Cloth," p. 45.

34. Ibid., p. 43

35. See Constantino, *Aquino Watch*.

36. Teodoro C. Bacani, Jr., "Church Is Against Military Takeover," letter to the editor, *Manila Chronicle*, October 17, 1987, p. 5.

37. See Clad, "Politics of the Cloth," p. 46.

38. Constantino, *Aquino Watch*; Clad, "Politics of the Cloth."

CHAPTER 12. THE SWORD AND THE CROSS: CHURCH-STATE CONFLICT IN LATIN AMERICA

1. Peter L. Berger, *Pyramids of Sacrifice* (New York: Basic, 1974), p. 3.

2. The doctrine of the two swords can be traced to such prominent early Christian writers as St. Augustine. For a stimulating account of the doctrine and its political ramifications, see Sheldon S. Wolin, *Politics and Vision* (Boston: Little, Brown, 1960), pp. 120–131.

3. A brilliant account of the struggle to create the Iberian nation-state, and of the role of church and state in the conquest of the New World is found in Claudio Véliz, *The Centralist Tradition in Latin America* (Princeton, N.J.: Princeton University Press, 1980), esp. chaps. 2, 3, 9.

4. See William Lytle Schurz, *Latin America: A Descriptive Survey* (New York: Dutton, 1964), pp. 30–31.

5. Véliz, *The Centralist Tradition*, p. 40.

6. J. Lloyd Mecham, *Church and State in Latin America* (rev. ed.; Chapel Hill: University of North Carolina Press, 1966), p. 11.

7. Ibid., p. 12.

8. Schurz, *Latin America*, p. 35.

9. Stanley J. Stein and Barbara H. Stein, *The Colonial Heritage of Latin America* (New York: Oxford, 1970), p. 76.

10. Mecham, *Church and State*, p. 37.

11. The obvious exception is the church's periodic defense of Indians against the exploitations that accompanied their use in systems of forced labor.

12. Donald E. Smith, *Religion and Political Development* (Boston, Mass.: Little, Brown, 1970), p. 24.

13. Ibid., p. 51.

14. Ivan Vallier, *Catholicism, Social Control, and Modernization in Latin America* (Englewood Cliffs, N.J.: Prentice-Hall, 1970), p. 8.

15. This phrase is also Vallier's. See his "Religious Elites: Differentiations and Developments in Roman Catholicism," *Elites in Latin America*, eds. Seymour Martin Lipset and Aldo Solari (New York: Oxford University Press, 1967), pp. 190–232. The concept of "new value movements" is discussed on pp. 194–195.

16. A detailed and informative discussion of this point can be found in Donal Dorr, *Option for the Poor: A Hundred Years of Vatican Social Teaching* (Maryknoll, N.Y.: Orbis Books, 1983), pp. 11–28.

17. Penny Lernoux, *Cry of the People* (New York: Penguin Books, 1982), p. 24. Lernoux reports that up to 70 percent of the Catholic clergy fled Cuba in the aftermath of Castro's triumph and the unsuccessful Bay of Pigs invasion of April 1961.

18. For an interesting discussion of the shock and disillusion among Church people that accompanied the discovery of "underdevelopment," see Gary MacEoin, *Revolution Next Door* (New York: Holt, 1971), esp. chaps. 1, 5.

19. Edward L. Cleary, *Crisis and Change: The Church in Latin America Today* (Maryknoll, N.Y.: Orbis Books, 1985), p. 22.

20. Walter M. Abbott and Joseph Gallagher, *The Documents of Vatican II* (New York: Guild Press, 1966), p. 244.

21. Ibid., p. 203.

22. *The Church in the Present-Day Transformation of Latin America in the Light of the Council*, vol. 2 (2d ed.; Washington, D.C.: U.S. Catholic Conference, 1973), p. 61.

23. Ibid., p. 64.

24. Lernoux provides an interesting and wide-ranging account of the development of CEBs in a variety of Latin American countries. See *Cry of the People*, pp. 389–408.

25. Cleary, *Crisis and Change*, pp. 125–142.

26. See the essays by Phillip Berryman, "El Salvador: From Evangelization to Insurrection"; and Michael Dodson, "Nicaragua: The Struggle for the Church," *Religion and Political Conflict in Latin America*, ed. Daniel H. Levine (Chapel Hill: University of North Carolina Press, 1986), esp. pp. 64–78, 82–87.

27. An excellent overview of the rise of authoritarian military regimes, even in seemingly developed countries such as Argentina and Chile, is *The New Authoritarianism in Latin America*, ed. David Collier (Princeton, N.J.: Princeton University Press, 1979).

28. H. Mark Roeloffs, "Liberation Theology: The Recovery of Biblical Radicalism," *American Political Science Review* 82 (June 1988): 553.

29. Ibid., 551.

30. Alfred Stepan, "The United States and Latin America: Vital Interests and the Instruments of Power," *Foreign Affairs* 58 (Winter 1979): 662.

31. Scott Mainwaring, *The Catholic Church and Politics in Brazil, 1916–1985* (Stanford, Cal.: Stanford University Press, 1986), p. 48.

32. Michael Dodson, "Comparing the 'Popular Church' in Nicaragua and Brazil," *Journal of InterAmerican Studies and World Affairs* 26 (February 1984): 132.

33. Rosa Maria Pochet and Abelino Martinez, *Nicaragua: Iglesia: Manipulación o profecía?* (San José, Costa Rica: Editorial DEI, 1987), p. 9.

34. Phillip Berryman, *The Religious Roots of Rebellion* (London: SCM Press, Ltd., 1984), p. 61.

35. Ibid., p. 62.

36. These leaders include the current president of the ATC, Edgardo García. For García's own account of his formation as a campesino leader, see Teófilo Cabestrero, *Revolutionaries for the Gospel*, trans. Phillip Berryman (Maryknoll, N.Y.: Orbis Books, 1983), pp. 45–54.

37. Dodson, "Popular Church in Nicaragua," 85.

38. Ibid.

39. Rollie E. Poppino, *Brazil: The Land and People* (2d ed.; New York: Oxford University Press, 1973), p. 280.

40. Brian Smith, "Churches and Human Rights in Latin America," *Churches and Politics in Latin America*, ed. Daniel H. Levine (Beverly Hills: Sage, 1980), p. 163.

41. Mainwaring, *The Catholic Church*, p. 85.

42. Ibid.

43. Ibid., p. 99.

44. Ibid., p. xii.

CHAPTER 13. THE ISLAMIC REVIVAL AS CONSERVATISM AND AS PROGRESS IN CONTEMPORARY EGYPT

AUTHOR'S NOTE: Useful comments were received from Dr. Ali Hilal Eddin Dessouki and others in a lecture before the Faculty of Economics and Political Science, Cairo University, July 20, 1988; from Dr. Gregory Gause; and from the opportunity to further share my thoughts publicly at a lecture at the Middle East Institute, Columbia University, December 5, 1988. I also want to thank the Department of Social Sciences, U.S. Military Academy, West Point for its support in my revision while a visiting professor there in 1988. I am especially indebted to Deborah Jefferson for her careful and conscientious typing of the original manuscript, and for Helen Pasquale's final version.

1. For sources on contemporary Islam in Egypt in addition to those cited, see Richard Dekmejian, *Islam in Revolution* (Syracuse, N.Y.: Syracuse University Press, 1985); Louis J. Cantori, "Religion and Politics in Egypt," *Religion and Politics in the Middle East*, ed. Michael Curtis (Boulder, Col.: Westview, 1981), pp. 77–90; and Hamid Ansari, "The Islamic Militants in Egyptian Politics," *International Journal of Middle East Studies* 16 (March 1984); as well as the comprehensive bibliography of works in foreign languages and Arabic compiled by Ibrahim Karawan, "Islamic Resurgence: A Preliminary Bibliography" (University of Utah, Middle East Center, 1988).

2. This comment is a carefully considered one not intended to detract from the scholarly merits of the important works whose quality of scholarship makes them mandatory reading on Islamic fundamentalism. Reference here is to Emmanuel Sivan, *Radical Islam: Medieval Theology and Modern Politics* (New Haven, Conn.: Yale University Press, 1985); Gilles Kepel, *The Prophet and the Pharaoh: Muslim Extremism in Egypt*, trans. Jon Rothschild (London: Saqi Books, 1985); and Adeed Dawisha, *The Arab Radicals* (New York: Council on Foreign Relations, 1986). As argued in the present chapter, the phenomenon of Islamic fundamentalism and radicalism is discrete and merits this separate treatment. When, however, an argument is made, as it is by Sivan that its importance is broader in that it represents leadership factors and issues that are dominant in society, then this tends toward overstatement. This is illustrated in a chapter entitled, "The Conservative Periphery," for example, a reference to what is in fact the majority of Muslim society (Sivan, *Radical Islam*, pp. 130–152). While Sivan's study is a brilliant one in illuminating the important relationship of the medieval scholar Ibn Taymiyya to contemporary radical Islamic thought, he tends to overlook the behavioral evidence presented here of the drama of mainstream Islamic revitalization that has effectively reversed since 1967 what he refers to as the "inadvertent secularization" taking place (Ibid., p. 152). This reversal constitutes the profound cultural change of Egyptian society since the 1970s.

This point is about a tendency to exaggerate the significance of Islamic fundamentalism to Egypt. Other scholars, notably the work of Dekmejian, but also importantly, John Voll, *Islam: Continuity and Change in the Modern World* (Boulder, Col.: Westview, 1982); James P. Piscatori, *Islam in a World of Nation-States* (London: Cambridge University Press, 1986); and John Esposito, *Islam and Politics* (Syracuse, N.Y.: Syracuse University Press, 1984), deal with revivalism. It is Voll's argument in "Renewal and Reform in Islamic History: *Tajdid* and *Islah*," *Voices of Resurgent Islam*, ed. John L. Esposito (New York: Oxford University Press, 1983), pp. 32–47, which parallels the present argument of "renewal" and "reform."

3. These alternative paradigms are discussed at length by Ronald Chilcote, *Comparative Politics: The Search for a Paradigm* (Boulder, Col: Westview, 1981).

Notes

4. Corporatism has received much attention since the publication of Frederick Pike and Thomas Strich, eds., *The New Corporatism: Social-Political Structures in the Iberian World* (Notre Dame: University of Notre Dame, 1974), especially the article by Phillippe C. Schmitter. The more inclusive meaning of the concept advanced here with normative and structural components is perhaps best presented by Douglas Chalmers, "Corporatism and Comparative Politics," *New Directions in Comparative Politics*, ed. H. Wiarda (Boulder, Col.: Westview, 1985), pp. 56–79, and reprinted in Louis Cantori and Andrew Ziegler, eds., *Comparative Politics in the Post-Behavioral Era* (Boulder, Col: Lynne Rienner Publishers, 1988), pp. 134–157. For the argument about a possible conservative corporatist research paradigm, see Cantori and Ziegler, Ibid., pp. 73–77; and Cantori, "Post-Behavioral Political Science and the Study of Comparative Politics," Ibid., pp. 417–426. For Middle Eastern applications of a corporatist approach, see John Waterbury, *The Egypt of Nasser and Sadat* (Princeton, N.J.: Princeton University Press, 1983), pp. 309–312; Robert Bianchi, *Interest Groups and Political Development in Turkey* (Princeton, N.J.: Princeton University Press, 1984), *passim*; and *Associational Life in Egypt* (New York: Oxford University Press, 1990); Salih Abd al-Rahman al-Manaa, "al-mudarrasa al-jamac. iyya kamidkhal lidirasa al-dawla wa alaqataha bi al-mujtamaa fi al-mashriq al-arabi" ("The State Corporatist Approach as an Introduction to the Study of the State and Its Relationship to Society in the Middle East"), *Dirasat* 2 (Jordan: Jordanian University, 1988), pp. 303–328.

5. For this general process in Germany and France and for details of much of the discussion that follows, see Ralph H. Bowen, *German Theories of the Corporate State with Special Reference to the Period 1870–1910* (New York: Whittlesey Press, 1947); Matthew H. Elbow, *French Corporate Theory, 1798–1948* (New York: Columbia University Press, 1953); and Klaus Epstein, *The Genesis of German Conservatism* (Princeton, N.J.: Princeton University Press, 1966).

6. This definition is a composite one arrived at from Albert Schaffle, "Uber den wissenschaftlichen Begriff der Politik", *Zeitschrift fur die gesamte Staatswissenschaft* 53 (1897); and Rene'de La Tour du Pin, *Vers un ordre social chretian, jalon de route 1882–1907* (Paris: Gabriel Beauchesne, 1929).

7. Karl Mannheim is well-known for his sociology of knowledge theory and Enlightenment spawned utopias, for example, liberalism and Marxism [*Ideology and Utopia* (New York: Harcourt, 1936)]. In this book, however, he was unable to explain conservatism in the same way and years after his death an incomplete manuscript appeared first in German (1984) and then in English as *Conservatism*, trans. David Kettler, Volker Meja, and Nico Stehr (London: Routledge and Kegan Paul, 1986). An elaboration of the subject of conservatism can be found in Louis J. Cantori, "Corporatism, Conservatism and Political Development in the Middle East," *Political Develop-*

ment Reconsidered: Political Change in the Middle East, eds. Cantori and I. Harik, in preparation.

8. The discussion upon the importance of the past as a guide to the future is similar to that of Yvonne Yasbeck Haddad, *Contemporary Islam and the Challenge of History* (Albany: State University of New York Press, 1982), "Conclusion: Towards an Islamic Understanding of History," pp. 134–144, which discusses the Islamic past as "progressive not because it changes but because it is equipped to cope with all change."

9. Sivan, *Radical Islam*, p. 70.

10. On this subject, see Denis J. Sullivan, "Islamic Associations in Egypt: A Development Alternative," Northeastern University.

11. On the theoretical conceptual points of *hegra, jahiliyya,* and *jihad,* see Sivan, *Radical Islam,* pp. 86–94, esp. *hegra* as internal migration and a countersociety.

12. The specifics of the effects of the 1967 defeat and the 1973 "Victory" and Islamic sentiment are discussed by Haddad, *Contemporary Islam,* pp. 33–45.

13. On the liberal period and its decline see Albert Hourani, *Arabic Thought in the Liberal Age* (London: Oxford University Press, 1962), esp. pp. 340–373.

14. See John Waterbury, "The Public Sector in Crisis," *The Egypt of Nasser and Sadat* (Princeton, N.J.: Princeton University Press, 1983), pp. 83–100 for a political economy analysis of the demise of the Nasser effort at state socialism.

15. This is the significance of Sivan's discussion of *jinn* (good spirits) and the prolonged funeral rituals common to Egypt but seldom found elsewhere in the Islamic world. Sivan, *Radical Islam,* p. 136. See also, Michael Gilsenan, "L'Islam dans L'Egypte Contemporaine: Religion d'Etat, Religion Populaire," *Annales: Economies, Societies, Civilizations* 35 (1980): 598–614.

16. The presence of angels has been related to the author by several soldiers and officers who made the assault. See also, Haddad, *Contemporary Islam,* p. 43.

17. Keppel's analysis of the sermons of Shaykh Kishk (Keppel, *The Prophet and the Pharaoh,* pp. 172–190) are revealing of this intermediate brokering role between popular and official Islam.

18. Keppel, *Prophet and the Pharaoh,* pp. 105–107, but also pp. 103–128 for the legal publication of *al-Da'wa* magazine of the Muslim Brethren that remained an "illegal," but tolerated organization.

19. Sivan, *Radical Islam*, pp. 131ff. for a content analysis of the newspaper's attention to religious issues.

20. Ibid., pp. 135–142.

21. The best general analysis is the classic work by Richard P. Mitchell, *The Society of the Muslim Brothers* (London: Oxford University Press, 1969), which covers the organization until its assassination attempt upon Nasser in 1954. Keppel's analysis of the radical fundamentalists, is one that traces the connections of more radical personalities and doctrines (importantly influenced by the organization's Supreme Guide, Sayid Qutb) from the Muslim Brethren to such groupings as Takfir Wa al-Higra and al-Jihad through the decades of the 1960s, 1970s, and into the 1980s. Keppel, *Prophet and the Pharaoh*, esp. chaps. 1, 2, 3. See also, Sivan, *Radical Islam*, pp. 73–82. For a treatment of the evolution of the Muslim Brethren to the parliamentary elections of April 1987 as well as Egyptian Islamic groups in general, see al-Sayyid Yasin, ed., *al-taqrir al-istrat i jiyya al-arabi 1987* (The Arab Strategic Report, 1987) (Cairo: al-Aharam, 1988), pp. 231–233 and 236–241.

22. See Keppel, *Prophet and the Pharaoh*.

23. The estimate of nine thousand, the greater part of whom are located in Cairo and Alexandria, is based on the author's consultancy experience with the U.S. Agency for International Development in Cairo. See also, Sullivan, "Islamic Associations in Egypt."

24. Abdel Monem Said Aly, "Egypt: A Decade After Camp David," *The Middle East: Ten Years after Camp David*, ed. William Quandt (Washington, D.C.: Brookings, 1988), p. 83. For a fuller discussion see Alain Roussillon, "Secteur Public et Societies islamiques de placement de fondsila recomposition du system redistribute if en Egypt," *Bulletin Du Cedj*, ed. Jean-Claude Vatin, 23 (Premier semester), pp. 277–322 (Cairo; Centre d'Etude et de Documentation Economique, Juridique et Sociale, 1988).

25. This is one of the conclusions in the by now classic article on the subject by Saad Eddin Ibrahim, "Anatomy of Egypt's Militant Islamic Groups: Methodological Note and Preliminary Findings," *International Journal of Middle East Studies* 12 (December 1980): 423–453.

26. "Egypt/8," Dossier, *Nord-Sud Export*, no. 146 (May 1988): 13.

27. Leonard Binder, *Islamic Liberalism* (Chicago, Ill.: University of Chicago Press, 1988); James Piscatori, *Islam in a World of Nation-States* (London: Cambridge University Press, 1986); Robert Bianchi, "Islam and Democratization in Egypt," *Current History* (February 1989); and Iliya Harik, "Liberty as a Criterion of Political Development," *Political Development Reconsidered*.

CHAPTER 14. WOMEN AND RELIGION IN A MODERN
ISLAMIC SOCIETY: THE CASE OF KUWAIT

AUTHORS' NOTE: The authors express their thanks to John Esposito for his comments on an earlier version on this chapter.

1. Evidence of the strength of Islamic attachments at the individual
level is provided by a 1976 survey of Kuwaiti and other Arab students at the
University of Kuwait. Students ranked Islam first in a hierarchy of group
affiliations that also included family, citizenship (Kuwaiti), ethnicity (Arab),
and political orientation, leading the author of the study to conclude that
"Islam was paramount in the lives of the vast majority of Arab undergrad-
uate students attending Kuwait University." See Tawfic Farah, "Group Affiliations of University Students in the Arab Middle East (Kuwait)," *Political
Behavior in the Arab States*, ed. Tawfic Farah (Boulder, Col.: Westview, 1983).

2. Useful discussions of the circumstances of women in Muslim society are provided in the introductory chapters and in many of the contributions in Elizabeth W. Fernea and Basima Q. Bezirgan, eds., *Middle Eastern
Muslim Women Speak* (Austin: University of Texas Press, 1977); Lois Beck and
Nikki Keddie, eds., *Women in the Muslim World* (Cambridge, Mass.: Harvard
University Press, 1978); and James Allman, ed., *Women's Status and Fertility
in the Muslim World* (New York: Praeger, 1978). For additional, more focused
treatment see Norman Anderson, *Law Reform in the Muslim World* (London:
The Athlone Press, 1976); Charis Waddy, *Women in Muslim History* (London:
Longman, 1980); and Ghada Al-Kharsha, *Islam and Liberty of Women* (Ku-
wait: Dar Al-Seyasa, 1974). Also highly recommended are Nikki Keddie,
"Problems in the Study of Middle Eastern Women," *International Journal of
Middle Eastern Studies* 10 (May 1979): 225–240; and Keddie, "Iran: Change in
Islam; Islam and Change," *International Journal of Middle East Studies* 11 (July
1980): 527–542.

3. For a forceful exposition of these arguments, written from the
point of view of a contemporary Muslim feminist, see Fatima Mernissi, *Beyond the Veil: Male-Female Dynamics in a Modern Muslim Society* (rev. ed.;
Bloomington: Indiana University Press, 1987), pp. 44–45. Mernissi also argues that Islam views women as active sexual beings and that Muslim theorists, considering this a threat to social order and civilization, have
accordingly insisted on the strict regulation and control of female sexuality.

4. For accounts of al-Afghani, Abduh, and other Islamic modernists,
see Keddie, *An Islamic Response to Imperialism: Political and Religious Writings
of Sayyid Jamal ad-Din al-Afghani* (Berkeley: University of California Press,
1968); Albert Hourani, *Arabic Thought in the Liberal Age* (London: Oxford
University Press, 1962); and Charles C. Adams, *Islam and Modernism in
Egypt* (London: Longman, 1933). See also Fazlur Rahman, "Islamic Modern-

ism: Its Scope, Method, and Alternatives," *International Journal of Middle East Studies* 1 (1970): 317–333; and Daniel Crecelius, "Nonideological Responses of the Egyptian Ulama to Modernization," *Scholars, Saints, and Sufis: Muslim Religious Institutions since 1500*, ed. Keddie (Berkeley: University of California Press, 1972).

5. Qasim Amin, *Tahrir al-Mar'a* [*Emancipation of Women*] (Cairo: 1899).

6. One contemporary affirmation to this effect is the Universal Islamic Declaration, issued by the Islamic Council of Europe in 1982. In one provision, the declaration calls for "ensuring that women enjoy full rights—legal, social, cultural, economic, educational and political—which Islam has granted to them. See Salem Azzam, ed., *Islam and Contemporary Society* (London: Longman in association with the Islamic Council of Europe, 1982), p. 263.

7. For a summary of this argument, which is commonly made by Islamic modernists, see Malise Ruthven, *Islam in the World* (New York: Oxford University Press, 1984), pp. 164–165. See also Dale Eickelman, *The Middle East: An Anthropological Approach* (Englewood Cliffs, N.J.: Prentice-Hall, 1981), pp. 151–152. A different point of view is advanced by Mernissi, *Beyond the Veil*, p. 64. Mernissi argues that the introduction of Islam increased male dominance, fostering "the transition from a family based on some degree of female self-determination to a family based on male control."

8. "Introduction," *Scholars, Saints, and Sufis*, p. 2.

9. Crecelius, "Nonideological Responses," *Scholars, Saints, and Sufis*, pp. 204, 208.

10. Noel Coulson and Doreen Hinchcliffe, "Women and Law Reform in Contemporary Islam," *Women in the Muslim World*, p. 48.

11. Tribalism in states of the Arabian Gulf is discussed in Muhammad T. Sadik and William P. Snavely, *Bahrain, Qatar and the United Arab Emirates* (Lexington, Mass.: D. C. Heath, 1972), pp. 119–120.

12. A recent comparative study of three Muslim movements in Tunisia nicely illustrates the ideological and political diversity of groups associated with the Islamic resurgence within a single country. See Douglas Magnuson, "Islamic Movements in Contemporary Tunisia" (Ph.D. Diss.: Brown University, 1987). Some of Magnuson's terminology informs the present discussion of differing ideological tendencies among Muslim groups in Kuwait and elsewhere. For a general examination of religious movements in the Arab Gulf region, see James A. Bill, "Resurgent Islam in the Persian Gulf," *Foreign Affairs* 63 (1984).

13. A like-minded movement in Kuwait is the Salafiyya party. In most other countries, groups bearing the name Salafiyya tend to be modernist in

orientation, but in Kuwait the party is similar in character to the Liberation party.

14. Sayyid Qutb, *Ma'alim fi al-Tariq (Guideposts along the Road)*; quoted in Gilles Kepel, *Muslim Extremism in Egypt* (Berkeley: University of California Press, 1984), p. 44

15. Saad Eddin Ibrahim, "Islamic Militancy as a Social Movement: The Case of Two Groups in Egypt," *Islamic Resurgence in the Arab World*, ed. Ali E. Hillal Dessouki (New York: Praeger, 1982), p. 122. Ibrahim's study is based on two groups that are smaller and more militant, but in the same ideological stream as the Muslim Brotherhood. He also notes that one group was more concerned than the other with equality for women and that one but not the other had female members.

16. Quoted in Yvonne Haddad, "Traditional Affirmations Concerning the Role of Women as Found in Contemporary Arab-Islamic Literature," *Women in Contemporary Muslim Societies*, ed. Jane I. Smith (Cranbury, N.J.: Associated University Presses, 1980), p. 81.

17. See John Esposito, *Islam and Politics* (Syracuse, N.Y.: Syracuse University Press, 1987), pp. 142–150. See also Ismail Raji al-Faruqi, "The Islamic Critique of the Status Quo in Muslim Society," *The Islamic Impulse*, ed. Barbara F. Stowasser (London: Croom Helm, 1987), pp. 226–243; Charles Adams, "Mawdudi and the Islamic State," *Voices of Resurgent Islam*, ed. John Esposito (New York: Oxford University Press, 1983), pp. 99–133; and Charles Butterworth, "Prudence Versus Legitimacy: The Persistent Theme in Islamic Political Thought," *Islamic Resurgence in the Arab World*, pp. 95–102.

18. Abu al-Ala al-Mawdudi, *Al Hijab (The Veil)* (Beirut: Ressaleh Foundation Union Co., 1973), pp. 11–12.

19. Ibrahim, "Islamic Militancy as a Social Movement," *Islamic Resurgence*.

20. It is notable in this connection that, contrary to the assessments of some Western observers, veiling and a separation of the sexes are not at all synonymous with political apathy or a withdrawal from modern life. For an account of the different reasons that a woman may decide to put on the veil, see John Alden Williams, "Veiling in Egypt," *Islam and Development: Religion and Sociopolitical Change*, ed. John Esposito (Syracuse, N.Y.: Syracuse University Press, 1982).

21. Kepel, *Muslim Extremism in Egypt*, p. 29.

22. Yvonne Haddad, "The Progressive Muslim Movement in Tunisia" (Paper presented at a conference on the Political Economy of Tunisia, John's Hopkins University School of Advanced International Studies, 1989).

23. For additional information about social change and modernization in Kuwait, both in general and as they relate to the circumstances of
women, see Farida Allaghi and Aisha Almana, "Survey Research on
Women in the Arab Gulf Region," *Social Science Research and Women in the
Arab World* (Paris: UNESCO, 1984); Suad M. al-Sabah, *Development Planning
in an Oil Economy and the Role of Women: The Case of Kuwait* (London: East
Lords Publishing Ltd., 1983); Jamal Sanad and Mark Tessler, "The Economic Orientations of Kuwaiti Women: Their Nature, Determinants, and
Consequences," *International Journal of Middle East Studies* 20 (1988): 443–468;
and Kamla Nath, "Education and Employment among Kuwaiti Women,"
Women in the Muslim World. For additional information about the economic
dimensions of social change in Kuwait, see Naiem A. Sherbiny, *Labor and
Capital Flows in the Arab World: A Critical View* (Kuwait: The Industrial Bank
of Kuwait, 1985); and Shamlan y al-Essa, *The Manpower Problem in Kuwait*
(London: Routledge, Kegan Paul International Ltd., 1981).

24. For general discussions of the nature and causes of the current
Islamic resurgence, see the introduction and many of the contributions in
Dessouki, *Islamic Resurgence in the Arab World*. See also Bassan Tibi, "The
Renewed Role of Islam in the Political and Social Development of the Mid-
dle East," *Middle East Journal* 37 (Winter 1983); Nazih N. W. Ayubi, "The
Political Revival of Islam: The Case of Egypt," *International Journal of Middle
East Studies* 12 (1980); Richard Hrair Dekmejian, "The Islamic Revival in the
Middle East and North Africa," *Current History* (April 1980); and Bernard
Lewis, "The Return of Islam," *Commentary* (January 1976).

25. Interview, July 1984.

26. See Sanad and Tessler, "Economic Orientations of Kuwaiti
Women."

CHAPTER 15. SHI'I ISLAM: BONYADGIRI
OR FUNDAMENTALISM?

1. For example, not a single work in the development and modernization literature prior to the Iranian Revolution suggested that Islam might
be compatible with rational economic development and modernization
strategies and, indeed, regarded it as a retrograde force that increasing
Western-style political participation and economic consumerism would
make increasingly relevant to the political and economic development of
the Middle East.

2. For a more detailed discussion of the ideological foundations of development and modernization theory see R. Packenham, *Liberal America and
the Third World: Political Development Ideas in Foreign Aid and Social Science*

(Princeton, N.J.: Princeton University Press, 1973); and M. Kesselman, "Order or Movement? The Literature of Political Development as Ideology," *World Politics* 26 (1974): 139–154.

3. Note that Parsons builds the secularist bias into his definition of the evolutionary universal: . . . [an] integrated system of universalistic norms, applicable to the society as a whole rather than to a few functional or segmental sectors, highly generalized in terms of principles and standards, and *relatively independent of both the religious agencies that legitimize the normative order of society* and vested interest groups in the operative sector, "particularly in government" (emphasis added). Talcott Parsons, "Evolutionary Universals in Society," *American Sociological Review* 29 (1964): 350–353.

CHAPTER 16. RELIGIOUS RESURGENCE AND POLITICAL MOBILIZATION OF THE SHI'A IN LEBANON

1. The standard reference is Michael C. Hudson, *The Precarious Republic: Political Modernization in Lebanon* (New York: Random, 1968).

2. For an excellent analysis see Samir Khalaf, "Changing Forms of Political Patronage in Lebanon," *Patrons and Clients in Mediterranean Societies,* eds. Ernest Gellner and John Waterbury (London: Gerald Duckworth, 1977), pp. 185–205.

3. Samir Khalaf, "Adaptive Modernization: The Case for Lebanon," *Economic Development and Population Growth in the Middle East,* eds. Charles A. Cooper and Sidney S. Alexander (New York: American Elsevier, 1972), pp. 567–598.

4. Evelyn A. Early, an anthropologist, conducted interesting research on the 'Amiliyah Society in the early 1970s. Though she has shared some of her insights with the author, most of her work on Lebanon remains unpublished.

5. For example, Elizabeth Piçard argues, in an otherwise very fine paper, that the "Shi'a have transmitted down the centuries a collective refusal to accept any political power which does not have its origins in the religious hierarchy of the community. Consequently, they are predisposed to join parties contesting established authority" ["Political Identities and Communal Loyalties: Shifting Mobilization Among the Lebanese Shi'a Through Ten Years of War, 1975–1985," *Ethnicity, Politics and Development,* eds. Dennis L. Thompson and Dov Ronen (Boulder, Col.: Lynne Rienner Publishers, 1986), p. 183].

6. Cf. Abbas Kelidar, "The Shi'i Imami Community and the Politics of the Arab East," *Middle East Studies* 19 (January 1983): 3–16. Kelidar observes, "The Shi'i community has shown a marked tendency for rebellion stemming from its general attitude and belief that the authority of Muslim rulers with the exceptions of Imam Ali's [sic], could not be recognized as legitimate."

7. For accounts of al-Sadr's role see Fouad Ajami, *The Vanished Imam: Musa al-Sadr and the Shi'a of Lebanon* (Ithaca, N.Y.: Cornell University Press, 1985); and Augustus Richard Norton, *Amal and the Shi'a: Struggle for the Soul of Lebanon* (Austin: University of Texas Press, 1987).

8. *Amal* means hope in Arabic, but it is also an acronym that stands for the "Lebanese Resistance Detachments." For a more detailed account of the political emergence of the Shi'a, and particularly Amal, see Norton, *Amal and the Shi'a.*

9. Hilal Kashan, "Antiwestern Perceptions among Lebanese Shi'i College Students," Beirut, 1987.

10. See Jim Muir, "Buying Hearts and Minds," *Middle East International,* no. 315 (December 19, 1987): 6–7.

11. David C. Martin and John Wolcott, *Best Laid Plans: The Inside Story of America's War Against Terrorism* (New York: Harper, 1988), esp. pp. 105, 133.

12. For an insightful analysis of the thought of three important clerics (Muhammad Jawad Mughniyya, Muhammad Mahdi Shams al-Din, and Muhammad Husain Fadlallah), see Chibli Mallat, *Shi'i Thought from the South of Lebanon,* Papers on Lebanon, no. 7 (Oxford: Centre for Lebanese Studies, April 1988).

13. Ahmad Nizar Hamzah, "Conflict in Lebanon: A Survey of Opinions and Attitudes" (Ph.D. Diss., University of Southern California, 1986).

14. *al-Shira',* September 19, 1988, p. 9.

15. Ze'ev Schiff, *Ha'aretz,* June 10, 1988, p. 28.

CHAPTER 17. THE POLITICS OF RELIGIOUS RESURGENCE AND RELIGIOUS TERRORISM: THE CASE OF THE SIKHS OF INDIA

AUTHOR'S NOTE: I wish to thank Professors John A. Booth, Margaret Reid, Frank Brooks, and Emile Sahliyeh for their help in the preparation of this paper. Booth, especially, took time to review this chapter and offered extensive comments and suggestions. And finally, I wish to thank Linda Strube for her invaluable assistance in typing and editing this chapter.

1. G. Singh, "Understanding the Punjab Problem," *Asian Survey* 17 (1987): 1277.

2. R. Aya, "Theories of Revolution Reconsidered: Contrasting Models of Collective Violence," *Theory and Society* 8 (1979): 39–99; L. A. Tilly and C. Tilly, eds., *Class Conflict and Collective Action* (Beverly Hills: Sage Publications, 1981); Barrington Moore, Jr., *Injustice: The Social Basis of Obedience and Revolt* (White Plains, N.Y.: 1978).

3. Tilly and Tilly, *Class Conflict and Collective Action*, p. 17.

4. Aya, "Theories of Revolution Reconsidered," 75.

5. T. Skocpol, *States and Social Revolutions: A Comparative Study of France, Russia, and China* (Cambridge, N.Y.: Cambridge University Press, 1979), pp. 19–24.

6. Lawrence C. Hamilton, "Dynamics of Insurgent Violence: Preliminary Findings," *Behavioral and Quantitative Perspectives on Terrorism*, eds. Yonah Alexander and John M. Gleason (New York: Pergamon Press, 1981), p. 229; John M. Gleason, "Third World Terrorism: Perspectives for Quantitative Research," *Quantitative Perspectives on Terrorism*, p. 243.

7. Aya, "Theories of Revolution Reconsidered," 79.

8. M. Olson, *The Logic of Collective Action: Public Goods and the Theory of Groups* (Cambridge, Mass.: Harvard University Press, 1971).

9. People's Union for Democratic Rights (PUDR) and People's Union for Civil Liberties, *Who Are the Guilty: Joint Inquiry into the Causes and the Impact of the Riots in Delhi from 31st Oct. to 10th Nov., 1984*.

10. *Facts on File Yearbook* (New York: Facts on File, 1985), p. 310.

11. Arthur W. Helweg, "India's Sikhs: Problems and Prospects," *Journal of Contemporary Asia* 17 (1987): 146.

12. M. S. Dhami, "Caste, Class and Politics in the Rural Punjab: A Study of Two Villages in Sangrur District," *Political Dynamics of Punjab*, eds. Paul Wallace and Surendra Chopra (Amritsar: Guru Nanak Dev University Press, 1981), p. 295.

13. Ibid., pp. 295–296.

14. Wolf, *Peasant Wars of the Twentieth Century* (New York: Harper & Row, 1969), pp. 289–291; H. Alavi, "Peasants and Revolution," *The Socialist*

Register (New York: Monthly Review Press, 1965), pp. 274–275.

15. K. Singh, *A History of the Sikhs*, vol. 1 (Delhi: Oxford University Press, 1963), pp. 14–15.

16. J. Pettigrew, *Robber Noblemen: A Study of the Political System of the Sikh Jats* (England: Routledge and Kegan Paul, 1975), pp. 25–26.

17. Singh, *History of the Sikhs*, p. 96.

18. Ibid.

19. Pettigrew, *Robber Noblemen*, pp. 26, 242.

20. *India Today* (New Delhi), January 15, 1988.

21. *Facts on File Yearbook* (New York: Facts on File, 1988), p. 650.

22. T. J. Byres, "The New Technology, Class Formation and Class Action in the Indian Countryside," *The Journal of Peasant Studies* 8 (1981): 445.

23. G. S. Bhalla and G. K. Chadha, "Green Revolution and the Small Peasant: A Study of Income Distribution in Punjab Agriculture," *Economic and Political Weekly* 17 (1982): 870.

24. H. Puri, "The Akali Agitation: An Analysis of Socio-Economic Bases of Protest," *Economic and Political Weekly* 18 (1983): 117; P. Kumar et al., *Punjab Crisis: Context and Trends* (Chandigarh, India: CRRID, 1984), p. 50; Pettigrew, *Robber Noblemen*, p. 35.

25. Helweg, "India's Sikhs," 151.

26. Byres, "New Technology, Class Formation and Class Action," 439.

27. H. P. Sharma, "The Green Revolution in India: Prelude to a Red One?" *Imperialism and Revolution in S. Asia*, eds. H. P. Sharma and K. Gough (New York: Monthly Review Press, 1973), p. 77.

28. Wolf, *Peasant Wars of the Twentieth Century*, pp. 289-291.

29. Byres, "New Technology, Class Formation and Class Action," 434.

30. Kumar et al., *Punjab Crisis*, p. 84; B. L. Kapoor, "Labor Market Discrimination against Migrant Workers in an Indian State: The Case of Punjab," *The Journal of Development Studies* 23 (1987): 402–417.

31. Kumar et al., *Punjab Crisis*, p. 48.

32. A. Ray and J. Kincaid, "Politics, Economic Development, and Second Generation Strain in India's Federal System," *Publius: The Journal of Fed-*

eralism 18 (Spring 1988): 159–163; T. V. Satyamurthy, "India's Punjab Problem: Edging Towards a Solution?" *The World Today* 42 (1986): 49.

33. A. De Tocqueville, "How, Though the Reign of Louis XVI Was the Most Prosperous Period of the Monarch, this Very Prosperity Hastened the Outbreak of the Revolution," *When Men Revolt and Why: A Reader in Political Violence and Revolution*, ed. J. C. Davies (New York: Free Press, 1971), p. 96.

34. Pettigrew, *Robber Noblemen*, p. 26.

35. Satyamurthy, "India's Punjab Problem," 47–48.

36. M. Tully and S. Jacob, *Amritsar: Mrs. Gandhi's Last Battle* (London: Jonathan Cape Publishers, 1985), pp. 57–58.

37. Victor D. D'Souza, "Economy, Caste, Religion and Population Distribution: An Analysis of Communal Tension in Punjab," *Economic and Political Weekly* 17 (1982): 792.

38. Tully and Jacob, *Amritsar*, pp. 58-59.

39. Puri, "Akali Agitation," 116.

40. Helweg, "India's Sikhs," 143; Tully and Jacob, *Amritsar*, pp. 52–73.

41. Puri, "Akali Agitation," 117.

42. Tully and Jacob, *Amritsar*, pp. 71–72.

43. J. S. Gandhi, "System, Process and Popular Ethos: A Study in Contemporary Politics in Punjab," *Political Dynamics of Punjab*, p. 59.

44. *Facts on File Yearbook* (New York: Facts on File, 1986), p. 926.

45. Tully and Jacob, *Amritsar*, pp. 63–66.

46. *Facts on File Yearbook* (New York: Facts on File, 1984, 1986, 1987), pp. 588–589, 798, and 45, respectively.

47. H. E. Hegland, "Conclusion: Religious Resurgence in Today's World—Refuge from Dislocation and Anomie or Enablement for Change?" *Religious Resurgence: Contemporary Cases in Islam, Christianity, and Judaism*, eds. R. T. Antoun and H. E. Hegland (New York: Syracuse University Press, 1987), pp. 248–250.

48. Singh, *History of the Sikhs*, p. 289.

49. Kumar et al., *Punjab Crisis*, pp. 78–79.

50. Singh, *History of the Sikhs*, p. 140.

CHAPTER 18. RELIGION AND POLITICS IN THE JEWISH STATE OF ISRAEL

1. Abba Hillel Silver, *A History of Messianic Speculation in Israel* (New York: Macmillan, 1927).

2. Arthur Hertzberg, *The Zionist Idea* (New York: Atheneum, 1979), p. 430. See also, Zalman Abramov, *Perpetual Dilemma: Jewish Religion in the Jewish State* (Rutherford, N.J.: Fairleigh Dickinson University Press, 1976), pp. 164ff.

3. Hertzberg, *The Zionist Idea*, p. 403.

4. Jean Real Isaac, *Party and Politics in Israel: Three Visions of a Jewish State* (New York: Longman, 1981), p. 40.

5. Herbert Feis, *The Birth of Israel: The Tousled Diplomatic Bed* (New York: Norton, 1969), p. 61.

6. Amnon Rubinstein, *The Zionist Dream Revisited* (New York: Schocken, 1984), p. 34.

7. Yaacov Morris, "Anti-Judaic Religious Politicians," *The Jerusalem Post*, February 13, 1987.

8. Reuven Hammer, "The Enemy Within," Ibid., October 6, 1986.

9. Quoted in Thomas Friedman, "Fight for the Religious Future Builds in Israel," *The New York Times*, June 29, 1987.

10. Daniel J. Elazar and Janet Aviad, *Religion and Politics in Israel* (New York: American Jewish Committee, 1981), p. 16. See also, Stewart Reiser, *The Politics of Leverage: The National Religious Party of Israel and Its Influence on Foreign Policy* (Cambridge, Mass.: Harvard University Center for Middle Eastern Studies, 1984), pp. 20–21.

11. Ehud Sprinzak, *Gush Emunim: The Politics of Zionist Fundamentalism in Israel* (New York: American Jewish Committee, 1986), p. 8. See also, Zvi Raanan, *Gush Emunim* (Tel Aviv: Sifriyat Poalim, 1980).

12. Sprinzak, *Gush Emunim*.

13. Quoted in Uriel Tal, "Foundations of a Political Messianic Trend in Israel," *The Jerusalem Quarterly* 35 (1985): 44–55. See also, Sprinzak, *Gush Emunim*, p. 10, and Ian Lustick, *For the Land and the Lord: Jewish Fundamentalism in Israel* (New York: Council on Foreign Relations, 1988), pp. 94–95.

14. Lustick, *For the Land and the Lord*.

15. Shaul Mishal, *The PLO Under Arafat: Between Gun and Olive Branch* (New Haven, Conn.: Yale University Press, 1986), p. 130.

16. A definition of *fundamentalism* in the present context is provided by Sprinzak, *Gush Emunim*, p. 1. "Because this [religious Zionist] system combines belief in the literal truth of the Bible and total commitment to the precepts of modern secular Zionism, it may be called Zionist Fundamentalism." See also, Ian Lustick, "Israel's Dangerous Fundamentalists," *Foreign Policy* 68 (Fall 1987): 118–139.

17. In addition to the studies just cited a useful overview of Gush Emunim is provided by David Newman, ed., *The Impact of Gush Emunim: Politics and Settlement in the West Bank* (London: Croom Helm, 1985).

18. Lustick, *For the Land and the Lord*, p. 120.

19. Use of the term *earthquake* is discussed by Isaac, *Party and Politics in Israel*, pp. 11ff. See also, Don Paretz, "The Earthquake: Israel's Ninth Knesset Election," *The Middle East Journal* 31 (1977): 251–266; and Howard R. Penniman, ed., *Israel at the Polls: The Knesset Elections of 1977* (Washington, D.C.: American Enterprise Institute, 1979).

20. Friedman, "Fight for the Religious Future."

21. For example, one defendant convicted of "weapons possession, membership in a terrorist organization and causing grievous bodily harm" received a four-month sentence.

22. See *The Jerusalem Post*, July 10, 1985. For additional information, see Sprinzak, "Fundamentalism, Terrorism and Democracy: The Case of the Gush Emunim Underground," *Occasional Papers of the Smithsonian Institution's Wilson Center*, no. 4, 1986. Much additional evidence of the lawlessness of the settler movement may be found in a 1982 report prepared by Yehudit Karp, at the time deputy attorney general of Israel. According to *Yediot Aharonot* (February 8, 1984), "The report examines more than 70 cases of lawbreaking, 15 of them in great detail, and from its findings and conclusions an alarming picture emerges of lawbreaking, of defects in police investigation . . . and of involvement by the military administration in attempting to disrupt investigations against Jews." For details see *The Karp Report: An Israeli Government Inquiry into Settler Violence against Palestinians on the West Bank* (Washington, D.C.: Institute for Palestine Studies, n.d.).

23. Shubert Spero, "Messianism in Context," *The Jerusalem Post*, June 17, 1984.

24. See Gabriel Sheffer, "Kahane, Kahanism and Racism," *Israel Yearbook, 1985*, pp. 68–72.

25. These quotations were recorded by officials of the New Israel Fund, a Jewish organization devoted to combating Kahane's growing influence. They were publicized in a NIF Newsletter dated October 14, 1985.

26. Raphael Israeli, "The Israeli Elections of 1984: Issues and Factions," *The Middle East Review* (Special Report) 1 (1984-1985): 4.

27. *Yediot Aharonot*, June 23, 1984. Quoted and discussed in Edward Witten, "Attitudes of Israeli Socio-Economic Forces toward the Question of Settlements," *Israeli Settlements in the Occupied Arab Territories: An International Symposium* (Tunis: The League of Arab States, 1988).

28. For example, in a paid ad in *Ha'aretz* in May 1984, Peace Now stated, in part: "We have been warning for years about Jewish terror and the soil for its growth. . . . The Jewish terrorist movement is not a deviation or a coincidence. It is the price of Greater Israel, it is the bitter fruit of fanatical nationalist ideology, an ideology of power. The settlements . . . have become the hothouse of terror."

29. *The Jerusalem Post*, July 11, 1985.

30. Ibid., July 23, 1985.

CHAPTER 19. CONCLUDING REMARKS

AUTHOR'S NOTE: I wish to thank Professor John A. Booth and JoAnn Lutz for their comments and suggestions.

1. See, for example, Peter H. Merkl and Ninian Smart, eds., *Religion and Politics in the Modern World* (New York: New York University Press, 1983); Myron J. Aronoff, ed., *Religion and Politics*, vol. 3, *Political Anthropology* (New Brunswick, N.J.: Transaction Books, 1984); Lionel Caplan, ed., *Studies in Religious Fundamentalism* (Albany: State University of New York Press, 1987); and Richard Antoun and Mary Elaine Hegland, eds., *Religious Resurgence: Contemporary Cases in Islam, Christianity, and Judaism* (Syracuse, N.Y.: Syracuse University Press, 1987).

Index